The East Coast
A pilot guide from
the Wash to Ramsgate

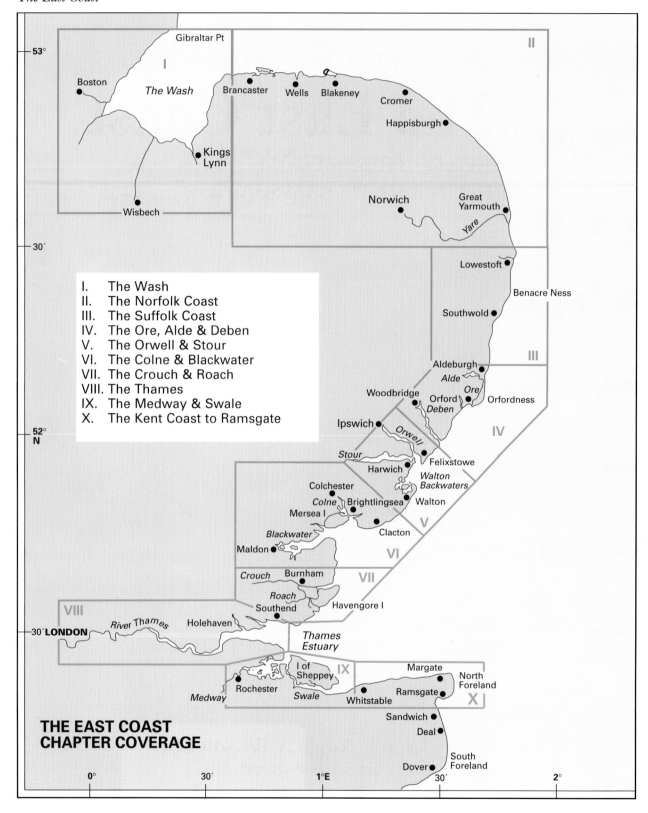

53°

Gibraltar Pt

Boston

I

The Wash

Brancaster   Wells   Blakeney

Cromer

Happisburgh

Kings
Lynn

Norwich

Great
Yarmouth

Yare

Wisbech

30′

Lowestoft

Benacre Ness

I.   The Wash
II.   The Norfolk Coast
III.   The Suffolk Coast
IV.   The Ore, Alde & Deben
V.   The Orwell & Stour
VI.   The Colne & Blackwater
VII. The Crouch & Roach
VIII. The Thames
IX.   The Medway & Swale
X.   The Kent Coast to Ramsgate

Southwold

II

III

Aldeburgh
Alde

Woodbridge
Ore
Orford
Deben
Orfordness

Ipswich

Orwell

IV

52°
N

Stour
Harwich
Felixstowe

*Walton
Backwaters*

Colchester

Brightlingsea
Walton

Colne

V

Mersea I

Clacton

Blackwater

VI

Maldon

Crouch   Burnham

VII

Roach

Southend

Havengore I

VIII

River Thames

Holehaven

30′ LONDON

*Thames
Estuary*

IX

Margate

North
Foreland

Rochester

I of
Sheppey

Ramsgate

Medway

Swale

Whitstable

X

Sandwich

**THE EAST COAST
CHAPTER COVERAGE**

Deal

South
Foreland

Dover

0°   30′   1°E   30′   2°

The East Coast

A PILOT GUIDE FROM THE WASH TO RAMSGATE

Derek Bowskill

Imray Laurie Norie & Wilson Ltd
St Ives Cambridgeshire England

Published by
Imray, Laurie, Norie & Wilson Ltd
Wych House, St Ives, Huntingdon,
Cambridgeshire PE17 4BT, England
☎ +44 (0) 1480 462114
Fax +44 (0) 1480 496109
e-mail ilnw@imray.com

© Derek Bowskill 1998
1st edition 1984
2nd edition 1987
3rd edition 1992
4th edition 1998
ISBN 0 85288 369 2

British Library Cataloguing in Publication Data.
A catalogue record for this book is available from the British Library.

PLANS

The plans are based on information contained in British Admiralty Charts and are reproduced with the permission of the Hydrographic Office of the United Kingdom and the Controller of Her Britannic Majesty's Stationery Office.

CAUTION

Every effort has been made to ensure the accuracy of this book. It contains selected information and thus is not definitive and does not include all known information on the subject in hand; this is particularly relevant to the plans, which should not be used for navigation. The author believes that its selection is a useful aid to prudent navigation, but the safety of a vessel depends ultimately on the judgement of the navigator, who should assess all information, published or unpublished.

CORRECTIONS

The editors would be glad to receive any corrections, information or suggestions which readers may consider would improve the book, as new impressions will be required from time to time. Letters should be addressed to the Editor, *The East Coast*, care of the publishers. The more precise the information the better, but even partial or doubtful information is helpful, if it is made clear what the doubts are.

The last input of technical information was February 1998.

Printed in Great Britain by
Bath Press Colour Books Ltd, Blantyre, Scotland

KEY TO SYMBOLS

⊼	Water
▮P	Fuel-petrol
▮D	Fuel-diesel
WC	Toilet
▣	Shower
↘	Public telephone
⌁	Electricity
⌑	Public House
Ⓥ	Visitors' berths/moorings
Ⓒ	Chandlery
⚓	Marina

Contents

Foreword

There have not been many months in the past eight years when I have not been cruising the area covered by this pilot guide. During that time, I have come to enjoy, respect, admire and fear this sometimes lush, sometimes bleak; sometimes remote, sometimes only-too-accessible; sometimes uncivilised, sometimes over-refined; sometimes vulgar, sometimes effete and decadent; sometimes ever-alert, sometimes torpid and somnolent; sometimes green, blue and white, but mainly muddy and grey; and never dramatically rocky but always potentially treacherous east coast of ours! I hope that my perception of it will be acceptable as a celebration; and, in addition, that this volume will be of actual, practical help. I shall be most grateful to hear personally from any skipper who can offer comment, advice, corrections, amendments or information that will enable me to improve the accuracy and/or increase the usefulness of this work.

So many people have helped me during the years I have been occupied with this guide that to mention them all would be to devalue each. However, some persons have been invaluable in ways they may never know about, and it is by way of paying tribute to their many and varied, if not indeed diverse and even disparate, contributions that I name them.

Sadly, the first two must now be in memoriam: Jack Toogood (of the Red Blood, the Blue Eyes, the Open Mind and Golden Heart); Jack Bradley (my Sea Man for all Sea Sons); Ian Rennie and Tim Ascot; both of Ramsgate and elsewhere; Sonny (The Cromer Light) a whelker (and so much more) from Wells-next-the-Sea; Charlie Brinkley and John Lineham, pilots both, from the Deben, the Wash; the master of Shuttlewood's Boatyard on the Roach, a certain Mr Norris; Chris Reynolds-Hole, the residing genius behind Bradwell Marina; the eponymous owner of Titchmarsh Marina, Walton-on-the-Naze; Captain David Garside, harbourmaster *extraordinaire* of King's Lynn: a Q.Fl navigational aid of few words, much sagacity and wit, completely (but unboringly so) reliable – and a scourge of all water-borne idiots.

I have been accompanied on this project (at times in the flesh, but more often wraithly in mind and spirit) by my First, Second and Third Mate. My lifeline in times of great joy or fear or sorrow (for the human condition is such that sooner or later we all need to express or at least try to communicate our significant experiences and feelings) was the telephone link with She who was (usually anyway) Standing By: Anthea.

However, this dedication must over-ride all other factors and acknowledgements, and I now make it with great surges of gratitude and humility, to the men of the RNLI.

Derek Bowskill
Pool-in-Wharfedale 1984

Foreword to the second edition

Much have I travell'd in the realms of gold
And many goodly states and kingdoms seen;

. . . so wrote Keats, and I wonder what kind of wild surmise he would have had, 'like some watcher of the skies', if he had been scanning Britain. I am still ambivalent to the east coast and North Sea. At best, they are what Brid and Skeggyites call 'bracing'; at less than best, they are heavy and grey, and can only too easily become drear and daunting.
Nevertheless, they have about them that which can engage and enthral. They have engrossed me by their constant state of flux; and although there is not always 'full fathom five' in their cruising rounds, it could well have been said:

Nothing of them that doth fade,
But doth suffer a sea-change
Into something rich and strange.

I am grateful to all who have told me of those special changes that, just like fate, are ready for you the minute you think you have worked it out.

Derek Bowskill
Pool-in-Wharfedale 1987

Foreword to the third edition

It is many years now since *Valcon* and I first left Ramsgate harbour and turned to port for the Thames Estuary and the east coast rivers. Since then, I have cruise-coasted, mainly single-handed and almost non-stop, from the Scottish border to the French Riviera and from Land's End to the Costa del Sol via the inland waterways of England and France.

In all that time, the force and spirit of the East have never left me, and as I look back on my frequently bleak but always challenging years on the coastal waters from Ramsgate to the Wash, they still arouse vivid memories tinged with awe and affection. Little that is 'of the essence' has changed, though there has been marginal mutation, occasional innovation and much refurbishment.

However, this guide has been through something of a radical sea-change; while it has not experienced a reversal in its fortunes it has been turned back to front. And why? Mainly because the cruising folk I have met who have been good enough to speak to me about the book have said, 'Don't you think it goes the wrong way?' or, alternative, 'Don't you know most people want to do it the other way round?'; and, in addition, 'What about the Broads, you don't say half enough!'

So, wanting to please and hoping to sell more copies, this edition has been completely revamped. It now travels southerly and with the consequential rearrangement, contains a special section relating to the Norfolk Broads. I hope the changes are improvements.

Derek Bowskill
Pool-in-Wharfedale 1992

Foreword to the fourth edition

After some years in the Mediterranean, it was with some apprehension that I returned to the East Coast to bring this volume up to date. By chance, the weather was good and the sun shone throughout my endeavours. Never before had I been so grateful for the consistency of the North Sea's tides and prevailing winds. The Med has a lot going for it – most of it sun – but what goes against it is the unpredictability of wind conditions; the swells that come from more than one direction at a time; and the lack of useable tide. I did not expect to be as grateful as I was for what the East Coast has to offer.

I cannot remember where I read the following, but it comes from the works of a writer of pilot guides published around the turn of the century; but this is pretty close to what the man had to say: 'Just to let the unthinking cruising skipper into the difficulties of writing such a guide as this, I will tell him that, after I had written the directions for the Barrow Swatchway, I found the Black Deep light-vessel had gone and the Barrow was lit instead. These contretemps are always happening, and the above-mentioned amateur skippers will never be bored, and can always have the joy of picking holes in other people's work for I am sure that many will gloatingly seize upon all they can find.'

But this is pleasantry – a circuitous way of thanking all those skippers who have, over the years, been so generous with their comments. I hope this edition will meet the suggestions many made with regard to the further improvement of the work. I am especially grateful to the staff of Imray's for their investment of so much time and effort in bringing new colour and vitality to the production.

In the past, I have mentioned how much I have appreciated the help and advice of the fishermen and members of the RNLI over the years, and my respect and admiration is as unstinting as ever. I have also mentioned one other person – Anthea – and it is to her that I now dedicate again the memories of all the joys and vicissitudes that have informed our lives ever since we left Ramsgate and turned *Valcon*'s bows towards the East Coast.

Derek Bowskill
Pool-in-Wharfedale, 1998

Acknowledgements

I am grateful to Ian Martin of *Challenger* at Gibraltar Point for keeping me informed and up to date on the ways of Wainfleet and the Wash.

Readers are occasionally good enough to write with good wishes and better info. One such soul is Patricia O'Driscoll who hails from London SE23. She says, 'I have been given a copy of the second edition of your book *The East Coast* and write to offer a little information. Some might be useful for a subsequent edition, and some is just by the way. My knowledge of these waters comes from 11 years commercial barging, 1959–1970.'

The index to this fourth edition was compiled by Elizabeth Cook. Patrick Roach, piloted by Pat Blenkinsopp, took the photographs from the air late in 1996.

Introduction

This volume is not intended for use as a pilot (in the strictly understood Admiralty usage of that word) nor as a set of sailing instructions (for those intrepid explorers who are never content until they have piloted themselves through every single puddle on any given patch). It is intended to be a practical cruising guide/companion: providing any visiting skipper with all the appropriate (that is, sufficient and necessary) information needed to navigate the area safely and efficiently – when used in conjunction with the relevant Admiralty and/or Imray charts.

The guide sections of the book offer hard facts in the form of diagrams, sketch maps, chartlets and clearly laid out details of port information and so on; while the companion sections set out to describe the areas and venues in a way that is informative but also discursive and entertaining. These comments and commentaries are meant to pass on not only useful thoughts and ideas about actually cruising the area, but also something of the *genius loci* that is to be experienced.

Chartlets and sketch maps

These have been provided with the intention of giving an overall 'view' of the area, or detailed sketches of particular approaches. It is quite clear when considering the information they offer whether or not they are suitable for 'navigation/ pilotage'. In fact, most of them are not, and are only to be used in conjunction with the appropriate Admiralty/Imray charts. Depths, where given, are in metres and all bearings are true.

The plans in this guide have been based on British Admiralty charts with the permission of the Hydrographer of the Navy.

Weather

Glossary of some terms used in shipping forecasts

Anticyclone

A region characterised in the barometric pressure distribution by a system of closed isobars, with the highest pressure on the inside. It is also known as a *High*. The circulation about the centre is clockwise in the northern hemisphere, anticlockwise in the southern hemisphere.

Backing

A change in the direction of the wind, in an anticlockwise direction.

Cold front

The boundary line between advancing cold air and a mass of warm air under which the cold air pushes like a wedge. Its passage is normally accompanied by a sharp shift of wind, a rise in pressure, a fall in temperature and dew-point, and a period of rain, often heavy; sometimes there may be a line squall or thunder. The cold front was originally called the squall line.

Cyclones

A name given to the tropical revolving storms of the Bay of Bengal and Arabian Sea. Sometimes used as a general term for tropical revolving storms of all oceans, or in the form *Tropical Cyclone*. Depressions of the Temperate Zones were formerly often referred to as cyclones, but *Depression* or *Low* is now used to distinguish them from tropical storms. The term *cyclonic depression* is still sometimes used for a depression, as also is *extra-tropical cyclone*. (See also *Winds becoming cyclonic*.)

Depression

A region characterised in the barometric pressure distribution by a system of closed isobars, having lowest pressure at the centre. The circulation about the centre is anticlockwise in the northern hemisphere and clockwise in the southern hemisphere. A depression is described as *deep* when encircled by many isobars close together and is said to be *deepening* when the pressure at the centre is decreasing. The word *shallow* is used to describe a depression which has few isobars. A depression is said to be *filling up* when the central pressure is increasing.

Fog

A term used when the visual range is less than 1000m.

Further outlook

A statement in brief and general terms appended to a detailed forecast and giving the conditions likely to be experienced in the 24 hours or more following the period covered by the actual forecast.

Gale

A mean wind of at least Beaufort Force 8 (34–40 knots) and/or gusts reaching 43–51 knots. The term *severe* or *strong gale* implies a mean wind speed of at least Beaufort Force 9 (41–47 knots) and/or gusts reaching 52/60 knots.

Gale warnings

The term *imminent* implies within 6 hours of the time of issue: *soon* implies between 6 and 12 hours: *later* implies more than 12 hours. Gale warnings remain in force unless amended or cancelled. However if the gale persists for more than 24 hours after the time of origin the warning will be reissued.

Gust

A momentary increase in the strength of the wind, much shorter lived than a squall and different in nature, being due mainly to mechanical interference with the steady flow of air, especially around large obstructions.

Land and sea breezes

Local winds are caused by the unequal heating and cooling of adjacent land and water surfaces. The sea breeze usually sets in during the forenoon and reaches its maximum strength during the afternoon. The land breeze may set in about midnight or not until early morning.

Pressure systems

In weather bulletins the terms used to describe the speed of movement of pressure systems are as follows:

Slowly – less than 15 knots
Steadily – 15 to 25 knots
Rather quickly – 25 to 35 knots
Rapidly – 35 to 45 knots
Very rapidly – more than 45 knots

Ridge

A ridge or wedge of high pressure is the converse of a trough, and is indicated by isobars extending outwards from a high-pressure area. It corresponds to a ridge running out from the side of a mountain.

Squall

A sudden increase of wind speed by at least 16 knots or by at least three stages of the Beaufort Scale, the speed rising to Force 6 (22 knots) or more and lasting for at least 1 minute.

Storm

A mean wind speed of at least Beaufort Force 10 (48–55 knots) and/or gusts reaching 61–68 knots. The term *violent storm* implies a mean wind speed of at least Beaufort Force 11 (56–63 knots) and/or gusts reaching 69–77 knots.

Trough

The word trough is used in a general sense for any 'valley' of low pressure, and is thus the opposite of a 'ridge' of high pressure. A special form of trough was formerly known as a V-shaped depression. Frequently a front lies in a trough.

Veering

A change in the direction of the wind, in a clockwise direction.

Visibility

In weather bulletins, the words *poor visibility* imply a visual range of between 1000m and 2M; *moderate* is equal to a visual range of 2–5M; *good* is applicable when visibility is greater than 5M.

Beaufort scale

Sea state	Beaufort No.	Description	Velocity in knots	Velocity in km/h	Term	Code	Wave height in metres
Like a mirror	0	Calm glassy	<1	<1	Calm	0	0
Ripples	1	Light airs rippled	1–3	1–5	Calm	1	0–0·1
Small wavelets	2	Light breeze wavelets	4–6	6–11	Smooth	2	0·1–0·5
Large wavelets	3	Gentle breeze	7–10	12–19	Slight	3	0·5–1·25
Small waves, breaking	4	Moderate breeze	11–16	20–28	Moderate	4	1·25–2·5
Moderate waves, foam	5	Fresh breeze	17–21	29–38	Rough	5	2·5–4
Large waves, foam and spray	6	Strong breeze	22–27	39–49			
Sea heads up, foam in streaks	7	Near gale	28–33	50–61	Very rough	6	4–6
Higher long waves, foam in streaks	8	Gale	34–40	62–74			
High waves, desne foam, spray impairs visibility	9	Strong gale	41–47	75–88	High	7	6–9
Very high tumbling waves, surface white with foam, visibility affected	10	Storm	48–55	89–102	Very high	8	9–14
Exceptionally high waves, sea covered in foam, visibility affected	11	Violent storm	56–63	103–117	Phenomenal	9	>14
Air filled with spray and foam, visibility severely impaired	12	Hurricane	>63	>118			

Warm front

This is the boundary line at the earth's surface between advancing warm air and a cold air mass. Precipitation usually occurs within a wide belt (some 200M) in advance of the front. Passage of the front is usually marked by a steadying of the barometer, a rise in temperature and dew-point, and a shift of wind.

Waves

Length of swell waves
Short   0–100 metres
Average   100–200 metres
Long   over 200 metres

Height of swell waves
Low   0–2 metres
Moderate   2–4 metres
Heavy   over 4 metres

Winds becoming cyclonic

A term used to indicate that there will be large changes in wind direction across the track line of a depression within the forecast area. Such changes are considered to be too complicated to be given in detail.

Buoyage

This is the standard representation of buoyage around the United Kingdom as used in all Imray publications.

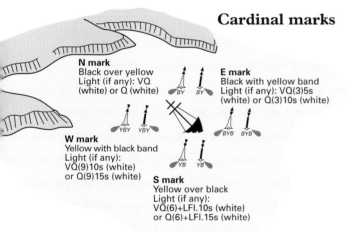

Cardinal marks

N mark
Black over yellow
Light (if any): VQ (white) or Q (white)

E mark
Black with yellow band
Light (if any): VQ(3)5s (white) or Q(3)10s (white)

W mark
Yellow with black band
Light (if any): VQ(9)10s (white) or Q(9)15s (white)

S mark
Yellow over black
Light (if any): VQ(6)+LFl.10s (white) or Q(6)+LFl.15s (white)

Lateral marks

Port hand
All red
Topmark (if any): can
Light (if any): red

Starboard hand
All green
Topmark (if any): cone
Light (if any): green

Navigation aids

RADIOBEACONS

Dungeness Lt 50°54'·77N 00°58°·67E
DU (−··/···−) 300·5kHz A1A 50M
North Foreland Lt 51°22'·49N 01°26'·85W
NF (−·/··−·) 311kHz A1A 50M DGPS service 310·5kHz 40M
Southend 51°34'·55N 00°42'·12E
SND (···/−·/−··) 362·5kHz Non A2A 20M
Great Yarmouth 52°38'·10N 01°43'·73E
ND (−·/−··) 417kHz Non A2A 10M
Cromer Lt 52°55'·45N 01°19'·10E
CM (−·−·/−−) 313·5kHz A1A 50M

HM COASTGUARD MRCCs AND MRSCs

Stations do not accept public correspondence (link calls). They deal with distress, urgency and safety traffic. The call in each case is the geographical name followed by 'Coastguard'.

They all keep watch on VHF Ch 16 and 2182kHz (H24) for distress, urgency and safety calls covering UK waters. Those indicated on page 4 also keep watch on VHF Ch 70 and/or 2187·5kHz DSC in accordance with GMDSS. Unless stated below, stations also operate VHF Ch 10, 67, 73.

Strong winds (Force 6/7) and/or gale warnings are broadcast on receipt and every two hours. Weather messages (local area forecasts) are broadcast every four hours or on request. Local navigational warnings are broadcast on receipt and before weather messages if required, and on request. All scheduled broadcasts are announced on Ch 16 and made sequentially from remote transmitter sites in each coastguard district on Ch 67 (Dover Coastguard on Ch 11) from the times shown below for each station. They may be suspended while search and rescue action is in progress.

Isolated danger marks
(stationed over a danger with navigable water around)
Black with red band
Topmark: 2 black balls
Light (if any): Fl(2) (white)

Special Mark
Body shape optional, yellow
Topmark (if any): Yellow X
Light (if any): Fl.Y etc

Safe water marks
(mid-channel and landfall)
Red with white vertical stripes
Topmark (if any): red ball
Light (if any): Iso, Oc, LFl.10s or Mo(A) (white)

COASTGUARD SERVICES

Dover Coastguard (MRCC) 50°08'N 01°20'E
☎ 01304 210008 *Fax* 01304 202137
Covers Beachy Head to Reculver. VHF Ch 16, 69
(H24). Ch 10, 11, 67, 73, 80 (HX). 2182kHz. Operates
Channel Navigation Information Service (CNIS) in
conjunction with Gris-Nez Traffic. Ch 69 is the primary
working channel for routine CNIS traffic (call direct on
Ch 69). CNIS broadcasts navigational and public
information on Ch 11 every H+40 (and H+55 in bad
visibility). Weather messages every 4h commencing 0400
LT. DSC MMSI. 002320010 VHF Ch 70.
Thames Coastguard (MRSC) 51°51'N 01°17'E.
☎ 01255 675518 *Fax* 01255 675249
Covers Reculver to Southwold.
Operates VHF Ch 16 (H24), 10, 67, 73 (HX). 2182kHz
(H24). Broadcasts every 4h from 0010 LT. DSC
MMSI. 00232008 VHF Ch 70.
Yarmouth Coastguard (MRCC) 52°37'N 01°43'E
☎ 01493 851338 *Fax* 01493 852307
Covers Haile Sand Fort to Southwold.
Operates VHF Ch 16 (H24), 06, 10, 67, 73 (HX).
2182kHz (H24). 2596 kHz (HX). Broadcasts every 4h
from 0400 LT. DSC MMSI. 00232008 HVHF Ch 70.
Humber Coastguard (MRSC) 54°06'N 0°11'E
☎ 01262 672317 *Fax* 01262 606915
Covers Anderby Creek to Port Mulgrave.
Operates VHF Ch 16 (H24), 10, 67, 73 (HX). 2182,
2226kHz (H24). Broadcasts every 4h from 0340 LT.
CSC MMSI 002320007 2187·5kHz.

WEATHER SERVICES

Marinecall – automatic telephone weather service

Recorded inshore forecasts are provided for 16 areas
around the UK coastline. In each case dial 0891
500, followed by the three-figure number of the area
required. See below.

The forecasts cover the inshore waters out to 12
miles offshore and are updated at 0700 and 1900
daily, which is additionally updated at 1300 daily.

The two-day forecasts are immediately followed
by forecasts for days three to five. Two-day forecasts
include: The general situation, warnings of gales
and strong winds, wind, weather, visibility, sea state
and temperature, and the maximum air
temperature.

A two to five day planning forecast for the English
Channel is available on ☎ 0891 500 992, and a
three to five day National forecast, covering the UK
coastline is available on ☎ 0891 500 450.

Marinecall current weather reports

For actual weather reports coastal locations ☎ 0891
226 plus the Marinecall inshore three figure number
below for the East Coast.

Each of the Marinecall areas contains three
weather reports (occasionally two), and are normally
updated every hour.

The reports include details of wind, weather
visibility, temperature, pressure and pressure
tendency. These reports are followed by the forecast
for that area.

454
Bridlington
Easington
Holbeach
455
Weybourne
Sheerness
Walton-on-the-Naze
456
Dover
Greenwich LtV
Newhaven
457
Thorney Is
Lee-on-Solent
St Catherine's Pt

MetFAX Marine

Weather maps, two-day inshore forecasts, two to
five day planning forecasts, satellite images and
weather reports are available by facsimile. An index
for all fax products can be obtained by *Fax* on 0336
400 401.

Two day inshore forecasts for the East Coast can be
obtained by dialling ☎ 0336 400 455.

Two to five day planning forecasts and 48/72h can
be obtained by dialling ☎ 0336 400 472.

Additional fax services available include:

24h shipping forecast	*Fax* 0336 400 441
Guide to surface chart	*Fax* 0336 400 446
Surface chart	*Fax* 0336 400 444
Surface forecast chart	*Fax* 0336 400 445
Chart of UK weather reports	*Fax* 0336 400 447
Index to chart of weather reports	*Fax* 0336 400 448
3–5 day inshore forecast	*Fax* 0336 400 450
Guide to satellite images	*Fax* 0336 400 498
Satellite image	*Fax* 0336 400 499

Weather Centres

Weather centres provide a range of services at a
charge. For a forecast ring:

London	☎ 0171 696 0573 or 0171 405 4356
Norwich	☎ 01603 660779
Newcastle	☎ 0191 232 6453

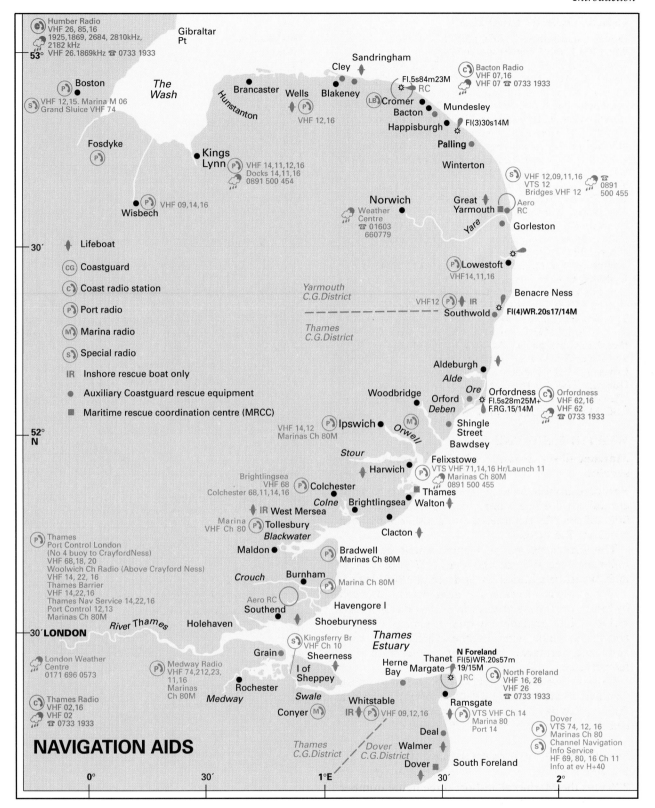

Humber Radio
VHF 26, 85,16
1925,1869, 2684, 2810kHz,
2182 kHz
VHF 26.1869kHz ☎ 0733 1933

53°

Gibraltar
Pt

Sandringham

Cley

Fl.5s84m23M

Bacton Radio
VHF 07,16
VHF 07 ☎ 0733 1933

Boston

*The
Wash*

Brancaster   Wells   Blakeney

Cromer

Mundesley

VHF 12,15. Marina M 06
Grand Sluice VHF 74

Hunstanton

VHF 12,16

Bacton

Happisburgh

Fl(3)30s14M

Fosdyke

Kings
Lynn

Palling

Winterton

VHF 14,11,12,16
Docks 14,11,16
0891 500 454

VHF 12,09,11,16
VTS 12
Bridges VHF 12

0891
500 455

VHF 09,14,16

Norwich

Great
Yarmouth

Aero
RC

Wisbech

Weather
Centre
☎ 01603
660779

Yare

Gorleston

30′   ↕   Lifeboat

CG   Coastguard

*Yarmouth
C.G.District*

Lowestoft

VHF14,11,16

C   Coast radio station

P   Port radio

VHF12   IR

Benacre Ness

Southwold   Fl(4)WR.20s17/14M

M   Marina radio

*Thames
C.G.District*

S   Special radio

IR   Inshore rescue boat only

Aldeburgh

Alde

●   Auxiliary Coastguard rescue equipment

Woodbridge

Orford

Ore   Orfordness

Orfordness
VHF 62,16

■   Maritime rescue coordination centre (MRCC)

Deben

Fl.5s28m25M+
F.RG.15/14M

VHF 62
☎ 0733 1933

52°
N

VHF 14,12
Marinas Ch 80M

Ipswich

Orwell

Shingle
Street

Bawdsey

Stour

Felixstowe

Brightlingsea
VHF 68
Colchester 68,11,14,16

Harwich

VTS VHF 71,14,16 Hr/Launch 11
Marinas Ch 80M
0891 500 455

Colchester

Thames

Colne

Brightlingsea

Walton

IR West Mersea

Marina
VHF Ch 80   Tollesbury

Clacton

Blackwater

Thames
Port Control London
(No 4 buoy to CrayfordNess)
VHF 68,18, 20
Woolwich Ch Radio (Above Crayford Ness)
VHF 14, 22, 16
Thames Barrier
VHF 14,22,16
Thames Nav Service 14,22,16
Port Control 12,13
Marinas Ch 80M

Maldon

Bradwell
Marinas Ch 80M

Crouch   Burnham

Marina Ch 80M

River Thames   Holehaven

Southend

Havengore I

Shoeburyness

30′ **LONDON**

*Thames
Estuary*

Kingsferry Br
VHF Ch 10

London Weather
Centre
0171 696 0573

Grain

Sheerness

Herne
Bay

Thanet

N Foreland
Fl(5)WR.20s57m
19/15M

Margate

RC

Thames Radio
VHF 02,16
VHF 02
☎ 0733 1933

Medway Radio
VHF 74,212,23,
11,16
Marinas
Ch 80M

I of
Sheppey

North Foreland
VHF 16, 26
VHF 26
☎ 0733 1933

Rochester

Swale

Whitstable

Ramsgate

Medway

Conyer

IR   VHF 09,12,16

VTS VHF Ch 14
Marina 80
Port 14

NAVIGATION AIDS

Deal

Dover
VTS 74, 12, 16
Marinas Ch 80
Channel Navigation
Info Service
HF 69, 80, 16 Ch 11
Info at ev H+40

*Thames
C.G.District*

*Dover
C.G.District*

Walmer

Dover   South Foreland

0°   30′   1°E   30′   2°

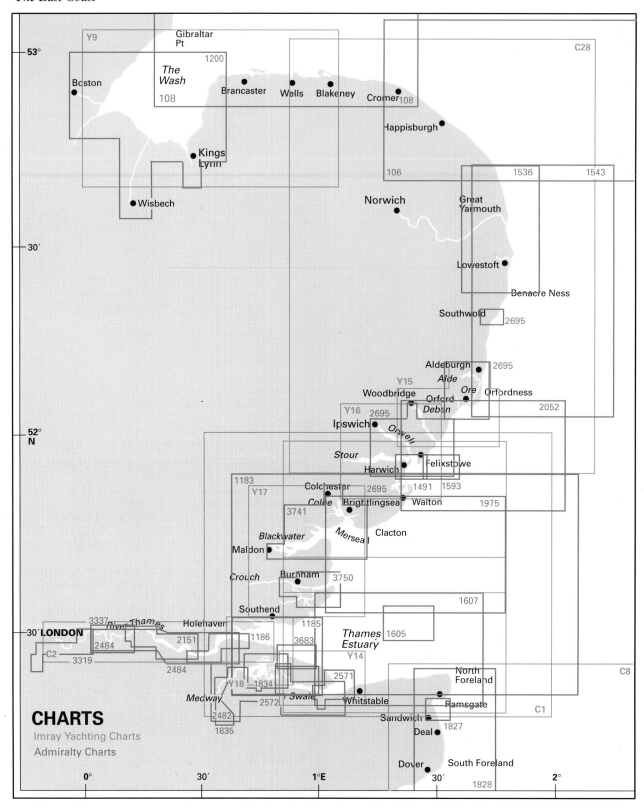

CHARTS
Imray Yachting Charts
Admiralty Charts

Appropriate charts for the East Coast

In the preparation of this volume (and indeed at most other times as well) the author has always used both Imray and Admiralty charts. The range of Imray charts for the East Coast fits very well with the divisions to be found in this volume.

BRITISH ADMIRALTY CHARTS

Passage charts

Chart	Title	Scale
1408	Harwich to Terschelling and Cromer to Rotterdam	300,000
2182a	North Sea – southern sheet	750,000

Approach/harbour charts

Chart	Title	Scale
106	Cromer to Smith's Knoll	75,000
108	Approaches to the Wash	75,000
323	Dover Strait – eastern part	75,000
1183	Thames Estuary	100,000
1185	River Thames – Sea Reach	25,000
1186	River Thames – Canvey Island to Tilbury	12,500
1190	Flamborough Head to Blakeney Pt	150,000
1200	The Wash Ports	Various
1491	Harwich and Felixstowe	10,000
1503	Outer Dowsing to Smith's Knoll	150,000
1504	Cromer to Orfordness	150,000
1536	Approaches to Great Yarmouth and Lowestoft	40,000
	Great Yarmouth haven: Lowestoft harbour	6,250
	Approaches to Lowestoft	20,000
1543	Winterton Ness to Orfordness	75,000
	Southwold harbour	10,000
1593	Harwich channel	10,000
1594	River Stour – Erwarton Ness to Manningtree	10,000
1605	Thames Estuary – Edinburgh channels	15,000
1607	Thames Estuary – southern part	50,000
1610	Approaches to the Thames Estuary	150,000
1698	Dover harbour	6,250
1827	Approaches to Ramsgate	12,500
	Ramsgate harbour	5,000
1828	Dover to North Foreland	37,500
1834	River Medway – Garrison Point to Folly Point	12,500
1835	River Medway – Folly Point to Maidstone	6,000
	Continuation of the River Medway to Maidstone	25,000
2482	River Medway and the Swale	25,000
	Ferry Reach	12,500
	Rochester	12,500

IMRAY CHARTS

Passage charts

Chart	Title	Scale
C1	Thames Estuary. Tilbury to North Foreland and Orfordness	122,000
C8	North Foreland to Beachy Head and Boulogne	115,000
C25	Harwich to the River Humber and Holland	239,300
C28	The East Coast. Harwich to Wells	126,000
C29	East Coast of England. Whitby to Harwich	261,000
C30	Thames to Holland and Belgium Harwich and North Foreland to Hoek van Holland and Calais	182,000

Approach/harbour charts

Chart	Title	Scale
C2	The River Thames. Teddington to Southend. Teddington to Vauxhall	17,000
	Vauxhall to Barking	14,000
	Barking to Southend	40,000
Y6	Thames Estuary – Northern Part	112,000
Y7	Thames Estuary – Southern Part	116,000
Y9	The Wash	87,000
Y14	The Swale	26,530
Y15	Rivers Ore, Alde and Deben	29,000
Y16	Walton Backwaters to Ipswich and Woodbridge	32,000
Y17	The Rivers Colne to Blackwater and Crouch	49,000
Y18	River Medway. Sheerness to Rochester with River Thames, Sea Reach	21,000

Further reading

North Sea (west) Pilot (NP 54)
Dover Strait Pilot (NP 28)
Both published by the Hydrographer of the Navy

North Sea Passage Pilot, Brian Navin, Imray, Laurie, Norie and Wilson Ltd
The Tidal Havens of the Wash and Humber, Henry Irving, Imray, Laurie, Norie and Wilson Ltd
East Coast Rivers, Jack Coote, Yachting Monthly
The Pilot's Guide to the Thames Estuary 1960, Lt Col W E Wilson, Imray, Laurie, Norie and Wilson Ltd
Macmillan Nautical Almanac
Cruising Association Handbook, The Cruising Association
London's Waterway Guide, Chris Cove-Smith, Imray, Laurie, Norie and Wilson Ltd
Inland Waterways of Great Britain, Jane Cumberlidge, Imray, Laurie, Norie and Wilson Ltd
The Shell Book of Inland Waterways, Hugh McKnight, David and Charles Ltd
The Coast of South East England, J Seymour, William Collins Ltd
Northeast Waterways, Derek Bowskill, Imray, Laurie, Norie and Wilson Ltd
The River Thames Book, Chris Cove-Smith, Imray, Laurie, Norie and Wilson Ltd

IMRAY MAPS

River Cam and Lower Ouse
River Upper Great Ouse – Pope's Corner to Bedford
River Nene
The Middle Level
The River Medway – Gillingham to Tonbridge

Tidal streams

The figures against the arrows denote mean rates in tenths of a knot at neaps and springs. Thus 06·11 indicates a mean neap rate of 0·6 knots and a mean spring rate of 1·1 knots.

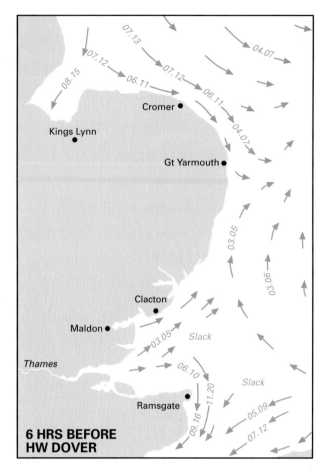

6 HRS BEFORE HW DOVER

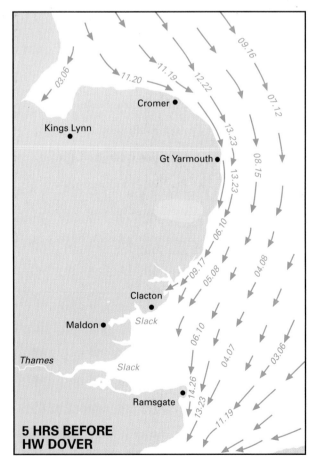

5 HRS BEFORE HW DOVER

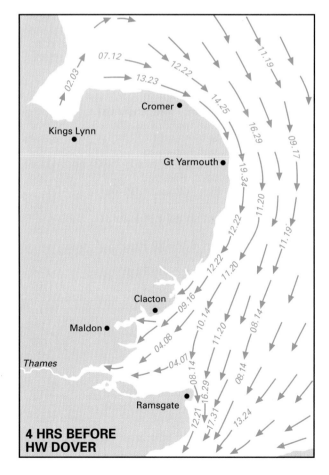

4 HRS BEFORE HW DOVER

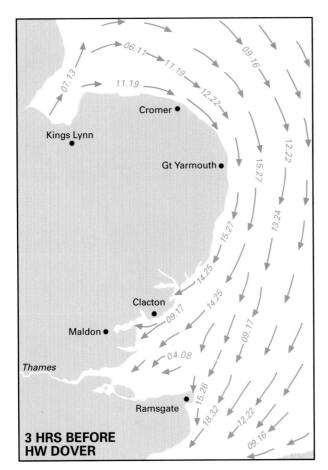

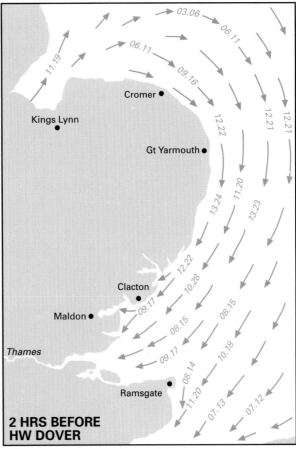

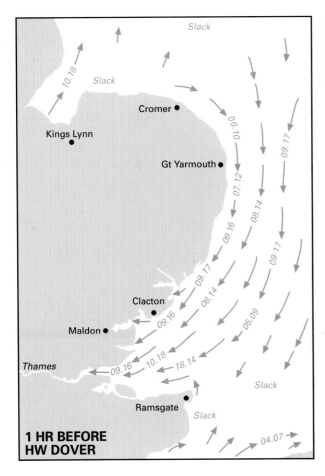

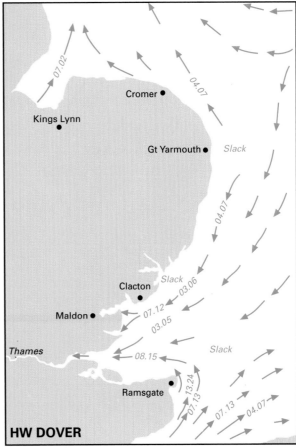

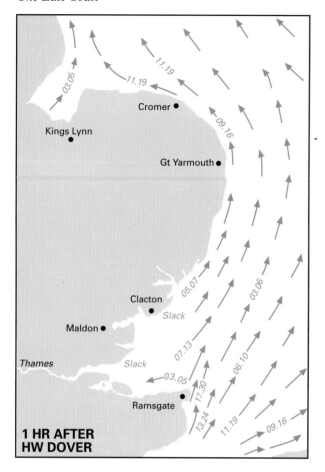

1 HR AFTER HW DOVER

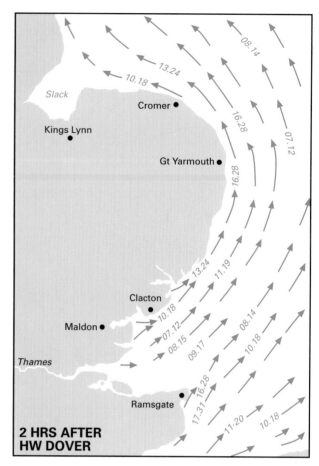

2 HRS AFTER HW DOVER

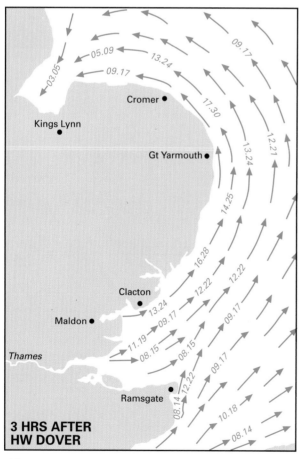

3 HRS AFTER HW DOVER

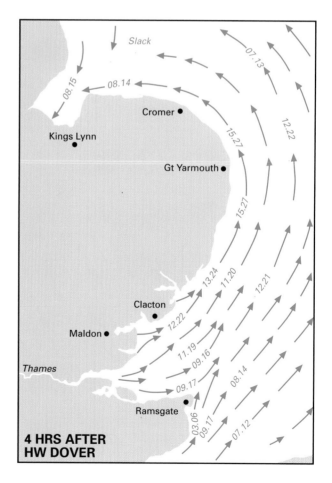

4 HRS AFTER HW DOVER

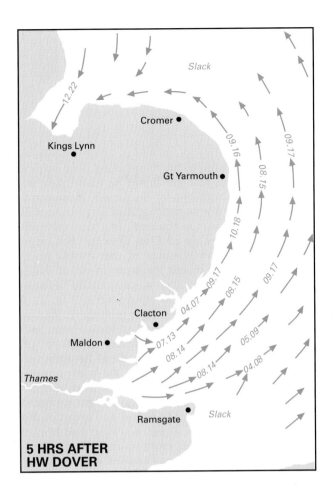

**5 HRS AFTER
HW DOVER**

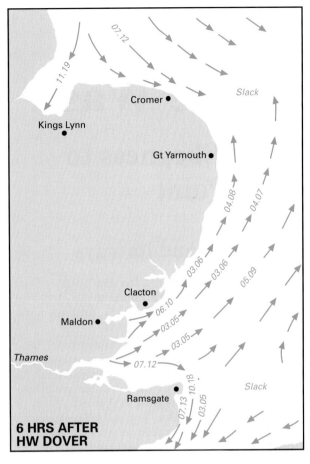

**6 HRS AFTER
HW DOVER**

I. The Wash

From Skegness to Gore Point

The Wash and its ways

I have written before that I feel the waters of the Wash to be more or less All Things to All Men. Not my phrase, of course, but St Paul's, from his letter to the Corinthians, in which he says:

I am a free man and own no master; but I have made myself every man's servant, to win over as many as possible. To the weak I became weak, to win the weak. Indeed, I have become everything in turn to men of every sort, so that in one way or another I may save some. You should understand, my brothers, that our ancestors were all under the pillar of cloud, and all of them passed through the Red Sea . . .

Most of that seems to me to be redolent of the grave waters of the Wash, in which many a soul has found a watery grave: both living man and the equally living element of water can be free; can be tamed into servitude; can be weak or strong; can save as well as destroy; and both are aware of the habitual presence of cloud in the area – and the tide-out sand-vastness which must surely surpass any land passage opened by Moses.

All pretty powerful and sombre stuff; but there is another facet: 'It will all come out in the Wash'; and although the phrase is well known, there is actually

Distance between ports (nautical miles)

	Denver	Lynn	Wisbech	Fosdyke	Boston
Denver	–	14	45	46	48
Lynn	14	–	31	32	34
Wisbech	45	31	–	30	32
Fosdyke	46	32	30	–	10
Boston	48	34	32	10	–

Distance to deep water (nautical miles)

King's Lynn to Cork Hole	8
to No. 1 light buoy	12
Wisbech to Bar Flat	16
to Sutton Bridge	6
Fosdyke to Clay Hole	8
Boston to Clay Hole	6

some serious doubt about its meaning. One school has it that all our sins will finally be revealed as we are washed in the Blood of the Lamb. However, I much prefer the one suggesting that 'Everything will turn out for the best in the end'. It is derived from Spanish, and crops up in Don Quixote. But since the philosophy and fortunes of that 'noble man' were probably as mixed as were those of King John, it is not, perhaps, a particularly reliable recommendation.

Nevertheless, I still maintain it is all there. Within the 250 square miles of waters and banks, braes and holes there is an extraordinary mixture of experiences to be found. The contrast between the Wash at high water and the Dry at low water is quite amazing to behold. Stories are rife of men, women and children being caught out by, caught up with, and quite taken over by the power and speed of the flood tide. Legend has it that not even wild horses can outrun the tide at its swiftest; and, when a good spring tide has receded almost out of sight, its sands extend for miles towards the North Sea and folk have been known to mount inter-tidal cricket matches on those far reaches – rather like those Kentish madcaps who do similar things on the Goodwins.

Great indeed are the rewards of the Wash, but it is not a calm inland sea, especially when those kinfolk *Boreas* from the North and *Eurus* from the East get together with their brother *Argestes* and rage at us from North through to East. Their combination, creating formidable forces, is not merely unpleasant but is also the prevailing condition of the weather in the Wash. Under such circumstances it is good to know that, although the situation can be bleak and desperate, once the ebb tide has made its presence properly felt, the sandbanks start to emerge – and, more importantly, begin to offer the protection for which they are so famous.

Mirages and fogs abound. But in season, when the heat of the sun stands some kind of chance, it can be very pleasant to observe the upside-downness of all the vertical stalks that inhabit the shoreline; fingers of all kinds from decaying withies to magnificent cranes and derricks – the mirages of which all shimmer apparently arse-uppards in the heat of the sun. Even at the height of summer, however, pleasing mists can develop into full-grown fogs in a fleeting moment – virtually in front of one's eyes.

I remember one occasion in the midst of the mellow fruitfulness of early autumn when the waters of the Wash were oily calm; the airs were so light

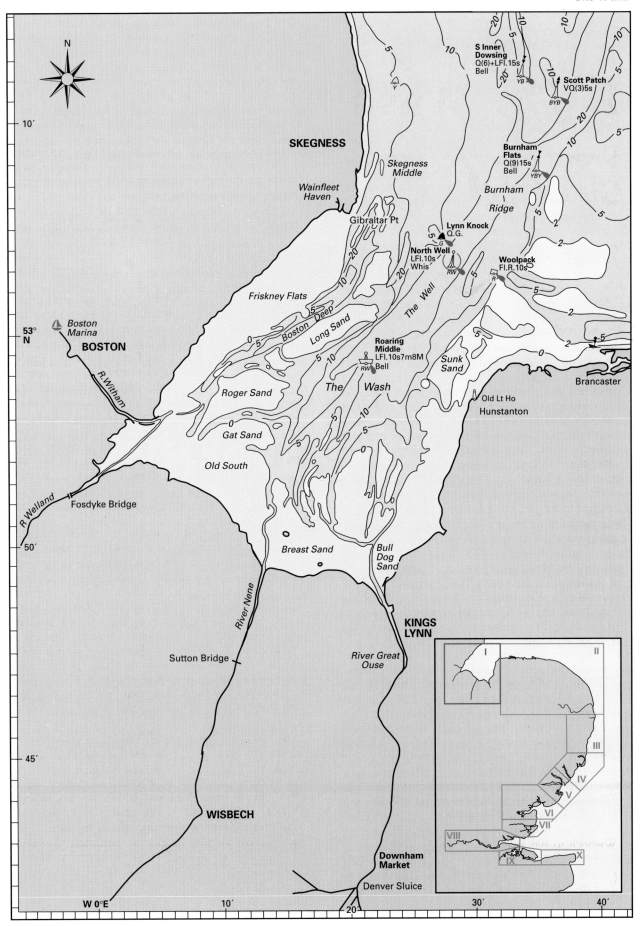

N

SKEGNESS

*Skegness
Middle*

*Wainfleet
Haven*

Gibraltar Pt

**S Inner
Dowsing**
Q(6)+LFl.15s
Bell
YB

Scott Patch
VQ(3)5s
BYB

**Burnham
Flats**
Q(9)15s
Bell
YBY

*Burnham
Ridge*

Lynn Knock
Q.G.
G

North Well
LFl.10s
Whis
RW

Woolpack
Fl.R.10s
R

Friskney Flats

*Boston
Deep*

Long Sand

The Well

10′

*Boston
Marina*

53°
N

BOSTON

R.Witham

**Roaring
Middle**
LFl.10s7m8M
Bell
RW

*Sunk
Sand*

The   Wash

Roger Sand

Old Lt Ho
Hunstanton

Brancaster

Gat Sand

Old South

R Welland

Fosdyke Bridge

50′

Breast Sand

*Bull
Dog
Sand*

River Nene

**KINGS
LYNN**

Sutton Bridge

*River Great
Ouse*

45′

WISBECH

**Downham
Market**

Denver Sluice

W 0°E   10′   30′   40′

20′

I   II

III

IV

V

VI

VII

VIII   IX   X

Wainfleet Ranges
Open daily 0900–1700
Wed. and Fri. night flying to 2100. 2300 in
summer
RAF Command HQ ☎ 01754 820777,
VHF Ch 12

they produced not a ripple on the glassy surface. There was no visible movement of any kind, nor any sign of life. Not even a seal enquiringly raised its head above the surface to probe what must have been my wraith-like presence. Although, in general circumstances, when there is much movement of fishing boats, pleasure-craft and big ships, it is uncommon to see many seals actually swimming around; and although, in addition, they keep their visible activities almost exclusively for sun- and sand-bank bathing, I still hoped and expected that one or two might emerge, just for company and to allay my anxiety. Usually birds are about in goodly numbers; but not on that day – and no vessel hove into sight nor blew its whistle. It seemed that *Valcon* and I were alone and exiled in the Wash. I could see for hardly any distance worth measuring: in fact, for some minutes at a time, it was impossible to discern the ensign from for'ard. The water surface merged so smoothly into the hanging water vapour that it was impossible to tell 't'other from which'. At times I was near to hallucinating; dreaming up the presence of sounds and sights that I would dearly loved to have had around. Indeed, I felt I knew what it was like to be an Ancient Mariner with an albatross clouding around like a vast umbrella. Yet, on other days, the air has been so clear that visibility has permitted the belfry of St Botolph's church to rise from the grave, as it were, and pierce the very heavens. In brief, the weather can change so quickly in the Wash that even the keenest of shipping forecast fans may be taken unawares by the qualities of its unique mini-climate with its characteristic speedy shifts in the weather.

But, as they say, there is no such thing as a free lunch, and the undoubted pleasures of these waters come with an equally undoubted price tag. If you want to navigate the cruising grounds without anxiety and in complete comfort and relaxation, you must ensure proper preparation. Some skippers approach cruising the Wash as they would crossing the North Sea; while others make as little effort as if they were going for a turn on the Stainforth and Keadby Canal . . . and not venturing through the massive lock gates thank you very much! The wise skipper does both, by attempting to prepare for all contingencies so that everyone can set out, and sit back and enjoy the day's experience before safely returning to base. For, don't forget, whichever exit you choose on the ebb, you will not be able to return to base until the next flood has at least reached half its rise (unless, of course, you have a very shoal-draught craft).

To keep in favour with the erratic ways of the Wash gods, one should acknowledge that the cost of survival is eternal vigilance; the *genius loci* being only too ready to test the heedless, the reckless and the over self-assured. Many there are who have been found wanting. I am always happy and relieved when I can get back to a berth or the tamed waters of the Great Ouse above Denver or those above the Grand Sluice at Boston without having lost anyone, bumped into anyone, or broken anything.

Outer approaches

So now to the knotty, nitty-gritty business of first finding, and then finding one's way around, the Wash. Coming in from well out in the North Sea, the buoys to check out first are, in order of approach, the South Inner Dowsing and Scott Patch cardinal marks, about 2 miles apart; they are followed in a more or less southerly fashion by the cardinal Burnham Flats at about 4 miles. This is the gate to the waters of the Wash, for to the east there are the sands of the Burnham Flats and to the west the encroaching drying banks of Friskney and Inner and Outer Dogs Head. Next, and almost equally at 5 miles are the green Lynn Knock, tending to the southwest; the safe-water North Well, tending to the south. Then there is the red Woolpack, tending just to the east of south. North Well establishes you well in the Wash: right in the middle of the Well itself, and the top end of Lynn Deeps. And deep they both can get at near to 50 metres. Finally, well grasped in the jaws of the Wash, come the famously infamous waters marked by the unmistakable float called Roaring Middle. At 2 miles from Long Sand to the east, and three from Sunk Sand to the west, it marks the patch that frequently lives up to its name. From here on in, channels and routes diverge for one of the four ports of the Wash, which are, reading from east to west: Boston; Fosdyke (not to be confused with the Fossdyke of the Witham-and-Fossdyke navigation above Boston); Wisbech and King's Lynn.

Easterly close approaches

Now for the closer approaches. First from the south, from which direction the tides are favourable and it is possible to choose a helpful, forward-looking stream all the way from Great Yarmouth. Cruising at 6–7 knots, you should be able to follow the stream straight into the Wash on the early flood, thus arriving at the ever-present Bar before your final destination just about half tide; and having been able to do so without having had recourse to flat-out pushing or forcing – either craft, engines or crew. Although the tides are agreeable when coming from Great Yarmouth, there are other factors to be taken into consideration: the coastline of North Norfolk, from Happisburgh and Cromer, to the southeast corner of the Wash is extremely exposed – especially to those devilish winds from the north that seem so to prevail. Conditions can often be severe enough to render every haven, no matter how modest, to be worth a ransom to caught-out mariners. Unfortunately, however, in conditions of strong winds (with or without the legendary mist and fog) they are difficult, if not indeed impossible, of access. Any attempt will put the vessel in danger of being stranded. In such conditions it is better to be impatiently waiting inside one of the havens, rather than being bravely at risk outside it.

Hugging the coast is fine as far as Wells. After that, I have always made for the red Bridgirdle buoy, the Woolpack and the North Well. This reduces to a minimum the power of the rip off the NE corner of the Wash. Using the Sledway can be an intriguing proposition at a low water spring tide. Sandbanks abound on either side and a careful watch is to be kept on the state and surface of the water if their dangers are to be avoided. Invigorating though!

Craft from Blakeney or Wells-next-the-Sea, or Great Yarmouth may decide on an outer passage to the north of the Stiffkey Overfalls, about 4 miles out, making for, first, the blind, red Bridgirdle, through the Sledway and on to the lit Woolpack, after that making a straight course to the Roaring Middle. Those with craft of suitable draught, and enough local knowledge and/or courage, can choose a course through Holkham Bay, Brancaster Road and past Thornham Harbour to the south of the Gore and Middle Banks keeping, for much of the time, ½ mile offshore and at no time much over a mile, and finishing off with the narrow channel known as The Bays – no more than a couple of cables wide at best. Being of a cautious, if not indeed anxious constitution, I have always opted for the Bridgirdle and Woolpack outer route; but one of these days I am sure I will find a wise and knowledgeable pilot who will guide me so that I can enjoy the landscape from close to. So much for the southerly approach, but we shall return to the havens in the next chapter, The Norfolk Coast.

Westerly close approaches

A similarly close inshore passage for those with local knowledge is to be found when coming from the Humber or further north. It is a perfectly safe short cut and, therefore, extremely tempting for any skipper bound for Boston or Fosdyke. Coming south, once you have passed the lit red Ross Spit buoy, it is possible to take a close inshore passage at about ½ mile out. To seaward you pass inside those with their memorable names: lit red Protector, the Inner Dowsing lightship and the cardinal S Inner Dowsing; none of which should be of serious concern on this route. You will pass those relics of a near-bygone age: Mablethorpe, Chapel St Leonards-and-Hogsforth and Ingoldmells with its yellow marker, until you finally arrive at Skegness, marked by its blind green buoy and gasholder. This stretch of the Lincolnshire coast is very much like that of the north coast of Norfolk over the water:

long, low, flat and with few really noticeable features. The major difference is that Lincolnshire possesses nothing remotely like a harbour so there is nowhere to run between Spurn and Gibraltar Point.

There is even more tourist-resort life ashore than when I was a teenager, keen to get away to the school conferences and courses that were held there. Anything from Greek to religious knowledge was grist to the grinding mill of 'boy in search of girl'. Rewarding it might have been then, and perhaps even more so now, but at sea it is nevertheless a fairly long and grim haul from, say, the northern delights of Brid, Scarboro' fair and Grimsby down the coast to the northeast corner of the Wash.

The close approach round the bend to the southwest takes you past the blind green Skegness and Skegness South buoys (guarding the Outer and Inner Dog's Head banks to the south) and to the blind red Wainfleet Roads; after which it is a straight southerly course past Gibraltar Point. Then, tending just westerly, comes the Wainfleet Swatchway that leads down to Boston Deep. The Swatchway is marked by the (all blind) red Inner Knock, the green Swatchway, the green Pompey, the green Long Sand, the green Friskney, the green Scullridge down to the cardinal Freeman Inner and the ever popular Roger Sand.

The Wainfleeet Swatchway is no longer as broad as it used to be, but it is still easily usable by leisure craft – even those with draughts up to 2·4m. There is also a special connection between the end of the Swatchway (just after the green Pompey) and the Well (in the main area of the Wash). It is known as the Parlour Channel and is marked by two starboard buoys, *P1* and *P2*, and two port buoys, *PA* and *PB*.

Slightly easier courses lie ahead once we have reached the cardinal Freeman Inner and join with the main channel into Lower Road down to Clay Hole, a popular waiting station when early on the tide. The well-marked clear channel takes us to the distinct and brightly lit beacons of green Dolly Peg, red Welland and white and green Tabs Head. Here, the channel divides: to port and tending to the southwest leads to the Welland and Fosdyke; while westward is the New Cut and the Haven into the River Witham and then to Boston.

Back to basics – Gibraltar Point and Wainfleet Haven

Before we retrace our steps to the waters of the Roaring Middle, we must take a look at the very northwest corner of the Wash, where, hidden away behind Gibraltar Point, is the first landmark, the first possible stopover berth, nearest to the North Sea. It is Wainfleet Haven, a famous resting place and watering hole, tucked well away from the sea; protected from visiting hordes by a tortuous approach channel which may, with good luck and fortitude, lead the inquisitive stranger eventually to

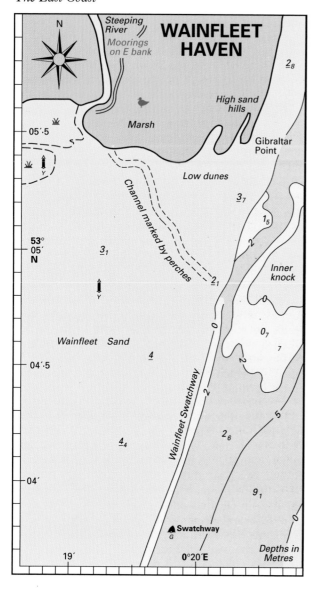

WAINFLEET HAVEN

Steeping River

Moorings on E bank

Marsh

High sand hills

Gibraltar Point

Low dunes

Inner knock

Channel marked by perches

Wainfleet Sand

Wainfleet Swatchway

Swatchway

Depths in Metres

the few berths that are jealously guarded by those lucky enough to have one.

Gibraltar Point must be somewhat incongruously named, since nothing could be less like the high-reaching 2½ square miles of hard rock that marks the Spanish peninsula overlooking the gateway to the Mediterranean. The almost concealed, or even secret, haven is the quiet refuge known variously as Wainfleet Swatchway, the Roads and Wainfleet Haven. If you wish, you can also refer to its upmarket appellation, especially if you are a strict riparian, for it is sometimes referred to as the 'Steeping River'. The area is thrice blessed in its coveted features: the modest Wainfleet Harbour; the nature reserve with its dedicated bands of minders and watchers; and the nearby and equally prestigious Seacroft golf course.

It is situate east of Wainfleet All Saints, which, although it now owns only a pale shadow of its former glory as a thriving harbour, is still a place of old-world charm, and virtually inaccessible except to the gifted explorer or the cognoscenti. Wainfleet

is said to stand on the site of the old Roman town of Vainona. It is probably best known for its famous family-run brewery. There is a special market on Fridays.

Only a little distance to the north is 'Bracing Skegness'. From seaward it is accessible only by beaching or breeches buoy; while by land in any week near to the 'summer season' there is always a mighty traffic jam. Wainfleet is not the kind of haven to be found by chance, offering as it does no easy in-and-out, lazy mains-powered weekend. In fact, it has naught but its rural charm and a commanding view of the Wash.

The Steeping River, at whose outfall Wainfleet Haven sits, is tidal up to Wainfleet All Saints almost 5 miles inland. It was, at one time, busy with commercial shipping, but silting and neighbouring competition put an end to those days. It is now little more than an attractive dream. Wainfleet Haven is approached by a channel that is narrow, tortuous, shallow and, in the main, given over to two kinds of wildlife: first, flora, fauna and birds of a feather; and, second, those eccentric sailors who are attracted by its idiosyncratic charm, the exigencies of time and tide and the frequently changing course of the channel. It is a most useful reserve destination should you happen to be running late on the tide for Boston (that is, if you are fairly sure of your entrances and your exits). It must be added that it is not a suitable harbour of refuge for any stranger or first-time visitor caught out by adverse weather conditions – or even a well-found local for that matter since the area can be very disturbed. Access is not dangerous but neither is it easy, so the best plan is to visit shoresides at low water and make as many friends as you can. Don't be afraid to ask for advice and be ready and willing to take the offer of the guiding hand which is more than likely to be proffered. The channel is not a place for nervous skippers or crews who don't keep their eyes skinned. The Skegness Yacht Club is active in the Haven, as are – still – one or two local professional fishermen. It is also a delight to find that the place possesses real live toilets, an unexpectedly welcome facility in such a remote haven!

Coming from the north, to find the River Steeping channel, you make for the green buoy marking Skegness Middle and then leave Skegness South to starboard tending southwesterly for Wainfleet Roads, continuing thus down to the red Inner Knock Fairway buoy by the Wainfleet Swatchway. From the south, via the Well or Boston Deep, you make for the yellow No. 1 *DZ* and the nearby green Swatchway which will take you more or less northerly to the Inner Knock. You then search out the first Wainfleet Channel buoy. The last series of legs of the approach channel is marked by the Skegness Yacht Club with spar buoys along the outer, seaward section and beacons for the final stretch up to the haven proper. While none of these is quite as obscure as the old Pye End buoy at the entrance to the Walton Backwaters used to be, it can take more than one pair of fine eyes in that kind of dark, misty grey that so often passes for light in the Wash; and while for Christopher Fry The Dark may have been Light Enough, that does not obtain on this part of the low-lying Lincolnshire coast.

The club has also managed to establish moorings for about thirty boats up to 10m LOA and 1·5m draught. However, the top range of such vessels cannot navigate the channel on neap tides. Two or three visitors can usually be accommodated if of shallow draught and with ability to sit up when dried out. If in doubt, and there is no one to assist, tie up alongside the fishing boat or motor boat astern of it. It is vital that you stay on board at subsequent high waters in case they are going to sea. Access is 2 hours either side of HW springs, 1 hour neaps. Offshore banks reduce the swell in onshore winds; and strong S winds reduce the height of HW, especially neaps.

Ian Martin is a worthy local contact, to whom I shall be ever indebted. He describes the channel in these terms: 'Where it traverses the beach, there are small spar buoys with light reflectors, red to port, green to starboard. Where it traverses the marsh, there are beacons, red can tops to port, black or green triangular topmarks to starboard. At night, there is an 'unofficial' light that can help – the north trap light on the nature reserve field station.'

For anyone staying more than a few days in the Wash, it will be impossible not to become aware that there is an RAF range in the vicinity of Wainfleet. The river marks its legal boundary, and anyone navigating the channel into Wainfleet Haven will be neither threatened nor stand in danger. However, the noise will be overwhelming.

Normally, the range is open daily from 0900 until 1700 (office hours even in the skies above!); and night flying takes place on Wednesdays and Fridays up to 2300 during the winter and 2100 during the summer. RAF Command HQ listens on VHF Ch 16 and the range can be contacted by land line on ☎ 01754 820777.

Whether on deck taking a strong sundowner; peering from the observation room of the nature reserve; or out on the no-man's-land that is the foreshore of Gibraltar Point's mud flats, Wainfleet Haven is the kind of place that permits a clear and undistorted view of the Wash; its glories, its many attractions and, from time to time, its extremely bleak perspectives. It is a splendid place to be safe inside after the arduous and tortuous business of getting there; but, upon being there, one is offered a splendid opportunity to view, if not actually encounter, the outer face of the North Sea Wash.

Steps retraced – to Boston

Approaches

The first and most important buoy to locate once the North Well has been left behind is the Roaring Middle, which is about 6 miles to its southwest. Not long ago, the float was a rather strange-shaped, yellow vessel that looked more like a surfing banana than an important aid to navigation. Now, it is red and white, but its new colours have done nothing but elaborate the colourful scheme and it now stands more proudly and more conspicuously than ever before. From the Roaring Middle, we tend to the west for the Boston Roads red and white buoy that marks the entrance to the Freeman Channel. The international buoyage system is owned and maintained by the Port of Boston Authority, and is easy and excellent to follow, as it leads you, station by station from Alpha the first in the actual channel, in impeccable alphabetical order, to Juliet, the last before the aforementioned Dolly Peg, Tabs Head and Welland. When used without cutting corners – for the channels are sometimes steeply edged and narrow – it makes the approach a simple, safe and straightforward matter.

A favourite spot to anchor while awaiting a tide to permit you over the bar and up to Boston is in the area of Clay Hole, and the nearby red Golf and green No. 11 buoys. Clay Hole is as well a protected spot as you can hope to find in the Wash, but in fact I prefer to go not quite to Clay Hole, and to use High Horn instead. However, no matter which place you choose, the chances are that you will be in the company of the local fishing boats queuing up just before opening time.

BOSTON
52°56'·00N 00°05'·00E (Tabs Head Bn)
Charts Admiralty 1200, 108. Imray C29, Y9.
OS Landranger 131

Tides Immingham +0010, Dover –0415

Authorities
Boston Harbour ☎ 01205 362328

Radio
VHF Ch 12 (–0300/+2000 HW and office hours).
Vessels between *Golf* buoy and Grand Sluice must listen on VHF Ch 12
Boston Grand Sluice Lock
☎ 01205 364864 (24-hour answering service)
Dual watch VHF Ch 16 and 74

Boston Marina Ltd
☎ 01205 364420
Tidal access
HW ±2hrs
Ⓥ (45), ⚓, ⚡, 🚾 (nearby), 🛟 (nearby), ⚓D,
Repairs (by arrangement)

BW Moorings
Ⓥ Available.

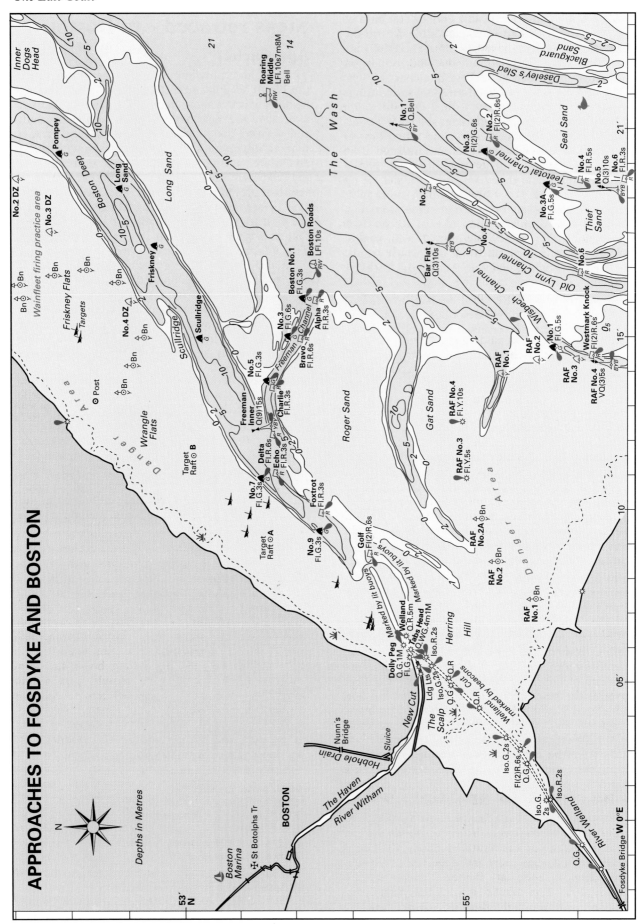

APPROACHES TO FOSDYKE AND BOSTON

N

Depths in Metres

BOSTON

Boston Marina

⚓ St Botolphs Tr

53′ N

Danger Area

Wrangle Flats

⊙ Post

Friskney Flats

Targets

Wainfleet firing practice area

Inner Dogs Head

Pompey
G

No.2 DZ
Y

No.3 DZ
Y

No.4 DZ
Y

Long Sand
G

Friskney
G

Scullridge
G

Boston Deep

Long Sand

Bn ⊕

Bn ⊕

Bn ⊕

Bn ⊕

Bn ⊕

Target Raft ⊙ **B**

Target Raft ⊙ **A**

Delta
G
FI.G.6s

Echo
R
FI.R.3s

No.7
G
FI.G.3s

No.9
FI.G.3s

Foxtrot
R
FI.R.3s

Golf
FI(2)R.6s

Freeman Inner
Q(9)15s

Charlie
FI.R.3s

Freeman Channel

No.5
G
FI.G.3s

No.3
FI.G.6s

Bravo
FI.R.6s

Alpha
FI.R.3s

Boston No.1
FI.G.3s

Boston Roads
RW
LFI.10s

Boston Channel

Roger Sand

Gat Sand

The Wash

Roaring Middle
RW
LFI.10s7m8M
Bell

No.1
BY
Q.Bell

No.2
R
FI(2)G.6s

No.3
FI.G.6s

No.2

No.4

No.4
R
FI.R.5s

No.5
BYB
Q(3)10s

No.6
R
FI.R.3s

No.3A
FI.G.5s

Thief Sand

Seal Sand

Teetotal Channel

Blackguard Sand

Daseley's Sled

Bar Flat
Q(3)10s

No.2

No.1
FI.G.5s

No.2
R
FI(2)R.6s

Westmark Knock
RW

No.1
FI.G.5s

Wisbech Channel

Old Lynn Channel

RAF No.2
Y

RAF No.1

RAF No.3
Y

RAF No.4
VQ(3)5s

RAF No.3
FI.Y.5s

RAF No.4
FI.Y.10s

RAF No.2A
Bn

RAF No.2
Y

RAF No.2
Y ⊕ Bn

RAF No.1
Y ⊕ Bn

RAF No.1
⊕ Bn

Danger Area

Herring Hill

Dolly Peg
Q.G.1M

Welland
Q.G.5m

Tabs Head
Q.WG.4m1M

Marked by lit buoys

Marked by lit buoys

FI.G
Ldg Lts
Iso.G.2s

The Scalp

Iso.R.2s

Welland marked by beacons

Iso.G.2s

Q.G

Q.R

Q.G

Cut

FI(2)R.6s

Iso.G.2s

Iso.R.2s

Q.G

Iso.G.2s

Q.G.G

New Cut

Nunn's Bridge

Sluice

Hobhole Drain

The Haven

River Witham

River Welland

Fosdyke Bridge W 0°E

55′

05′

10′

15′

21′

10

21

14

5

2

2

5

10

10

5

0

5

10

0

5

2

0

5

10

2

5

0

2

0

2

After that, Tab's Head and Dolly Peg show the way into the New Cut to the Haven and the River Witham. Leave Tabs Head to port for Boston. It is possible to get closer in by watching your water through the channel almost up to the well-known trio of beacons. When I was there last, I determined to pass over the bar as soon as I possibly could, although I knew that would mean a necessarily slow trog up the New Cut and The Haven since the bottom is always close until well after half tide – and even if you succeed in getting up to the lock at Boston Grand Sluice you will have to wait for the first-level opening of the Sluice. In order to do that, you need to be off to a good start and with no more than a metre's draught, there will be no problem. Much more will require high-quality skill to keep you out of keel-scraping trouble. In addition, the riverbed is over-supplied with debris and detritus in a variety of forms, from the occasional old car chassis to heavy tyres and supermarket trolleys. More still: there are concrete works on the steeply sloping banks; while eel nets and plastic bottles, harnessed together in mid-stream, also form some keel and prop-threatening formations. An inspection of the river at low water will convince you of the need for caution and accurate pilotage. Basically, tide times for entering the river are the same as the others in the Wash: no better than 3 hours before high water.

Be that as it may, I decided to stand watch by the Welland beacon and move into the New Cut as soon as I could – that is, if I could get to the beacon in the first place. Eventually, I got within striking distance after a long series of stirring soft mud humps and touching slightly harder bottoms – and consequently using a lot of fuel by much use of *Valcon*'s 56-horsepower engines to go astern. In the event, I found that sitting just to the north of the Welland beacon was not a happy occupation. While I was on the bottom looking at the Welland beacon itself and hoping to go afloat, everything was fine, for it was an extremely pleasant evening. But when I did eventually come off, I found myself propelled powerfully to the beacon itself and not into the Bar Channel. It was no easy matter to avoid going aground yet, at the same time, trying to ensure that I moved in the right direction. All in all, it proved that such an exercise is pointless; patient waiting being the name of the game; but nevertheless, the achievement of having tested it for myself gave me modest gratification.

The New Cut and the Haven

Once over the bar and in the New Cut, joy and despair may await you in equal measure. The channel is more or less central, with only the normal hazards of tide-time port and river navigation to be overcome – and, at Boston, these are not formidable. The banks are well marked with beacons, but normally they are needed only for

At the confluence of the man-made-straight streams of the River Witham's New Cut (at left) and the River Welland's Straight Cut, North and Southflow from the East into the everlasting arms of The Wash – here pictured with its channels and sandbanks clearly to be seen.

interest or just to plot your progress and speed over the ground; and all is plain sailing until you reach the area of the docks, where life can become a bit hectic. A radio request to the harbourmaster (VHF Ch 12) will bring information regarding shipping movements; information of some import since room to manoeuvre is never generous and, in the immediate vicinity of the entrance, it is at a premium – there is little space for amicable flirtations between commercial traffic and leisure craft. It is comforting to know that co-operation has always been the order of the day at Boston, with none of the aggravation that sometimes mars relationships between big fishing boats and even bigger commercial shipping vessels, and leisure craft. The meeting of these different worlds has always been a pleasing aspect of Boston's river.

The docks are not available to yachts except in an emergency, and the nearest feasible moorings are just below the first bridge on the port hand where the bottom is soft mud. Under favourable circumstances, craft can stay afloat at all states of the tide. However, laying alongside this short length of wall is a risky affair, only to be considered if you have a robust vessel with sturdy tackle and a stalwart crew who will be staying on board. To move any further upstream for yachts with masts means that they must be lowered in order to negotiate the river bridges and the lock at Grand Sluice.

There are also other possible moorings beyond the railway swing bridge to the docks. They are private jetties and berths, near-berths and so-called berths where, even if you could find the owner, it would take only one tide to convince you that they are not really suitable for leisure craft – fragile or otherwise. Nevertheless, they are in great demand, much valued by local fishermen and pleasure boaters since they afford access to the Wash without the constraints and disciplines that the Grand Sluice enforces. There have been what might be euphemistically termed 'vague ideas', 'sketch plans' and 'proposed projects' around for years to improve, refurbish or even to renew and reorganise the area and its facilities. But, as usual, riparian interests and the delays of local office stand in the way of boaters' progress. At the moment, boats are frequently tethered to unstable jetties and most of them take to the (soft mud) bottom every tide.

If you have lowered your gear to pass under all the bridges up the Boston River, you will be able to get through the Grand Sluice lock without any trouble. The last stretch of the river before the lock is the one where extra care must be taken especially if you are 'early' on the tide, trying to catch the first pen. The bottom is tricky – although there are fewer eel nets than there used to be, there are still enough to warrant a watchful eye. Rocks and a generally foul bottom are to be found reaching from the port bank out as far as mid-stream. Keeping the railway signal in line with the last lamp standard on shoresides will keep you clear of all the obstructions. The worst area is just after the footbridge, where it is foul on both sides and the stretch is generally shoal.

Finally, there is the immediate approach to the lock itself, Grand Sluice! It is an ugly-looking, threatening affair, with gates that can spew out its races at a tremendous rate of knots, and special care is required if sluicing is going on. The whole process can be vicious enough to turn and spin a small boat, so that the skipper really needs enough power to counteract the forces. From time to time, you may need to manoeuvre about or just 'jill around' while awaiting the keeper's advice, instructions or pleasure – and there are powerful eddies to be watched out for, avoided or accommodated.

Overmuch unnecessary hanging around can be avoided by letting the lock-keeper know of your ETA (preferably by phone since VHF reception is poor) he can then ask the sluice-controlling engineers to co-operate, and so ensure that cruising folk are put out as little as possible.

The lock office is equipped with a telephone and answering machine (Boston ☎ 01205 364864) and also on VHF Chs 16 and 74, on which dual watch is maintained. As a final resort, Captain Franklin, the Boston harbourmaster, will consider passing on a message from you via the telephone should necessity demand. The lock is in fact available at tide times during both night and day for anyone making a genuine seagoing passage or requiring a haven from the Wash, but since there is only one keeper, he appreciates not having to work nights as well as days. When the lock-master at Boston lays down the

Just to the right of centre, St. Botolph's mediaeval church (Boston Stump) presides majestically over the River Witham and its Grand Sluice lock to be seen almost parallel with its 'spire'.

law – as he frequently does for he knows it well and is more than ready, willing and able to pass it on – he who disregards it or fails to take proper action, is indeed a sad and sorry man (although later he may well become a wiser one). The lock-keeper is one of the longest serving on the local waterways and, during that time, he has accumulated a great deal of comprehension and apprehension of the ways of leisure craft and is thus well prepared for the vagaries of his job. His characteristic and particular style is singular to a degree (master's, of course).

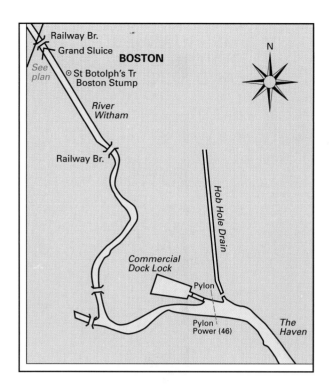

If you have to wait outside the lock, moor only between the ladders, where if you draw less than 1·5m you will be able to stay afloat at all times. If you draw more, you may touch bottom on springs and it is hard concrete. It is quite flat, but since it is hard, exposed engines or outdrives are at risk. The traffic signals are standard. While the navigation is theoretically open from October to April, the river is often run low, so passages are often well nigh impossible.

British Waterways (BW) which runs moorings on the 'fresh' side of the river only, has issued a guide for boaters wishing to pass through the Grand Sluice lock (see page 20).

Halfway between the Wash and the town of Boston is the Pilgrim Fathers' commemorative tablet. The best view, if you have an eye for that kind of thing, is from the river, and not many manage to find it overland; certainly not many of those contemporary Americans who make the pilgrimage to Boston (Lincolnshire) from Boston (Massachusetts, USA). The heart of Boston itself, is totally out of sight from the navigation that actually runs right through the centre of the town. What is, however, remarkably visible and obvious is the tower of the Church of St Botolph, known locally as the Stump. Actually, so high and mighty is it that it is almost impossible not to feel overawed by its dominating presence – you will not be out of its oversight or purview for many a mile. Its higher echelons are now prohibited to the public on account of the growing popularity of suicide attempts from its balconies.

There is little point in going to Boston, with all the trouble of taking down masts (if necessary), without going through the Grand Sluice lock into the fresh water of the river. The first mooring facility is

Boston Marina. Doris Farmer has now retired to her next-door bungalow and keeps a welcoming eye open for old friends. The new proprietors, keen to follow the keen tradition, are John and Christine Guille. There is mains water and electricity at the berths, with the marina's diesel pump nearby. You can telephone the marina at Boston ☎ 01205 364420. A phone call is a wise precaution since it is a very popular spot in the summer season.

For further information on the Witham & Fossdyke Navigation, please refer to the author's *Northeast Waterways* guide, also published by Imray.

Boston

No skipper ever finds himself in Boston by chance. It is so far inland from the North Sea as to make a 'chance' call out of the question. Its position at the end of the Witham and Fossdyke Navigation demands that real thought must be given to getting there; and any navigation from salt to fresh, or vice versa, for any yachtsman not based in the area, is one that requires serious thought. But positively acting on that serious thought will bring its own reward since there are so many excellent reasons for making such a special trip to this out-of-the-way capital of South Holland. The trip is worthwhile on two counts: the welcome you will find on the upstream of the lock, at both the BW moorings (now much improved) and Boston marina moorings; and that from the local clubs on the other (west) side of the river.

Then there is the town itself. Many of the local shopkeepers seem to be related to one another, and if they are not, then they are close friends. If they cannot get what you want, they generally know a man who can. The town has kept up with the times sufficiently for small family butchers and bakers to be in short supply, but those who have not gone under are in great demand. No doubt there are

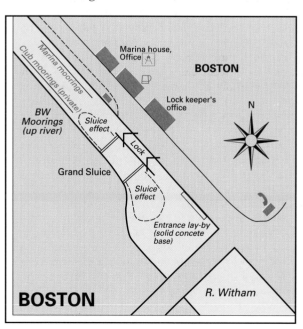

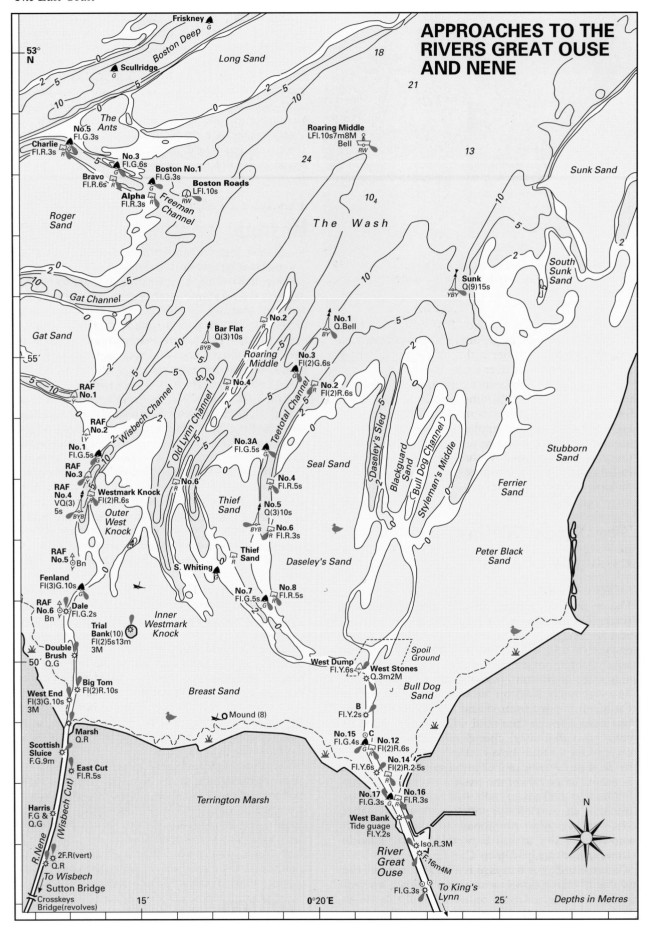

APPROACHES TO THE RIVERS GREAT OUSE AND NENE

Friskney
G

Boston Deep

Long Sand

18

53°
N

21

Scullridge
G

2
5

10

0

The Ants

No.5
Fl.G.3s

Charlie
Fl.R.3s
G
R

No.3
Fl.G.6s
G

Boston No.1
Fl.G.3s
G

Roaring Middle
LFl.10s7m8M
Bell
RW

13

Sunk Sand

Bravo
Fl.R.6s
G
R

Boston Roads
LFl.10s
RW

24

Alpha
Fl.R.3s

Freeman Channel

The   Wash

10₄

10

Roger Sand

0

5

2

Sunk
Q(9)15s
YBY

South Sunk Sand

Gat Channel

0

10

Gat Sand

5
10

0

No.2
R

Bar Flat
Q(3)10s
BYB

Roaring Middle

No.1
Q.Bell
BY

55'

5

5

10

No.3
Fl(2)G.6s
G

Daseley's Sled

RAF No.1
Y

10

5

No.4
R

No.2
Fl(2)R.6s
R

5

Blackguard Sand

Bull Dog Channel

Styleman's Middle

Stubborn Sand

RAF No.2
Y

2

Old Lynn Channel

5

Wisbech Channel

No.3A
Fl.G.5s
G

Teetotal Channel

0

Seal Sand

5

Ferrier Sand

No.1
Fl.G.5s
G

RAF No.3
Y

2

10

No.6
R

Westmark Knock
Fl(2)R.6s

0

No.4
Fl.R.5s

Thief Sand

No.5
Q(3)10s
BYB

RAF No.4
VQ(3)5s
BYB

Outer West Knock

No.6
Fl.R.3s
R

Daseley's Sand

Peter Black Sand

RAF No.5
Bn
Y

S. Whiting

Thief Sand

Fenland
Fl(3)G.10s
G

RAF No.6
Bn
Y

Dale
Fl.G.2s

Inner Westmark Knock

No.7
Fl.G.5s
G

No.8
Fl.R.5s
R

Trial Bank(10)
Fl(2)5s13m 3M

Double Brush
Q.G

50'

Spoil Ground

Big Tom
Fl(2)R.10s

Breast Sand

West Dump
Fl.Y.6s

West Stones
Q.3m2M

Bull Dog Sand

West End
Fl(3)G.10s 3M

Mound (8)

B
Fl.Y.2s

Marsh
Q.R

Scottish Sluice
F.G.9m

East Cut
Fl.R.5s

No.15
Fl.G.4s
G

C

No.12
Fl(2)R.6s
R

(Wisbech Cut)

Fl.Y.6s

No.14
Fl(2)R.2·5s
R

Terrington Marsh

No.17
Fl.G.3s
G

No.16
Fl.R.3s
R

Harris
F.G & Q.G

West Bank
Tide guage
Fl.Y.2s

Iso.R.3M

2F.R(vert)

R.Nene

Q.R

River Great Ouse

F.16m4M

To Wisbech

Sutton Bridge

Crosskeys Bridge(revolves)

Fl.G.3s

To King's Lynn

15'

0°20'E

25'

N

Depths in Metres

There are private jetties and berths, near-berths and so-called berths where craft are frequently tethered to unstable jetties.

thieves, rogues and vagabonds in Boston but I have never encountered a single one, and Boston must be Lincolnshire's contender with Norfolk for the most appealing East Coast river town.

From Boston, with proper timing, you can cruise the waters of the Wash, almost endlessly at leisure for they have so much of contrast to offer. You can also begin the long exploration of the inland waterways of the northeast, starting perhaps with the deliciously named Witham Navigable Drains. Boston is one of my favourite ports of call, and it is difficult to think of a river port that can offer more.

The River Welland to Fosdyke

Approaches

The regime for getting in and out of the River Welland is the same as for Boston and the New Cut; but, if anything, it is better to leave any attempted entry until a little later for the Welland Cut. There are some areas of the bed of the river which are not only uneven but also 'close'. Moreover, the flood tide can really shift on its way up to the bridge. Classically, it is unsound and unsafe to have your bows stuck fast on the mud with a spring flood up your stern. For more thoughts on this, please see under 'Great Ouse' below. It is prudent, therefore, to consider access to be no better than HW ± 2 hours at the mouth of the river.

The Tabs Head and Welland beacons are the manifest signposts for the Welland Cut, with Tabs Head being left to starboard. The first stretch, known as The Cut, lies between the sandbanks of Herring and Scalp. Up to Cut End and the River Welland itself, the buoyage is standard and well lit. Welland Cut channel is straight, trained by walls and marked by beacons on its bank. They are lit, and most have radar reflectors.

In general, Fosdyke Bridge is the head of navigation for visitors, certainly for masted vessels. If you cannot pass under the bridge, turn well before it so that you have plenty of time to stem the tide, which can get up to 5+ knots. A good idea is to start turning just before you reach the moorings on the starboard (north) hand. Your turn should be made to the south, and it is essential to have plenty of power. Mooring is problematic below and above the bridge. A prior visit or telephone call should be made to the Port of Fosdyke Ltd.

Fosdyke Bridge

Welland Cut runs through low-lying marshlands where, shortly after entering, there are to starboard one or two 'last ditches' (they can hardly be called channels) where those with a mind to get well away from it all can navigate at springs, to find truly better 'oles. It is a pleasant, wildlife anchorage in back-of-beyond Boston, provided you are fully self-supporting or enjoy tripping the light fantastic in the dinghy. The only risk is that you will become so lotus eater-like that you will get neaped. An alternative entertainment is to search out one of the Lineham family. They have been in the area for centuries. Wherever you find one, especially if it be John, you will get a good tale, excellent conversation, first-rate assistance and as much advice as you can take. All the time and effort expended on getting there and finding a berth somewhere, will be well rewarded. You may become overwhelmed by the looming silhouette of Fosdyke bridge at sundown and will no doubt turn to the Ship Inn for sustenance. You will certainly find a warm welcome awaiting, for (a) hardly anyone will believe that you have a managed to get there at all, and (b) that you wanted to get there in the first place.

The quayside at Fosdyke (on the starboard hand going upstream just before the bridge) is a dramatic place to berth. Not only is there the usual amazing rise and fall of the Wash tide with its equally amazing fast flood; but there is also the complication of strong back eddies created by the masonry and support of the bridge. The now closed-to-navigation Fosdyke bridge is a very substantial affair that will see off any assailant. It is best not to become in any way involved with it. Reserve power is essential so that you can turn easily and hold your own against the flood tide without stress.

The Port of Fosdyke Ltd is a small commercial quay which lays claim to neither official, unofficial or even informal facilities for yachts; and even if there were, getting a line to that high, high-and-mighty jetty is a demanding and potentially fraught job – especially when there is no one ashore to help. With prior permission, you may be able to lie alongside a big ship – also a somewhat problematic exercise. But, Fosdyke is undoubtedly 'special', if only for being one of the few remaining 'open' ports left in the UK.

Sutton Bridge. There are stagings not far from the swing bridge. Some moorings are still used by local fishermen. It is best to obtain prior permission, and essential not to disrupt their routines.

If you can get under Fosdyke bridge, you will then be able to see that there are some private moorings on the starboard hand. From Fosdyke it is no distance back to Boston for that matter and, for once, it is possible to move between two of the Wash ports on one tide; that is, not having to anchor outside. All it needs is a simple manoeuvre of turning the corner at Tabs Head. Even more than at Boston, it obtains that no one arrives at Fosdyke by chance.

From Fosdyke it is not far to Spalding, which, years ago, was a thriving seaport situated deep in the heart of agriculture. Some of the merchants' magnificent mansions still stand as a tribute to the commercial drive and success of the local businessmen and entrepreneurs. In the town of Spalding itself, the waters are above a lock; and since they are no longer tidal, there is no sign of the ferocity that can reign at the river mouth nor the tide rip further towards Fosdyke Bridge. Craft drawing no more than a metre can attain the upper reaches outside the town on good tides, but there is little to attract the boating fraternity per se, although the town offers much in the way of historical monuments, cultural singularities, botanical features and strong vegetables.

Back at Fosdyke Bridge, the isolated countryside possesses little in the way of clichés or plastic Brummagem, and for that reason alone is often felt to be worth what can be an experimental-to-troublesome trip and mooring; whether it is accomplished by boat, by dinghy, by foot or by public transport, for – as I have hinted above – Boston is only just around the corner. There is a well-stocked shop; the beer is of Bateman's best; and the company is even better. In the wise locals you will find friendly advisers who are expert on the ways and wiles of the Wash. Those with a mind to listen and look will not fail to be impressed by the sensory input. Not only is there always much to read, mark, learn and inwardly digest – but most of it is rich beyond the general ways of these Flatlands . . . for mind and body alike.

It is true that Agriculture Rules, but this form of rural husbandry is a hard and harsh taskmaster and many of the indigens have a really hard time. Some of them do no more than scratch a living from meagre smallholdings – rather like the Poor Whites in the Deep South. But that does not prevent them from leading lives that, while physically under the hammer, sickle, forceps and tongs of still-lingering Thatcherite market forces, are nevertheless to be found psychologically, humanly and emotionally in good grace, better fettle and best spirits. Indeed, I still recall with warmth that on one of my many weather-bound stopovers at Fosdyke, I found myself dejectedly looking at a tiny patch of cauliflowers. It was hardly any time at all before I was encouraged out of my miserable pondering, by the grower; proudly carrying a sack filled with four gorgeous exhibits. The phrase 'Beware of Yellow-bellies Bearing Gifts' was entirely inappropriate, insulting even, for the man would permit no money to change hands. I managed, however, to put the matter to rights later in the day at the pub. Fosdyke is an unique experience; best appreciated by those with a penchant for the recherché.

There are also plenty of good yeoman stock to see that you are looked after like a gentleman: some of these vocal locals have ancestors who were there before the Romans – and they know what's what. They can also sniff out who's who; and all get treated accordingly – and that usually means generously.

The River Nene to Wisbech
Approaches
Yet again, the access is no better than half tide. Prudence recommends, here particularly, that it is better not to try to set off other than 2 hours before high water at the mouth of the river. To approach the River Nene, the first buoy to locate after Roaring Middle is the cardinal Bar Flat, the pilots' station for Wisbech and Sutton Bridge. In fair weather, that is, as in bad weather, they stand by at the RAF No. 5. After the Bar Flat, the next buoy is the lit green No. 1. Almost all leisure craft will be able to reach the cardinal wreck buoy RAF No. 4, where there is usually at least 5m. In the area to the west of Outer Westmark Knock and to the north of the cardinal Kerr, there is plenty of space for all-comers to anchor. Extra care need be taken only when tending to the south on a big spring tide, when it is risky for those without local knowledge. Then it is a case of waiting for at least an hour after the flood has started, even with little more than a metre's draught if you want to be sure of not finding the bottom. For some years now there has been a trial bank about 2 miles to the south of the anchorage, monitoring the movement and strengths of the surrounding conditions. A local rule of thumb is that, once there is water all round its base wall, it is possible for 1·5m craft to gain Wisbech. It makes sense to wait for this event and set off with a fair amount of assurance.

The Wisbech Channel itself is well marked by a combination of buoys and beacons. After RAF No. 4, there is one more cardinal to be left to port before the well-known green Fenland buoy hoves into view. The channel then is marked by a few buoys and a series of beacons, all of which are starboard hand. Although the chart shows variety, if not indeed whimsy, with regard to the channel in this area, there is little point in trying to find it, as a directly straight course (just west of south) 1 hour after the flood will keep you safe. The RAF beacon No. 5 should be kept well to starboard. After the Fenland buoy, there is a smart turn to starboard (much sharper than the charts indicate) to pick up the beacons which are all starboard hand until you come to the last, Big Tom.

These beacons are best left about a cable away; but you do need to be close enough to make sure that you are not lining up one of the derricks, chimneys, posts and perches that abound on the shore. The beacons lead to the intriguingly named Big Tom and West End, with the former being left to port and the latter to starboard. They mark the start of the training wall. Just after Big Tom, to port and on the other side of the training wall is a classically named spot, 'Crab's Hole'. From this point, the channel is straight ahead. The first feature to catch the eye is the pair of (now disused) lighthouses, one of which was home to painter/naturalist Peter Scott. They are still not entirely decayed and stand as reminders of the days when this was a channel much used by the big ships that once visited what is claimed to be the Capital of the Fens, Wisbech. Before gaining the town, however, there is another feature to be encountered, one which is of much more navigational significance, and that is Sutton Bridge.

Sutton Bridge
Sutton Bridge, just like everything else on the Nene 'Cut' to Wisbech, is straight ahead. The bridge master keeps radio watch on Chs 9 and 16 every hour. But with advance notice he will co-operate on Ch 14 via 16. The area below Sutton Bridge is the last place where it is possible to moor before Wisbech itself. There is a staging by the West Old Light, and near the swing bridge the remains of an old dock. In the summer there is the pontoon facility of the Peterborough Yacht Club. Moorings are still used by local fishermen and it is essential not to disrupt their routines. It is best to obtain prior permission. An over-tide stop is actually possible at all of these places by negotiation, should the need arise. However, that would be only for the skipper on his way out, awaiting his best departure time. It is not likely that any inward-bound skipper or crew would want to delay their arrival at the town quay for the unusual experiences that are on offer in the capital of the Fens.

Wisbech
In Wisbech itself, there is often a mooring space to be found on either hand just below the bridge; but the only sure way of obtaining a good berth is by getting on with the locals. Without a first or second thought, the folk on the jetty, be they fishermen, coaster crew or local marketers will deny all knowledge of the port. In particular, they will protest complete lack of erudition on the subject of the likely movement of any of the berth-holders. They will also claim absolute ignorance about who actually is the proud and proper occupant of any or

WISBECH

52°40'·00N 00°09'·65E

Charts Admiralty 1200, 1190. Imray Y9, C29, Landranger OS 132.

Tides

Immingham +0005, Dover −0450

Access to Wisbech 4·8m at springs, 3·4m at neaps

Authorities

Sutton Bridge harbourmaster ☎ 01406 351530

Radio

VHF Ch 09, 14, 16 (from HW −4hrs to HW when vessels are expected)

Pilots

Louis Doubleday ☎ 01945 773285

all of the berths. What is more, there will be a paucity of opinion as to whether he/she will be using it on that tide . . . or indeed on any subsequent tide. Hardly anyone seems to understand the need of yachtsmen to find a suitable berth before the tide starts to leave them high and dry at a quite unsuitable spot.

This pretence at ignorance of the whereabouts of berthing spots and/or their owner is a well-known ploy at many mooring spots, but the Wisbech locals have learned the skills in very truth and have taken them to the level of fine art. Should you be so bold as to tie up without local consultation (no matter how brief or pointless) or, more pertinently, consent, there will immediately appear on the scene a quayside lawyer who will inform you at length, and usually lugubriously, that 'Bill' or 'Fred' or 'Jim' is coming up the river on the last of the flood. It will not be until you have made fast your lines to the berth where it seemed least likely that you would be assaulted or cast off, that there will always be someone 'just passing by' who thinks he 'just ought to tell you' that the berth belongs to an irascible local who has a way not only with words but also with yachtsmen – and even more so with their lines.

When you have finally unmade those very lines and cast off, you will probably be lucky and just in time to get out of trouble (that is, out of deep water and into deeper water) by taking the tide of your affairs (and those of the river) at the ebb and letting it lead on to fortune; thus avoiding a voyage bound in shallows and in miseries. Better to float down just ahead of the ebb and achieve Sutton Bridge than to linger longer perhaps unhappily by the quay and accomplish nothing but grief.

Searching out the local fisherman with the kindest-looking features and gaining his blessing is probably the best ploy. Most of the time such a blessing is given: sometimes willingly, other times reluctantly . . . it all depends on prior politeness. Seriously though, although accommodation for leisure-craft yachts is severely limited, in the end there is usually 'just one more space, if you don't want to stay too long'.

For all but shallow-draught boats (less than 1·2m), below the bridge at Wisbech is considered to be the head of navigation. Skippers wishing to go further up river should contact the lock-keeper at the lock with the intriguing appellation 'Dog-in-a-Doublet' well in advance, since there is often a shortage of water, thus preventing passage to Peterborough.

Wisbech's 'Town Bridge' contrasts quite unfavourably with the cast-iron railings and beautiful façades of the 'Heritage' merchants' Georgian houses. Close by, just below the bridge by the 'traditional' visitors' berths, is the much more impressive edifice of the police force.

The town is remarkable in a number of ways. When the draining of the Fens took place in the 17th and 18th centuries, the farmland created brought great prosperity and greater riches to the area; and this, in turn, brought trade and commerce. The produce of the surrounding farmlands was dispatched via the port. Some of the results of the wealth it brought can still be seen today in the well-preserved and extraordinarily elegant houses and mansions. For example, the Crescent and Museum Square have very fine buildings, including the amazing Wisbech 'Castle' – a splendid example of Regency building. There are two Brinks, the North and the South; presumably named because of their situation on opposing banks of the river. It is said that the North Brink is among the most famous and beautiful Georgian streets in England.

In particular, situated on the North Brink is Peckover House which, with its famous gardens, is administered by the National Trust. The walled garden is classic Victorian, quiet and secret. The house was built in 1722, and bought by one Jonathan Peckover at the end of the century. He came from Fakenham and founded a local bank which was to become part of Barclays. The house is open to the public. William Godwin was also a Wisbech man. He married Mary Wollstonecraft, and their daughter Mary, married Shelley. Mary Shelley is more remembered in the town than is her father − no doubt for her (in)famous novel *Frankenstein*. The town was also the birthplace of Octavia Hill, one of the early creators of the National Trust, and there is museum to her memory in South Brink.

If Fosdyke represents the recherché, then Wisbech characterises the eccentric. It is a collection of opposites; and while they are not actually warring factions, they create an ambivalent atmosphere in the town. I have been told sinister tales and legends, not only by amateur gossips, but also by those professional prattlers, the police; but in spite of all the supposed mayhem that inhabits the town and its locale, I have always found the Wisbech people to be friendly to a degree and ever ready to serve without fear or favour. I have never been knowingly overcharged for anything I have bought in the place – not even the market. In this unusual township you will find the old and the new, the stylish and the plebeian, the rich and the poor, the generous and the greedy, the licentious and the prude, side by side and almost hand in hand; for it is a place of captivating contradictions.

While Wisbech is undoubtedly a place of superb interest and character, and well worth a visit for domestics, food and drink, it does not cater much for the boater's specialised needs.

If you want to proceed to the calmer waters above the intriguingly named Dog-in-a-Doublet lock, you must first navigate the fixed road bridge in Wisbech. The heights and states of the tide, your draught and air draught all enter into the complicated equation that must be worked out before you will know whether or not such a project is feasible. You will discover that you are likely to need to add 2 hours on to those listed for the mouth of the river for the lock to be in your favour. From Guyhirn, the lock is 8 miles upstream. Headroom clearance at Guyhirn Road Bridge, as at Wisbech, varies with the state of the tide. Whittlesey Washes (Moreton's Leam) discharges above Guyhirn on the right bank and can be strong enough at times to require careful attention.

The locks at the Dog-in-a-Doublet are manned most daylight hours. In common with standard practice, no mooring is permitted within 100 metres of the lock except in passage. Water point and toilet facilities are available with a lock key. A pay-phone in the lock office may be used during opening hours. The eponymous pub is nearby and has a restaurant and, in Whittlesey, no more than a brisk mile away, all basic needs can be met. The first 2 miles upstream of the lock are completely straight. After that, the twisty channel starts as it means to go on with two sharp bends. Above the lock, close by Stanground Backwater, there is a single-span road bridge. Fitzwilliam Bridge is a double-span, and marks the de-restricted speed limit 1 mile stretch. It is clearly marked at both ends and caution is to be exercised when water skiing is in progress. After this, the quieter, calmer and more casual life of canal-boating takes over and progress can be made to Peterborough – and right up to Northampton if wished – but by no stretch of the imagination has such a trip anything in common with the East Coast.

The Great Ouse to King's Lynn

Approaches

Decades ago, the main channel to King's Lynn was what is now known as the Old Lynn Channel, and was the main approach to the west side of Roaring Middle and Thief Sand. In 1966, a training wall was built to prevent the severe scouring caused by the power and swiftness of the tide, and it served its purpose well. Partly as a result of this artifice there are still semi-secret channels across the sands at high water to Wisbech – for those in the know. Namely

those on whom the mantle of wisdom sits and who, like London taxi drivers, have 'The Knowledge'.

Recently the channel was through Cork Hole from the Roaring Middle light float. A straightforward southeast route, easy to follow and with no navigational hazards. The pilot boats used to wait around the area of the tide gauge – a great help to visiting yachtsmen. The buoyage was well-laid and, if followed exactly, with no corners cut, was problem free. When the tide was out, some of the buoys could be seen sitting on the very edges of the banks, high and mighty above the channel itself. Close encounters were not unknown; and, to improve the shining hour, the tide was swift and strong – reaching, at times, more than 2 knots. This channel was used for many a year.

But, in late summer 1995, Captain Garside (tugmaster and HM to King's Lynn Conservancy Board) and his staff rerouted the approach back to the old Teetotal Channel. During the autumn, some sad souls who had not seen the notes to mariners, found themselves in trouble by just following their old ways or their uncorrected charts. Indeed, the Admiralty *3364/95 Notice* now offers the following, sad to read, correction: 'King's Lynn Apps, Stylemans Middle, insert stranded wk' – right in the middle of the old channel. Even with the new buoyage, it is still wise to call Lynn Harbour for advice of traffic movements, and to take any appropriate instruction. Once the buoys have been spotted, they serve extremely well and there is little chance of any watchful skipper getting into error.

Ignoring any wilful foolhardiness, the time to start from the Wash for King's Lynn and in all probability Denver Sluice, or to leave the Great Ouse for the Wash will depend upon your draught, air-draught, speed and destination. There is no point in steaming faster than the rate of the flood tide, for that will only bring about an encounter with the bottom. Conversely, it is unwise to be late if you are en route for the lock at Denver Sluice, since the question of air draught and headroom under the many bridges on the Great Ouse is paramount. This is a matter for some study, and prospective navigators should contact the lock-keeper at Denver and/or a local pilot who will advise and/or assist.

KING'S LYNN
52°49'·72N 00°21'·30E (West Stones Bn)
Charts Admiralty 1200, 108. Imray Y9.
OS Landranger 132
Tides Immingham +0030, Dover −0445
Access to dock HW −1½ hrs to HW
Authorities
KLCB Harbourmaster ☎ 01553 773411
Radio
KLCB VHF Ch **14**, 16, 11, 12
Pilots
Louis Doubleday ☎ 01945 773285
John Lineham ☎ 01205 260618

I was originally advised to let the flood run for about an hour before even trying to begin to make my way inland, and I still find nothing wrong with this counsel. True, some local fishermen do set off earlier, but they all know the shifting grounds well, and not many of them draw as much as the 2m that some of the Boston boats do. Unless you know who is in front, it is better not to follow. On the whole I think it is best to consider access as being no better than half-tide from outside and 2 hours to high water from the mouth.

I can still remember one of my earliest visits to the Wash and King's Lynn. I was anchored towards the southeast corner of the Wash near the Sunk Sand waiting for the tide into the Ouse. I reported my position and my intentions to King's Lynn Radio and relaxed. As usual, I pretended to fish. 'Pretended', that is, as in 'pretender: one who makes baseless, false or insupportable claims'; for I am successful in the piscatorial stakes only when mackerel are shoaling like the crazed Gadarene, with their fishy eyes fixed on the tackle for their self-immolation. Even then, my hooks, lines and sinkers are more perilous to me than to the fish. As if to confirm my inefficiency and lack of intimidation to surrounding life, wild or otherwise, I was closely encountered by three seagulls, all of a particularly impertinent bent. For a long time, I thought I could hear them in telecommunication with a band of seals, letting them know how pathetic this human was. In keeping with this wheeling indifference, I was solicited, or so I thought, by a solo seal; but all he/she did was to sidle close to *Valcon*'s stern and wallow off after a massive show of indifference.

It was relaxing to be in waters where every buoy was on station with a name that could be easily read and a light that showed at the advertised times and intervals. Up to that moment the Wash had disclosed nothing of its inmost nature and little of its deep-seated disposition. It had been a trouble-free inland sea. Not wanting to overtake the young flood, for I wasn't really late on the tide, I glided slowly and effortlessly along with it, looking to discern something of its special qualities.

As I moved slowly through the narrow channel, the still-exposed banks of mud unfolded to each side in sad but splendid grandeur. The ribbon of the rising tide showed me the way as clearly as ever did the Yellow Brick Road to its four arcane space travellers. It led me on through an apparent maze of undulating contours, where steep mounds and elongated humps lay like the carcasses of prehistoric amphibians. As the setting sun slanted on the banks and the relatively motionless waters, it seemed to sculpt mountains emerging from a slow stream of lava.

Occasionally, the shriek of a seagull or the baying of a seal would filter through the slight mist to add yet another aspect of other-worldliness to my circumstance. It was a vast vista; the whole scene majestic and compelling. I only wish that all my

entrances to the Great Ouse could have been so mild and wonderful.

I was jolted back into the other world of the Wash by a timely VHF call from King's Lynn Radio wanting to know why I wasn't on the move and telling me that if I didn't get up there soon I would lose the light. Captain Garside and his staff are more caring than they have need to be, especially when they are busy with big ships on the tide. Of course, there is no doubt an element of self-interest in their solicitations, wanting no trouble from leisure craft – but I am convinced it is, in the main, the gentle co-operative art of humane mariners.

But back now to the new channel: features to note in particular are the West Dump yellow buoy and the cardinal West Stones which mark the long training wall that goes all the way into Lynn Cut from that point on the west side, and from the new cut itself on the east. After the first mile of the training wall, which is virtually southerly, the channel tends to the southeast when approaching King's Lynn, and the route is straight ahead for the docks, the port and the town.

King's Lynn

King's Lynn itself has not yet made up its mind whether to stay plebeian or to take on the more upmarket Lynn Regis as its nomenclature. Since there is a North and South, as well as a West Lynn, it is ironic that there is no sign of the best known of all: East Lynne.

However, there is more to this argument than Kings and Cardinals (no matter how pointed) since, before 1537, the area was called 'Bishop's Lynn', after Herbert de Losinga, one of the Lords Spiritual. He had an eye not only for the Three Estates, but also for real estate, and bought himself into the top drawer by bribing King William II to give him the office and title of Bishop of Norwich. When Pope Paschal II got to know of this at the opening of Norwich Cathedral (1101) he made the bishop build priories and churches all over the place. One of the biggest was built at Great Yarmouth on the sand: '. . . and the rain descended, and the floods came, and the winds blew and beat upon that house; and it fell: and great was the fall of it.' The other huge affair was Holy Mary Magdalene and St Margaret (see below), and All Holy Virgins: only one degree better in siting, it was erected on salt-marsh, one of Herbert de Losinga's own plots at an encampment known as Linn – Saxon for a small lake. The fact that it already had a church was as nought; and to seal the matter and his ego at one fell swoop, it became 'Bishop Losinga', later turning into Bishop's Lynn – with one of the prized markets. There is more: another Bishop, Turbe of Norwich, envied Herbert, and tried to outsmart him by building a completely new town just to the north, merely in order to be able to erect a church (St Nicholas) – and have a market. So came about the two towns, hardly twinned, and the two markets, forever foes. King John united the towns and chartered the markets in 1204.

There is one drawback to King's Lynn: while the town has many and manifest attractions, it has no facility for visiting leisure craft. The problem is twofold: King's Lynn port and docks are extremely busy with big commercial shipping traffic; and the rise and fall of tide is such that any quayside berthing is a very difficult operation. It is almost impossible to envisage how, without a major and massively expensive excavation and building scheme, the situation could ever be improved for visiting yachts. A great sadness this, since King's Lynn itself is such a pleasingly built, welcoming community, as soaked in history as were King John's jewels in the Wash – except, of course, that all that happened in another county . . . miles away.

The following quote establishes the pride that the City Fathers have in their history:

Built in the 1420s, the magnificent Guildhall of the Holy Trinity Saturday Market Place is one of Lynn's most important buildings. Next-door is Tales of the Old Gaol House – opened by HRH Prince Charles in March 1993, where stories of local witches, murderers and highwaymen are recreated in original atmospheric 18th- and 19th-century cells. Ticket includes entry to the Regalia Rooms, where artefacts including the priceless 14th-century 'King John Cup' are displayed.

Also in the Saturday Market Place is the 12th-century Church of St Margaret, a beautiful building with some impressive original windows and brasses. Priory Lane features the 15th-century archway of a 12th-century Benedictine Priory; Nelson Street includes the exterior of Hampton Court, a medieval merchant's house and warehouse; the 15th-century Hanseatic Warehouse is visible from St Margaret's Lane; and Bridge Street features the late medieval Church of All Saints. Queen Street and King Street are lined with Georgian-fronted medieval buildings, and are close to Purfleet Quay, where the famous Custom House overlooks the river. Further along King Street is St George's Guildhall, the largest surviving medieval guildhall in England, now housing the King's Lynn Arts Centre. Behind the Guildhall is the Red Barn Gallery, where regular exhibitions are mounted. A short walk through the town is the Lynn Museum near the bus station, where a range of local treasures are housed in a former chapel. St Nicholas' Chapel, St Ann's Street, is the largest early 15th-century chapel of ease in England and overlooks the charming cobbles of Pilot Street.

King's Lynn. The crosspiece of the 'T' is the Wash; the slanted 'upright' the Great Ouse: 'Water, water, everywhere. Nor any drop to anchor – nor any spot to berth?

Nearby is True's Yard Museum – a fascinating record of Lynn's fishing heritage. On London Road is the Red Mount Chapel, a curiously shaped 15th-century building, and further along London Road is the South Gate, last remaining of the three 15th-century entrances through the Town Defences.

But, back to other business. The docks are exclusively for commercial traffic, except for emergencies. Tradition has it that, alongside the quays, there are 'barges' that stay afloat at all states of the tide; and against which a yacht may moor without fear or favour and free of fee. This is not the case in many ways: the barges do not stay afloat; the bottom in that region is foul in the extreme; leisure craft are not permitted to moor there; and, since no berth exists, it can be neither f.o.c. nor paying. Yachts may moor there just as sheep may safely graze in the company of wolves.

Tradition also informs that you may berth free of charge in front of the very Customs House; and finally that you can 'arrange something' with the fishermen who use Fisher Fleet, Purfleet and Mill Fleet. More likely, they will 'arrange' something with you; and to their advantage. As T S Eliot said, 'tradition without intelligence is not worth having'. In this case, certainly, intelligence can often be the better part of tradition. There are some isolated sunk concrete buoys below the road bridge, but none commonly available to visitors.

Recent changes have brought some slight improvement with mooring buoys (see below); but even so, visitors should start to make enquiries about a possible booking well ahead of their expected arrival; and should you, by the greatest of good fortune, get allotted one of the Port Authority moorings, just across from the harbourmaster's office and within hailing distance of the East/West Lynn ferry, you will find that the ferrymen are more than pleased to help you to and fro.

Just below the road bridge, the Great Ouse Boating Association (GOBA) maintains three moorings of its own strictly for members, while the Denver Cruising Club similarly has two. There is also one noticeable yellow Harbour Authority buoy, and use of this requires even more prior organisation and permission than those of the Association and the Club. Even if prior permission can be obtained, it is not easy to pick them up as many of the lines and markers are pulled under by the strength of the tide – and it can be a patience-exhausting activity to wait for the flood to lose its sting.

Some brazen souls have tried for a berth with the fishing brethren in Friars Fleet. They have regretted it only slightly less than those who have been reckless enough to leave their boats at Boal Quay, unattended, failing to think of local 'trespassers' and completely ignoring, or being in ignorance of, the rate, rise and fall of the Great Ouse. The tide rip is indeed a thing of wonder, the rise easily achieving 25ft. For single-handed skippers, it can make mooring/jilling fraught with complications and adversity.

King's Lynn Port Authority officers will advise about tide heights and times (and of course help in emergencies); and, in any case, it is always a good idea to let them know what you are doing and to request a traffic report from them.

Before we move on upstream, let us consider the procedure for leaving Lynn for the Wash. You will still need to leave King's Lynn about HW and anchor in the Wash to await the flood for one of the other three Wash ports. If for any reason you should quit King's Lynn on the flood, don't be surprised to notice that people walking on the banks are likely to overtake you. It is only the river doing its usual stuff.

There are many who boast of making the passage from the Great Ouse to Boston Grand Sluice on one tide. The requisites are that you should know exactly where you are going; exactly what you are doing; and have a craft that can move at a great rate of knots. It is over 40 miles from Denver Sluice to Boston Grand Sluice, and about 30 from King's Lynn to Boston. Simple arithmetic gives an idea of the Speedy Gonzales cruiser needed for such a project. Surely, far better to plan for decent weather and enjoy the peace of a leisurely trip and, if predictions should fail to meet your best desires and expectations, the protection of the sandbanks at low water will help you make the best of the disappointment; and, if the weather is fine, you can crop and reap the mussels which abound in many of the stretches en route.

It is possible to make one inter-port trip without the need to anchor off. As mentioned above, this is the passage between Boston and Fosdyke; but even so, you still need to have your speed and draught in the right combination. As for the rest, they are routes used over the centuries by fishermen, pirates and smugglers. The buoys or marks (if there at all) are not easy to see or locate; and, even when spotted, it is no mean task to read their meaning and direction. Many are they who have come to grief trying these 'short cuts' over the sands and in the final resort have achieved merely a long-drawn-out and boring haul. Some rash skippers have even found themselves stranded on a training wall. It is well to remember that, in some places, there is a vertical drop on one side of the wall and a long,

KING'S LYNN TO BEDFORD
Restricting dimensions
Draught 1·75m to Ely; then decreasing until more than 1·3m is a liability; particularly at the sides, especially for bilge keelers
Length 25·8m
Beam 3·1m
Air draught 2·2m
Authority
Environment Agency ☎ 01733 371811
Middle Level Commissioners ☎ 01354 653232

DENVER SLUICE
☎ 01366 382340. Radio VHF Ch 6/8

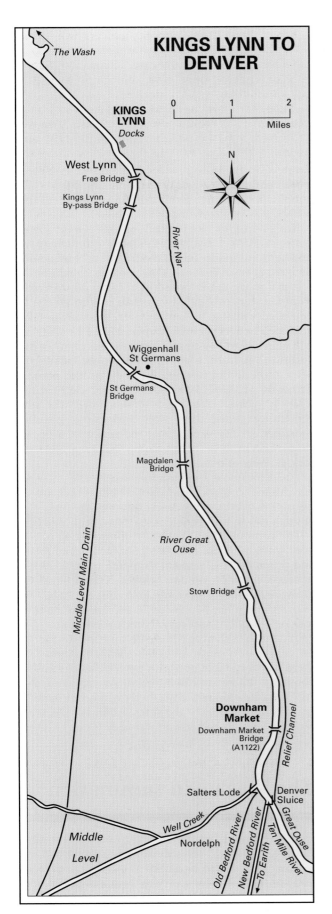

KINGS LYNN TO DENVER

The Wash

KINGS LYNN
Docks

0   1   2
Miles

N

West Lynn
Free Bridge
Kings Lynn
By-pass Bridge

River Nar

Wiggenhall
St Germans
St Germans
Bridge

Magdalen
Bridge

Middle Level Main Drain

River Great
Ouse

Stow Bridge

Downham
Market
Downham Market
Bridge
(A1122)

Relief Channel

Salters Lode

Denver
Sluice

Middle   Well Creek

Level   Nordelph

Old Bedford River

New Bedford River

To Earith

Ten Mile River

Great Ouse

gradual slope on the other; no soft mud berth to plop safely into by mistake.

So, having safely quitted the Lynn Cut, the next step is to get out through the Teetotal Channel to the No.1 cardinal buoy and from there to your favourite sandbank. The Wash is completely exposed to northeasterly winds and, when the wind is against the ebb, even the best-found boat becomes uncomfortable in the nasty conditions that can arise in as little as a Force 3. Shelter is to be found in the protection of the sandbanks at low tide and these are the places to make for even if you have to sweat it out in lumpy conditions before they top out. The Freeman Channel and especially the famous Roger Sand are popular for this manoeuvre because they are central and afford the best shelter.

The Great Ouse: King's Lynn to Denver Sluice

The river deserves its adjectival Great, being long, strong and tortuous, with its deep water at the extreme edges of some of its very tight bights, where unfortunately the bottom can be foul. It floods for between two and three hours, consequently ebbing for all of nine to ten. The *Admiralty Pilot* quotes the streams at four knots but, at times, I have been able to make only minimal headway against a spring flood; and *Valcon*'s Parson's Pike twin 56hp diesels, will, at full throttle, push her at 7+ knots.

At a few specified places in King's Lynn, it is safe to moor to the wall for a time if you need to wait for the tide for any reason. Permission must be obtained and there must always be competent crew on board. For most skippers, the plan is to pass through King's Lynn so that the tide will get them safely to Denver for the locking. The following factors must be considered: the tides; their rise and fall; and thus the

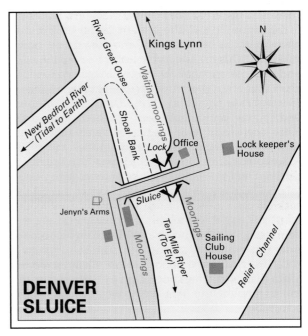

River Great Ouse

Kings Lynn

N

New Bedford River
(Tidal to Earith)

Waiting moorings

Shoal Bank

Lock   Office

Lock keeper's
House

Jenyn's Arms

Sluice

Moorings

Ten Mile River
(To Ely)

Moorings

Sailing
Club
House

Relief Channel

DENVER SLUICE

amount of water below you in the river and the amount of air above you under the bridges. Departure times will depend upon the individual measurements of the craft; but in general, it is not a good idea to move past King's Lynn until the flood has been running for about two hours – the intention being to achieve a smooth trip, no encounter with bed or bridge, and to arrive at the lock when there is plenty of water all round and the flood is beginning to lose its ferocity. As usual, good advice can be obtained not only from the harbourmaster's office at King's Lynn but also from the lock-keeper at Denver Sluice and the marina at Ely. Above Denver, the waters are controlled, and it is a delight to cruise slowly up to the splendid cathedral and find a really well-cared-for stretch of river under its mighty shadow.

An extra caution is necessary, particularly at springs, and not even big ones – if you are navigating early on the tide, the young flood is up your stern. Should you dig into a mud bank or just catch an unexpected hillock in the channel, you can be keeled over with the wheel snatched out of your hands and the boat suffering scouring in minutes. In such cases, fast and expert action is essential, for to run fully aground under such circumstances is to risk the loss of the vessel.

Moving upstream from the harbourmaster's office, past West Lynn and the hazardous Boal Quay we prepare to pass under the first of the many bridges before Denver. It is now known as the Free Bridge but, when it was first erected in 1821 (in wood), users had to pay a toll. Now it looks hardly any different from its next neighbour, the A47 bypass road bridge. After Eau Brink Cut and its relief channel are pylons and pipelines that cause no headroom problem. Just before the first of the 'problematic' bridges, on the starboard hand going upstream, is the entrance to the Middle Level Drain. The bridge is known as St Germans Bridge, taking its name from one of the many St Germans villages in the area, this particular being Wiggenhall St Germans. It was also a wooden toll bridge, but once again has been brought into the present times and style. There is noticeable feature before the next bridge at Wiggenhall St Mary Magdalen, where there is another shortened version of its eponymous village, being known as 'The Magdalen'. Just after that, power cables pass high overhead and, once more, there is little to see on the banks other than the occasional house or clump of bushes and trees. Next comes Stow Bridge, which was also originally wooden, and this is followed by another high power cable. There is a nasty double bend after this bridge and, on one occasion, I had to pass so close to the port bank that I was afraid of seriously bruising the boat along its side; but the flood tide has scoured a deep-water channel very close in. The bottom is foul and the bank immediately above encumbered so much that, with a big spring tide, all types of detritus will be brought into the mainstream. The last bridge before Salters Lode Lock, the Old Bedford River,

BRIDGE HEADROOMS

	Springs		Neaps	
	HW	LW	HW	LW
Downham Market	2·6m	7·5m	3·7m	7·0m
Stow	2·4m	6·5m	3·8m	6·6m
Magdalen	2·3m	7·3m	3·7m	7·1m
St Germans	2·5m	7·6m	3·9m	7·4m

the new Bedford River (called by some the Hundred Foot) and Denver Lock is Downham Market. It goes back more than five centuries and, like all the others, was originally made of wood.

Bridge heights are critical on the Great Ouse between King's Lynn and Denver, for there is nowhere to moor on that stretch of potentially dangerous river. It is not a place to get caught out.

It is a much easier proposition to go downstream from Denver to King's Lynn than it is to go up. If you need a pilot at all for this river, it is only to take you up. The Denver lock-keeper, Mike Fairweather, will help to sort you in and out and, like many of his vocation (in truth, for it is an eccentric calling) is often to be found working well beyond the normal demands of duty. 1990 saw 'Denver Bert' retire after 42 years. Users and Ousers alike will still remember those days well and carry grateful thoughts. In my experience, the majority of lock-keepers seem to be called Bert – but God bless all lockies, Bert or no!

The table above was promulgated by the Environment Agency and should help. There are also some overhead pipelines, but they are high enough not to be a problem.

The community at Denver is an interesting one and, while there are only the basic facilities of food and drink, there is pleasant shopping to be found not far away at Downham Market. Things have changed at Denver since my first visit; the full refurbishment has been completed, and guillotine locking is smooth and easy. Nevertheless, I am confident that Denver will never succumb to the rat race or be a centre of *la dolce vita*; although there is a hospitable pub with noisy peacocks for company. There are Environment Agency limited-stay moorings along the northerly bank, but there tends to be shoaling at the sides. All in all, Denver Sluice guards its secrets too jealously for any visitor to find himself there by chance.

The Wash – in summation

The most important piece of advice ever given to me regarding the Wash was about Not Doing Things. Don't try to save time. Out there, more haste means less speed and even less safety; or you might end up needing your life to be saved: 'Too swift arrives as tardy as too slow!' Don't try to work a doubtful tide by cutting corners, or you may end up cornered yourself. Don't be tempted to use those secret, private, fishermen's mini-channels, or you will end up being very secret and private yourself – and some have indeed gone to a watery grave in the deeps of the Wash. 'The grave's a fine and private place, But none, I think, do there embrace.'

If there is another 'one' thing not to do in the Wash, it is not to follow one of the local fishing boats that, with amazing serendipity, seems to be going the way you want to go. It is likely that the skipper can perceive, discern and read the signs and portents in the water much better than the average leisure skipper; and that his vessel, although looking deep-draughted, is in fact of a very shallow design. You may well conclude the experiment with mud on your hull and egg on your face.

The Ouse, Nene, Welland and Witham all suffer from banks, braes and bars, and all must be deemed inaccessible until about three hours before high water. Craft of 2m and more are advised to wait at least half an hour longer. Make no mistake – the streams can attack you. The *Admiralty Pilot* quotes them at 4 knots saying, 'The streams are reported to be strong,' but in both the Great Ouse and the Welland, *Valcon*'s 56hp twin diesels have, on occasion, been unable to deliver much more than 2 knots over the ground.

Since the rise and fall can achieve 9m, sound, long, strong warps are essential and so is reliable ground gear. It is asking for trouble to try to moor on the tidal stretches of any of the Wash rivers except in the Nene by the Towers and near Sutton Bridge. It is essential to keep to the buoyed channels and to maintain a close lookout for the training walls.

The cruising man who has not tried the Wash is to be envied for all the many contrasting experiences that lie ahead of him. While it is not, perhaps, the ideal place for the novice (but anyone having been initiated into boat handling in it will seldom find more challenging grounds) there is no long haul between landfalls and the main buoyage is well-nigh impeccable. Indeed, novice and expert should both find the Wash worthwhile, for it is a place of mystery, magic and continuing challenge: a veritable trap for the unwary; falsely comforting to the unheeding; temptingly seductive to the overconfident; apparently without hazard, horror or even minor obstacle to the foolhardy; yet always rewarding to any realistic skipper who is, as he should be, respectful, appreciative and cautious.

II. The Norfolk Coast

From Thornham to Great Yarmouth

Any cruise from King's Lynn up the close-in waters of the east side of the Wash will reveal the soft underbelly of North Norfolk as it stares sullenly across the waters of the Wash to its arch enemy, South Holland. That granted failing visibility – a frequent visitor to the area – neither hinders nor frustrates. Across the sands, the mainland is low and most of what is upstanding is connected with leisure, pleasure or tourism; from the most humble of caravans on the most modest of estates to the most sumptuous of castles on the most magnificent of grounds.

And now, last before going round the bend, comes Hunstanton. Built in Victorian times, it achieved fame and stature when Edward, Prince of Wales, stayed there to recuperate after an attack of typhoid. Another soul was not so lucky: according to St Mary's parish records of 1286, one Nicholas Bagge was beheaded after being convicted twice for larceny.

It has other contradictions: this essentially prim and unpretentious small town, has decided to designate itself a 'Fun Resort'; and just like St-Tropez on the south coast of France, it faces an unexpected direction. St-Tropez is the only French Mediterranean resort facing north, and Hunstanton is the only English East Coast resort facing west.

For another, more intriguing, actual hands-on (or perhaps more feet-on) view shoresides, I turn to Patrick Hamilton's description of George Harvey Bone, the anti-hero of his novel *Hangover Square*, at leisure one Christmas Day afternoon:

And now he was walking along the cliff . . . on his left, down below, lay the vast grey sweep of the Wash under the sombre sky of the Christmas afternoon: on his right the scrappy villas in the unfinished roads. A light wind struck him in the face and roared in his ears, and he looked at the feeble sun, in the nacreous sky, declining behind the bleak little winter resort. The little pier, completely deserted, jutted out into the sea, its silhouette shaking against the grey waves as though it trembled with cold but intended to stay where it was to demonstrate some principle. He turned left, and went upwards and away from the sea – the Wash in which King John had lost his jewels – towards the street which contained the semi-detached villa in

which tea, with Christmas cake and cold turkey (in front of an electric fire at eight o'clock), awaited him.

Hunstanton, pronounced 'Hunston' by the real lords of the community, is still, more or less, just the old-fashioned railway resort that George Bone experienced. A pity that little can be seen from seaward and nothing at all visited, since there are also the remains of St Edmund's Chapel. St Edmund's Point is where the Saint himself is supposed to have landed when he arrived by boat from Schleswig Holstein to become King of All the East Angles. However, there is some consolation to be had since the first actual sea haven just round the corner (Thornham) can be reached by boat – although, it must be said it is done much more easily by car or public transport.

So back to our maritime muttons . . . the most outstanding feature, when it does outstand, is the old but unmistakable lighthouse of Hunstanton. Situated at the northeast corner of the Wash, it is not always easy to pick out the light or St Edmund's Point on which it stands – or, for that matter, Gore Point, which may be of decided importance to any skipper who is knowledgeable, brave or foolhardy enough to attempt to navigate the inshore passage between Sunk Sand and the shore and through the Bays to, or past, Thornham haven. The corner is as famous as the Isle of Wight when it comes to its birthday-cake cliffs, triple-layered with carr stone, red chalk and white chalk, piled one upon the other. Poor visibility is most annoying when one can read, even in that most austere of publications, the *Admiralty Pilot*, that there is 'a cliff composed of marl, and grey and red chalk; it is remarkable both for the variety of its colouring and as the only cliff in the vicinity'. It goes on to say, however, in typically dismal tones, 'The rapidity of the tidal streams in this bight, the low elevation of its shores, and the mist which almost constantly prevails, render its navigation difficult, and a more than common degree of care is necessary.' In this case, I think the Admiralty has got it right.

Round the corner and into the channels brings three choices. The first takes us well past St Edmund's Point and well to the north. It is furthest out, going up to the Woolpack, across the Sledway, and then southerly towards the Thornham channel, leaving Gore Middle to starboard. In fact, it can be a good idea to set a course for Brancaster and then go back along the coast until you can pick out the entry.

Ower Bank

Leman Bank

10

5

5

10

10

10

10

5

10

Production wells
Fl.(4)Y.10s
Y Bell

Fl.Y.10s
Y Bell

Production Well
Fl.(4)Y.10s
Y Bell

23

25

22

19

18

15

19

E Hammond
Knoll
Q.(3)10s

Hammond Knoll
Q.(9)15s
BYB
YBY

Newarp
Fl.10s10m21M₅
Horn 20s
Racon(O)
O

wrecks

wrecks

Haisborough Sand

18

26

23

10

5

S Haisboro'
Q.(6)+LFl.15s
YB Bell

5

NE Cross Sand
VQ(3)5s
BYB

E Cross Sand
Fl.(4)R.15s
R

Cross Sand
LFl.10s6m5M
Racon(T)
RW

2°

19

18

5

5

10

5

10

Cockle
V.Q(3)5s
Bell
BYB

N.Scroby
V.Q.
Whis
BY

Fl(5)Y.20s5M
Mast (50)
Fl.R.3s

Q.G.6M
Fl.R.11M
Horn(3)

*GREAT
YARMOUTH*

5

10

10

10

5

5

10

Mid Haisboro'
Fl.(2)G.5s
G

N Haisboro'
Q
Bell
BY

The
Would

15

23

17

10

10

Fl(3)30s41m14M

Fl.R.5s5M

Fl.R.5s5M

Sea Palling

WINTERTON NESS

Hemsby

Caister-on-Sea

*Breydon
Water*

2 Ldg Oc.
+F.R.6M
10M

30'

HAPPISBURGH

Bacton

Mundesley

CROMER

Fl.5s84m23M

Fl.R.2.5s
R

RC

E Sheringham
Q.(3)10s
BYB

W Sheringham
Q.(9)15s
YBY

Sheringham Shoal

10

5

5

5

5

10

10

5

Cley-next-
the-Sea

Sheringham

Blakeney
Overfalls
Fl(2)R.5s
Bell
R

Blakeney Overfalls
R

S Race
Q(6)+LFl.15s
Bell
YBY

E Docking
Fl.R.2.5s
R

Fairway
RW

Wells
Fairway
RW

BLAKENEY

*WELLS-NEXT-
THE-SEA*

Stiffkey

10

5

5

5

5

5

10

5

10

15

Docking Shoal

Scott Patch
VQ(3)5s
BYB

S Inner Downing
Q(6)+LFl.15s
Bell
YBY

Burnham
Flats
Q(9)15s
Bell
YBY

Woolpack
Fl.R.10s
R

Lynn Knock
Q.G.
G

North
Well
LFl.10s
Whis
RW

05'

Burnham Flats

Bridgirdle
R

Stiffkey
Overfalls

Scott Head I

BRANCASTER

Old Thornham
Lighthouse

HUNSTANTON

2

2

2

0

55'

53° N

50'

45'

40'

35'

30'

N

1°E

35

This route has the advantage of deep water all the way until the actual channel is approached.

The second is the middle-of-the-road way – still leaving St Edmund's Point well to starboard, but going no further north than the deep cut which runs between Middle Bank and Gore Bank to the north and Sunk Sand to the south, with its close but small neighbour running up northeasterly to the Bays. This route also has deep water all the way, if you tend to the north – that is, towards the drying Gore Middle. It is fairly steep-to and sea conditions can inform almost as well and easily as the depth sounder.

The third choice is to venture easterly towards the old lighthouse at St Edmund's Point. This, however, is a tortuous affair, going first southeasterly just to the south of the wreck on the southern edge of Sunk Sand; then east; then northerly; then easterly close round Gore Point and on to the Thornham channel This is, of course, a top-of-the-tide job, and best taken after some kindly local boater or fisherman has shown you the way, the truth and the life – and what a life that inshore way is! To sum up, any skipper going to Thornham, Brancaster or Overy Staithe, should possess the right craft (boat), and the other right craft (skill) that will take him safely along the close inshore route between Sunk Sand and Middle Bank through the channel and on to the Bays and Gore Middle. In addition, the benefits of a third eye wouldn't go amiss.

Let us turn again to the *Admiralty Pilot*:

Small craft are cautioned that there are no accessible harbours along the North Norfolk coast under conditions of strong onshore winds, i.e. N of E or W. In these conditions the outer entrances of the small harbour along the coast become a mass of broken water and marks are difficult to see. Conditions rapidly worsen when the ebb stream begins to run or if there is swell as a result of a previous onshore gale.

Not only is this worth committing to memory; it should be burned into the brain, especially that of skippers planning a first-time visit to this stretch of coast where the people are so warm and welcoming and the conditions so cold, menacing and implacable.

There is, of course, much more to the tale than just that small warning from the *Pilot*. Further handicaps are the continuing difficulties of identification along the low-lying coastline, worsened by the frequency of the haze, mist, frets and fogs. Combined with the shortage of conspicuous landmarks from Hunstanton down to Cromer lighthouse, this can make for a difficult time in spotting marks and entrances. In addition, once 'safely' across the bars, the channels inside can be just as difficult (a) to observe and (b) to identify one from another, when actually located; for there are many that will lead you into ways of shallow impropriety. In this low coast of creeks, streams and near ditches, many seem to appear obvious, plain and clear. Indeed, many channels are called, but few

should be chosen – and only one followed. Spotting and following that right one can often involve real detective work. All very pleasant on a sunny Sunday afternoon at high water spring tide, but much less enticing of an autumn evening with an onshore breeze and an ebb tide.

The North Norfolk coast, from the northeast corner of the Wash to Cromer on the bend, is an exposed stretch of coastline and so severe can be the conditions that every solitary haven, no matter how modest, is worth a ransom to mariners. In particular, they are blessed refuges from the dangers of those strong winds that infest the area almost as much as the legendary mist and fog. Quite clearly, with a spiteful wind from the north, the cautious mariner will be inside waiting, and not outside wanting. These conditions, and their accompanying dangers, have been known to local fishermen and lifeboatmen, every coastguard and harbourmaster from Thornham to Winterton Ness over the years and even centuries. Happily for the cruising yachtsman they take for granted their obligation not only to be on hand whenever the need should arise, but to be alert, and almost waiting, for the stranger's call for help. This is the most reassuring feature of an otherwise quite inhospitable 50 miles. It is also worth noting that, if conditions get really bad, it can be worse in the Wash than further out in the North Sea; and it is a long haul from Great Yarmouth to Grimsby. Since all of these close approaches have hazards (including some of the obscure ones having no buoys), any skipper contemplating their assault should ensure that he is equipped with substantial ground tackle.

So, settled conditions, a good forecast and decent visibility must surely be obligatory for a first visit to the North Norfolk coast. It may mean waiting for longer than you would wish, but the people and the places in the nearby Wash will more than repay the insurance premium of waiting rather than risking. Boston, Wisbech and Wainfleet Haven are all good bad-weather halts from the north; and from the south there is the choice of Southwold, Lowestoft (made even more attractive now that Mutford Lock has been refurbished and reorganised) or, in an emergency, Great Yarmouth. The first two are well fitted out and hospitable, but the third is last in all those things looked for by yachtsmen and is best avoided.

All the havens (that is, Thornham, Brancaster, Burnham and Overy Staithe), except Wells, are best suited to shoal craft, and only easily negotiated if you draw no more than around the 1m mark. It is not merely that there is little water in the entrance channel; once inside, with much more than a metre's draught and more than 7 or 8 metres' LOA, there will hardly be anywhere you can find a place where you will not dry out, or where you will be safe, comfortable and, at the same time, within accessible range of shoreside facilities. Any skipper seriously intent on the smaller havens should call the local experts, prior to any attempt at entry. Their expert

Just round the bend from The Wash, Thornham is one of the smallest havens in the UK. Although the indigens try to keep the channel well buoyed, the combination of the surrounding flatness and the plenitude of trees (a near petrified forest) make it difficult to identify anything.

knowledge is usually freely given, and even the charges of the professionals are not expensive when the value of their advice and pilotage is considered. In addition, Henry Irving's *The Tidal Havens of the Wash and Humber* (Imray) offers helpful reading.

Thornham

Thornham is the most westerly haven, closest to the Wash, and also the smallest. The approach channel to what is euphemistically called Thornham's Harbour crosses a broad sandy foreshore and is constantly changing in depth and direction. In good conditions, a vessel drawing 2·7m can reach Thornham Staithe, about a mile above the actual entrance; but, generally speaking, any craft near even the 2·3m mark will experience difficulty except near calm springs. On very low neaps, not even craft with as little as 1·5m will be able to get there. The local fisherman do their best to keep the channel buoyed but the combination of the surrounding flatness and the plenitude of trees makes it very difficult to identify anything. There is also a near-replica of the classic Petrified Forest to add further to the confusion.

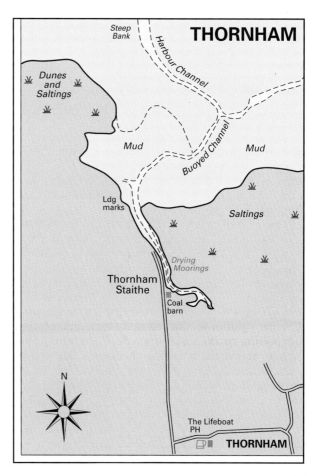

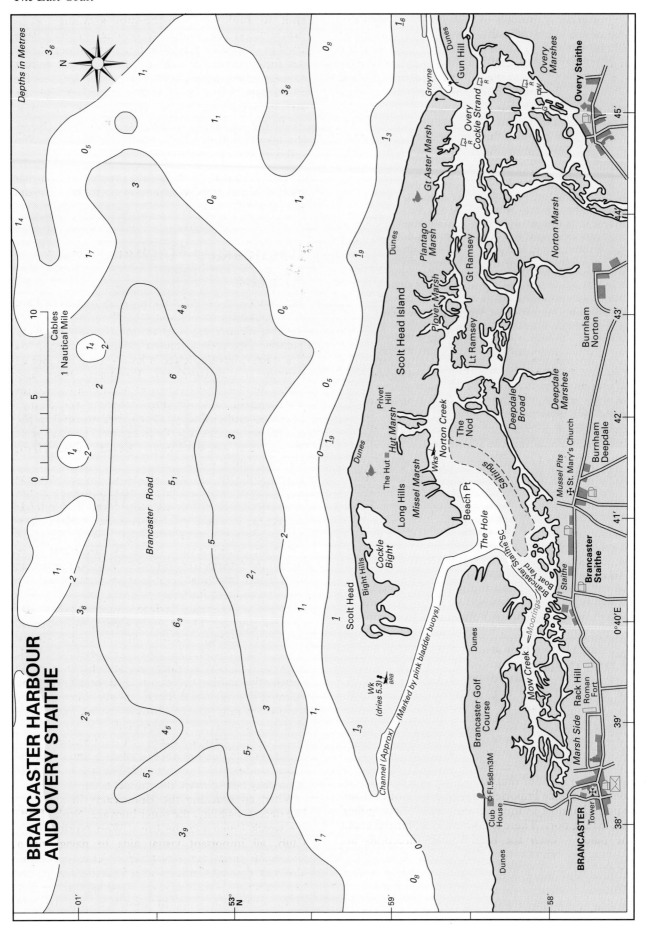

BRANCASTER HARBOUR AND OVERY STAITHE

Depths in Metres

Thornham is difficult to pick out from seaward. One of the most difficult – if not indeed, *the* most difficult in fact – from seaward, since trees obscure anything like a noticeable mark. Westward, it may be possible to pick out the spire of Titchwell church, inland to the east of Thornham; and, once Hunstanton corner has been rounded, it may be possible just to pick out the dip in the dunes that is about all that signifies the presence of the entrance channel. Eastwards, West Norfolk Golf Club (situated above Brancaster Marsh on the very shore, as it were) is occasionally easy to pick out. On the marshes next the sea, near the spreading foreshore, it is to be found between Mow Creek and its adjacent saltings and the North Sea approach channel. Although the course is protected by locked gates with monumental pillars, at least the sands are free and its clubhouse provides a useful landmark. In the event, it is a case of keeping the eyes skinned for the fall-away of the dunes, as this is the only worthwhile and ultimate pointer to get you in. A good eye must also be kept on the depth sounder for the bottom is eccentric to say the least.

The shelter within the small creek is middling to good but you must be prepared to take the ground dependent upon the tides and the kind of berth that you can find. All the moorings in the tiny harbour are private, but visitors are welcome to take a vacant one, or to pull up alongside another, when weight and LOA permit; and when the proper courtesies have been observed. About 1½ hours round high water is the maximum, and most would recommend no more than ½ hour. Of course, shoal craft with nothing of significance standing proud on the keels can come and go with much more flexibility. On the whole, the marks are starboard-hand, and they should be adhered to (as in 'stuck together') since they mark a route which is not only serpentine but also has some major twists and turns. All is not over yet – after the buoys come the (sometimes topmarked and sometimes beheaded) wooden posts that lead the way through the salt-marsh. Finally, the last lap of the east bank is marked by smaller brethren in three post stakes. These should not be approached too closely. Of course, none of this presents a serious hazard or even a problem in fine, settled weather, on a good tide in the sunshine; nevertheless though, it is one of the havens that most qualifies for a necessary prior visit by road.

However, as with many of the small havens on our east and southwest coasts, once gained it is to be valued as the fisherman's pearl. Thornham is now a diminutive harbour that has 'gone' as a commercial concern (it once imported vast quantities of coal and exported almost as much grain), and is now 'going' as a fishing port. There is nothing at all formal about the place – even the local sailing directions are couched in relaxed terms: 'Coal barge to Olive's garage'. Now, it is important to know that Olive's garage is next door to The Lifeboat, the pub that draws crowds with its reputation for good food and real ale. I, for one, cannot think of a more unlikely

spot to find made-on-the-spot gravadlax as a lunchtime snack. There are facilities in the village itself (a short walk inland) but many mariners never get further than the hostelry. It is a quiet retreat (except when the holiday crowds race in) and for this reason alone, it is worth the effort. But its strange scenic setting at large (one of the most intriguing in Norfolk) and the singularity of the unique old flint coal barn make it an imperative call – not forgetting the camera.

I am indebted to John Conder, skipper of the gaff cutter *Zhivago*, for his generous assistance with the sailing notes.

Brancaster Harbour and Staithe

Just easterly of Thornham is a pair of havens that are at one and the same time very alike, yet also very unalike: Brancaster Staithe and Burnham Overy Staithe. The first is known always and simply as Brancaster; but the latter is known by a number of denominations: Burnham, Burnham Overy and Overy Staithe. There are many surrounding villages with appellations bringing together the names Burnham and/or Overy, so it is best to stick to the full cognomen title, or, if you are trailing your boat, you may find yourself trying to launch it from a farm some distance inland.

The outstanding natural feature in the area is Scolt Head, a remarkably long sandhill. It is the most northerly point on this coast and affords protection for both the havens. Scolt Head is a nature reserve particularly inhabited by breeding common and sandwich terns. Brancaster is approached from its west and Burnham from its east. There is a great feeling of openness about the approaches, both harbours and villages.

To reach Brancaster Staithe, a very long entry has to be negotiated. The *Admiralty Pilot* gives its usual stern commentary: 'should only be used by those with local knowledge; the approach channel, between sandbanks which dry out for a mile, is constantly shifting in depth and direction. The channel buoys are difficult to see in moderate onshore winds, due to broken water, when the entrance should not be attempted'. No matter who advises me, I have always found the channel inside to be almost unbelievably twisted – and, what is more, confused by the plenitude of small buoys that are locally laid to mark the mussel beds.

When approaching the Brancasters in anything like decent visibility, the outer buoyage, Scolt Head, the wreck *Vinna* and the Royal West Norfolk Golf Club, all important visual aids to navigating a successful entry, are easy to spot. Then come the closer markers: the port-hand red bladder buoys; the beacon on the wreck; and the fixed light at the golf club. Instructions as proffered to me by the commanding character of the harbour, Mervyn

Brancaster is invaded more often by cars than it is by boats – but the sea is so close that even cars can be driven to within yards of the beach. In the harbours creeks and inlets, there is a plenitude of mullet, bass and sea trout – and a dearth of folk fishing for them. Brancaster's famous 'Hole' can be seen just to right of centre.

Nudds, the master, take a different tack and are couched in an altogether contrasting tone: 'There are two channels. The buoys are all numbered. No. 1 buoy is west of the golf club; and the wreck channel No. 1 is northwest of the wreck, the *Vinna*. Going out over the bar, we have a green topmark buoy for the two channels. Moorings are available when they are not in use, or the owners are out visiting or on a long cruise. If not, I can always anchor one safe.' Visitors are made welcome to use Brancaster Staithe Sailing Club. It is worth noting that there is a bye-law as follows: 'Vessels in the harbour must muffle their rigging.'

You will have to go a long way to find mariners more sensitive, sensible and straight up and down than those of this coast; and among them, Harbourmaster Nudds is known for his expertise, his friendly co-operative manner and his incorrigible attitude to all things of the sea. Any intending skipper would be well advised to book him as their pilot. His services as guide, philosopher and friend come in train.

A telephone call to Mr Nudds will give you a lot of information; and, if you need more help than telephone instructions, he will generally be able to arrange for one of the local fishermen to meet you on his normal return at tide time. It is well worthwhile making preliminary arrangements and, indeed, a preparatory visit if at all possible. I would personally urge any skipper with a draught of more than 1·2m not to come for the first time by boat without having visited the shoresides well ahead, got advice and arranged for help.

There are one or two professional whelkers; but, at fine weekends with high tides, the amateurs take over and the place can get crowded with all kinds of racing enthusiasts – boaters, surfers, sand-riders and the like. On the open sand-flats, a special class of drag-racing is the modern fad. While on the other side of the tracks there is the aforementioned Scolt Head, the untamed and solitary National Trust island which is a birdwatcher's fantasy and a botanist's dream but restricted as to landing.

Brancaster was the Branodunum fort of the Romans, situated on Rack Hill, between Brancaster and the Staithe. There is little there now to show its importance as an important naval base, and a Saxon coastal fort, with a full complement of soldiers; for it is given over to those, hardly less warlike, pastimes of golfing, sailing, and larking about on sands and holiday sites.

Burnham Overy Staithe

Burnham Overy Staithe is very much a sequestered and confined community, with a tiny harbour and a very tight run in; indeed, its approach channel has been described as a mere tidal creek. The approach is from the east side of Scolt Head, by the quite unmistakable gap between that island and the threateningly named Gun Hill. The administrative authority is Burnham Overy Harbour Trust, and the centre of all life is to be found at its small jetty overlooking the modest mooring area. Across the road is The Boathouse, a chandlery and boatyard facility run by one Peter Beck, who is the Cruising Association representative and boatman and also auxiliary coastguard. His place is a real Aladdin's Cave for seamen.

The entrance is generally deemed to be more difficult than Brancaster's. Although it is not so long, it is more arduous since it changes even more frequently and, although buoyed, is of a complexity to confound even some of the local fishermen from time to time. As at Brancaster, it is not too difficult to spot where you are because of the unique configuration of Scolt Head and Gun Hill, but after that it is a tortuous and confusing affair. The place

is such a small paradise that it is easy to understand why they may try to keep it secretly to themselves. However, once you are there, you will be made extremely welcome.

There is a red bladder buoy for the harbour entrance, and small yellow floats. There are also beacons and various posts that are markers to those with local knowledge or enough native wit to work them out. There are a few swinging moorings. The best plan for any visitor is to arrange a shoresides look at low water and fix a date with Mr Beck for pilotage. He is decidedly modest about the need for help and advice, saying only: 'Do not attempt to enter harbour with northerly winds unless guided.' Any visitor with a boat of much more than 1m draught should consider pilotage obligatory for a first entry.

Burnham Overy, once proudly sported the cognomen, Overy Town. It is, in fact, a small community that could never hope (nor wish, no doubt) to be described as more than a village; and in reality has the air of living, thriving hamlet more than anything other. Like so many harbours and havens now deserted, lost, sunk or silted, it was once a flourishing centre. But the thousands of tons of sand and shingle that have been tidally shifted down from the eroding coast of Yorkshire, combined with the forces of the North Sea at large, have made their deposits, made their inroads and done their damage here, perhaps even more than elsewhere on the East Coast. Later, as a direct result of these ruinous changes, Overy Staithe came into being as a separate entity. Long ago, Overy and Overy were the centre of a brisk sea trade humming with movements of substantial schooners, large barges, and big brigs and brigantines.

Nothing is there now that remotely resembles this past in concrete terms; however, the spirit of the people is indomitable – and it is easy to imagine the life that was once here. Notwithstanding the power of the days of yore, there is no sounding of sunk bells; nor the voices of seductive merman; or even dead sailors crying out their doom.

Burnham Overy Staithe has a warm feeling about it that is not usually associated with the North Sea's East Coast, making it a charming harbour and one of the prettiest havens on this stretch of coast, rivalling even those of the remoter parts of Cornwall.

Horatio Nelson lived in the rectory of one of the many other nearby Burnhams – Burnham Thorpe – and Overy locals have made much of that ever since he became famous. This is now 'Nelson Country', although Beccles on the Broads claims it taught him all he knew. The village where he was born, gives testimony by its hanging signs of hostelries and tea-rooms. There is actually no evidence that he ever came near the place; and he is known to have shown little interest in the sea at all until he was rudely introduced to its ways courtesy of his uncle's man-o'-war.

BRANCASTER STAITHE
52°59'·00N 00°46'·50E

Charts Admiralty 108, 1190. Imray Y9, C28.
OS Landranger 132.

Tides
Immingham +0050, Dover −0430

Tidal access
HW ±2hrs. *Min. depth* Dries

Caution
Boats drawing more than 1·2m should seek local assistance

Authorities
Harbourmaster ☎ 01485 210638
Sailing Club ☎ 01485 210249

Facilities
Ⓥ (poss.), D, P, , , WC, , Provisions (nearby), Repairs (by arrangement)

BURNHAM OVERY STAITHE
52°59'·00N 00°46'·50E

Charts Admiralty 108, 1190, Imray Y9.
OS Landranger 132.

Tides
Immingham +0050, Dover −0430
Tidal access HW ±2hrs. *Min. depth* Dries

Caution
Do not attempt to enter in northerly winds. Boats drawing more than 1–1·5m should seek local assistance.

Facilities
Chandlery: The Boathouse ☎ 01328 730550
Burnham Overy Staithe Sailing Club ☎ 01328 738348

Burnham Overy was once Overy Town; and the whole area a thriving business community with a brisk sea trade. Above and below, it is seen at its fishing village best.

Wells-next-the-Sea

The first time I visited Wells was under conditions vividly described in the *Admiralty Pilot*: 'Vessels should never attempt to enter Wells harbour at night, nor without local knowledge, especially with onshore winds.' To be fair, I was actually being towed in by the *Isabella*, a local whelking boat, after an unpleasant contretemps with crab-lines off Cromer. Even so, the rough and tumble experience across the double bar provided me with enough misgivings to accept every word the *Pilot* had to offer. But there were compensations – one moment we were being tossed around at the end of a long rope from the ex-lifeboat, and the next we were deep in a shadowy night of enchantment with the lights of the buoys flashing in fairytale array against the thick darkness of the enveloping banks and trees, all of which lent an air of mystery to our near-silent journey. Then, all on a sudden, we were face to face with the raucous road and sideshows that comprise the quay: bazaars and bingo; fish, chip and burger bars; pubs and snackeries; and lights and music all the way.

The men of Wells looked after me and sorted out *Valcon*'s props and attendant problems without fuss or payment. Not one of those who helped would take a penny – and it took a lot of arm twisting before my original rescuers, Sonny and Alan, would accept a bottle of whisky. That, however, is typical of Wells-next-the-Sea.

Access is from an 1½ hours before to 1 hour after HW. The bar at the entrance is locally acknowledged as being 3m maximum, with 'winds from the northwest causing heavy swell over it'. I have found such conditions to be much more than threatening, but no matter what descriptions are given, the conditions themselves are still to be avoided.

It is essential to identify and approach the red and white Fairway buoy, otherwise there is a good chance of getting caught on the notorious Bob Hall's Sand. The most common problem is being blown on to the lee shore and, in spite of the reputation of Bob Hall (not to mention the bar), some skippers are still careless and these mishaps do occur. There is special constraint enforced on yachts: they should not proceed east of the conspicuous silo without prior permission since there are extensive mussel lays which are extremely vulnerable to damage.

Wells-next-the-Sea is not well known. Indeed, on many occasions when I have telephoned friends from there, they have automatically jumped to the conclusion that I have been miraculously transported to Bath and Wells. It is still a busy commercial port but, with a population of no more than 3,000, it doesn't feel like it from the outside. It is also described as a small sea town, a harbour and haven, and nary a soul would quarrel with that last, but for me it is quintessentially Wells, just Wells – a place in its own right, and quite the friendliest place between Ramsgate and King's Lynn.

Wells and its worthies are deeply attached to their history, rooted to it but not bogged down in it, and while the flavour of the past has been well preserved, the community has kept up with the times. However, it is still something of a contradiction to discover that this quite busy port, with its bingo halls, an excellent and up-to-date caravan site, a plethora of television aerials, and a narrow shopping street of character and urban 'busyness' has such poor public-transport connections. The only railway connections Wells has are the Wells to Walsingham Light Railway, situated on the coast road to Stiffkey, and the Harbour Railway from the quay to the beach. The nearest main-line station is 14 miles away at Sheringham. There is also a public bus service that carries so few passengers it feels private and runs so infrequently that it barely justifies the claim 'service'.

The core of Wells' 3·4 square miles is its charming 'village green' with its nearby public houses and hotels, a real attraction on a blustery summer day, when it affords protection from all but the worst of winds. But this centre is neither the heart nor the core of Wells. Like any well-proportioned photograph, its focal point is off-centre and, in the case of Wells, it is the quay. Old, well-used and much-loved, it is often busy with coasters and the fishing vessels that serve the adjacent whelk houses. It is no longer as thronged as it was in the days when vessels filled the haven and their crews burst the

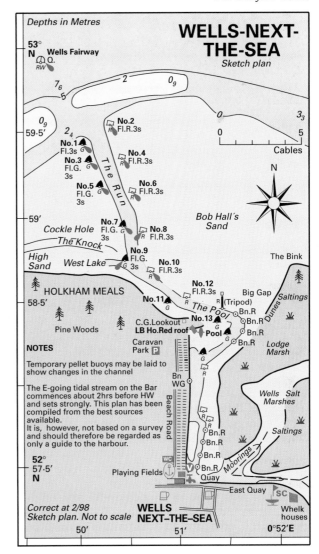

seams (and much more) of the 32 taverns the port then boasted. But there are still all the facilities, the bustle and the inherent dignity of a place alive with a continuing reliance on its harbour and the sea; and the inns that remain provide plenty of friendly entertainment and vitality.

Wells is dedicated to its quay, and little happens there that is not subject to the passionate interest and keen scrutiny of the many small groups that people it. Hardly an event occurs that is not closely observed, reported at length and discussed in detail; and what transpires in the morning, no matter how unobtrusive, inconsequential or guarded, come the evening, will be broadcast and debated as a matter of some concern. The quay symbolises the town's dependence on the sea and the men who go down to it in little ships, small boats and penny numbers to wrench from it a hard-gotten and not always rewarding living. They are mainly whelkers and, for some of them, there is a trip of up to 30 miles before they even start at their pots. It is a totemistic spot for a community in which families of the seagoing fishermen listen to their VHF radio monitors for news of the port's fleet of whelkers and shrimpers

WELLS-NEXT-THE-SEA
52°59'·30N 00°49'·75E

Charts Admiralty 108, 1190. Imray C28, Y9.
OS Landranger 132.

Tides
Bar +0020 Immingham, −0500 Dover
Quay +0100 Immingham

Tidal access
HW −1½hrs to HW +1hrs (max. draught approx. 3m).
Min. depth Dries. Entrance dangerous in northerly winds.

Authorities
Wells Harbour Commissioners Harbourmaster
☎ 01328 711646

Radio
Wells Harbour Radio VHF Ch 12, 14, 16, 8, 6, 37
(HW −2hrs and when vessels due)

Facilities
Ⓥ, 🅳D (nearby), 🅿P (nearby), ⚓, ⚡, WC (nearby),
⚓ (nearby), Provisions (nearby), Repairs: William
Cracknell (boatbuilder) ☎ 01328 710551; James
Case (boatbuilder) ☎ 01328 710550
Chandlery: Standard House ☎ 01328 710593

Shining like 'a good deed in a naughty world', the red roof of the Wells coastguard lookout is the halfway house along the broadly turning channel from seaward to the safety of the quay and the sale marshes. It is essential to identify and approach the red and white Fairway buoy (the white blob above top right), otherwise there is a good chance of getting caught on the notorious Bob Hall's Sand (middle right).

echoing, in contemporary terms, the age-old anxieties of those who wait and watch.

Wells-next-the-Sea is one of the most intriguing, fascinating and appealing harbours on the East Coast. This is the kind of welcome you might expect:

Dear Harbour User

As we look forward to another enjoyable year on the water, we would like to welcome to Wells our many visiting craft, some for the first time. The town has much historic interest and we hope you will have time during your stay to explore the area and sample some of it's delights exploring the many 'nooks and crannies' in the town.

There have been considerable improvements to the Harbour in recent years. The purchase of yet another 3 navigation buoys this year and a replacement Fairway Buoy will bring to an end our programme totalling 10 new buoys in all providing an excellently marked channel. The new Harbour boat storage area, provided at very competitive rates, has gone from strength to strength with further improvements planned for the future. The welcome and helpfulness given to all by harbour staff has further enhanced the popularity of the port, encouraging visitors to return again.

This brochure contains information on the local area as well as essential Harbour details. Should you have further needs or enquiries please do not hesitate to contact the Harbour Office, we will be only too pleased to help you.

We hope you enjoy your stay. Have a safe passage and we hope to see you again in the near future.

To our resident Harbour Users our good wishes for a safe and enjoyable season in 1998.

Lorraine Marshall
Clerk to the Commissioners

Commercial ships no longer visit Wells, and the Commissioners are even now improving facilities for pleasure craft and making the small port even more attractive to visitors. Boats that cannot safely take the ground can often be found a spot if they do not exceed a metre in draught.

Blakeney and Morston Quay

Blakeney is the last of the small fishing villages on the East Coast before Great Yarmouth for the yachtsman who is heading south. It is an intriguing spot, with a host of attractive features, many of which are so tucked away as to be almost hidden from view – except for the most avid and fervent explorer. For holidaymakers, tourists, ramblers or boaters, it is an excellent HQ for all kinds of excursions. In addition, for ecologists, conservationists and birdwatchers it is special insofar as it is protected and in the hands of the National Trust. However, for the sea-going mariner it is unique: being the first and last stop between the Wash ports and the River Yare at Great Yarmouth. These two harbours are separated by 40 miles which could not be more different; and they are 40 miles without a single refuge and little by way of coastal landmarks.

One of the Blakeney folk best qualified to assist, as well as being guide, philosopher, pilot and friend, is a character by the name of Stratton Long. He is the chief chandler in the place, running a store that is a cross between a fisherman's hut and an Anglican Aladdin's Cave. He is the local boatbuilder extraordinaire, the Blakeney boatman, the lifeboat expert, the unofficial harbourmaster, the chandler, and, to use his own words, 'the general fiddler and diddler of the place'. At one time, he was even in the airplane salvage business. His business is Stratton Long Marine, known to one and all as 'Stratton's'. It is not a place to venture if you are feeling one under the eight, for it is an experience to be lived up to. Predictably, I feel it is pointless to visit Blakeney without calling on him.

It is difficult to decide whether entry to Blakeney has more twists and turns by road or sea. There are two major landmarks – Blakeney church and the long, steeply shelved shingle bank that runs down to the sand dunes that mark the end of the Point. Visibility on this part of the coast is still not always reliable, although we have moved a little south; and it is still just as wise to keep a regular watch on the depth sounder and not try to effect an entry until you have found the green-and-yellow buoy that is laid April to October (with a quick-flashing light); the red bladder buoy; and the green wreck buoy. The wreck is of an old cod-fishing smack. It can be a threat up to half tide, and a constant reminder of the hazards of shoal cruising at all times. About 200m will clear the danger.

The channel is now well buoyed with marks that are all to be left to starboard when entering. Everybody in Blakeney connected with the sea plays a part in keeping them up to scratch. However, as Stratton Long says, 'The entry is generally very difficult, for the sand bar is moving all the time; and if there is any north in the weather at all it will be extremely difficult and often dangerous.' An unassisted entry is possible, but only under ideal conditions. Stranded vessels have little chance, and it must be prudent to wait for settled weather and daylight.

From the west, or even from the north, it is not easy to spot the actual entry, since you are heading more or less straight into it. The low sand dunes seem to melt and meld with the water so smoothly that there is little contrast. The most noticeable feature is the tower of Blakeney church. From the south and east, however, spotting the lower dunes indicating the entrance is easier and plainer to see – the approaches are straightforward and extremely simple, and the church tower is very noticeable from this approach. I find the cliffs of Sheringham and Cromer suggest all kinds of mysteries to do with the sea and its gods; but the significance of these cliffs to the cruising skipper coming from the south is that they will give him excellent notice that, when they fall away, he is well on his way to the entrance. The vast ridge of shingle, as dramatic as Dorset's Chesil Beach, will then take him on to Blakeney Point.

From hereon southwards, crab pots abound, some with very obvious cans, and some merely with bubbles of plastic hardly more than a balloon, and they will accompany you well on the way to

Yarmouth. When the sand dunes level out, you will be almost on top of the buoys that mark the entrance.

Craft of 1·5m can enter about 2 hours round high water, except on neaps when it is best to wait as long as you can to high water, and certainly no better than an hour to be on the safe side. There are strong rips on the tide and both ground tackle and engines need to be substantial – or perhaps the buzzword is 'robust'. The main channel leads past Stanley's Cockle Bight to the Pit and, once past Tibby Head, to Blakeney Channel and the quays. There are two quays: the Low Quay is the smaller of the two and is situated to the west of the larger. There is no official harbourmaster, Blakeney being one of the few remaining completely 'free' harbours in Britain.

The first, and probably the best place to try for an anchorage is the pool just after the entrance channel to the south of the Point. It is called the Pit, is marked by beacons and has some moorings near to it. There is water there all the time and it is well protected. The chances of picking up a spare mooring are not high and it may be necessary to move more westerly into the 'harbour' itself, by the Morston Marshes to the south, where it may be possible to find a spot to anchor. At these places it will be necessary to take the ground. The miniature channel into Stiffkey Marshes leaves the main one just before the last green No. 10 buoy. Withies mark the way for shoal craft between the mussel beds which must be carefully avoided. This is a remote spot from which you have to take a dinghy to reach pubs and shops.

The old port of Blakeney has a small quayside, and it seems impossible to imagine that big commercial sailing ships ever managed to get in – never mind manoeuvre. Larger craft are likely to encounter the bottom somewhere along the twisting channel that is occasionally marked by a withy or a buoy. There are plenty of shops; certainly enough to meet the visiting yachtsman's needs. Stratton Long run a very good chandlery.

Approaching from the road, there are some quaint and charming names to notice: Cabbage Creek, Muckledyke, Stiffkey Freshes and Morston Meals; or, from the other direction, Bard Hill, the Skirts and Cley Eye. It is worth trying to stand back and view the flint buildings of the village from a good vantage point, but this is not easy as the streets are narrow and often busy. Blakeney is one of those places where you get a strong whiff of its reality the minute you step off your boat (or get out of your car); nor does it disappoint you the longer you stay, repaying investigation by offering you jewels of art, architecture and people. Its only drawback is its popularity for visitors with cars. Happily, however, Blakeney is a place with a spirit and rhythm so all its own that it can survive all comers. To stand on the quayside from tide to tide and watch the comings and goings of those who are earning their not-much-more-than-meagre livelihoods, as well as those who are spending their equally hard-earned leisure, is to

Once you reach the aegis of the Wells Harbour Commissioners, the delights of the saltings, the whelk houses and the inner secrets of this intriguing place are there for the taking.

experience something of the flavour of the days when Blakeney was a full-blown working harbour of substance and stature. Wool, grain and other exports were despatched to the ports of the Wash, Hull, Newcastle and London and, as late as the 18th century, sailing vessels were still working Blakeney and its near neighbour Cley-next-the-Sea.

BLAKENEY HARBOUR
52°59'·10N 00°58'·35E

Charts Admiralty 108, 1190. Imray C28, Y9. OS Landranger 133.

Tides
Immingham +0300 (Point), +0050 (Quay), Dover −0500

Tidal access
HW ±2hrs (max. draught approx. 1·5m)

Authorities
Harbourmaster ☎ 01263 740362

Pilot
Stratton Long Marine ☎ 01263 740362

Facilities
Chandlery: Stratton Long Marine

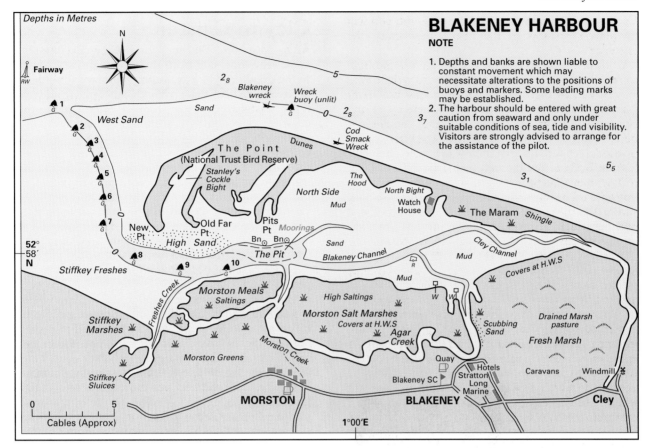

Blakeney is flanked by small communities with creeks. On the Wells-next-the-Sea side there is Morston, and on the Yarmouth end is Cley. Morston is little more than a quay and Cley is hardly a quay at all. So, first to Morston, the deepest and best channel associated with the Blakeney harbour complex. As such, it is in much use by the professional boatmen ('ferrymen') who regularly take out parties to the National Trust bird sanctuary at Blakeney Point. There are few facilities; in the main it consists of dunes with minimum services for holidaymakers. The boatmen have no objection to visitors making use of whichever of the landing stages is not in use and they are very firm on that. Visiting yachtsmen who understand the ways and needs of the boatmen are offered a friendly and helpful welcome, but woe betide those who expect to use a landing stage as if by right. The creek is not a place where you want to be stranded, at the mercy of justifiably angry boatmen.

While the Morston Greens, Meals and Marshes are not to be compared to any of America's salt flats, there are still plenty of enthusiasts who use the area for land sailboarding.

Cley-next-the-Sea is an experience of quite another kind. If Morston is epitomised by its channel, creek and salt marshes, then Cley must be noted for its flint, both in the village itself and on the massive pebble ridge to be seen to full advantage down at Cley Eye. The ridge is a splendid barrier to the encroachment of the North Sea and it is to be seen at its dramatic best when those waters spend

their force furiously on its shelf. It is another spot where it seems impossible that a large port could ever have existed – never mind prosper. There is still, however, the tiny, narrow and tortuous Cley Channel that snakes away to the east past the Watch House, unmarked save for a sporadic buoy or withy. It is so narrow and shoal that only the most devoted mud crawlers will wish to pursue it. Far better just to observe it from land, or try it in a dinghy or dayboat.

Cley is equally as charming in the centre of the village, where there is much lively life – a butcher, general store, smoked fish shop, delicatessen, garage, pub and two residential hotels. But, perhaps the most conspicuous features of Cley are the beautiful windmill (extremely well preserved) the Custom House; the colossal Cley church; and the nearby mill at the virtual head of the navigation. Whether the visit is by road or by the tortuous Cley Channel, this beautiful mill is a worthwhile objective.

Morston, Cley-next-the-Sea and Blakeney form a trio of communities that hang together with a unified will and spirit that face the rigours of the North Sea with a panache that is only equalled by the fortitude with which they face the demands of the touring multitudes. The locals know that they stand as much in threat from inundation by the one as they do by the other; but, in true Norfolk tradition, they calmly persevere, respecting both but deferring to neither.

Blakeney is a busy spot. Road traffic from the hinterland streams in and, in the holiday season in particular, it is difficult to park – in spite of the efforts of the Village Fathers.

Cley to Caister

After Morston, Blakeney and Cley-next-the-sea, comes the long slog from the great light of Cromer to the great dark of Yarmouth, with nary a bolt hole between. As the three villages fall astern, and we move eastward to the north of Sheringham, the coastline rises gently to a thickly wooded skyline of hills and cliffs. The small and keep-it-in-the-family community of Sheringham lies in a hollow between the cliffs and hills. Nestling, as it does, by the water's edge like a village in a merman's fairy-tale, in the early summer sun with a slight haze, or a late October moon, it can form a mysterious spectacle. Only those with an exclusively fierce and fixed attachment to the harsher realities of life, and without a vestige of imagination will find it possible to cruise past this domain without succumbing to its potent magic.

My first boating experience off Sheringham was of a different order. Standing off about a couple of miles, so as to leave all the crab pots well to port, I noticed the marker of an isolated pot about two cables to starboard. 'Safe distance', I thought; but I was wrong, for the line stretched ominously in front of our bows. Too late I cut the engines and, Sod's Law ruling yet again, I picked up the line around starboard prop. Full investigation showed that it was an already cut line. Later, taking avoiding action from an apparently unmanned coaster, I succeeded in wrapping most of the line round both props and the rudder. The tale had a happy ending in so far as the whelkers of Wells rallied round to get me in and sort me out; but, to this day, I cannot see a crab pot marker without my anxiety level rising. They still abound, prevail and even predominate.

The general tendency southwards is still towards a low-lying coastline; but, within this overall view, some cliffs proper can be seen beginning to make their mark. Indeed, on either side of Cromer, the cliffs rise steeply while the hinterland stands out conspicuously, being dramatically well-wooded. Where the cliffs begin to lose some of their grandeur towards the southeast of Cromer they are topped by bungalows and chalets that do nothing to improve the skyline. This marks the end of the 2-mile expanse of cliffs, which, although they are not particularly tall, fall at a dramatically steep-to angle to the sea and, in their entirety, are beautifully sculptured. At one point, below an isolated white bungalow, one section of the cliffs is just like a massive replica of Old Father Time, with looming eyes, a hook nose and a v-shaped beard.

This represents perhaps the best cliff frontage and profile to be found between Flamborough and Beachy Head; indeed, it is the last before the North Foreland except for the slow emergence of a short sequence by Caister-on-Sea. While still of miniature proportions, they offer an attractive frontage with modest spans that look almost primeval.

After Cromer, we move on down past Bacton and its conglomeration that is of so much assistance to

In contrast, leisure craft filter in in ha'penny numbers, but it is still a case of foxes having holes, birds of the air having nests, but the Sons of the Sea having not where to lay their lines.

yachtsmen wanting VHF contact with the mainland. Just a little further down we come to the coastal strip of the Norfolk Broads. The first real contact comes with Happisburgh (pronounced 'Haysbrer'). The lighthouse stands sentinel for the Haisboro Sands. The nearby church tower is also a well-known and much-used mark. Happisburgh had a church recorded in the Domesday Survey. Some Norman bits are still supposed to be there. The 110ft tower and its battlement parapet were built in the 15th century. In the mid 19th century a likeable fellow with the unlikeable appellation of Jonathan Balls was finally put in his place by being laid out to rest. He was a man with something of a reputation, and it was not with a comb and a glass in his hand that he was encased, but with a bible, a cake, a poker and a tong. The reason is not noted; but it is mooted

that poison was found in his remains and also in those of two of his associates.

After Happisburgh, the cliffs finally disappear, giving way to the dunes that are typical of the holidaymaking area, much of it is protected by a sea wall. Both Eccles and Palling have suffered badly in wind-swept sea gales and sand storms. In 1953, when the great tide hit Wells-next-the-Sea very badly, these two communities were ravaged with much flooding and seven deaths. After Sea Palling, on the way now nearly south, we pass most closely to the Broads themselves; namely at Hickling and Horsey Meres.

Next comes the full fall, as the low-lying house-peppered land starts its slow march down to Winterton Ness foreland and its disused lighthouse, on a long promenade of sand that slowly slopes into the sea from its attractive undulating dunes. Also proud on the landscape is the 132ft 15th-century flint tower of Winterton church; known well by all mariners who pass by. The old lighthouse is the most noticeable feature in the area; standing out starkly, as it does, against the almost Mediterranean-style dunes and their flowers. Such a perception is reinforced by the fact that, perhaps unexpectedly and certainly quaintly, Norfolk has its own version of California just to the north of Yarmouth. While its climate can never approach the Mediterranean style of the American state, it does manage to support pretty grass-covered banks that steeply shelve down, almost to the water's edge. Here, they front lines of camps, beach huts, bungalows, chalets and other holiday homes, all proclaiming the move towards the centre of the fully matured tourist territory of the town. Not only has Yarmouth deemed itself to be Great Yarmouth over the decades, but it now proclaims, even more loudly than before, that is to be promoted as Great*er* Yarmouth.

This part of the coastline is archetypally disregarded, but not so disgraced as many parts of the UK; our natural heritage is still alive, if somewhat threatened by so many scattered and jumbled holiday camps. It is no problem to conjure up images of those submarine forests that are to be found just off this coast, and to visualise the coastline itself as the long-suffering, silent and historic victim of those landslides and general eroding decay that have had their way as the sea has reclaimed, inch by inexorable inch, its own inheritance, the land.

Caister-on-Sea was, at one time, much more 'on the sea' than it now is, since it used to be the former estuary of the combined Yare, Bure and Waveney rivers. Shifting sands cut them off from the sea by the formation of an amazingly substantial bar. That 'bar' finally led to the creation of those many 'bars' that together are now known as Great Yarmouth. More soberly, it is interesting to note that in the 2nd century AD, the Romans built a town at the mouth of the rivers. It was well protected from invasion by both sea and enemies by a ditch, a bank and a

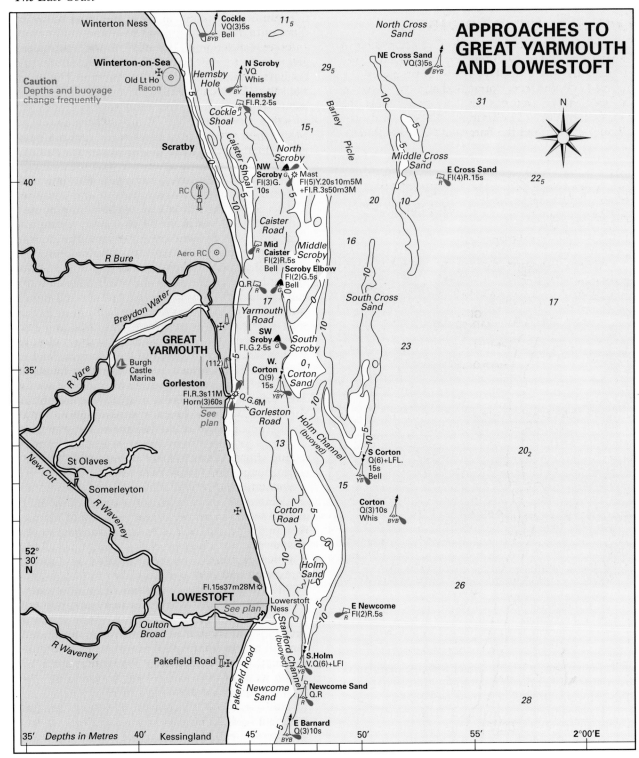

APPROACHES TO GREAT YARMOUTH AND LOWESTOFT

wooden palisade. It is in the tradition of such warlike sea-going vigour that the volunteers who run the lifeboats in the area make supreme efforts to gain the funds to carry on. They even penetrate the calm waters of the Broads in search of support. They show splendid stubbornness and guts in the face of so many petty but frustrating obstacles. Their fundraising is almost to be compared with their lifesaving work and bravery at sea.

Great Yarmouth Haven

On the whole, my unfavourable first impression of Great Yarmouth in 1975 remains unchanged. From seaward, the place displays a face of no appeal – a dejected countenance, dominated and oppressed by the mélange of factories and power stations; the conglomeration of chimney stacks; and the silhouetted hump of the fairground's rollercoaster.

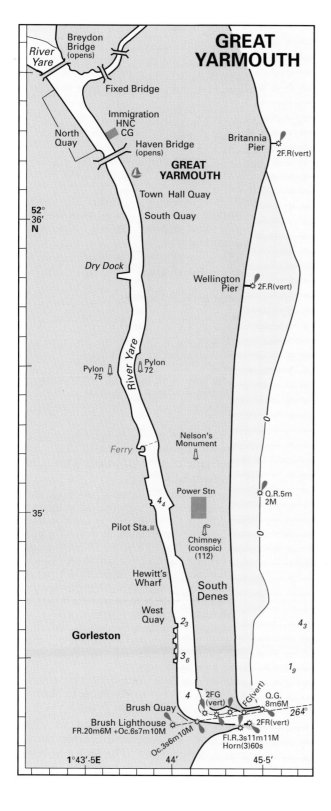

From a scenic point of view, the coast to Great Yarmouth, from both the north and the south, while offering a lot to the seeking eye, has some intriguing features, but also long stretches of what tend to be ho-hum camps and low-lying tedium. Not even Nelson's Column stands out as an identifiable monument in its own right. In spite of the profusion of lights, I must say that there is nothing about the place about which it can be said, 'So shines a good deed in a naughty world.'

From the north, after the well known Cockle cardinal off Winterton Ness, the approach lies between the north shoals of Scroby and those off Caister – inside Scroby and outside Caister, and straight down through Caister and Yarmouth Roads. From the south, the obvious choice is a straightforward run inshore through the Lowestoft Roads. Take care when looking for the cardinal Barnard, the green and red Newcomes, and the cardinal Corton; the first can be repositioned and/or taken off station frequently; up-to-date information is important here – although a close inshore run with an eye on the sounder should keep the coast clear as it were, since there is much to look at. Both lead to Gorleston Road, situated immediately to the south of Yarmouth Haven entrance. From such a southerly position, at about ½ mile off, the entrance shows as a long, low line in dark rust colour. A green silo shows to the right hand; a green and white silo is to the centre; and, just to west of north, the power station chimney shows prominently, and is the most obvious landmark for the port.

The immediate entrance into the Haven, between the north and south piers, is difficult to identify exactly until you are very close, since both sides of the piers are the same dreary colour not only as one another but also as most of the background. So, a cautious approach is best until they are clearly recognised and fully open, when the old red-brick lighthouse on the Brush – not one that can be called conspicuous – will lead you in on a near-westerly course. To effect entry, substantial power may be needed if you are to make it on the ebb, for the rate can achieve anything up to 6 knots. Although there is complete access at all times, when there is any SE in the wind in excess of 3/4 entry against the ebb should not be attempted.

I still recall with unpleasant vibrations my first experience of Yarmouth's entrance. While it was stimulating, it was not the kind of stimulus that brings out great poetry, or even impressive acts. Conditions were 5/6 southeasterly with a spring tide on the ebb. Had it not been for current gale warnings and an already rising wind (with my next port of call northwards, namely Wells-next-the-Sea) I would never have tried. What the *Admiralty Pilot* says in no way overstates the case: 'Light-draught vessels may enter at most times, but high or low slack water is recommended. There is risk with a heavy sea in the entrance particularly during strong SE winds with an outgoing stream; under these conditions the roadstead is recommended for refuge.' The roadstead held no appeal as a refuge for me, so I braved the mass of broken water for a 10-minute struggle that seemed to last an hour. *Valcon* succeeded in lurching in all three planes at once and was apparently ready to capsize. It was I, of course, who was ready to founder; and the minute I had made the right-angled turn to starboard into the river itself, I had recourse to the medicinal brandy.

Great Yarmouth

After the Brush, a dramatic right-angled near-blind turn to starboard, the Haven proper takes over with a wide and deep channel all the way up to the Haven Bridge – a journey through murky waters, past the residual tugs and rig support vessels that at one time covered the waterfront. Almost immediately after Brush Bend, on the port hand, is the fuel station, the RNLI and the pilot boats, wasplike in orange and black with a yellow stripe. Most of the rest of the bank is taken up by the boats of the local professional fishermen, who, to put it at its kindest, have no interest in yachtsmen; and at worst will cast you off without the blinking of an eye. Just over ½ mile up the Haven there is a cross-river ferry to be avoided.

The Haven Bridge, and the 'new' Breydon Bridge must be negotiated to reach the Broads; the Haven bridgemaster is on VHF Ch 12 and the Breydon master is in contact with him. When closed, both bridges offer no better than 2·8m headroom. There are now only two openings a day for leisure craft, and if you wish to pass through on Sunday (or even Monday morning, according to some of the staff) you must make the booking before 1600 hours on the preceding Friday. You are usually permitted to wait at the Town Hall Quay. Occasionally you may be given something resembling a smile, and something of a warm tone from a bridge-master; but attitudes have changed little since my first unhappy visit. On that occasion there was hardly anywhere to moor and it was only with the greatest difficulty that I managed to make one line fast, ascend a badly bruised ladder to the almost insurmountably high wall, and somehow get over it to make fast the other lines on the unsuitably placed bollards on the other side. I was later told to cast off. Happily there was a coaster across the river. The crew who had observed all, shouted across, 'Come over here mate; you'll be all right with us', and took our lines.

It is some long time since I have seen a coaster on that quay. Fortunately, I have had no need of such help since then, and access to the quayside wall has been much improved. There are now ladders and rings that are well paved. But it really is time a floating pontoon was put into position and more done to substantiate Yarmouth's claim to welcome leisure craft. It still lacks facilities, co-operation and friendly services.

GREAT YARMOUTH
52°34'·33N 01°44'·50E

Charts Admiralty 1536, 1543; Imray C28, C29; OS Landranger 134

Tides
Lowestoft –0025, Dover –0210 (Haven Bridge: Lowestoft +0300)

Caution/notes Strong tides at the entrance and in the river make navigation difficult for small craft. There are more than 16,000 ship movements annually within the port.

Authorities
Harbourmaster ☎ 01493 855151
VTS (24 hrs) ☎ 01493 855153
Breydon Bridge ☎ 01493 651275
Broads Navigation Authority ☎ 01603 610734

Radio
Port VHF Ch 11, **12**, 09, 16. Call *Yarmouth*
Haven & Breydon Bridges VHF Ch 12

Traffic signals
Traffic signals and VTS instructions (VHF Ch 12) must be obeyed at all times
S pier: 3R(vert)
vis 235°–340° = Entry prohibited
VTS office: 3R(vert) = No vessel to go downriver
                              S of the LB shed
Haven/Breydon bridges:
3R(vert) = Passage prohibited

Leading lights at Brush Quay
Front Oc.3s6m10M
Rear F.R.20m6M & Oc.6s7m10M

Haven Bridge
Northbound traffic
Blue flag or F.Bl over F.W light on SE buttress exhibited 5 mins before bridge due to open.
Southbound traffic
Red flag or F.R over F.W light on NW buttress exhibited 5 mins before bridge due to open.

My most recent intelligence comes from the harbourmaster, Captain Alex Goodlad. This is his outline of the present situation.

'Great Yarmouth is a busy commercial port built on a narrow river. Strong tides at the entrance and in the river make navigation difficult for small craft. In addition there are than 16,000 ship movements annually within the port.

Berthing for visiting craft is limited to a 50-metre length of quay. The quay is of steel-pile construction topped with a flood wall. Access is by vertical ladder of 4·2 metres from MLWS to the top of the flood wall with another vertical ladder of 1·1 metres from the top of the flood wall to the quay. Fresh water is available.

You will have deduced that the difficulties in navigation and the limited facilities, access and availability of berths make Great Yarmouth suitable only for experienced yachtsmen having local knowledge.

I therefore request that Great Yarmouth is not entered as a port for leisure craft, but as an alternative to Mutford Lock for access to the Norfolk Broads.'

The alternative, Mutford Lock, used to offer nothing better than an expensive weekly ritual. Happily, things have changed. The lock has been

A dramatic view of The Brush, the right-angled near-blind turn to starboard that leads into the deep and wide channel of the River Yare as it sweeps up to the Haven Bridge.
Below Both Haven and Breydon Bridges can be clearly seen below. 'Breydon' is from the Danish for 'water broadened from narrow'; and there is no question of Water not being Broadened here. Breydon Water was the sea estuary of the local rivers, before they united to rush through the Haven at Yarmouth . . . Nearly four miles long and over a mile wide, it is to be compared to an inland sea – and, at low water, more a large mud flat . . . but always an impressive spread.

refurbished and now affords easy and comparatively inexpensive access into Oulton Broad. (For full details of the organisation and method at Mutford Lock, see page 59.)

Yarmouth's appeal may not be universal, but it has some features worth exploring and, in the season, promotes a carnival way of life – cockles and rock; bangers and burgers; boat trips, birds and booze. Yarmouth's 'harbour and haven' claim to fame and usefulness for yachtsmen was its easy access to the Norfolk Broads, compared with Lowestoft's laborious methods a few years ago. But now Lowestoft has got its act together at Mutford Lock, this attraction no longer obtains. The new Broads Authority has brought about many much-needed changes, but there seems to be no sign of obvious co-operation between the imaginative and welcoming Broads services and staff and the Yarmouth set-up. Once through the bridges with Yarmouth astern and into classic Broads territory, be it north or south, you could not wish for a warmer welcome, friendlier officers or a more efficient service.

III. The Suffolk Coast

From Lowestoft to the Harwich Estuary

Lowestoft

Approaching Lowestoft, after quitting Great Yarmouth by way of the Haven and the River Yare, the navigation tends just to the east of south with little danger when cruising close in. On what is virtually a straight southerly course, you just drop down, leaving the cardinal Holm Sand to the east and enter Corton Roads, past the mainland village of the same name, with the unmistakable tower of the local Corton Roads Holiday Camp. The last buoy is the green West Holm which leads you to Lowestoft North Road. A similarly plain approach marks the course from the south via Newcome and Pakefield, but see also below.

It is worth noting that the well-known red East Newcome stands outside the Lowestoft sandbanks and caution should be exercised if using it as a waypoint or entry marker for the harbour. I have jilled around the site more than once and now know that careful study of the chart and regular soundings are required as the buoys are moved quite frequently. That is if you feel you must approach that way.

Long before Nelson sailed the seas, the tall west tower of St Bartholomew's church at Corton, just down the coast from Hopton, was an important guide to seafarers. Down the road, the tiny village of Gunton is to be seen just to the north of Lowestoft, with Pleasurewood Hills by its side. Gunton is an old village with a splendid round Norman tower. It is actually now impossible to separate it out from Lowestoft and it must be considered its suburb, made up entirely of housing estates, holiday camps and country clubs.

Just to the north of the harbour is Lowestoft Ness, famous for being the most easterly point of the UK. There is a pub which brilliantly, and justifiably, exploits the fact to boost its trade.

Lowestoft harbour is virtually impossible to miss, to overlook or mistake, mainly because of its distinctive, rocket-like light towers at the entrance and the high-rise silos behind them. Just to the north of the entrance is the coastguard station. It is a prominent concrete building with the appearance of a luxury liner's wheelhouse. It looks reassuringly seaworthy. Safe access can be had into the harbour at all times, but wind against tide, especially an ebb, makes for a rough five or ten minutes.

Entry into the harbour and Lake Lothing is strictly regulated by traffic control lights, but since the harbourmaster and his staff are completely friendly and co-operative towards leisure craft, it is not often that a yacht is held up for very long waiting for the town bridge to open. Anyway, for those who do not like jilling around at all, there is always the Royal Norfolk and Suffolk Yacht Club. They welcome visitors and can usually offer a berth. Since Lowestoft is a mass of leisure and pleasure for land-grabbers and sea pirates alike, a few days spent exploring its milieu can be of appeal.

It is important to check with the harbour radio (VHF Ch 14) for commercial shipping movements. This will also give you some idea of how long you might have to wait for the lights to come in your favour and allow you to get in. It can also inform you of the next opening of the bridge that permits you to 'cross the road' into Lake Lothing and make for the Inner Harbour and up to Mutford Lock.

Visitors' moorings are to be found in the South Basin, and the normal plan is to tie up to the North Wall at the Inner South Pier or lie next another boat. The basin is usually busy and it is customary to seek instructions from the Royal Norfolk & Suffolk Yacht Club's berthing officer. The moorings were renowned throughout the North Sea cruising community for years because of their famous/infamous giant sausage fenders that would roller-paint your hull with whatever oils, flotsam or other detritus happened to be floating in your vicinity. Happily, there has now been a rapid change, as is shown in the plan at top of page 58. The entrance now faces a much more sea-kindly direction and a whole series of flexible pontoons has been installed.

I always think of the Royal Norfolk & Suffolk Yacht Club as an amazing establishment – in spite of being a relic, redolent of those dear, dead Edwardian days well beyond recall, it is alert and alive with the kind of humming activity that is not usually associated with yacht clubs. Stringent regulations control your sartorial style in various rooms and, while they don't actually have a string quartet for your leisure and pleasure at afternoon tea, they should, for it would complete the *mise en*

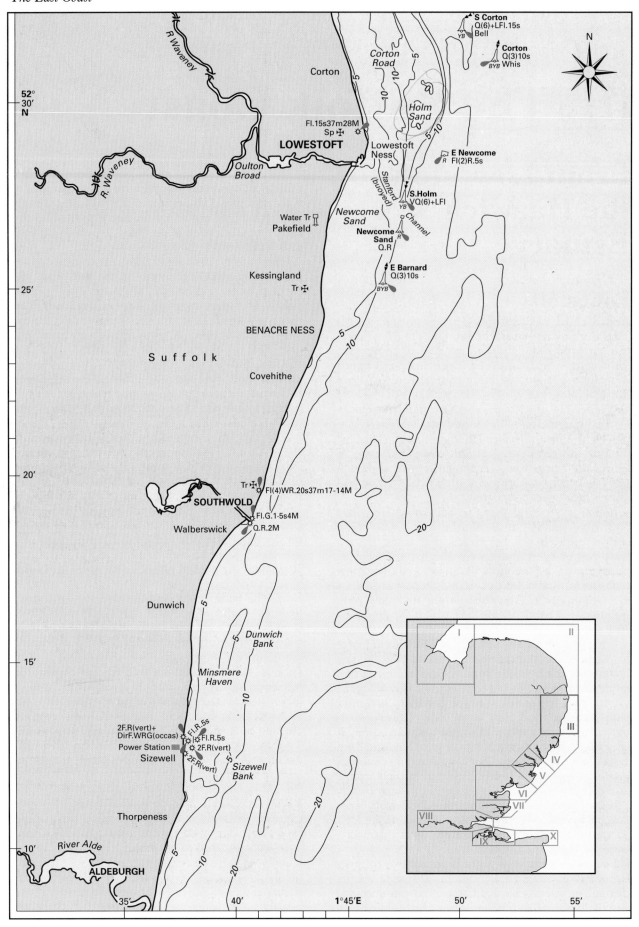

S Corton
Q(6)+LFl.15s
YB Bell

Corton
Q(3)10s
BYB Whis

Corton Road

Corton

Holm Sand

N

R Waveney

52°
30'
N

Fl.15s37m28M
Sp

LOWESTOFT

Lowestoft Ness

E Newcome
R Fl(2)R.5s

Oulton Broad

R. Waveney

Stanford (buoyed) Channel

S.Holm
YB VQ(6)+LFl

Water Tr
Pakefield

Newcome Sand

Newcome Sand
R Q.R

25'

Kessingland
Tr

E Barnard
Q(3)10s
BYB

BENACRE NESS

Suffolk

Covehithe

20'

Tr
Fl(4)WR.20s37m17-14M

SOUTHWOLD

Fl.G.1·5s4M
Q.R.2M

Walberswick

Dunwich

Dunwich Bank

15'

Minsmere Haven

2F.R(vert)+
DirF.WRG(occas)   Fl.R.5s
Power Station   Fl.R.5s
Sizewell   2F.R(vert)
2F.R(vert)

Sizewell Bank

Thorpeness

10'   River Alde

ALDEBURGH

35'   40'   1°45'E   50'   55'

I   II

III

IV

V

VI

VII

VIII

IX   X

Lowestoft harbour is virtually impossible to miss, to overlook or to mistake, mainly because of its distinctive, rocket-like light towers at the entrance and the high-rise silos behind them. This picture was taken before the changes were made to the Yacht Basin. Please see note on page 55. The fishing basins are on the right, and to centre left the road bridge can be seen, giving access to Lake Lothing.

scène. But none of this in any way stands in the way of modern facilities and up-to-date services with a smile.

There has been talk, and it is even more lively than ever now, of a new marina development closely linked with the club, with the essential idea being to extend the Inner South Quay. This would provide leisure craft with moorings that are separate and safe from all docks traffic and with much-improved protection from swell. There is also rumour that the old clubhouse would go in the general furore of a modern development scheme. However, we can all cease from worrying for at least a year or two . . . or three. Long live the RN & SYC!

Another well-established organisation is the Lowestoft & East Suffolk Maritime Society, to whom I am indebted for the following:

The objects of the Lowestoft and East Suffolk Maritime Society as defined in the Constitution are to educate the public in shipping, old and modern in Lowestoft and the County of Suffolk, and in the trades and crafts associated with shipping lore in general, and in particular to maintain a museum.

MARITIME MUSEUM

This is a private Museum of the Lowestoft and East Suffolk Maritime Society, which is a registered charity. The Museum is self-financing, and does not receive any monetary grants. It is maintained by members of the Society on a purely voluntary basis.

It was established in 1968, and extended in 1978 – the extension being opened by HRH the Duke of Edinburgh. A further extension was added in 1980.

The Museum specialises in the history of the Lowestoft fishing fleets, from early sail, to steam and through to the modern diesel vessels. Methods of fishing are also recorded, namely trawling, and the no-longer-practised art of herring driftnet fishing. Also depicted is the town's wartime association with the Royal Navy, together with a fine exhibition of the evolution of lifeboats.

Museum attendants are ex-seamen and others interested in the history of the Port of Lowestoft, and, given half a chance, will spin a 'salty' yarn, and will be delighted to answer any questions you may have about the Museum and its exhibits.

WATCHES ABOARD SHIPS . . .
How they are arranged

For many, many years the hours seamen are required for duty aboard ships have been arranged in 'watches' or

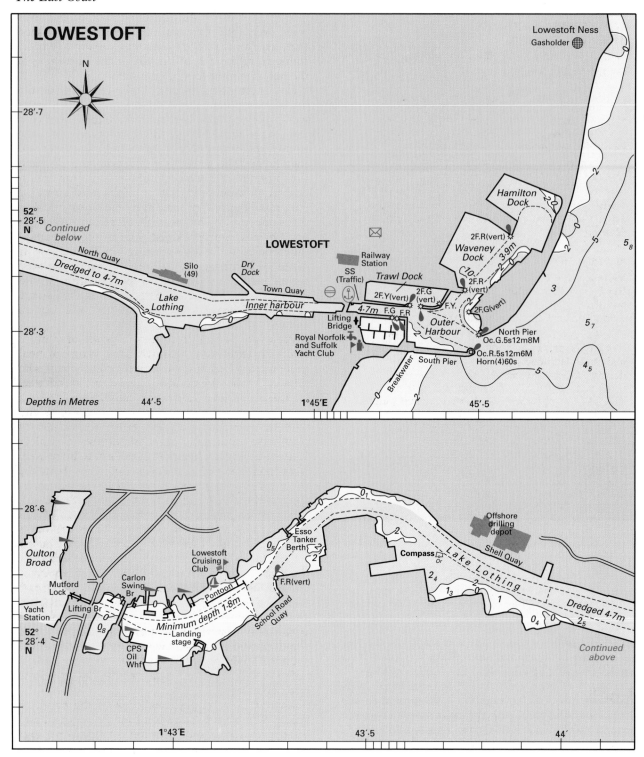

LOWESTOFT

Lowestoft Ness
Gasholder

Hamilton
Dock

2F.R(vert)

Waveney
Dock   3.9m

2F.R
(vert)

Trawl Dock

2F.Y(vert)   2F.G
(vert)   2F.G(vert)

F.Y.

4.7m F.G F.R

Outer
Harbour   North Pier
Oc.G.5s12m8M

Oc.R.5s12m6M
Horn(4)60s

*Continued
below*

LOWESTOFT

North Quay

Dredged to 4.7m

Silo
(49)

Dry
Dock

Town Quay

Lake
Lothing   *Inner harbour*

Railway
Station

SS
(Traffic)

Lifting
Bridge

Royal Norfolk
and Suffolk
Yacht Club

Breakwater   South Pier

Depths in Metres   44′·5   1°45′E   45′·5

Offshore
drilling
depot

Esso
Tanker
Berth

Compass

Lake Lothing

Shell Quay

Oulton
Broad

Lowestoft
Cruising
Club

Mutford
Lock

Carlon
Swing
Br

Pontoon

F.R(vert)

Minimum depth 1.8m

School Road
Quay

Or

Dredged 4.7m

Yacht
Station

Lifting Br

Landing
stage

CPS
Oil
Whf

*Continued
above*

1°43′E   43′·5   44′

'tricks' of 4 hours each and the passing of each half hour indicated by ringing the ship's bell.

Middle watch	midnight to 0400
Morning watch	0400 to 0800
Forenoon watch	0800 to noon
Afternoon watch	1200 to 1600
First dog watch	1600 to 1800
Second dog watch	1800 to 2000
First watch	2000 to midnight

The purpose of dividing the period between 1600 and 2000 into two 'dog watches' is to permit the 'tricks' or duties to change every day. Without this arrangement men

would have the same duty, day in and day out.

The commencement of the Mutiny at the Nore on 13 May 1797 was indicated by the ringing of five bells at 1830 (6.30pm). Since that date five bells have not been rung in British ships at that time; the bells of the first dog watch are repeated in the second watch.

It is also customary in British ships to sound one bell 15 minutes before the new watch commences. This is known as 'little one bell' and is the time the new watch is aroused.

Also in British ships it's customary to ring eight bells twice on New Year's Eve. Once for the old year and once for the new!

LOWESTOFT HARBOUR
52°28'·28N 01°45'·50E

Charts Admiralty 1536, 1543. Imray C28, C29.
OS Landranger 156/134.

Tides
Dover −0133

Caution Sands are continually shifting. Beware shallows and drying areas and do not cross banks in bad weather or strong tidal conditions.

Authorities
Harbourmaster ☎ 01502 572286
Mutford Bridge & Lock ☎ 01502 531778/523003

Radio
Lowestoft Harbour Control VHF Ch **14**, 16, 11 (24hrs)

Pilot
☎ 01502 560277 VHF Ch 14

Visitors' moorings
Royal Norfolk & Suffolk Yacht Club ☎ 01502 566726
Oulton Broad Yacht Station ☎ 01502 574946

Local regulations
The Lowestoft Harbour Bridge (between the Inner and Outer Harbours) will only be opened on demand for commercial shipping. Commercial shipping is discouraged from passage: 0815–0900, 1230–1300 and 1700–1730. Small craft and yachts may use a bridge opening for commercial shipping provided that prior arrangement has been made with Lowestoft Harbour Control: VHF Ch 14, ☎ 01502 572286 or personal visit. In addition, and subject to prior notification of at least 20 minutes, small craft and yachts may be given a bridge opening at the following times:
Mon–Fri. 0700, 0930, 1100, 1600, 1900, 2100
Sat, Sun, bank hols. 0745, 0930, 1100, 1400, 1730, 1900, 2100
Navigation in the bridge channel is controlled by VHF advice with additional amber and green ëtraffic lightsí when the bridge is operated. Small craft passing under the bridge have a clearance of 2·2m at mean HWS (approx. 2·4m on the tide gauge) with a reduction of 0·5m for the arch sides.

Lake Lothing and Mutford Lock

Once past the opening road bridge and through the inner harbour, you reach Lake Lothing. This is a favourite spot for large sailing yachts to undertake repairs and refurbishment.

At the head of Lake Lothing, the Cruising Club ('Long waiting list . . . full for years') appears with its congregation of many pretty craft tucked away all neat'n'nice in the midst of the vast assembly of commerce, industry, wrecks, hulks and the general mess epitomised by the paperworks storage. Nearby is the International Boatbuilding Training Centre, and the extraordinary shapes and colours of the many and various sizes of the survival capsules. There is good photogenic stuff all round this area.

This takes us to Mutford Lock. The original was built over 150 years ago, and gloriously claimed that, like Janus, it faced both ways, ready to handle traffic from the end of the old or the beginning of the new; from the fresh to the salt.

Lowestoft is a composite of the pretty old and the not-so-pretty new; and after many a sojourn in its well-protected yacht harbour, I have come to review my first judgements on this town that mixes the trendy, the broken-down, the soiled, the ribald and the choice. The gentry, the plebeian, the elite and the nondescript rub shoulders in this semi-egalitarian community. It is a curiosity affording entertainment and relaxation to the tourist, and at the same time being worthy of serious study by psychologist and sociologist. Life in the harbour is different from the days when it was famous for its gangs of herring girls, but recent years have seen something of a revival of the port's fortunes, and fishing and commerce are both on an upward surge, as the development plans and the new buildings all show.

From the visiting yachtsman's point of view, it offers an excellently comprehensive range of boat gear, marine facilities and services run by staff who know what they are doing . . . and don't overcharge. In these respects, Lowestoft cannot be bettered; and, bearing in mind that it is easy of access and without attendant hazards, its strange blend of peculiarly charming and singularly charmless features must make it a port of call not to be missed. This cannot be said with much conviction about any other harbour to the north until you reach Grimsby (up the Humber) or Blyth (on the way to Scotland).

The older part of Lowestoft is between Gunton and the harbour and Lake Lothing. There are lots of narrow alleys and, tucked away, are still some family artisan fish smokers. Lowestoft was looked up to in the past as chief town in the Lothingland Hundred. At the time of the Spanish Armada, Lowestoft mustered itself a small but powerful army with hand guns and longbows. In 1588, the Spaniards met with total disaster and never got there. The important and well-known lifeboat society was founded here in 1800, and the present Ladies' Lifeboat Guild is even today known for its efforts and successes.

Lots of Lowestoft is touched with the brush of gaiety. While north Lowestoft slowly developed into a large residential area with many tourist trappings and attractions, south Lowestoft was, from the very beginning a happy holiday tourist amenity by the day, the week, or the fortnight.

So, as the sun sets on the roller coaster of Lowestoft, we say farewell and move down the coast past less frolicsome areas. There is no hazard on a close inshore passage, until you reach the cardinal South Holm; the red Newcome Sand; and the cardinal East Barnard. This keeps you out about a mile which is a good distance for arriving off Southwold and being able to manoeuvre in comfort

Lake Lothing coming in from the top right, leads through a
rather old and broken down waterside area to the quite new and
rather modern lock construction, with the intriguing appellation
'Mutford'.

with plenty of sea room while setting a course for
entry.

First to stand out as a small feature on the coast,
after all the hotels and bed and breakfast joints, is
the water tower at Pakefield. In the past there may
have been small fires on the cliff to call in the little
ships with the big contraband, for which the locals
were famous. After no time at all, the church tower
at Kessingland hoves into view. It was here that
Rider Haggard wrote *She* – surely nothing further
from an adventure at sea can be imagined.

The sandbanks that were well out to sea off
Lowestoft have closed the coast and almost joined it
by the time we get to Benacre Ness. Keeping about
a mile off avoids any difficulty and takes you outside
the Barnard shoal off Benacre Ness but, inside the
buoy and straight on to the S Newcome and the
Pakefield buoys. After Benacre Ness there is little
left of the cliffs due to continuing erosion. Indeed,
the *Admiralty Pilot* warns against such debris as tree
trunks after springs or storms.

Mutford Lock

Transit bookings are advised: ☎ 01502 531778
(Lock) or 01502 523003 (office hrs). Mutford Lock,
connecting the Lowestoft Inner Harbour with Oulton
Broad, is operated daily under the direction of the
Broads Authority. The Lock, with safe usable
dimensions of 22m × 6·5m, has a water depth of 2m
plus tidal variations and should only be used by craft
suitable for the water depths of Oulton Broad. Non-
local craft with a draft exceeding 1·7m should seek
advice from Mutford Lock staff and consider the
Oulton Broad tide which is approx. 3 hours after
Lowestoft with a mean range of 0·7m.

Mutford Road Bridge

Adjacent to the Lock, Mutford Road Bridge has a
clearnce of 2·1m at mean HWS (approx. 2·4m on the
Lowestoft tide gauge) and it is therefore advisable for
all craft requiring an opening to make an advance
booking and to be prepared to wait. Such bookings
will automatically include the Railway Bridge located
close eastward. VHF Chs 9 and 14 are monitored on
an occasional basis by Mutford Control, which is
attended daily in response to bookings and at the
following times: 0800–1100, 1300–1600 (BST),
0900–1200 (standard time).

Southwold

Whether approaching Southwold from the north or the south, the conspicuous lighthouse to the NE of the harbour entrance, and the water tower are the confirming visual aspects. There are two very good 'unofficial and informal' leading-line marks from seaward in the form of the lighthouse and church in Southwold.

When making for an entry from the north, it is best to stand off about ½ to ¼ mile until you have a good sighting of the south pierhead. Then make a course of 90° and go straight for it. This will keep you well away from the shingle shoal that is building up around the north pierhead. The north and south piers have about 40m between them. Having arrived at the south pierhead, make immediately for the well-known 'Knuckle' at the end of the North Pier. From the south, it is best to keep at least 300m off until you have reached the same position, as if coming from the north. 'Large' vessels can, by arrangement with the harbourmaster, be berthed near this area. *Valcon* is not a 'large' vessel and so not eligible, but I have never been tempted by the appearance of that quay. I am sure it is all properly shipshape, boatshape and Southwold-fashion, but I still find it of sinister aspect.

You should pass the Knuckle very close – no more than about 2·0m off. Then tend to the north by the mooring posts as there is a shingle patch towards the

east. Once at the green beacon, you can then tend to the centre of the river until you reach the harbourmaster's office, when the yacht moorings will be in sight.

There is never less than 2·0m between the piers these days, and never less than 1·5m at the Knuckle. The cross-streams can be strong and capriciously treacherous, so it is important to know exactly what they are doing and what you propose to do regarding them. Offshore winds with an ebb tide can be very bad. Southwold is a harbour where it is usually difficult to change your mind, or even manoeuvre at times, when you have once committed yourself to an entry.

When I first visited Southwold in the late 1970s, not only was it a strange 'Wild West' kind of place but it also possessed an entry that was downright inhospitable to visitors. Between the piers, strangers would find it impossible to discern the channel, which, in any case, was unpredictable almost from tide to tide. There was a disreputable red flag permanently flown at the entrance, denoting 'entrance inadvisable'. There were broken-down jetties, huts, shacks and decaying hulls. The floating pontoons, which clearly found it difficult to live up to their description, were a miscellany of small unstable berths for pleasure craft (permanently private, but not always occupied); larger but hardly more stable catwalks; and piles for the few professional fishermen. A few unattractive berths were for those visitors who had chanced their all at the entrance and had actually made it to just below the bridge. In brief, confusion reigned – and the fact that the harbourmaster was also the supervisor of the caravan site seemed entirely fitting.

I remember that first visit clearly. I had noticed through the binoculars the torn and tattered entrance flag on its unsteady pole. The *Admiralty Pilot* said briefly, 'A red flag, unreliable, means that entry is inadvisable.' The fact that it rhymed and nearly scanned was amusing but of little help or consolation; but since the wind, weather, tide and time were all in my favour I decided to risk an entry in spite of the warning. After I had been there a day

Exiting Lowestoft at its sublime summer best.

SOUTHWOLD HARBOUR
52°18'·75N 01°40'·65E
Charts Admiralty 2695, 1543. Imray C28, C29.
OS Landranger 156
Tides
Dover −0105
Caution/notes The entrance, which is liable to change, is dangerous in N winds.
Authorities
Harbourmaster ☎ 01502 724712   *CH 12*
Radio
Southwold Port Radio VHF Ch 12, 16, 09
Ⓥ

Harbour Marine Services
☎ 01502 724721
⬧D, Ⓔ, Repairs, Engineer

or two, I was baptised into local lore and the reason for the red flag flying by day and night. The then harbourmaster and caravan-site supervisor himself addressed me, 'That self-same flag has been there for years. We leave it there all the time. It puts visitors off, and that's how we like it. But you should see what the charts say we've got. We're down for all kinds of things we've never heard of. That's always good for a laugh, that is.'

It is pleasant to be able to record that the situation has changed dramatically. The navigational aids are exactly what they are supposed to be, and the Admiralty has given the place a thorough survey. The visitors' pontoons are now quite splendid affairs, sound and new, with ladders and planks provided by the harbourmaster.

Most yachts will want to go straight to these moorings by the harbourmaster's large office and opposite the Harbour Inn. The moorings can actually accommodate 100 yachts, although I must say that, at first glance, the berthing facilities suggest that a sardine-like proposition of even 75 would be on the generous side. Southwold is very popular with the foreign sailing fraternity, especially the Dutch. It usually hosts 40 to 50 boats in an average week in the season and visitors can find themselves rafted together up to four or five deep.

At low water springs, deep-keeled craft on the inside moorings will probably take the bottom, but on the outside there is a sharp drop to 6·0m or more. The harbourmaster will pilot you in if required. He is usually around at tide times to guide and assist you into a berth. At one time, as mentioned above, you needed your own planks; but under the new regime, together with a good water hose, they are now provided. However, you will need good strong warps – although the rise and fall is not more than 2·0m, there is tremendous power in the stream.

The Harbour Inn (which can get its deliveries from the Southwold Brewery by horsedrawn dray) is a classic of an old-fashioned East Coast hostelry. Its floors are uneven and prone to flooding; its timbers dark and unyielding and the staff can be similar unless (and until) you are elected to the chosen few; and its beer is of a high quality. Meals are available, but they are up to date and, although they are no longer of old-fashioned excellence, they are still good.

Harbour Marine Services is an excellent establishment with a good range of books, charts and chandlery. It undertakes all the standard services associated with a boatyard. Also in operation is Blackshore yacht sales. This is what its brochure says:

The entrance to Southwold Harbour, with the River Blyth disappearing into the top left distance. The notorious 'Knuckle' can be seen at the end of the right-hand wall, with the new look-out post just above. Fishing and leisure moorings can be seen at mid left.

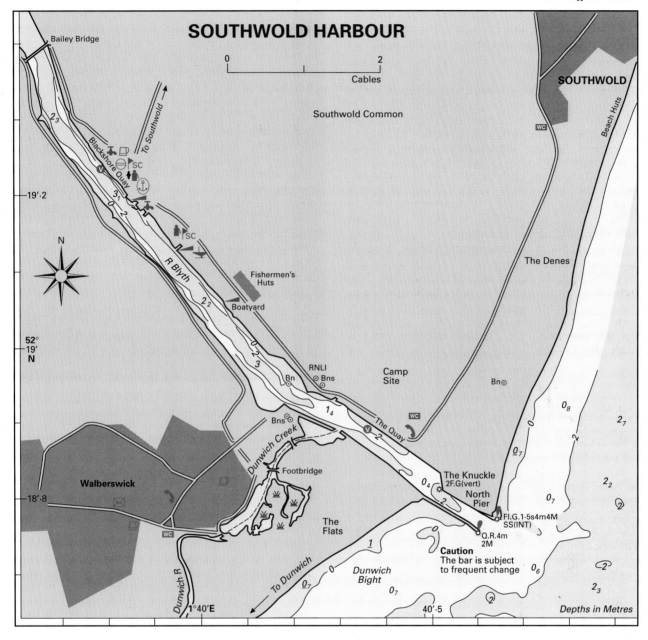

SOUTHWOLD HARBOUR

0   2
Cables

Southwold Common

SOUTHWOLD

Bailey Bridge

To Southwold

Blackshore Quay

SC

19'·2

N

R Blyth

SC

Fishermen's Huts

Boatyard

52°
19'
N

The Denes

Bn

RNLI
Bns

Camp Site

Bns

Bn

Bn

wc

wc

Dunwich Creek

Footbridge

The Quay

Walberswick

The Knuckle
2F.G(vert)

North Pier

18'·8

wc

The Flats

Fl.G.1·5s4m4M
SS(INT)

Q.R.4m
2M

Dunwich R

1°40'E

To Dunwich

Dunwich Bight

Caution
The bar is subject
to frequent change

40'·5

Depths in Metres

Harbour Marine Services has been at Southwold since 1988, and aims to provide reliability, along with a friendly and personal service. Until 1988 there was no working boatyard at Southwold, since then the business has expanded and we are now able to provide full boatyard facilities with lifting and launching to 10-ton and slipping to 20-ton. We have extensive hardstanding with storage available both inside and out, and encourage our customers to use our facilities whilst working on their own boats.

Nancy Blackett, previously owned by Arthur Ransome, is one of the many vessels completely restored by Harbour Marine Services.

In addition, there is a nearby establishment that advertises itself as a chandlers, but inside I have never seen many items associated with boats on its shelves, nor have been given the impression that its staff know a lot about them. What is more, it takes a devil of a long time to get a cup of coffee . . . another of their specially advertised services.

The fresh fish 'sheds' are still there. Christina Cara's fish sales (whole cod, £0.80lb), 'Willie's Plaice' and the like. The fish could not be fresher; nor could the jokes; nor the air – the air around or the air of the fishermen. While the red flag no longer flies at the entrance to the River Blyth, it still flies above one of the sheds: a relic of the days when 'milord' up the hill used to have his steward, his valet or one of his skivvies watch for it to be raised. That was the signal that 'his' fish had arrived.

From these small 'offices' is sold the fresh fish that is landed from the boats before your very eyes. Once upon a time, really dishy-fishy bargains were to be had there, but those times have gone and you now pay the proper rate. Nevertheless, the real fresh thing is so different from the pale imitations that flop on most supermarkets' slabs or on the few townie fishmongers' stands that still exist, that it seems, by comparison, to be half price. Indeed, it is hardly too much to say that nothing can beat the taste of sea-fresh fish at any price.

Southwold itself is well distanced from the harbour by an excellent walk, the road is used by motor traffic that is notorious for its careless speed. The town has a long history and is much livelier than nearby Aldeburgh which is twice its size. It is a pleasant walk from the moorings into the town which is famous for its two 'landmarks'. Their order of priority will depend upon your taste; they are the lighthouse and the brewery. The splendid old lighthouse is to be found right in the centre of the town and, while it shows its age, it is also manifestly well cared for.

There is a working bustle at Southwold, indicative of a truly busy place, that exposes the sham that is the 'business' of the other place. The town is remarkably well supplied with public conveniences and possesses a cross-section of contemporary life, from poorly patronised pseudo arts and crafts centres to one fish and chip shop that was so over-patronised that it seemed pointless to join the queue.

Nearer to the river mouth and the caravan park, the beach is bordered by a concrete apology for a promenade and a line of beach huts including those with names as incongruous as Dodge City and High Chaparral. Touristic and domestic accommodation is generally to be found on the road behind the sand dunes that are neither land- nor sea-scaped, but merely sparsely covered with gorse and sea grass.

Almost on the edge of the sea are a few outposts of what might once have been holiday homes. Bleak, and suggesting the kind of hospitality redolent of a Brontë father-figure, it takes little imagination to see them slowly disappearing under the waves like the dream home of a forsaken merman. They must provide fantastic experiences for anyone who can enjoy or even survive a winter in such splendid isolation.

Although Southwold hosts a summer tourist brigade that has been consistently growing ever since Michael Palin's gentle TV satire, *East of Ipswich*, gave it national prestige, it has not fallen victim to the dreaded faceless holiday resort strips that seem to swallow so many of our coastal towns and villages. Southwold has retained its sense of identity – there is witness to the strange spirit of the place all around Gun Hill by Southwold Common and Town Marshes.

You can get to the other side of the River Blyth by dinghy, by the ferry not far from its entrance, or across the Bailey Bridge upstream from the pontoons. The former is a good way to spend a few hours just looking and/or messing about in boats. It is quiet, rural and intriguing. Whichever way you cross, it is impossible not to be interested in Blythburgh and intrigued by Walberswick.

At Blythburgh the principal objects of interest are the old Court House and the Abbey, of which the latter is an extremely fine building, although dilapidated. Blythburgh is on the edge of the

Southwold and its environs offer intriguing experiences: the town centre and sea front are redolent of days gone by with the hostelries, beach huts and B&B's presenting façades that, in spite of the best endeavours, cannot quite keep up with the present . . .

surrounding marshes, struggling to keep itself from the ravages of the sea which almost reaches it. Long ago, like many settlements on this part of the coast, it was a thriving place. It still retains some of its old houses and its huge church to signify something of its past glory. Inside the church there is a vast flagged area that reinforces the sense of space and size. The carvings are a positive delight.

In the beginning, Walberswick was a fishing village, but even as far back as the early 1890s, it was deemed to be quaint, with ancient decaying wooden piers and well-regarded picturesque cottages. Its visitors were chiefly self-styled artist-painters and the like. It is still quaint and picturesque, but the properties bear the legend of affluence, and the penniless artists have been ousted by the flavour of the theatrical month. Indigens are in short supply.

It would indeed be outrageous to leave the Southwold area without some reference to the other 'landmark': Adnam's, Suffolk's oldest brewery. So from the obscure, the old-fashioned and the effete on the side of the water, we now return to heart of the matter. I called in out of the blue in the summer of 1995, and was most kindly and obligingly shown round the whole shoot by the MD himself. That's what I call service. A little history . . .

From Suffolk's oldest brewery
Adnam's of Southwold is heir to an unbroken tradition of brewing which can be traced back for over six and a half centuries, to the medieval ale wines. The Sole Bay

Brewery was originally the brewhouse of The Swan, Southwold's oldest inn, and its history parallels that of the town. In both cases there is a strong sense of local identity, the desire for independence and a habit of 'doing different'. Such characteristics have ensured the survival of both, to the delight of every visitor and the quiet satisfaction of locals. It is a tradition we are determined to preserve.

From English ale to bitter beer

Ale, of course, was the common drink of all classes and all ages of society, in the days when coffee and tea were unknown and the water supply was frequently unfit for human consumption. But one important change was taking place: the East Coast mariners were beginning to acquire a taste for the bitter beer brewed by the Dutch, their neighbours across the sea. By the time that Southwold was granted its Charter in 1490, hops were being imported from Holland to add bitterness to the soft English ale and in the mid-16th century Bullein's 'Governance of Health' talks about hops being grown in England, 'As proof I know in many places in the country of Suffolk, whereas they brew their beers with the hops that groweth upon their own grounds.' One of the earliest hop farms in the county was nearby, at Bruisyard. You could enjoy a flagon of bitter in the alehouses of Southwold long before Burton-on-Trent became famous.

But, to move on and out to sea again. Leaving behind Southwold's church and its very noticeable old lighthouse, we are now going to cruise non-stop down to Harwich and then return for a more leisurely look at the Rivers Ore and Alde, and the River Deben. The most noticeable feature en route is the 30m lighthouse at Orfordness. With its white tower and red stripes it is even more difficult to miss than Sizewell and it has always been a friendly signalling sentinel on this sometimes bleak and unwelcoming coast.

. . . and while this red flag signifies neither that is unsafe to enter the harbour nor that His Lordship's Fish has landed and been gutted – nevertheless flying the flag still carries its own important legend!

. . . while some of the fishing boat jetties near the harbour mouth still cling to their occupation, when a cursory inspection would suggest they are incapable of living up to their expectations . . .

Both the Dunwich and Sizewell banks can throw up frequently troubled waters with many short, sharp disturbances. The two banks are configured quite separately, a combination guaranteed to cause maximum interference under minimum provocation. There is a perfectly safe, close inshore passage all the way from Southwold to Orford Haven. However, a wary watch must be kept, not just for the standard crab-pot markers and their gear, but also for the massive array of some that are laid with cable lengths just on or just below the surface.

Also to be watched out for, although for very different reasons, are the light brown 'cliffs' of Dunwich and their sparse, indeed scarcely grassy, banks. Steam past them slowly and reverentially, for somewhere below may be the salt-sea pickled or bleached remains of our early ancestors, their forests, churches, castles, their feudal domains and their walled cities. Ever since the natural disasters of the 13th and 14th centuries, much of the history,

Upstream River Blyth: the black rectangular roof (with lights) indicates the HM's office, and close by the visitors' moorings.

heritage and residuals of the domain of Dunwich have been dispersed over this sea bed. Sadly, it is extremely unlikely that much will ever be traced. For divers, the frequently inclement conditions, and the murky waters that often restrict visibility to a few feet, make serious research problematic.

The exact location of the ancient sunken city of Dunwich is about ¼ mile out to sea in 7 fathoms in Dunwich Bay, between the Dunwich Bank and the Dunwich Cliffs. During the time of Henry II (1154–1189) the city of Dunwich was probably in its prime. One 18th-century historian credits the city with 52 churches, chapels, religious houses and hospitals, one king's palace, one bishop's seat, one mayor's mansion, one mint, as many top-ships as churches, and no fewer windmills. Its forest extended to a point 7 miles southwest of the city and probably stretched many more miles to the east before falling victim to the sea. It was surrounded by a great wall within which were set massive brazen gates.

Today, there is little to remind anyone of that past glory and pride – a history going back to the times before the Druids. It seems, somewhat sadly, that it will not be long before all that is left of even the present modern, condensed Dunwich, moved inland centuries ago, will be memories and legends. The cliffs crumble and fall casualty and sacrifice to the inexorable demands of the harshly elemental North Sea. Left behind after the devastation that is

sometimes caused by the combined assaults of wind and water, are to be found human bones that have survived much longer than their brief bodies.

But now for something quite different, although deeply concerned with matters of life and death: Sizewell. Recent developments on the site have made it even more outstanding than it was before. It will in all probability be our Alpha and Omega – with Omega/Armageddon coming well before its time. Its A, B and C (and no doubt ultimately D to Z) Sizewell power stations make it conspicuously unmistakable.

Coming to Thorpness there is slightly less water close in but ½ mile will clear all hazards. The background trees and the water-tower make the Ness itself easy to spot. From seaward, Aldeburgh is demandingly eyecatching, with its variegated houses hugging the waterline in one colourful, charming and rustic array. They add the final scenic touches to a model illustration of our domesticated coasts at their very best.

After the slight shallowing at Thorpness, one can safely make a close-in passage to Aldeburgh Bay and continue to do so down to the Onion, leaving Aldeburgh Ridge buoy to seaward. It is essential to note that there is a change of direction of buoyage at this point and, for those who want to make the 'outer' passage round the Aldeburgh ridge, the red can is to be left to starboard.

Even more eyecatching is the 280m-tall white tower at Orfordness. Its light may no longer burn as bright as it used to, nor does it any longer occupy the prime place it once had in coastal navigation, but it is still a significant symbol and an important

No longer the brightest and best teller of good news for those navigating northward or southward, but, nevertheless, still a tall marker and bringer of good news for those who prefer the balmier waters of the south. Tall stories tell of those who have spat tobacco juice from the stems of passing craft to reach the very lighthouse, so close can one steam to shore.

landmark for all East Coast yachtsmen. Londoners may believe that Watford Gap marks the beginning of rule and reign by North of England savages, but all coastal cruising folk know that the light at Orfordness marks the end of the North Sea at its most threatening, and the beginning of the solace and succour of calmer waters. The rounding of Orfordness can be as much of a close encounter as you wish, for the deep water is right up to the shingle beach, which in itself is remarkably steep-to. No more than a stone's throw from the beach there is a good 8·0m at low water.

This inshore passage provides not only something of a thrill by the very nature of the proximity of the overpowering light, but it also avoids the overfalls which can be a real trial to boats in the cruising class.

Now we move down through the Hollesley Channel, situated between Hollesley Bay and the shallow Whiting Patch, and on the entrance to those symbiotic rivers, the Ore and the Alde. It is quite intriguing to look across the flatland to Havergate Island, where you can easily see the castle ruins, yet still have to travel many miles and round many bends before you reach it. The river itself approximates closely to the shore and it is possible to pick out a barge in the river, apparently sailing on the land, with absolutely no trace of the river from the sea.

So we pass well inside the Whiting Bank, where, in the Hollesley Channel, there is a least depth of 14 fathoms at LW springs. The Whiting Shoal, which is about 3 miles along, is well buoyed from beginning to end and from side to side. This will bring us to the red and white offing buoy of Orford Haven. After Orford Haven, there is a short close-in leg down to the red and white Woodbridge Haven buoy.

From the general quietness (traffic, not necessarily of entrances) of Orford and Woodbridge Haven we make our way down to the busier waters that come after Cobbolds. I prefer to make a course that keeps about a mile offshore and leaves the green Wadgate Ledge and the red Pitching Ground to seaward. The Harwich Harbour Authority has some very useful instructions and guidelines for yachtsmen for the Harwich approaches. We shall return to those technicalities at the beginning of Chapter V on the River Orwell.

Harwich, Felixstowe container port and Parkeston Quay provide much delight for the eye to marvel at; they must rank as a positive wonderland for a photographer. They combine, in fact, into one of the busiest ports in the UK, with a host of speedy tugs and pilot cutters in the harbour. Their masters are always well prepared to spot yachts, errant or otherwise, in advance of any difficulty, but all cruising skippers must be particularly vigilant when negotiating this port area. The official harbour launch *Valentine* is on station at summer weekends to advise, assist and discipline leisure craft if necessary. You can call in on VHF Ch 71.

The large ferries bound for the continent contrast dramatically with the few Trinity House light vessels still left at their moorings just off Shotley Gate. Seen in their seldom-disturbed berths, it is difficult to imagine how their majestic forms and masterful turrets could ever be menaced by the coastal waters of the North Sea.

IV. The Ore, Alde & Deben

The River Ore

Some prefatory remarks

It is long time since I cruised these rivers for previous editions of *The East Coast*. Usually the weather had been poor and I had been short of time; but the summer of my most recent visit was very good and, for once, I managed to make the time to visit at length all those byways I had never visited before. While I found little that was changed where I had been before, I discovered there was more to invite, detain and entertain than I had previously thought. So, viewed with at least a partly new eye, here is a slightly different view of these 'two' rivers (really only one) that have only one likeness on the East Coast – that being their neighbour, the Deben

There is no hazard on the way from either the north or the south to gain this river. The challenge, if challenge it be, comes with the entrance. Just down the road apiece, the Deben has a notorious bar but, if anything, I have found that the entrance to the Ore tends to be even more difficult.

Opinions are divided almost equally on the comparative difficulties of their entrances. My view

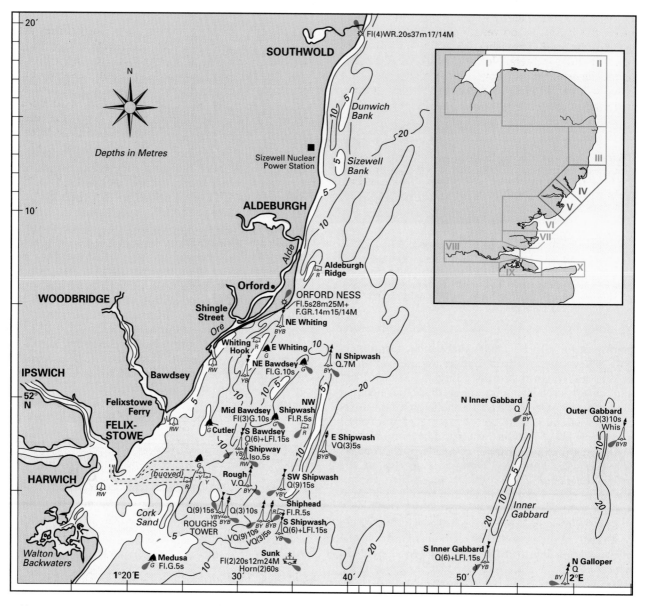

is simplistic – on a certain tide, on a certain day, one will be more difficult than the other. It really is a case of go and find out . . . or telephone the local (wise) experts before you set off. In his *Coastwise Cruising*, published in 1929, Francis B Cooke says:

If it was necessary to take a pilot into Woodbridge Haven it is infinitely more so here, for, to put it bluntly, it is the very devil of a place. The tide during the first 2 hours of the ebb attains a velocity of 7 knots or more, the entrance is obstructed by knolls of shingle, that frequently shift – sometimes in a night – and the entrance is difficult to locate until one is quite close to it. The stranger who attempts this passage perilous without the aid of a pilot is not a hero but merely a fool, for even local vessels often enlist the services of the pilots.

I agree with most of what he says, but unfortunately his dictate that we should all use a pilot is now impossible of realisation, since there has been no such officer at Shingle Street for many a long year.

There are specific reasons for my worries about the Ore entrance. Although the Woodbridge Haven buoy is not one of the easiest to spot, the Orford Haven buoy is frequently so heeled over by the local races that it is only too vexatiously simple to lose it against the undistinguished shoreline in what are often disturbed waters. Not until you have identified it and have begun to move into position to try an entry will you be able to make use of the Martello tower and the cluster of cottages at Shingle Street. It

Orford Haven safe water marker.

is very difficult for strangers, particularly if they are noviciates as, in essence, there is just the single buoy and the one leading mark. True, there are quite a few 'leading lines' that will bring you in safely, but these require 'local knowledge' at a level denied to most visitors. In any case, they all depend upon getting a 'just open' view between (say) 'the third chimney' and (say) 'a conspicuous clump of trees'. And that is if you can see any or all of these in what is often misty visibility.

The best information comes with the special chart of *Orford Haven with River Ore & River Alde*. It is published and promulgated by the Alde & Ore

The Orford River is separated form the sea by no more than a long slender finger of sand; a finger that is always changing – and in recent times growing longer and longer. Perhaps Auden might have said, 'Look, stranger at these islands now the shifting sands for your delight discovers.'

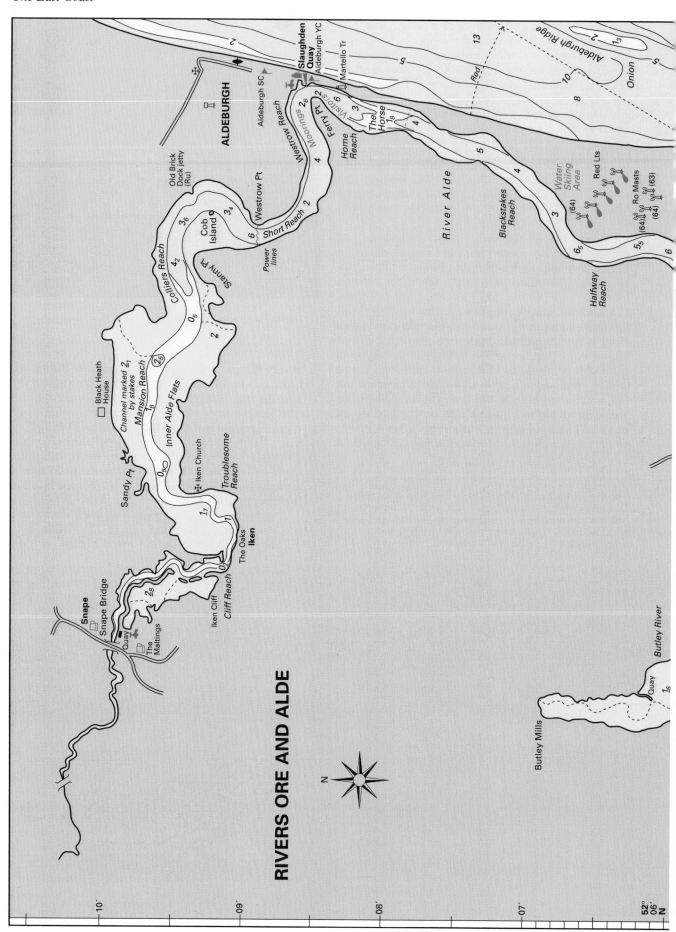

RIVERS ORE AND ALDE

The East Coast
ALDEBURGH
Slaughden Quay
Aldeburgh SC
Aldeburgh YC
Martello Tr
Westrow Reach
Moorings
Ferry Pt
Visitors
Home Reach
The Horse
Old Brick Dock jetty (Ru)
Westrow Pt
Short Reach
Power lines
Cob Island
Colliers Reach
Stanny Pt
River Alde
Blackstakes Reach
Water Skiing Area
Red Lts
Ro Masts
Halfway Reach
Black Heath House
Channel marked by stakes
Mansion Reach
Inner Alde Flats
Iken Church
Troublesome Reach
Sandy Pt
The Oaks
Iken
Iken Cliff
Cliff Reach
Snape
Snape Bridge
Quay
The Maltings
Butley River
Butley Mills
Quay
Aldeburgh Ridge
Onion

N

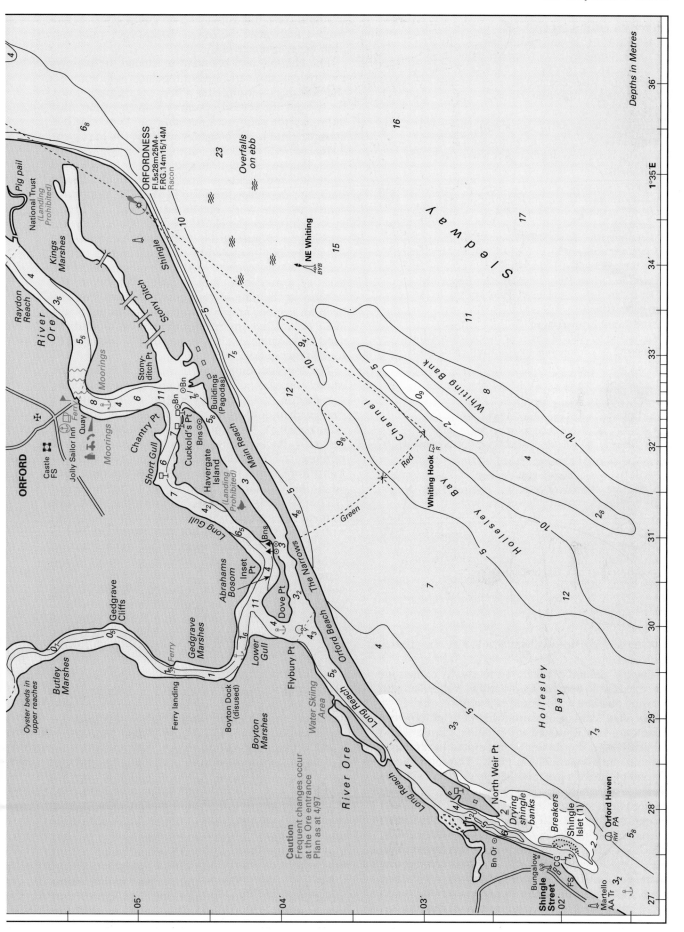

Depths in Metres

ORFORD

ORFORDNESS
Fl.5s28m25M+
F.RG.14m15/14M
Racon

Overfalls on ebb

NE Whiting
BYB

Siedway

Whiting Bank

Whiting Hook
R

Whiting Bay

Hollesley Bay

Red Channel

Green

Pig pail

National Trust
(Landing
Prohibited)

Kings
Marshes

Raydon
Reach

River
Ore

Stony Ditch
Shingle

Stony-
ditch Pt

Bn
Bn

Moorings

Buildings
(Pagodas)

Moorings

Castle
FS
Jolly Sailor Inn
Quay
Ferry

Chantry Pt

Short Gull

Cuckold's Pt

Bns

Main Reach

Havergate
Island
(Landing
Prohibited)

Bns

The Narrows

Abrahams
Bosom
Inset
Pt

Dove Pt

Gedgrave
Cliffs

Butley
Marshes

Oyster beds in
upper reaches

Long Gull

Gedgrave
Marshes

Ferry

Ferry landing

Boyton Dock
(disused)

Boyton
Marshes

Lower
Gull

Flybury Pt

Water Skiing
Area

Caution
Frequent changes occur
at the Ore entrance
Plan as at 4/97

River Ore

Long Reach

Orford Beach

North Weir Pt

Drying shingle
banks

Breakers

Shingle
Islet (1)

Orford Haven
RW PA

Bn Or

Bungalow

CG
FS

Shingle
Street

Martello
AA Tr

RIVERS ORE & ALDE
52°01'·10N 01°27'·60E (Entrance)
Charts Admiralty 2052 (entrance only), 2695.
OS Landranger 169. Imray Y15, C28. A guide and
chart of the River Ore and Alde is published annually
by the Ore and Alde Association.

Tides
Entrance: Dover +0015; Slaughden: Dover +0155

Tidal access
Orford Haven least depth in best water 1m (1998)

Authorities
Orford
Harbourmaster ☎ 01394 450481
Quay Warden ☎ 01394 450713
Aldeburgh
Harbourmaster ☎ 01728 452896/453047
Snape
Maltings Quay ☎ 01728 688303

Caution Orford Haven Bar changes frequently.
Depths are liable to change. Tidal streams in the
river are strong.

Additional information
Contact: The Alde & Ore Association, Woodlands,
Snape ☎ 01728 688602 or 15 Drury Park, Snape
☎ 01728 688744

ORFORD
Orford Town Trust ☎ 01394 450481
Ⓥ (140 – swinging moorings), WC (nearby),
🅿 (poss.), ⚓, Provisions (nearby), Ⓖ (nearby),
🅳 (nearby), 🅿 (nearby), Repairs (by arrangement)

Orford Sailing Club ☎ 01394 450759
Ⓥ (swinging moorings), WC (nearby), 🅿 (nearby), ⚓,
↘ (nearby), Provisions (nearby), Ⓖ (limited),
🅳, 🅿, Engineer (nearby), Repairs (limited)

ALDEBURGH
Aldeburgh Yacht Club ☎ 01728 452504
Ⓥ (swinging), WC, 🅿, ⚓, ⚡, ↘, Provisions (nearby),
Ⓖ, 🅳, 🅿 (nearby), Engineer, Repairs
(☎ 01728 452019)

Association and is usually available just after Easter
each year.

The old *Admiralty Pilot* used to say, 'A dangerous
place except in settled fine weather. A mistake with
a strong onshore wind would probably mean the loss
of the boat.' And again, somewhat unhelpful in view
of the above mentioned information, 'Entrance to
Orford Haven should not be attempted by strangers
without the assistance of a pilot.' The most recent
edition of the *Pilot* has modified its view and is by no
means so threatening: 'The approach is from the SE
end of Hollesley Bay Channel, but no directions can
be given due to the irregular and constantly
changing shingle banks lying S of North Weir Point,
which are dangerous. Care is necessary to establish
the vessel's position before approaching the
entrance. Entrance is best attempted between 1
hour after local low water, when the drying banks
are visible, and local high water depending on

draught. The out-going and in-going streams run
from 1 hour after the times of local low water and
high water respectively.'

The channel and bar tend to change frequently;
perhaps not dramatically but regularly and often. So
the best plan, certainly for a first engagement, must
be to wait for settled conditions and to time your
approach for about an hour after the flood tide has
started, unless, of course you draw in excess of
1·5m, when you wait until nearer high water
according to draught. It will then be possible to
interpret the surface-water signs which clearly
delineate the deeps from the banks. The best water
tends to the west on entering and a careful
approach, when the shingle is still uncovered, will
enable you to make a slow safe and sound way in.
Do not be not be misled by the apparently tempting
channel which seems to exist just to the north of the
tiny separated-out shingle isle. Whatever the
weather at the time of your entry, it is important to
keep an eye on, and a good clearance from, North
Weir Point since the rush of the stream around the
sand and shingle spit can be powerfully confusing to
look at or to negotiate.

The long-standing 'classic' advice, is to keep the
black topmark of the famous (position fixed)
conspicuous grey chimney almost in line with the
orange diamond topmark of the famous (position
approximate) beacon. The chimney should
generally be kept slightly open to the west, but
nothing can be guaranteed to keep you dead to
rights from winter to winter, although this does offer
an entrance that tends almost dead to north.

The old Imray pilot says, 'When strong winds and
a rough sea prevail, entry should not be attempted.
Entry against the ebb is not recommended and is
possible only in quiet weather for yachts having
plenty of power. Local knowledge under these
conditions is essential'. I can endorse all of that,
having once had to sweat it out to Southwold, due
to an entrance that was demonstrably 'impossible',
and that was with no more than a Force 4 against a
spring ebb. The entrance is particularly bad with a
strong wind from the east and at its worst when it is
ESE.

There is a solitary beacon shoresides which is
intended to be used in transit with the offing buoy to
give a course into the entrance. I have tried this
approach three times, twice being followed by
foreign visitors who recognised *Valcon* from using
earlier editions of this pilot guide, and on each time
have had to head dramatically off course to the SW
in order to keep the water. In balance, it must be
favourite to wait for settled conditions and try an
entry at about half tide when it is probably easiest to
read the surface of the water. The rising flood will be
with you, more or less towards the mouth proper,
and that will help should you hesitate, touch or find
bottom.

In late 1997, the entrance was much more
straightforward. The shingle spit had grown and
nearly reached the buoy. This helps because the

South Shoal has disappeared and the river is a bit deeper. Best available advice is to keep the buoy 200 yards to the E and the shore 100 yards to the W. The more obvious landmarks are the Martello tower and the Shingle Street cottages. With the aid of binoculars, Hollesley Church, the flagstaff and the orange beacon can all be spotted. One word of caution in the midst of all this joy – the South Shoal has been eroded by the growth of the North Shoal, which is now somewhat eccentrically edging SSW at a goodly pace. Indeed, even as I write, the growth upwards of the sand/shingle bottom is Topsy-like. There is now a permanent 'drying' island. A good sounder would be a wise investment. Once inside, having hung on tight as you went round the bend, the river settles down almost immediately.

Just after North Weir Point, by the not-very-distinguishable orange Ore beacon on the west bank, there are some isolated drying patches (almost small islands). The way to avoid them is, once the solid bank proper of North Weir Point has grown fully out of the sand and shingle fingers, to move over to the east of centre, and so continue upstream in deep water. Once that manoeuvre has been successfully adopted and completed, the Ore should present no further problem, provided you remember that good ground tackle is needed for any anchorage, and to treat the mud flats-and-banks and saltings with the respect that those East Coast singular features deserve. It is the rate of the stream that is the really threatening thing to watch out for. Then, at last, you can start to enjoy some of the finest river scenery in England.

The Ore & Alde is certainly a most extraordinary river. For about 10 miles it is so close to the sea in

places that you could easily throw a bowline across the shingle. After Aldeburgh it makes a dramatic turn to the west and starts to search out the soft underbelly of the environs and runs inland.

A certain amount of controversy is attached to the two names of this (now) one river. Imray's *Inland Waterways of Great Britain* mentions only the River Alde, and makes it quite clear that it runs from Snape Maltings to the sea. A common-sense view would seem to be that, at one time, the Alde – rising far to the NW – entered the sea near Aldeburgh; while the Ore, rising near Framlingham, exited at Shingle Street. Common sense has little to do with territorial claims and there is no chance that the idiosyncrasy is going to be tidied. So, somewhere between Orford and Aldeburgh, the River Ore becomes the River Alde, changing its name but not its nature. The bad news is that there is little chance of finding a vacant mooring on either of the rivers. The good news is that there are plenty of attractive anchorages with good holding ground – as near or as far from civilisation as you may wish. Right up Long Reach to Dove Point, on Havergate Island, there is a good 2m in mid-channel. The NW bank tends to be vague and shallow, while the SE is all shingle and steep-to virtually up to Havergate Island.

After the long run parallel to the beach, Dove Point will hove into view. To starboard, running still with the beach, are the Narrows and Main Reach. This route is the shorter – if Orford or even further is your target – but the prettier, and with more anchorages is to port. In three parts, it is known as Lower Gull, Long Gull and Short Gull.

The oyster-famous Butley River is the first watering hole of note. It is to be found on the port hand, after Flybury Point and Lower Gull – that is, a couple of cables after from the red-and-white buoy marking Dove Point's spit. Don't be tempted to cut corners; Boyton Marshes reach out well into the Butley at the bend. The Butley River affords the first

---

Close to, Orford Quay always appears to be busy – and the more you need moor at the quay . . . the busier will it be . .

possible anchorage – depending on your draught, you can go up to a mile or so, near Ferry Cottage, Gedgrave Cliff and the ruins of the old jetty, but always on the lookout for the oyster beds with their markers, stakes or legends, especially to port.

Marked by withies, the immediate entrance is a popular anchorage. It is possible to take a 2·0m vessel further up, but the channel becomes narrower and shallower almost by the yard. An exploration of the upper reaches is certainly worthwhile but is properly, and best, accomplished by dinghy. The Pinney family shop and restaurant in Orford are supplied from the oyster beds here, so anchoring anywhere after the disused Boyton Dock must be done with great caution. A good row up to Butley Mill through reeds, marshes and saltings will bring sights of all kinds of nature wild and wilful – including widgeon or pheasants in their seasons. At the head, however, is a true goal – the really remote pub past the Butley Mills and up through the mud to Chillesford. A Betterer Watering 'Ole would be difficult to find; and the fodder is first rate.

The Butley is the first anchorage that can be used without constant anxiety about the strength of your ground tackle. Some folk have it that there is a secure anchorage by Flybury Point, but I have found the power of the middle ebb is such that it requires a continual watch, something that can be circumvented by going further upstream or just that bit further into the creek. There is another anchorage just after the Butley entrance at the back of Dove Point, deliciously and variously known as Abraham, or Abram's, Bosom/Besum/Bosum/Bosun according to taste. It is also susceptible to

. . . yet from afar, all seems pacific and still: untroubled as it nestles under the protection of its wooded slopes and the custody of its village church. From water level, the fairway never seems this broad.

strong streams and eddies. The Butley itself is, however, straightforward, provided care is exercised with due regard to the obvious pitfalls of shallows, foul banks and oyster beds.

Out of the Butley, Long Gull leads to Short Gull, Horse Hard and, opposite Chantry Point, Cuckold's Point at the most northerly point of Havergate Island. There is no shortage of depth and little to choose between them. The final anchorage in the Ore is just below Orford Quay in more than 4m, but it is close to the moorings and tends to be a busy area.

My favourite spot on the river is just off Cuckold's Point by Havergate Island. It is well sheltered and just far enough away from Orford not to make it too popular.

Strange military manoeuvres and antics no longer occur and, since their demise, the area has had a chance to begin to settle down into something of a more natural existence once again. Moreover, where once it was almost impossible for tourists to contemplate taking out binoculars for fear of being accosted or arrested and charged with contravening MoD whims; there is now a National Trust ferry that actually aids and abets visitors to hear all and see all . . . uninterruptedly enjoying the pleasure of viewing the wildlife in its many and varied forms.

Havergate Island is an RSPB reserve, and reputedly one of the most famous haunts of the avocet. But, with my luck, I have spent many hours behind binoculars, in my regular quest for these curiously beaked birds, and have espied not a one – not even the suggestion of one on which my imagination could have worked. The colony was believed to have forsaken the UK around 1824.

Havergate's sandy island wilderness is also host to godwits and curlew pipers. I saw not one of these either. My fruitless search brings to mind the words of Gerard Manley Hopkins:

Thou art indeed just, Lord, if I contend
With thee; but, sir, so what I plead is just.
Why do sinners' ways prosper? and why must
Disappointment all endeavour end?
Birds build – but not I build: no, but strain,
Time's eunuch, and not breed one work that wakes.

However, never out of sight and more than obvious are, first, the low-lying military buildings known as the 'Pagodas' and, second, the reaching finger of the Orford Ness Light. Its flashes through the night have always been a comfort, no matter how troublesome the Times or the Reach. As the river turns to flow north/south, it becomes increasingly occupied with moorings from well before to well after the busy Orford Quay.

Across the other side of the river, it is a pleasant morning walk on the 'mainland' bank to Orford, where the village possesses all kinds of cultural joys – castle, church, plebeian pub, elitist 'hotel', fish-smokers and keep.

Nor is it any distance by boat, but reaching its quay to be able to savour Orford's unique form of civilisation with a boat bigger than a dinghy requires a little study. Access to the town quay is predictably best at HW; but, with care, both quay and surrounding waters can be approached at almost any state of the tide. There is very little room for either manoeuvring or parking at the quay, so any visit must be made with all proper circumspection. Perhaps the best idea is to find a decent spot to anchor (and they do exist; all it takes is jilling around with patience).

Facilities for yachts are neither comprehensive nor sophisticated. Diesel and fuel can be had by can, via the jetty where there is also a standpipe water tap. Minor repairs can be arranged, but this is not the place to break down or decide on a major overhaul. There are scrubbing posts, a small slipway and modest mobile crane.

There are moorings, but they are all private (with a long waiting list) and none are specially set aside for visitors. For use of the moorings or the quay, contact the harbourmaster: Ralph Brinkley, East View, Quay Street, Orford, Suffolk ☎ 01394 450481. Although he is not always immediately accessible, diligence and application usually prevail. Orford is indeed thrice blessed in its harbourmaster, Ralph, unmistakable with his beguiling smile and gold tooth.

Orford is neither quaint nor *outré*; but it is undeniably *recherché* and, as such, well worth a row from any of the river anchorages. It has a long, wide avenue that leads from the quay to the historic castle and church; and, on each side of the continental-style approach, there are walls, cottages, gates, doors and gardens (not to mention cats and dogs) that just cry out for observation and inspection. There are two hostelries – the Crown and Castle and also the Jolly Sailor. In the square there is an unexpectedly comprehensive grocer with a penchant for welcoming visitors.

The village has an olde-worlde flavour and a small community of excellent shops and eating places. It is, of course, famous for its smoking, and the Pinney establishment is known throughout the land – but there is also a smaller smoker who works in an unique fashion in a smokehouse that must be seen to be believed.

Orford is also one of those places where, not all that long ago, it was still an active practice for the majority to be convinced of the need to watch the wall my darling while the gentlemen go by! To this day, there is a hint of curtain-twitching and quick door-closing when there are strangers about. Indeed, in many ways, it is not very different from Staithes way up north, just above Whitby.

Orford ancient castle, was built for Henry II. It is famous as the fortress of Robert Malet, with its round tower keep and three square 'forts' attached. The entrance is up an imposing stone stairway. The one-time owner of the castle, the Marquess of Hertford, is supposed to have been the model of Thackeray's Lord Steyne in *Vanity Fair*; and it is only too easy to fly, fly away into the land of *Ivanhoe*. The castle is a huge place, the walls being some 20' thick in places. From the top, the view is supreme.

I have heard tell of a yarn here, the first variation of which frightened me to death when I heard it as a child in the Yorkshire seaside village of Ulrome. The tale tells of a wild and wild-eyed man with a hypnotic stare, who was netted by local fishermen. He was fancifully described as a merman, with the mien and dress of John the Baptist, except that he was fishlike and scale-headed. He was a thing of exhibition, like the Elephant Man, and crowds came from far and near to see the Wild Man from the Sea. Even Thomas à Becket was not immune, although he claimed merely to bless the poor thing. He is supposed to have escaped in the manner of the Flying Dutchman and reappeared from time to time to haunt and taunt the living and the dead. And if there were a spot where all this could be true, it is Orford – a village of the legendary receding past living cheek by jowl with the only too real invading present.

The River Alde

The sense of mystery persists as we move upstream towards Aldeburgh. Just above Orford, the River Ore suddenly becomes the River Alde (for no reason I have been able to discover); in just the same way as there is mystery about the Yorkshire Ouse changing to the River Ure at one sharp bend. But then again, there is also mystery about the derivation of Cuckold's Point and Abram's Bosom; and for that matter I am not sure whether it is only the one Cuckold or not.

After Orford, the river bends to the NE, and there is little of special interest until you see the long lone rows of aerials. Strange-looking, sky-seeking metal fingers, they are now more happily serving as radio masts for the BBC World Service than they were as servants of warlike intentions. They are to be seen between Raydon Reach, Eel Hole and Blackstakes After this point, the river turns to the N and NE again. Don't miss the two 'holes' on the east bank that are known as Upper and Lower Dans.

My first foray into the Alde River section of the river(s) was from the anchorage at Cuckold's Point in a small Avon dinghy, complete with oars and something approaching the smallest extant *Seagull*. First up to Orford Quay, then the MoD establishments, past Town, King's and Lantern marshes, past Halfway Reach and Blackstakes, predictably with no stake, black or otherwise, and finally into Home Reach by Sudbourne Marshes.

With a slight following wind and the tide in my favour it was a most agreeable trip; and it was just about lunchtime when I dragged the dinghy up the hard at Slaughden Quay. The wind had picked up slightly, but it had done nothing but help me; and I had neither the common sense nor, in those days, the experience to think that it could be a hindrance on the way back.

I returned to launch the Avon at the turn of the tide, looking forward to being an Easy Ebby Rider on the way back. No way! When I reached Slaughden quay the tide was OK, but the wind had become stiffish. As soon as I saw the waves roughing up the dinghies on the hard and the wind roughing up the water into frequent white horses (good title for a book I have always thought), it was clear I was in for a rough trip.

Just to launch the Avon took a fair amount of energy and, by the time I was out of hailing distance of the quay, I was exhausted. Imagine my dismay, after the *Seagull* had been swamped for the third time, when it would no longer start. I tried rowing, but found it impossible to do more than hold my own. The ebbing tide was with me all right, but the wind, now in its fives and sixes, was not and the lightweight dinghy stood no chance. Nor did I, with the wind and spray against me, as well as the rain since that was now against me too.

Fortunately, fate was on my side that time: dead on cue, along came a yacht with folk who not only recognised my plight but immediately did

Esoteric and outlandish to some; but romantic, fascinating indeed magical to others; Snape Maltings is an unique miniature experience . . .

something about it. They could not get close because of the danger of grounding, but they stood off in mid-stream until I managed to manoeuvre myself near enough for a line; and soon we were both under way. I was hauled on board and treated to rum and coffee and it seemed minutes only before I was back on board *Valcon*, in the anchorage so sheltered that hardly a ripple disturbed the surface; while, round the bend and out of Havergate's lee, the water was as turbulent as ever.

Aldeburgh's first landmark proper is the Martello tower that stands sentinel over the moorings, the yacht clubs and Slaughden Quay. Many visitors, including those Thames barges that still inhabit the area, use the deeps to the east to anchor well clear of the moorings and the fairway. But it is undoubtedly Aldeburgh's Slaughden Quay that is the Mecca. You don't have to make a long pilgrimage but you must remember that access is best at the top of the tide. At Slaughden, the man to see is Mr Upson. He is to be found in the yard at the quayside. This time I missed the notice which reads, 'Dogs and owners please use your wits. The quay is not a place for meditation'. In a way, the same must be said for the Ore and the Alde, for the bottom is perverse in its shelving.

There are better-than-basic facilities, and the boating fraternity is approachable and helpful. Between them, Messrs Upson and Wilson (of the Aldeburgh Boatyard Company) will fit you out with what you want; and if they can't it they will either know a man who can or send you where you can get it for yourself. But everything takes time, and you must move at an appropriate pace. Many a simple request can prompt a debate.

It is not easy to get a categorical promise from the boatyards for a mooring, and so the proper courtesies should be specially observed when picking up a buoy. Sometimes the owner may leave a note in a bottle: 'We shall be back on such and such a day. Enjoy your stay!'. What thoughtfulness; what bliss!

Access to the town of Aldeburgh is by grace and favour of the yacht clubs, via Slaughden Quay, which is accessible by dinghy at most states of the tide. The boatyards are close by and the town is a few minutes' walk away on the main road or along the sea wall. The part of the town that faces the sea does so bravely and with some style: there are hotels with balconies; real East Coast working fishing boats with all their gear and huts; the lifeboat station; and the Moot Hall, a splendid early 16th-century piece that was once the very physical centre of the town – demonstrating only too dramatically the power of erosion in these parts. After all, the 'lost' city of Dunwich is only a couple of miles out to sea to the north.

The power of erosion has also been at work more recently. Only a few decades ago it was still perceived as a diminutive but bracing coastal resort with a famous shingle beach and was well-renowned for its bathing and its two rather grand hotels; the Brudenell and the White Lion. The fact that it also had an important Lloyd's signalling post gave it a stature that was the envy of many lesser resorts. Its golf course was well-used, lauded and applauded even as far away as London.

Now, however, as a small town, Aldeburgh has lost the significance it had when it was a thriving port. The poet George Crabbe (1754–1832) lived there, and Crabby he was indeed in his view of his birthplace, carping and captious about the town and using such words as 'cranky' and 'cantankerous' about the people. It was only recently that my attention was drawn to the following lines by George Crabbe in which he describes the Aldeburghers as:

> *. . . a wild amphibious race,*
> *With sullen woe displayed in every face;*
> *Who far from civil arts and social fly,*
> *And scowl at strangers with suspicious eye.*

And Wilkie Collins says this:

At Aldborough, as elsewhere on this coast, local traditions are, for the most part, traditions which have been literally drowned. The site of the old town, once a populous and thriving port, has almost entirely disappeared in the sea. The German Ocean[1] has swallowed up streets, market-places, jetties, and public walks; and the merciless waters, consummating their work of devastation, closed, no longer than eighty years since, over the salt-master's cottage at Aldborough, now famous in memory only, as the birthplace of the poet Crabbe.

Thrust back year after year by the advancing waves, the inhabitants have receded, in the present century, to the last morsel of land which is firm enough to be built on – a strip of ground hemmed in between a marsh on one side and the sea on the other. Here – trusting for their future security to certain sandhills which the capricious waves have thrown up to encourage them – the people of Alborough have boldly established their quaint little watering-place. The first fragment of their earthly possessions, is a low natural dyke of shingle, surmounted by a public path which runs parallel with the sea. Bordering this path in a broken, uneven line are the villa residences of modern Alborough – fanciful little houses, standing mostly in their own gardens, and possessing here and there, as horticultural ornaments, staring figure-heads of ships, doing duty for statues among the flowers. Viewed from the low-level on which these villas stand, the sea, in certain conditions of the atmosphere, appears to be higher than the land: coasting vessels gliding by, assume gigantic proportions, and look alarmingly near the windows. Intermixed with the houses of the better sort, are buildings of other forms and periods. In one direction, the tiny Gothic town-hall of old Aldborough – once the centre

---

. . . best approached (if not in miniature boats) in craft of modest draught.

of the vanished port and borough – now stands fronting the modern villas close on the margin of the sea. At another point, a wooden tower of observation, crowned by the figure-head of a wrecked Russian vessel, rises high above the neighbouroughing houses; and discloses through its scuttle-window, grave men in dark clothing, seated on the topmost story, perpetually on the watch – the pilots of Alborough looking out from their tower, for ships in want of help. Behind the row of buildings thus curiously intermingled, runs the one straggling street of the town, with its sturdy pilots' cottages, its mouldering marine storehouses, and its composite shops. Towards the northern end, this street is bounded by the one eminence visible over all the marshy flat – a low wooded hill on which the church is built. At its opposite extremity, the street leads to a deserted martello tower, and to the forlorn outlying suburb of Slaughden, between the river Alde and the sea. Such are the main characteristics of this curious little outpost on the shores of England as it appears at the present time.

No Name Wilkie Collins

In 1810 he published *The Borough*, a work that, on the whole, decries life in a 'country town'. Benjamin Britten got to hear of one of the characters, a certain Peter Grimes, believed cruel to the point of tyranny and eccentric to the point of insanity. The consummation of this rendezvous with Crabbe was the opera *Peter Grimes*.

Apart from the pleasant walks along the front, the town is almost entirely given over to the main drag. Aldeburgh itself is a place apart – exclusive to a degree (bachelor's not master's); genteel but with little gentility; and seemingly socially, culturally and financially insolvent. Situated so close to Britten's beloved Snape Maltings, it is ironic that Aldeburgh should seem to have neither unison nor harmony. Aldeburgh attracts the epithet 'mixed-up'; and a typical example is the contiguity of the yacht club and the car park. The first is privileged, while the second is makeshift and in such disrepair that it is a barren and distressing place. However, in charity, I should report that in 1970, John Seymour wrote, in *The Companion Guide to East Anglia* that 'Aldeburgh can hardly fail to please.'

I have heard consistently that Slaughden Quay is accessible at all states of the tide for craft drawing up to 1·50m; or, if not actually accessible in the full meaning of the word, then that you can at least stay more or less afloat. My experience is that 1·0m is about the mark. So the alternative for those wishing to stay in the area is the anchorage upriver of the Horse and downstream of Slaughden; namely, before the moorings near the Martello tower, still frequently used by a few Thames barges. Immediately upstream of Slaughden Quay, the long lines of moorings (almost always occupied) clearly show the fairway.

Once past Slaughden Quay, the river tends generally to the W and is still busily attended by moorings until the turn to the NE at Westrow Point, which marks a dramatic change in its format.

Previously, the deep-water channel has been clearly delineated by the banks which have never been much more than 10 yards apart. Here, the river spreads out into the vale of Iken to become more of an inland tidal lake than a river. Happily we are introduced into this new experience quite gently. After the point, the first half mile or so tends to the NE, and the saltings and drying patches on Cob Island to the W are marked by the occasional withy. There is a very good landmark straight ahead on the hill in the form of the Aldeburgh Brickworks. This marks the site of the old Reade's Brick Dock Jetty, which is now in a ruinous state, although still allowing – a clambering if unsure – access to the muddy environs. There are five or six moorings here, in what must be one of the quietest and most attractive locations on the river. The last time I was there I was fortunate enough to meet one of the owners who was just leaving for the weekend and told me to 'feel free!'. If you want to anchor out of touch, right out of any dredged channel and be disturbed by nothing but the sound of lappings and lapwings, then the upper reaches of the Alde will be your Elysian cruising fields.

After this come Blackthorn Reach, Collier's Reach and Barber's Point; and while they make a turn from southeast to nearly southwest it is gentle one and there is, as yet, no problem staying in the deep water. For a long time, the stake on Cob Island will be visible as will the tide-threatened mainland of Stanny Point. There are landmarks of a sort – the headlands of Stanny Point to the south and Barber's Point to the N, and, standing out proud on the mainland to the S, can be seen the short sharp rise known as Yarn Hill.

Cob Island itself is actually marked by a few withies. They are no doubt of tremendous help to those who know them for what they are and make regular use of them. This qualification of 'regular use' applies consistently up to Iken and almost to within spitting distance of the quay at Snape. Visitors must try to read the surface of the water with extra care as the withies are, at times, very close to the channel but, at others, quite a distance.

When the tide is up, this is a quite exposed stretch of the river and, with its shallowness, it is, of course, a prime candidate for troubled waters when the wind is unkind – that is, mainly from the east. Once you start out for Iken and Snape, you are, by modern cruising standards, in uncharted territory. The domain becomes not only rustic and rural but runs the gamut from wild to sylvan.

The reaches named Stanny, Mansion, Bagnold's (or Bagnall's) and Church broadly drift through the low, flat countryside while their navigable channels meander between the extensive marshes of Hazlewood and Iken until they present you, penultimately, with their own versions of the classic 'Troublesome Reach'. Some reaches are short while others are long; some are almost wide while others are indubitably narrow. Yes, they come in all shapes and sizes; are many and various; and each is stamped with a unique quality that can entrap even the most wary.

Nevertheless, the tribulation of the 'tributaries' is worth what comes next: the tower of Iken church; the near-concealed and no doubt well-named Troublesome House; the unmistakable manor of Iken Hall; and, just a little later, the attendant, modest cliffs called Iken. They are the outstanding features that are not only worth observing in their own right but can also be used by the stranger as reliable marks in this marsh area. Once the river turns NS from its generally EW direction, these landmarks are very much needed to keep a sense of proportion . . . and direction. For those with bold heart and little draught, there is a secluded anchorage in the area near Iken Hall, between Iken Cliffs and The Oaks, in what is called Cliff Reach. It is a remote spot, with little space to manoeuvre or jill around. Nor is it over-blessed with much depth at low water, but the place has enough singular charm to make the search worth the candle. Expert local advice is needed to find the 'best 'ole' easily; that is, without seeking out the elongated nooks and crannies in the soft mud that serve as navigable channels in these parts. Careful sounding, even to the old extreme of dropping the lead will finally succeed.

From the anchorage it just over a mile to Snape Maltings. The old river banks and retaining walls clearly show the way, even at high water. Slowly moving through this last narrow channel, with nature's tall and slender growths on the banks of the river was one of the most pleasing excursions I have even made. The countryside was at its best, and the river at its quietest. Finally, when you actually close the quay, the first view of the classic oast houses, proud and lofty guardians overlooking the approach, is as beautiful as it is imposing. It is sad to discover that Snape is a snare and a delusion.

Arriving at the quay, you will find that some parts are designated 'Reserved', with a special place understandably set aside for the River Tour Boat. Generally, it is possible to lie alongside the wall or hang on to a friendly barge, but be prepared to take the ground not very long after high water. Be prepared also to find yourself sitting at a brave angle – although, of course, on the softest of soft mud. Personally, I am quite put out by even the slightest list (no doubt an over-reaction on my part) so prefer the nearby anchorage, and to use the dinghy for visiting.

The quay is old and solid with its history manifest in its enduring fabric; and the rise and fall of the tide is, as always, of mesmerising interest. The village is charming and, at no more than a mile away, a refuge where you can eat and drink.

Snape Maltings is a façade: courtly notices for car parks at the front, decaying windows at the rear; and the surrounding buildings, while old and attractive, tainted by the make-up of commerce – which, by and large, falls well short of the artistry you might expect. It is, of course, a place of irresistible appeal and exceptional interest for devotees of Benjamin Britten and Peter Pears. The Plough and Sail also has its fans.

For those who do not share my views and have a passionate enthusiasm for what happens at Snape Maltings, I mention the following from the PR handouts:

On the banks of the River Alde a remarkable collection of mellow red-brick granaries and malthouses makes up Snape Maltings. At low tide the river is a mere trickle of fresh water. At high tide it brims with salt water enough for 100-ton sailing barges to come alongside the quay. Snape Maltings retains its unspoiled rural charm yet has plenty to offer today's visitor to the Suffolk Heritage Coast.

I take exception to 'unspoiled rural charm'; but then, as Professor Joad used to say, 'It all depends what you mean by . . .'

Fortunately, however, it is only a small part of the Two-Rivers Experience; and while it may be the head of navigation and the end of an exploratory journey, there is much more to this tale – and the rest is attractive and appealing. Lovers of the mainly solitary and hidden delights of the Ore and Alde belong to a small section of the boating fraternity that wants nothing to do with mains water or power, and is all for getting the last ounce of innocent enjoyment from the lightest of airs. This is a romantic way of life and, sadly, part of a disappearing world. However, this little corner of the East Coast rivers world is likely to linger on in yesteryear; with Sizewell being the biggest blot and threat on the nearby land and waterscape.

The Ore and Alde make a strange combination of (river)bedfellows. There is no doubt that they offer something quite different in the cruising experience and possess many unique qualities. On a sunny day, it is a striking and picturesque river scene – uncomplicated and even idyllic. On a typically British grey autumn evening, the leftover Ministry of Defence pagodas, not quite lost in the mist, and the Orford light flashing to seaward, lend an unreal and transcendental air.

Be it summer or winter though, the vision of Orford's church and castle on the skyline create a *genius loci* that is redolent of Suffolk at its most appealing – and its most enigmatic.

The Deben

The coast from Orford Haven to the Deben is mainly one of low shingle beaches with little variation and only Martello towers for landmarks. It is only a short leg to the river entrance. From afar, the Bawdsey radio mast is plain to see, indicating the general location; and, from closer, the Woodbridge Haven buoy stands out bright red and white well out to sea, and is now much easier to spot.

The grim-looking manor at Bawdsey is like something from the more miserable works of Dickens and casts a strange atmosphere over the whole seafront. Bawdsey Manor has always been a secretive spot. A London stockbroker, one Quilter by name, got his hands on the land from Bawdsey to Methersgate Hall. In the late 1880s these same Quilters destroyed a Martello tower and its battery to 'decree' their own version of 'a stately pleasure dome' on the headland. In 1937, Bawdsey Manor was bought by the government for research and, by the time the war was under way, it was a working radar station. It then became a training centre and has had a chequered on-off relationship with the RAF until the final link in the chain was broken in 1991.

On the SW bank the Martello towers 'T' and 'U' keep watch over the entrance, and make good markers for the first approach. By the Woodbridge Haven red and white safe-water mark is a good place to prepare yourself for the tough rocking and rolling that can greet you at the bar of what is one of the most famous of the East Coast rivers.

The normal approach is first to pick up the Woodbridge Haven buoy and then take it slowly until the green bar buoy is spotted. In spite of its radar reflector, it can be difficult to identify and can easily be taken for a crab-pot marker, especially since the waters are frequently troubled. In poor weather it may be necessary to be on top of it before you actually see it. It can get pulled down by the tide and, in bad weather, is difficult to spot let alone confirm. The two best landmarks are the Martello tower 'T', which is close inshore on the west bank, and the leading marks close by to the north. The metes are a reddish/orange and white and not too difficult to pick out with the help of good binoculars. Once the tower and marks have been found, a combination of reading the water, common sense, intuition and luck, should bring the little green fellow into sight. There is usually a good metre over the bar at all states, but I have always preferred to wait until the last hour of the flood – if for no other reason than to have let the main force of the tide spend itself. Once inside the run, you are committed until well past the red Horse buoy after Felixstowe Ferry. Predictably, a reliably powerful engine is essential. Until the Haven and the Bar buoys have been identified, strangers should not attempt to

The changing highs and lows of the entrance to the River Deben at Woodbridge speak for themselves. The grim-looking manor at Bawdsey can just be seen (above centre to the right) amidst the green clumpery . . .

... however, any grimness of grey stones is more than compensated for by the warmth of the reception offered by the Felixstowe Ferry Sailing club.

enter. In particular, a rough southeast wind on an ebb tide will make conditions almost impossible.

My first visit to the Deben was under the watchful eye of Charlie Brinkley, who had responded promptly to my flagged request for a pilot. Ever since those early visits, I have always made a point of trying to get good advice well before attempting an entry; and my best contacts have been Robert and Charlie Brinkley at Felixstowe Ferry and the helpful staff at Small Craft Deliveries in Woodbridge, under whose sponsoring and ever-watchful eyes the actual chartlet is promulgated.

... but even its grimness is as naught when compared with Martello Tower 'U' on the west bank ...

Neither Charlie nor his son Robert would ever take payment for their help. It was always, 'Don't bother now. We'll see you another time.' Back at the beginning of this century, the situation was different – the going rate was 1s 3d per foot draught.

In 1995, the entry was straightforward, the single green buoy indicating the beginning of the channel proper. Then you look for the leading marks on the land across the river. These metes are: front marker, a red and white triangle; rear marker, an all-red square. The theory is that you line them up exactly and follow that course straight for the shore until, just in the nick of time, you make a sharp turn to starboard with the stream carrying you in. On my unaccompanied approaches to the Deben I have found that the best water requires you to keep just to port of the leading line. The notorious bar shifts fairly often and, if there has been a really big blow, it can change overnight. In summer, the buoy and leading beacons don't need to be moved; but since the banks often change substantially through the winter, it is best to wait for settled weather and check it out before trying for an entry – or to use the pilot.

The shingle shore is steep and the channel is close; so close that, only a few years ago, when the leading marks were near the Felixstowe Ferry crossing, it was virtually impossible to line them up without going ashore to do so. In 1982 the channel, which can be less than a cable wide, ran virtually north/south. In 1984 it broke through the Knoll to run virtually at right angles.

DEBEN ENTRANCE & FELIXSTOWE/BAWDSEY FERRY

Woodbridge Haven 52°59'·35N 01°23'·69E

Charts Admiralty 2693, 2052. Imray Y15, Y16, C28. A chart/plan of Woodbridge Haven is produced annually by the Tide Mill Yacht Harbour. OS Landranger 169.

Tides
Woodbridge Haven: +0025 Dover; Woodbridge: +0110 Dover

Authorities/Pilot
VHF Ch 8. Call *Late Times*. Harbourmaster Felixstowe Ferry ☎ 01394 270853
Tide Mill Yacht Harbour ☎ 01394 385745. VHF Ch 37, 80 M

Caution
The entrance is liable to change and local assistance should be sought.

Felixstowe Ferry Boatyard ☎ 01394 282173
Tidal access 24 hrs (with local knowledge)
Ⓥ (40 swinging), 🚾 (nearby), ⚓, ⚡ (nearby),
↘ (nearby), Provisions (nearby), Ⓖ, ⬤D, ⬤P (1 mile), Engineer, Repairs

Waldringfield Sailing Club ☎ 01728 748094
Tidal access
24 hours
⚓, 🚾 (nearby), ⬤P

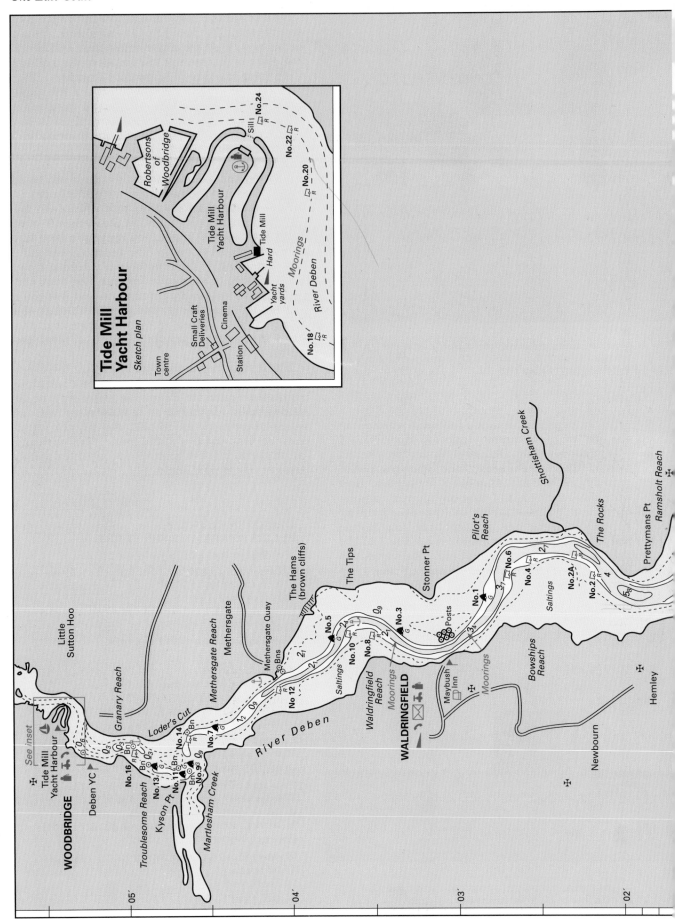

Tide Mill
Yacht Harbour
Sketch plan

Robertsons of Woodbridge

No.24
R

Sill

No.22
R

No.20
R

Tide Mill Yacht Harbour

Tide Mill

Hard

Yacht yards

Small Craft Deliveries

Town centre

Cinema

Station

Moorings

River Deben

No.18
R

Shottisham Creek

The Rocks

Ramsholt Reach

Prettymans Pt

Pilot's Reach

Stonner Pt

No.6
R

No.4
R

2

2A
R

3

No.1
G

3

No.2
R

4

5

The Hams
(brown cliffs)

The Tips

Saltings

Bowships Reach

Hemley

Newbourn

0

No.3
G

Posts

Moorings

Maybush Inn

WALDRINGFIELD

Waldringfield Reach

Little Sutton Hoo

Methersgate Reach

Methersgate

Methersgate Quay

Bns

No.5
G

No.10
R

No.8
R

2

2

No.12
R

Saltings

Granary Reach

Loder's Cut

Bn

No.16
R

No.13

No.11

No.9
G

No.14
R

No.7
G

Kyson Pt

Troublesome Reach

Martlesham Creek

River Deben

WOODBRIDGE

Deben YC

Tide Mill Yacht Harbour

See inset

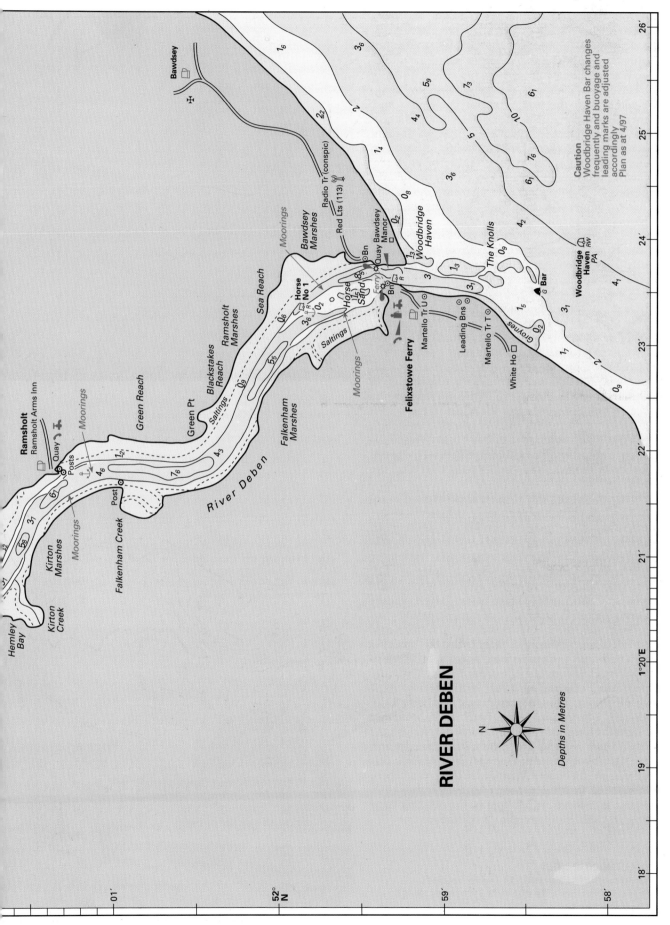

RIVER DEBEN

N

Depths in Metres

Bawdsey

Radio Tr (conspic)

Red Lts (113)

Bawdsey
Marshes

Bawdsey
Manor

Quay Bawdsey

Woodbridge
Haven

Moorings

Sea Reach

Horse
No 1

Horse
Sand

Bn

Ferry

Bn
R

The Knolls

Ramsholt
Marshes

Blackstakes
Reach

Green Pt

Saltings

Saltings

Falkenham
Marshes

Moorings

Felixstowe Ferry

Martello Tr U

Leading Bns

Martello Tr T

White Ho

G Bar

Groynes

Woodbridge
Haven
PA
RW

Caution
Woodbridge Haven Bar changes
frequently and buoyage and
leading marks are adjusted
accordingly
Plan as at 4/97

Ramsholt

Ramsholt Arms Inn

Quay

Posts

Green Reach

Moorings

Post

Moorings

Kirton
Marshes

Falkenham Creek

River Deben

Hemley
Bay

Kirton
Creek

52°
N

1°20'E

At the beginning of the 1992 season, the bars, banks and braes had so extended themselves that the actual (as opposed to the apparent) entrance channel was something of a dogleg, requiring you to keep easterly after you have passed to the north of the Haven buoy, clipping the green Bar buoy just to the south until the leading marks come into line. Generally speaking, it is safe to enter the Deben (if 'safe' is ever the word, that is) with 1.5m draught around one hour each side of low water. About two hours after, the broken water areas are plain to see, and while this usually shows quite clearly the relative positions of the channel and the bar, this is not entirely reliable, especially for a first-time visitor.

However, it is still true that the Bar usually carries 1m at LW springs, and there is a very fast rise of tide at the bar on the new flood with a likelihood of nearly 2m an hour after low water. Nevertheless, I would still advise strangers not to enter before half tide.

In late 1997, the channel was more or less straight in, but we must await the next chartlet for more up-to-date detailed information. It is usually ready just after Easter (see this page for details).

It can be quite an eerie experience near to high water, with the tide urging you along, to pass almost within hand-shaking distance of folk walking on the bank. In no time, you are in the midst of the waters of Felixstowe Ferry with all its busy traffic. Although modest in size, there are usually so many vessels on the move at the same time that it requires a lively eye from the visiting skipper – and a steady hand on the wheel.

Once inside, past the hospitable Felixstowe Ferry Sailing Club on the west shore – as I mentioned – there is usually a bustle of one kind or another. In addition, any wind-against-tide confrontation in this crowded area can create a rough and tumble of water enough completely to confuse progress. For those who want to stay at this attractive but tidally active spot, the best chance is to find a vacant mooring. This is difficult but can sometimes be arranged with the harbourmaster or the boatyard. The tide rip is strong and, frequently, the mooring buoys and lines are pulled well below the surface of the water. However, the effort can be worth it – the Felixstowe Ferry Sailing Club is friendliness itself with no one standing on ceremony; the Ferry Café and the Ferry Boat Inn both have enviable reputations for good food, drink and hospitality; the boatyard can meet all but extraordinary needs; and there is usually a tempting supply of fresh fish available at the huts. There was hope that there would be a floating pontoon ready for the 1998 season, accessible at all states for loading and unloading, but more specifically for diesel.

WALDRINGFIELD
Waldringfield Boatyard ☎ 01473 736260
Ⓥ (51, 25 visitors'), ⚓, 🚽, ⚡, ⭢, Provisions, Ⓖ, ⛽D, Engineer, Repairs

The Ramsholt Arms is one of the most popular spots on the River Deben. The HM's office is the (no-longer-sea-going) vessel that is to be seen by the (no-longer-working) jetty – just to left of centre . . .

. . . while another of the most popular spots is at Waldringfield – just a little way upstream. If you can find an 'ole, you will seldom want to find a better 'ole, for it is a joyful spot: popular and busy by land and water – but as yet nowhere near being ruined for indigens or visitors.

The moorings have been expanded and are now absolutely packed together at what must surely be saturation point. There are still a few places to anchor and, for these, you take advice and instruction from those on duty ashore. You need to be fairly self-sufficient to maintain a stay at Felixstowe Ferry. All the shops are in Old Felixstowe, 1½ miles away, but there is a bus service. Social life is not unrestricted and what there is centres on the pubs, the café and the fishermen, but local charm, character and friendliness are generous and unfettered. It is a splendid spot for photography and boasts a climate for which Skegness coined the concept 'bracing'. A bit of the East Coast at its best.

Less than a hundred years ago, there used to be a steam ferry known as the 'Bridges' here. Before that, legend has it that horses would swim across with their riders seated; later they used an ordinary rowing boat. But, from 1894 to 1931, there was the aforementioned steam chain-ferry service. It could even carry vehicles.

Charlie Brinkley told me about all this, because for years his family was in the ferry business. Once the chain went out of service, the elder Charlie used a launch until 1939, when the war put paid to it. Others ran it for a time but, in 1962, the present Charlie was in business; first with *Delia* and later with *Odd Times*, *Our Times* and *Late Times*. 'Times' of all kinds have changed; and son Robert is now back fishing.

Once past the tumble of sea over the bar and the tumult just within, there is one last hazard to be negotiated before the river settles down. That is the Horse Sand. It can seem an impossible task to leave the red Horse buoy to port at first, so close does it stand to the east bank, but it must be properly rounded, for it marks the isolated drying patch after which it is named, and which is more than ready to catch the unwary. I remember feeling ill at ease the first time I went through; but there is, of course, plenty of water, both abeam and below, and my worries were quite unnecessary.

With a good spring tide, you will swiftly pass Horse and be carried into the broader reaches of what quickly becomes a classic East Coast river – low-lying banks, far-reaching mud flats, frequent saltings, and a narrow channel in the middle of the broad expanse of shoal waters.

In this area, on the Felixstowe Ferry side, in a silted creek, it is still possible to see a few remains of the medieval harbour known as Gosford Haven. In its prime, it was known also as King's Fleet; because kings' vessels often sheltered there. Indeed, Edward III probably gathered his armada there to sail for Calais. Two and half centuries later, Woodbridge, almost at the very head of the navigation, and so much further upstream, robbed the creek of its trade to became the major port for goods brought in by sea. Historic remains are currently being researched.

The first sign of organised hospitality up the river comes with the small community of Ramsholt.

Approaching it, along the aptly named Green Reach you first pass Falkenham Creek (to port on the right bank) where some folk anchor but I have always shied off, not being sure of the bottom. On the other hand I have never heard anything but good reports of the spot and certainly never seen anything untoward. Upstream, the river becomes crowded to its maximum with moorings, so much so that you don't really see the fairway until you are in the middle of it. Flood and ebb move fast enough here to make it particularly hard work for small outboards to make much progress against the stream. Most visitors use this, the first of many attractive stopping places on the river, as a first port of call – the Ramsholt Arms, where there are moorings off the (now unused) old quay and the (now very much used) younger pub. The old quay was once a thriving trading post for barges, but it is now virtually untended and uncared for. It must stand as a prime candidate for refurbishment into a 'Port Deben Marina', complete with yachtsmen's residences. Perish the thought, but it may happen.

It is a popular spot, and the permanent moorings have been taken for years. There are no moorings set aside for visitors. The harbourmaster, George Collins, explains: 'We could never have more than a few visitors' moorings at best and, with just a few, you always have trouble. Somebody's always quarrelling about who got there first. Visitors should contact me and I will try to sort out a mooring.'

Being harbourmaster at Ramsholt runs in George's family. His father was master of the moorings back in the 1950s when there were only 25 boats. With the coming of Organisation and Method, the Administration appointed him as the first harbourmaster. There are now 200 moorings and that is how it is going to stay. (In fact, that is the general view in the river: no more moorings; no more boats.) George is usually found in one of three places: on his workboat on the river; in his office, which is a no-longer-sea-going vessel by the old jetty; or in the Ramsholt Arms, a good pub with a superb location given to glorious sunsets. Over the years it has collected notices that prohibit all kinds of things from dogs to picnicking.

Just a few cables upstream are to be found the attractive alternatives, the Deben anchorages. Two of them have good holding ground and are particularly well protected. Consequently they are popular. The first is on the west side of Hemley Bay and has good ground and splendid views. It is just past the enticing-looking Kirton Creek; but beware – do not be bewitched – the latter dries almost completely, and much of the ground is encumbered. The second is found on the stretch known as the Rocks, just off Prettyman's Point. There are one or two patches towards the upstream end where the holding quality is not absolutely first rate, but trial and error will sort that out. In the downstream section there are some foul patches, mainly in the area near the drying creek that is useable only during spring tides. Both, though, can be uncomfortable

Woodbridge at the top of the tide tends to be a busy place. Approaching on the last leg, the river broadens out moving towards the church and the boathouses. The restored Tide Mill (middle right, dating back to 1170) presides over all; nearby are the tiny, colourful rotunda of the bandstand (dating back hardly any time) and the classic cricket pavilion style HQ of the Deben Yacht Club. Come in willow, leather and cucumber sandwiches.

enough to be untenable when a strong wind is gusting against a spring ebb. A judicial move, made well ahead of time, up or down stream depending on prevailing conditions, usually achieves a substantial amelioration.

Prettyman's Point, only seriously crowded at weekends in the season, has a slender strip of firm sandy beach, a tree-covered slope that drops steeply to the shoreline and plenty of pathways and shrubbery. The river bank and saltings offer a variety of colour, pattern and texture rich enough to delight even the most exacting of artists. There is also a profusion of wildlife, including a number of resident swans. When there are not too many humans around, the hymns of the larks can be breathtaking. I am no ornithologist, so they might well be something else – but I would like to believe them to be larks. Most of the area is redolent of primitive Nigerian bush and jungle, while the rest mixes rock pools, saltings and almost untouched rural chaos with what are never more than modest essays into agriculture.

There is a really good walk to the Ramsholt Arms, where you are overlooked by the strangely shaped church tower that was, in its day, notorious as a smugglers' staging post, trafficking station and house of ill fame. Of an evening, you will be unlucky not to hear at least one nightingale singing on the way there. Care may be needed when returning after hours in the dark.

In spite of the derivation of the river's name ('The Deep One' or 'The Deep'un') its channel carries less and less water upstream from this point on. However, craft drawing up to 2·0m will be in no danger of finding bottom, even at low water, until abreast the picnic area known somewhat strangely as The Tips. This is roughly opposite the No. 10 red can buoy and well past the moorings at Waldringfield, which is itself a favourite weekend haunt for local cruising folk as well as visitors.

After Prettyman's Point, on the port hand opposite Stonner Point, comes the maze of moorings that denotes Waldringfield, an attractive and predictably busy spot. A phone call, in advance of a visit, to Waldringfield ☎ 01473 736260 will put you into touch with the boatyard of one Mr Brown whose patch it is. He is a most co-operative, approachable and affable gent who will see you well served. Anchor to port downstream of the moorings, just after and opposite green No. 1, or pick up a vacant mooring buoy and go ashore to the boatyard or the Maybush. You may be able to get a deep-water or half-tide mooring; but this is not as sure as death and taxes, for the river is increasingly busy – witness the plethora of mooring buoys extending from Waldringfield's tip to toe. Vacant ones can easily mislead newcomers about the direction of the fairway since many of them are red, and the size of buoys. The channel bends, twists and turns; is none too wide at best; and all around are shoaling banks of solid East Coast mud. Anchoring off, to the east, towards Stonner point has become more popular recently because of the difficulty of finding a vacant mooring.

Indeed, over the last ten years, the Deben has seen a vast increase in demand – one that cannot be met without filling the river and killing its joy. As a result of this, many craft are to be seen anchored outside the Waldringfield fairway on the edge of the shoals and shallows; while others lie above or below the trots and enjoy the long dinghy haul up to the mud/shingle beach or the old quay by the boatyard. There are two major attractions for visitors here: the

---

The Tide Mill Yacht Harbour has plenty of waiting buoys off the entrance, and an accurate tide gauge on the port hand side giving the depth over the cill. Richard Kember and his staff do all they can to make berthing facile and a stay a pleasure. While there is never a plethora of French or German visitors, there are always many Dutch boats to be seen – and it wise to book.

Maybush Inn and the Deben Stores. The renowned Maybush, with its display of cartoons personally signed by Sailor Giles, occupies a commanding position on the high ground overlooking the river. It is an extremely popular rendezvous by boat, car, bike and foot, and the staff are kept well occupied restlessly dispensing food and drink to all and sundry. The Deben Stores is not quite 'Open All Hours' but is open most of the time there is likely to be any business. It has expanded quite a lot since I first bought a rump steak there 20 years ago, and it is good to be able to report that the friendly service has kept pace with that growth. For those needing to buy or mend a boat, facilities are at hand.

There has been onshore development, bringing the place into today's commercial league of tourism. Waldringfield now sports a new feature: day trips on the Deben (on the good ship MV *Jahan*) embarking from a new jetty that extends helpfully into the river. It all looks neat, tidy and efficient; not a bit like the old Waldringfield image. Bye-laws are posted on the beach, informing all and sundry of what they must not do. One prohibition in particular shows how far our national weakness with regard to silly rules and regulations will let officialdom go: 'No digging for worms on the foreshore'. The river frontage still proliferates with its mix and match of the old and

WOODBRIDGE
51°58'·36N 01°24'·20E

Tide Mill Yacht Harbour ☎ 01394 385745
VHF Ch 80 M

Tidal access
2·5m over cill at MHWS
🅥 (40 visitors'), 🚾, 🅿, ⚓, ⚡ (16 amps), ⚓ (nearby),
Provisions (nearby), ☉ (nearby),
⚓D (nearby), ⚓P (nearby), Engineer, Repairs

Robertsons of Woodbridge ☎ 01394 382305
Tidal access 3 hrs before HW, 2 after for 3' draught
🅥 (40+ swinging moorings) 🚾, ⚓, ⚡ (quay),
Provisions (nearby), ☉, ⚓D (nearby), ⚓P (nearby),
Engineer, Repairs

Woodbridge Cruising Club ☎ 01394 382028
Tidal access
HW ±2
🚾, 🅿, ⚓, Provisions (nearby), ☉ (nearby),
⚓D, Engineer (nearby), Repairs (nearby)

Deben Yacht Club ☎ 01394 386504
🚾, 🅿, ⚓, Provisions (nearby), ☉ (nearby),
⚓D (nearby), ⚓P (nearby), Engineer (nearby),
Repairs (nearby)

the new and the classic beach bungalows still cling stubbornly not only to their last square feet of sandy fringe benefit but also, no doubt, to their dwindling last days. They still offer discreet testimony to the concept that some things do not change – these miniature holiday mansions are all variegated replicas of a *fin de siècle* archetype, spanning the style spectrum from the plainly plebeian to the luxuriously eccentric.

So, upriver to the two landing spots for those with reliable wellies: the Tips and the Hams. They are both on the east bank, just below Methersgate Quay – which always looks in a very sorry state. In about a mile, their pleasant features make ideal spots for both a break and a picnic. The anchorage around here is about the furthest upriver you can stay afloat with a draught of 2·0m at springs. From here on, the only hazard is one of running out of water; the channel upstream begins to deviate, and craft drawing more than 2·0m should not attempt to proceed past Methersgate Quay until after half tide. Running out of water, either by being too early on the tide, or by ignoring or clipping the first rate buoyage, is the only hazard up to Woodbridge. It is worth noting that the buoyage can, in the strong winds and harsh streams that can frequent the Deben, get dragged off station. Indeed, although the channel is well and clearly buoyed, the bottom does move around and you need a considerable amount of local knowledge not to meet it. However, joy of joys, the bottom is good-old-soft-gooey mud and no harm will befall. This stretch of the Deben is now even busier than ever, with the ribbon development of moorings reaching downstream to Methersgate quay almost non-stop from above Woodbridge.

This is a pretty part of the river, and it improves all the way up to Troublesome Reach. Many rivers have their Troublesome Reaches, but this is one par excellence. It comes just before Kyson Quay and Martlesham creek and, in fact, is no real trouble at all. There are three possible ways forward, each with its own problem. There are two channels to Woodbridge, the short road and the long road as it were; and another into Martlesham Creek. The main channel to Woodbridge, being the main road, has no name; but the short one is known as Loders Cut. It is the dodgier of the two.

The general area is headed by most attractive scenery and properties, well kept by zealous riparians, especially the miniature headland opposite Kyson Point. It is well trimmed, barbered and presented, all smartly green and tree clad right down to the last metre by the riverside. More power to their lawn-mowing elbows!

Let us turn our attention to Martlesham Creek first. It is the preferred choice for many locals who want just to pop out of Woodbridge itself on a tide for fish, beer or pipe, but there is by no means as much water as in the main channel and such a project should be approached with care. A low-water dinghy inspection may be best first. The Creek was renowned in the 1700s and the early 1800s; the Deben was host to much smuggling and Martlesham Creek and Shottisham Creek (by Prettyman's Point and the Ramsholt Arms) seem to have played a central part. Generally they had the support and vested interest of the whole population, so that farm labourers, farmers' wives, curates, magistrates, judges and even customs officers all had their hand in. For example, one vicar made his horses available at night and, at another church, there was a tunnel to one of the smugglers' hideaways in the farmhouse close by.

The honour of being second in line in the trickiness stakes goes to the intriguing rivulet known as Martlesham Creek. After the first big bend to the west, and near green Nos. 9 and 11, the creek runs more or less directly straight ahead, although the narrow navigable 'dyke' is not dead central. It is a loner's haven; quiet and peaceful, yet with the facilities of the small and welcoming boatyard to hand. The marked channel is not easy for strangers to identify and craft will take the mud very early on the ebb. It is something of a walker's and birdwatcher's delight. Both Creek and Kyson Point are well known as the indigens' favourite holiday spot when they want to hide from the visitors.

Back in less muddied waters, there is a real and challenging need for sharp eyes in these last legs before Woodbridge itself, for the channel twists and turns as if it had been designed to tease and cheat. Turning to Wordsworth for solace will only delude: 'Ne'er saw I, never felt, a calm so deep! The river glideth at his own sweet will'. This is no place for calm if you are to spot the beacons and buoys that mark the dramatic doglegs of the next half mile or so. In particular, it is easy to let the eyes hover on the well-kept riparian property that sits well up on the bank high above NE corner red No. 14 buoy.

Eye-catching sunsets are not all that common on the East Coast – and stunning ones are few and far between. One of the best viewpoints is the balcony or lawn of the Ramsholt Arms – when judiciously imbibed spirituous liquors will certainly enhance even the lowliest.

Much more likely to cause aggro than Troublesome Reach is the tempting short route known as Loders Cut, marked by three red beacons at the beginning, middle and end. It is the shortest by a long chalk – but not guaranteed the quickest unless you are of shoal draught, stout heart and an even stouter engine. The whole area dries out and the withies, excellent though they may be, can easily be misinterpreted by strangers. More than once have I seen visitors come to grief by following a local shoal-draught boat. Such craft use it frequently and

quite happily, and some locals say it is good for 2m craft at HW springs. I have never been tempted to try it.

Woodbridge at the top of the tide tends to be a busy place. Approaching on the last leg, the waterway, but not the channel itself, broadens out and opens up as you move towards the church and the boathouses. The main landmarks are attractive, with the restored and refurbished Tide Mill (dating back to 1170) presiding over all; while the tiny, colourful rotunda of the band-box bandstand (dating back hardly any time) is demonstrably in another school of architecture. It stands next the classic cricket pavilion-style HQ of the Deben Yacht Club. You can almost hear the thwack of leather on willow.

From here on, both the channel and its many moorings are, on the tide, often filled with craft, apparently jilling around. The channel runs the gamut of compass points, and is not susceptible of immediate identification. Consequently, this last leg is not one for letting attention wander. Moreover, it impossible to find a safe spot to anchor. The boats are many and the buoys but few; and there are intriguing sights to catch the eye. Careful searching with the eyeglass will locate the last reds that lead to the Tide Mill Yacht Harbour. For most visitors, this is the end of the road: a spot from which to enjoy all that this small town has to offer. The marina, run by master of operations, Richard Kember, is not the only place where you can moor at Woodbridge, but I recommend it as the best for a first-time visitor.

There are plenty of waiting buoys off the entrance, which has an accurate tide gauge on the port-hand side giving the depth over the cill. At HW Springs this has an average depth of around 2·5 metres. The new cill retains the water at its proper level. Once inside, you find that most of the pontoons are new; and all of them are substantial, clean and fully serviced. The facilities are comprehensive, and more new pontoons and steel piles are being introduced into the north arm. All the dredging in the south arm was completed in 1996. Richard, with his henchman Carl and staff, make berthing seem facile and a stay a pleasure. While there is never a plethora of French or German visitors, there are always many Dutch boats to be seen.

There is still more ahead, for this is not the head of navigation and time is well spent exploring upstream. There is much more to see and do than appears at a cursory glance. The trip can be taken in a yacht on the tide, and a mooring will probably be made available to you. They may be limited, but they are extremely peaceful – and equipped with good facilities. Predictably, you must be capable of taking the ground. It is a small, almost self-contained, but very approachable community. Of course, first quest is best done on foot or in the dinghy, since the muddy gutways can easily confuse – in spite of (or perhaps because of) the bountiful supply of withies. In any case, it is a most pleasant walk.

The boatyard that first takes the eye is known as Robertson's, and has been established here since 1887. Not only does it succeed in practising fine skills, but you will also find a warm welcome. The present chief will invest all his concentration on you, even if you want to talk exclusively about your fantasy. Nearby are more services from chandlery to insurance and surveys.

Towards Melton, a little further up, is another small group based on boating. It consists of the Granary Yacht Harbour, Larkman's, Skipper Yachts and the Coach and Horses, and you will find a warm welcome at all. They are all on the same side of the river as the marina and the town itself. On the other side of the river you can search out an experience of an entirely different kind – the famous Sutton Hoo burial ship site. When they were first unearthed, almost all the 'Mounds' had been vandalised and robbed. Only one slight hump had retained its treasures intact: the remains of a young man with his sword, spear and shield. Not far away his horse and bridle were also found. Sutton Hoo was probably a ritual burial ground for an important dynasty, based here and on the continent.

The drama of the actual site has always eluded me, but many find it of sombre atmosphere and intense ambience. Some even claim to have been approached by practising ghosts. If you don't want to face what can be bleak, many of the relics can be perused, out of the cold, back in the Woodbridge Museum.

It is only a short walk into the centre of Woodbridge from the marina and back to reality. The town is old – and looks it. Since the bypass took away most of the heavy traffic, it feels it. The first recorded settlement was in the 10th century, but there are artefacts that date back to the Neolithic Age. Walking its streets one can gain the impression of a small market town with its spiritual home in the 1830s; though not averse to today's prosperity. Nowhere can that be seen to better effect than at the main cross of Quay Street and The Strand, where stands the Crown Inn. Once a 17th-century coaching inn, it has been modernised in the style of Trusthouse Forte – and so has the service.

Woodbridge, a decorous and thriving little town, is the essence of contemporary classic East Anglia, and, except for busy Saturdays, is an excellent place to explore, particularly good on bookshops, fresh fish and deli's.

My selection of visitors' specials are to be found, first on the quay, where Frank Knight still runs his classic boatyard. Shortly after, comes a real contrast: Andy (Aladdin) Seedhouse's caves of boating gear and bric-a-brac. Then towards the town, on the first corner, Small Craft Deliveries runs a splendid bookshop. In fact, it is much more than a bookshop, for in its slightly cramped space there are all the books, charts, information and advice that you could wish for. Off the 'Thoroughfare', in the centre of town, there is a butcher of special note. He is a certain Mr Creasey, a 'high-class family butcher' who purveys his lamb, pork and beef in Hamblin Walk in the Turban Centre.

And, to finish, there is a real treat at the top of Market Hill: Le Provençal. The English husband and French wife team run a restaurant that offers food and friendship, with a table of your own for the night. Their 'bouquet' of vegetables is unforgettable and, happily, their prices are not exotic. The cuisine is not exclusively Provençal, but the food is delicious, and not to be missed. There are other eating houses in the area, notably the Captain's Table, at which many boaters predictably put down their land anchors.

My peroration turns to that extraordinary man Edward Fitzgerald, of *Rubaiiyait of Omar Khayyaim* fame, who frequently sailed from here. Strangely rigged and eccentrically garbed he became a legend in his lifetime, and it was only right and proper that he was buried nearby. He wrote his own epitaph: 'It is He that hath made us and not we ourselves'.

Woodbridge, the one-time thriving sea-port, together with its present flourishing community deserves better than that. They have themselves built a cruising man's resort of the highest order and are to be congratulated.

V. The Orwell & Stour

It is only a short leg from the Woodbridge Haven buoy, and the grim Bawdsey Manor to Landguard Point that marks the entrance to the vast watery municipality of Felixstowe and Harwich. During the trip down there are gentle alterations in the coastline and a few quiet contrasts to enjoy – cliffs, grassy banks, low shingle beaches and a façade of holiday huts; with tanks, towers, churches, a pier and a few more Martello towers also to be spotted. From shoresides, however, the huts are less than gay and sport little connection with Joseph's coat, for many are dressed in drab seaside-resort green, with terminal wood rot at their feet and noxious rubbish in their bins to the rear.

Detailed information on the regulations that apply to leisure craft navigating within the area of the Harwich Haven Authority are as follows:

Harwich Haven

The Harwich Harbour, and its adjacent rivers, is one of the UK's busiest port areas; over 121 million gross tons of shipping called at the Haven ports in 1995. Despite this commercial activity, the harbour and the delightful estuaries of the Rivers Stour and Orwell provide excellent sailing and recreational activities for large numbers of visiting or home-based pleasure craft.

Part of Harwich's busy container port and the contrasting nothingness of Bathside Bay are only part of this vast watery complex which, with Felixstowe, seems to attract trade like bees to blossom. The River Stour, quiet and doleful, keeping itself to itself, stretches away into the top misty distance.

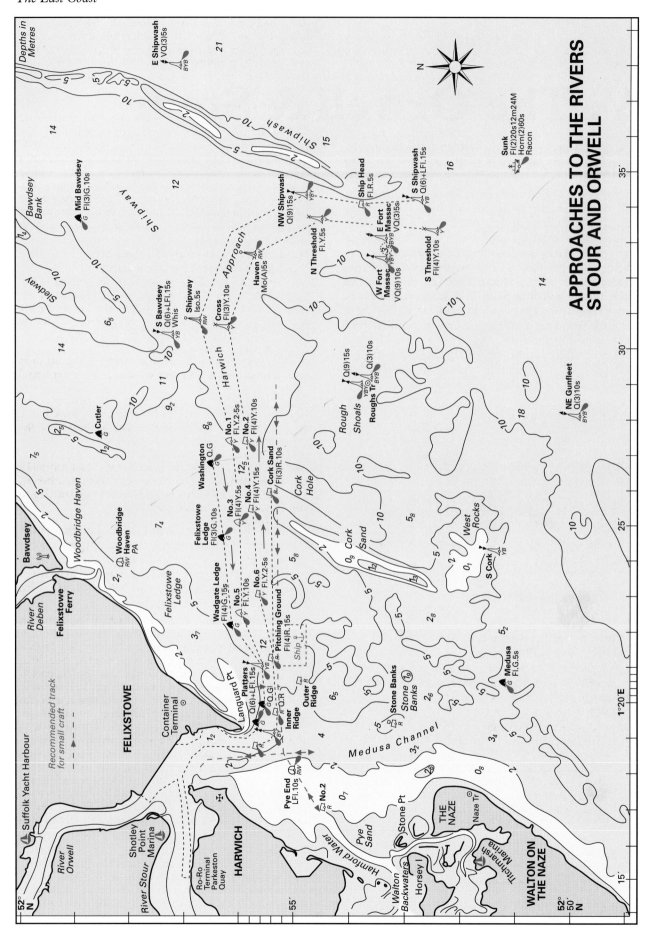

APPROACHES TO THE RIVERS
STOUR AND ORWELL

VHF radio

The harbour operations frequency, Ch 71, is extremely busy with commercial shipping. Yachts are requested not to use it except in an emergency, although it is beneficial to monitor this frequency in order to obtain information on commercial vessel movements.

Reporting

All vessels of more than 50GT entering or leaving the seaward approaches to Harwich Harbour by the approach channel must report by VHF Ch 71 to the harbourmaster when passing the appropriate reporting points (indicated on Admiralty charts) and report to Ipswich Port Radio Ch 14 on entering the River Orwell.

Navigational safety

The principal deep-water navigational channels within Harwich Harbour are well marked by buoys and lights. These channels are in constant use by large, deep-draughted container vessels, ferries and other traffic. Yachtsmen are advised to keep well clear of these main channels whenever possible and use the recommended yacht tracks (see chart). When main channels have to be crossed, this should be done as nearly as practicable at right angles. Avoid crossing the bows of oncoming commercial traffic. Large container ships, in particular, have very restricted visibility for quite a distance ahead when carrying a deck cargo of containers. (You may be able to see her clearly, but can she see you?) Most yachtsmen take a justifiable pride in the responsible way they conduct themselves. Part of this is a realisation that hindering the passage of large commercial vessels is not

HARWICH/FELIXSTOWE

Harwich 51°57'·03N 01°17'·88E

Charts Admiralty 1491, 2052, 2693. Imray C1, C28, Y16. OS Landranger 169.

Tides

Harwich: Dover +0050; Pin Mill: Dover +0100; Ipswich: Dover +0110

Authorities

Harwich Haven Authority ☎ 01255 243030
Harwich Harbour ☎ 01255 243000 (24hr). VHF Ch 16, 71, 11, 14 (24hrs). Call *Harwich Harbour Control*. Yachts should listen in Ch 71.
Orwell Navigation Service ☎ 01473 231010. VHF Ch 12, 14, 16 (24hrs)

Harwich Harbour Operations frequency, Ch 71, is extremely busy with commercial shipping. Yachts are requested not to use this channel, except in an emergency.

Useful telephone numbers
Weather
Marinecall Anglia ☎ 0891 500 455
Latest current coastal reports for the area are available on ☎ 0891 226 455

Coastguard
Thames Coastguard ☎ 01255 675518
(VHF Call Ch 16; working Ch 67)

HM Customs and Excise
Harwich	☎ 01255 244700
Ipswich	☎ 01473 235700
(24 hrs)	☎ 01473 235704
Felixstowe	☎ 01394 303030
Drugs Hotline	☎ 0800 595000

only bad manners, but downright dangerous to themselves and their crews. Yachtsmen are particularly requested to remind themselves and observe the content and spirit of Rules 9(b) and (d), 18(b)(ii) and 18(d)(i) of the *Collision Regulations* and also the *Harwich Haven Authority Byelaws*.

Harbour control

The Harwich Haven Authority maintains a regular patrol of the Haven throughout the year. In addition, during the summer months at weekends, between the hours of 0800 to 1800, these patrols are maintained to provide assistance and advice to yachtsmen, and to ensure that the main channel is kept clear for the transit of commercial shipping. The weekend harbour-patrol launch maintains a listening watch on VHF Ch 11. The crew will be pleased to offer advice and information on the harbour and its approaches.

Harwich Haven Authority Byelaws 1994
Vessels to keep clear of deep-water channel
No.18 A vessel which is not confined to the deep-water channel by reason of her draught shall keep clear of the deep-water channel when necessary to avoid impeding the movement of a vessel which is proceeding in, and by reason of her draught is confined to, that channel.
Vessel Entering Navigable Channel
No.19 A vessel shall not enter the navigable channel so as to hazard or impede the movement of any other vessel under way in that channel.
Small Vessels to Keep Clear of Berths and Anchorages
No.49 A small vessel shall not obstruct or impede the movement of any other vessel in any anchorage or the approach to any berth.
Obstructions to Large Vessels
No.50 Yachts, cruisers and power boats shall not make use of the navigable channel or approaches to wharves, piers and jetties in such a way as to cause obstruction to large vessels using the harbour.

Shotley Point Marina stands at the junction of the Orwell and the Stour, but since many more people use it for the Orwell than the Stour, for our purposes it is the starting point of our trip up the River Orwell. The marina offers the following advice to visitors for approach and locking:

Entrance Channel – Yachts approaching from seaward must keep to the track recommended by the Harwich Harbour Board until reaching the Shotley Spit beacon (YB) then steer west until the piles marking the outer channel limits are reached. From there the channel is controlled by an Inogon light mounted on the east side of the lock buttress which indicates when a vessel is on the correct bearing. A vertical black stripe indicates the correct track and a broad arrow indicates direction in which to alter course to come back on track. On arrival at the lock approach there are some waiting pontoons with an access bridge to the shore at the lock buttress on the port side. Passage through the lock is controlled by red (no go) and green (go) lights operated by the lockmaster. He can be contacted on VHF Ch 37 (Ch 'M'). At all times please comply with the lockmaster's instructions over the public address speaker.

The Lock – The cycle when the lock is being worked takes about five minutes after all boats have been secured. Be prepared for some turbulence in the lock as the penstocks are opened, vessels need to be well secured to the floating fenders as there is a strong surge usually towards the inner mitre gates. Please advise the lockmaster of the name and length of your boat as you pass through and new arrivals or visitors are asked to pay a call on the marina control tower after they have secured at their berth. The lockmaster will direct visitors to a berth.

The marina was opened in 1988 by Lord Lewin, Admiral of the Fleet, with a ritual entrance of the sailing barge *Ethel Ada*, to be the centrepiece of the Classic Boat Centre. This marina-based leisure facility has a capacity of 350 berths in a locked basin that affords access at all states of the tide.

A full range of up-to-date services is available, all within the marina complex, and the harbourmaster's office is extremely well sited. There is a yacht club and sea school for sail and motor cruising, and there is the Shipwreck hostelry.

Shotley Point has also had its day, and I am grateful to the Shipwreck for the following brief history:

It was the home for the HMS *Ganges*, the ship that never floated (in naval parlance a 'stone frigate'). Officially born on 4 October 1905, when the first young trainees arrived, HMS *Ganges* stood proudly on the edge of Shotley Point, covering some 173 acres, until it was finally taken out of service in 1976. During its 71 years in naval service it was one of the most famous, or some would say infamous, of all naval shore depots.

The marina, situated as it is at the tip of the Shotley Peninsula, has an excellent position for cruising the East Coast rivers at large; and has within its easy range the Orwell, the Stour, the Deben, the Ore and the Alde, the Blackwater and, of course, the very close-by Walton Backwaters.

It is, of course, no distance at all from the green Ganges, which tends to the southeast of the marina entrance channel to the Rivers Orwell and Stour, at the confluence of which it stands. The Orwell proper is entered between those two points on opposing points of the river with names that give cause for contemplation: Bloody Point and, on the other side of the water, in opposition, Fagbury Hill.

The Orwell is not a very long river, being no more than 10 miles from its entrance to Ipswich Docks; but is does pack an enormous variety into its short course. The inexorable progress of its commercial traffic contrasts markedly with the serenity of its peacefully changing scenery which shows a variety of trees, smaller greenery and mixed veg. The banks of the river grow in stature until, at times, they are quite substantial. (Novel on the East Coast, this.) The lower reach of the river has marshes on each side backed by wooded hills which shortly march directly down to the river, establishing the Orwell as different from anything to the south almost until the Dart.

The standard buoyage is well designed and maintained, as one would expect in a river that is busy with commercial shipping. The buoys are laid at intervals frequent enough for only the poorest East Coast visibility to defeat the careful navigator. The channel itself is dredged to 5·8m all the way to the head of navigation at Ipswich. It is no more than 2 cables wide at some points, misleading in a river

that spreads so far between its banks when the tide is in. For most of the time, it is possible to see the way ahead well and clear; and with such a deep channel, often straight, it is permissible for even first-time visitors to let their eyes wander over the attractions of the passing scene.

Full fathom five is not what the river carries; neither is there coral from bones nor pearls from eyes; but of the Orwell in very truth it can be said, 'Nothing of him that doth fade, / But doth suffer a sea-change, / Into something rich and strange.' Of all the areas covered by this volume, this is the one that has altered more than any other. Indeed, it has been transformed, and nothing that has not been for the good. Not only are there now more marinas than there were before, but two of the three that have been there some time have themselves been refurbished in accord with what is happening around them.

As for anchorages in the river, the first comes after Shotley Point Marina on the port hand. It is towards the west bank, above Fagbury Point and green No. 1 to the east and off the Shotley Marshes. Lots of folk use it quite happily, but I prefer to go a little further upstream, where there are two more. Both

'When the evening is spread out against the sky, Like a patient etherised upon a table': Craft at rest (and all being well at peace) in the locked and protected Shotley Marina.

are on the port hand; the first, a quite restricted area, is near the red No. 2, not far below Collimer Point, where there is an old hard and a tide gauge. The second, a much longer stretch, occurs towards the south bank of the river, from just above the north mile marks on the bank, to the red buoy 'Foxes Bottom'. It is essential to be well clear of the main channel, but there is plenty of good ground in which to be able to do this. Anchor lights are obligatory by the laws of good seamanship, but also essential for self preservation when close to such a big shipping channel. However, by the time we have reached this anchorage, Pin Mill on the south bank is no more than a couple of cables, but, more importantly for the moment, we have already passed one of the most popular marinas on the river: the Suffolk Yacht Harbour.

Suffolk Yacht Harbour has now had to surrender to Shotley Point Marina its claim to fame as the first of the welcoming hosts on the Orwell; but it certainly has not abdicated it claim to be the one that attracts more visitors, especially from across the North Sea and the English Channel. It still proclaims itself 'East Anglia's Leading Marina'. It is a well-protected facility, so much so that you see little of it, apart from masts, until you have fully opened up its entrance. The approach channel, a straight run in at right angles to the fairway, is well marked and dredged and is to be found just past the green Collimer buoy to the northeast shore; that is, on the starboard hand going upriver. Craft up to

HARWICH
Harwich & Dovercourt Sailing Club
☎ 01255 551153
Tidal access
HW ±2hrs
Ⓥ (swinging moorings, 2 visitors') WC, ⚓,
ᕽ, Provisions (nearby)

Royal Harwich Yacht Club
☎ 01473 780319
Tidal access
24 hrs
Ⓥ (30, no visitors'), WC, 🖼, ⚓, ⚡, ᕽ,
Provisions (nearby), Ⓖ (nearby), ⬩D, Engineer (by arrangement), Repairs (by arrangement)

RIVER STOUR
Shotley Point Marina Ltd ☎ 01473 788982,
Radio VHF Ch 80 and 37 (M)
Tidal access
Via manned lock 24 hrs (2m draught)
Ⓥ (350, 100 visitors'), WC, 🖼, ⚓, ⚡, ᕽ, Provisions, Laundrette, Ⓖ, ⬩D, Engineer, Repairs

---

RIVER ORWELL
Suffolk Yacht Harbour Ltd
☎ 01473 659465/659240, Radio VHF Ch 37 (M) and 80 (0800-1700)
Tidal access
24 hrs
Ⓥ (500+20 visitors. 24 swinging)

Pin Mill
For moorings, contact: Jack Ward & Son, Orwell Yacht Services ☎ 01473 780276. All services (no petrol)

Woolverstone Marina
☎ 01473 780206, Radio: VHF Ch 80 M
Tidal access 24 hrs
Ⓥ (200+140 swinging, 50 visitors'), WC, 🖼, ⚓,
ᕽ (nearby), Provisions, Ⓖ, ⬩D, Laundrette, Engineer (nearby), Repairs (nearby)

Fox's Marina Ipswich Ltd ☎ 01473 689111,
Radio: VHF Ch 80
Tidal access 24 hrs
Ⓥ (100, inc. visitors'), WC, 🖼, ⚓, ⚡, ᕽ,
Provisions (nearby), Ⓖ, ⬩D, Engineer Repairs

1·5m have access at all times through the channel. Deeper-draught vessels will have to wait accordingly. Reception, consisting of two 9·0m pontoons, is dead ahead on entering; that is, to the east of the fuel bay which is just inside the entrance.

Inside, you will find that manychanges have made a stop here a pleasure, for cruising amenities are all up to date, thanks to recent alterations and refurbishment. Because of this and the established personal attention to yachtsmen's needs, Suffolk Yacht Harbour has an EU-wide reputation and is usually busy. Permanent berths are at a premium. Power and water are now available at all jetties. The Haven Ports Yacht Club lightship clubhouse, recently brillianted even brighter red, is known throughout the worldwide cruising fraternity. I have been shown its picture in France taken by a Dutchman; in Spain taken by a Frenchman; and in

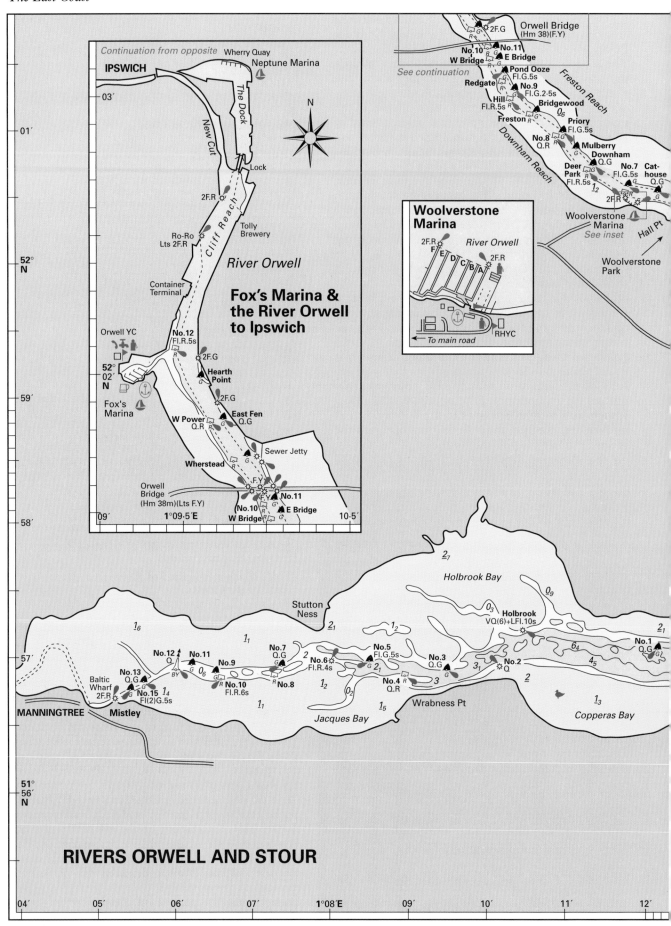

Fox's Marina & the River Orwell to Ipswich

Woolverstone Marina

RIVERS ORWELL AND STOUR

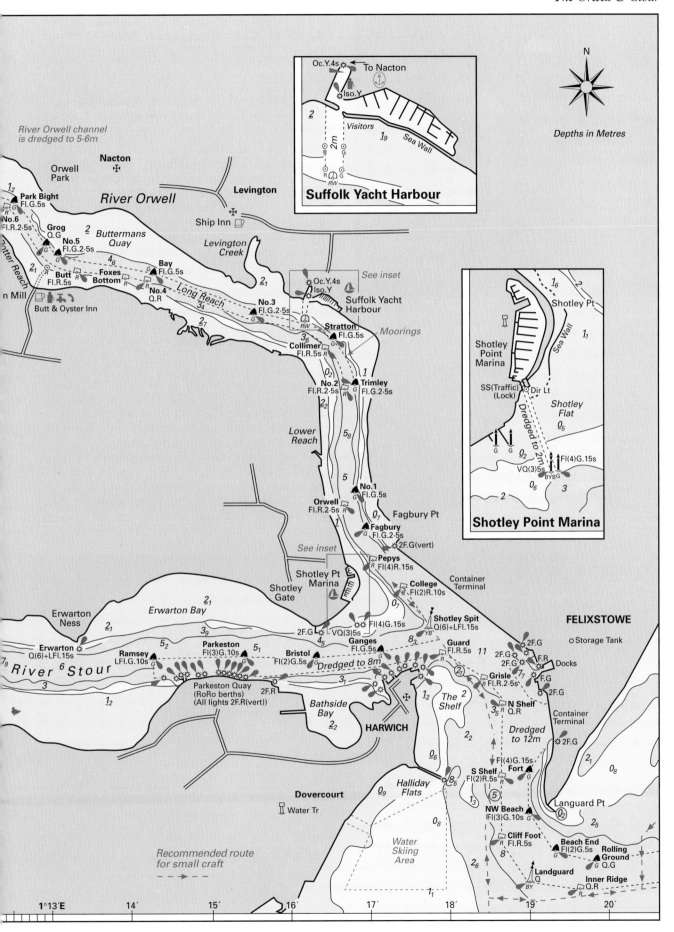

N

Depths in Metres

Suffolk Yacht Harbour

Oc.Y.4s
Iso.Y
To Nacton
Visitors
Sea Wall
RW

Shotley Point Marina

Shotley Pt
Sea Wall
Shotley Point Marina
SS(Traffic) (Lock)
Dir Lt
Shotley Flat
Dredged to 2m
G G
VQ(3)5s
BYBG
Fl(4)G.15s

River Orwell channel is dredged to 5·6m

Nacton
Orwell Park
River Orwell
Levington
Ship Inn
Park Bight
Fl.G.5s
No.6
Fl.R.2·5s
Grog
Q.G
No.5
Fl.G.2·5s
Buttermans Quay
Levington Creek
See inset
Suffolk Yacht Harbour
Oc.Y.4s
Iso.Y
Butt
Fl.R.5s
Foxes Bottom
Bay
Fl.G.5s
No.4
Q.R
Long Reach
No.3
Fl.G.2·5s
Moorings
n Mill
Butt & Oyster Inn
Stratton
Fl.G.5s
Collimer
Fl.R.5s
No.2
Fl.R.2·5s
Trimley
Fl.G.2·5s
Lower Reach
No.1
Fl.G.5s
Orwell
Fl.R.2·5s
Fagbury Pt
Fagbury
Fl.G.2·5s
2F.G(vert)
See inset
Shotley Pt Marina
Pepys
Fl(4)R.15s
College
Fl(2)R.10s
Container Terminal
Erwarton Ness
Erwarton Bay
Shotley Gate
Shotley Spit
Q(6)+LFl.15s
FELIXSTOWE
Erwarton
Q(6)+LFl.15s
2F.G
VQ(3)5s
Fl(4)G.15s
Ganges
Fl.G.5s
Guard
Fl.R.5s
Storage Tank
2F.G
2F.G
F.R
Docks
Ramsey
LFl.G.10s
Parkeston
Fl(3)G.10s
Bristol
Fl(2)G.5s
Dredged to 8m
Grisle
Fl.R.2·5s
F.G
2F.G
River Stour
Parkeston Quay (RoRo berths) (All lights 2F.R(vert))
2F.R
Bathside Bay
N Shelf
Q.R
Container Terminal
2F.G
HARWICH
The Shelf
Dredged to 12m
Dovercourt
Water Tr
Halliday Flats
Fl(4)G.15s
Fort
S Shelf
Fl(2)R.5s
NW Beach
Fl(3)G.10s
Cliff Foot
Fl.R.5s
Languard Pt
Beach End
Fl(2)G.5s
Rolling Ground
Q.G
Water Skiing Area
Landguard
Q
Inner Ridge
Q.R
Recommended route for small craft

1°13′E   14′   15′   16′   17′   18′   19′   20′

The upper reaches of the River Orwell have some glorious picture postcard sights to offer.

and gas. There is a well-stocked food shop and chandlery.

A particular landmark is the former Cromer light vessel which, rather than warning seamen to stay clear, welcomes hungry and thirsty visitors. The light vessel is the Haven Ports Yacht Club and has been converted into bars and a restaurant, while retaining many of its original features. The marina was developed, and is still managed by yachtsmen for yachtsmen and prides itself on being the number-one choice for discerning boat owners.

Little has changed in essence since I first came nearly 20 years ago; but there have been many advances in the services and improvements all round. In particular, there are new shower and toilet blocks with laundry facilities; and the old much-loved lean-to shanty-town shed that used to dispense all the domestic goodies that it had (and at that time they were not comprehensive) has now given way to a modern shop with much more, and a greater spread, of stock.

When I was there last, I made a complete mess of mooring up in unfavourable wind conditions; but all I got was the maximum of speedy help with not a raised eyebrow in sight. How warm, welcoming and kind!

There is an extremely pleasant walk to the village of Levington which stands at the top of the drying Levington Creek. The Ship Inn is a deservedly popular pilgrimage – especially since events of an eccentric but eclectic nature are apt to be in progress if you arrive in the middle of the evening.

As I suggested earlier, it is now not far in terms of physical distance from Pin Mill. But in terms of atmosphere, culture and history, it could hardly be further removed from the more cosmopolitan Suffolk Yacht Harbour. It was one of Arthur Ransome's favourite spots; indeed, it would have

Ibiza taken by a German. They all mentioned the excellence of the food, and that kind of publicity speaks for itself.

The marina brochure has this to say:

First-class facilities, sheltered berthing and a wealth of tidal estuaries to explore, go a long way to justify Suffolk Yacht Harbour's claim to be East Anglia's leading marina. (It is near the village of Levington, only 3 miles from the sea, 3 miles from the open sea, which goes a long way to explaining its popularity with continentals.) The marina has its own slipway, boat-hoist and crane facilities, fuel

been strange if it hadn't been since, at one time, he lived just across the river at Levington. Visiting Pin Mill frequently in his Hillyard-built cutter, *Nancy Blackett*, led to his 35ft cutter being built there by Harry King in 1938. He also built for him his eight-ton ketch *Peter Duck* in 1946. It was there that Ransome wrote much of his children's tale of the same name.

Pin Mill is one of those places where change is not the keynote; indeed, change is welcomed neither by indigens nor visitors. Pin Mill is archetypally unsuited to mutation and most folk who have anything to do with it believe it still to be the Thames bargee's idea of the 'Great Mooring in the Sky' – a heavenly haven. It has a singular fascination . . . it is curious, peculiar, unbelievable yet solid and authentic; at least that is the impact it has had on me. Pin Mill will never win silver anchors for the most prestigious, well-equipped moorings in the UK; nor gold stars or platinum shields to be mounted on panelled walls. It will never win any kind of prize unless it be one for friendliness and charm – but no such for that exists except in the hearts of those who have experienced it. Pin Mill has nothing to with being chic, *à la mode* or even just fashionable. Nor does it possess a craftsman sporting cider, straw hat and a clay pipe, making model barges in birch or Spanish oak.

Pin Mill is still as solid and substantial as ever. It is an abode where gravel from the boulders of epochs has fused with the bed of the vigorous river by its portals to create not only a symbolically concrete-hard-fact of riparian life but also a hard for all men, all boats and all seasons. Its inhabitants come from that stock that really does know the proper value of things, yet are hesitant to put the full going price on anything – and they certainly never try to make a fast buck from a visitor who knows no

Top Every Picture Tells a Story – and what words can add to this evocation of one of the most famous moorings in the UK: Pin Mill?

Opposite Suffolk Yacht Harbour: here seen fully exposed in its nearly fully enclosed rural and riparian state . . .
.. and here seen Head On with visitors' reception at dead centre.

better. They also know that too swift arrives as tardy as too slow; and can see no reason why the passing of the past in places elsewhere should forecast the demise of the present or threaten the future of any or all of its livelihood. Pin Mill will surely never try to emulate Shotley Point Marina nor Port Solent. And therein lies its strength – it cares little for the current gusts of change and will quietly wait for them to die away before it does. Pin Mill is *sui generis*; and likes itself that way.

Top Pin Mill from elsewhere. As Browning might have said: It was saltings, saltings all the way. The air broke into a mist with bells.
Bottom Woolverstone. The black and white buildings at the left of centre are the HQ of the HM. Visitors are usually well spotted in advance. It is usual practice to tie up on the outer hammer heads and await instructions.

With regard to facts, figures and facilities, Pin Mill is not without detail. The Ipswich Port Authority's representative, the official designation for the non-existent post of Pin Mill harbourmaster, is Tony Ward, of Ward's chandlery and moorings. Harbourmaster he may not be, but master of the harbour and hard taskmaster he certainly is.

His headquarters are at the top of that hard. The end of its concrete run is marked by a red can. Access isn't seriously restricted by tides, but landing can be a messy, muddy affair 1 hour each side of LW. Swinging moorings are available and, during the summer about half a dozen are reserved, and all clearly marked, for visitors. There are possibilities of anchoring, and the prudent skipper will take advantage of Tony Ward's presence and expert local knowledge before thinking of dropping anything. Mrs Ward will also serve, minister and advise from the small but well-stocked chandlery, marked in the lane by the fuel pumps.

Most boating facilities are to hand – in addition to Orwell Yacht Services, there are King's boatbuilders (Harry King and Sons, contact Geoff King). Although I must sadly report that Fred Webb, the yacht and boatbuilder who specialised in repairing Thames sailing barges, died early in 1996, his moorings and chandlery are to continue. Pin Mill Sailing Club looks after all kinds of interests and is a good and friendly contact for visitors (they have showers as well). There is no post office or shop, although Webb's carries a supply of groceries and possesses an off licence. Most village services are found in nearby Chelmondiston (and if you want to be ahead of the yuppies, you must try calling it 'Chelmo').

Character and characters abound all round; but the talented floating tattoo artist has moved his pitch landlubbingly upriver, and perhaps upmarket too? Sadly, the scene is dominated by the backdrop of barges that have seen better days and a wooden half-submerged structure that in silhouette on a murky evening stands like a gibbet at the ready. But to take the sting out of that, there are some who hang on in there, just below Pin Mill itself, living not on the breadline but on the waterline in a variety of constructions that defy belief even through the most powerful of binoculars.

In the words of John Wesley, 'Time like an ever-flowing stream bears all her sons away. / They lie forgotten as a dream dies at the opening day.' Sadly, 'Golden lads and girls all must, / As chimney-sweepers come to dust.'

After Pin Mill come two contrasts – the esoteric Royal Harwich Yacht Club and the exoteric Woolverstone Marina. The Royal Harwich is an eminent club to which access is restricted not by sills, tides, times or winds but by less perceptible, more elusive shibboleths. It possesses a few moorings and members of other yacht clubs are welcome. Planning permission has been obtained for a staging development on the riverside. All that is now needed is hard cash. It publishes a most useful guide to local facilities for visiting yachtsmen. Its rituals go far back and members seem intent on keeping them here to stay. It is not quite cucumber sandwiches on the lawn under spreading trees; but it comes close and suggests the exceptional gifts of not only sailing on water but also walking on the stuff. I was once introduced as 'that writer chappie'.

I am indebted to another writer chappie, Frank Cowper, who, when writing in 1893, said:

The Royal Harwich Yacht Club acknowledges only seven yacht clubs, out of a total list of thirty-eight such establishments, as its seniors. The venerable Royal Cork Yacht Club, which was founded in 1720, is the *doyen* of the yachting associations. Nearly a century elapsed before England started a club of her own. In 1812 the Royal Yacht Squadron was formed, followed by the Royal Thames in 1823, and the Royal Northern in 1824, then came the Royal Western of England in 1827. After another eleven years two yacht clubs were started in 1838: the Royal London, in England, and the Royal St. George, at Kingston, Ireland. Then the eastern counties caught the enthusiasm for this manly sport, and Harwich became the headquarters of the Royal Harwich. In 1893 it will celebrate its Jubilee, and the club is bestirring itself to mark the event with some suitable distinction. The Duke of Hamilton is the commodore.

The RHYC is very close to the next station up the river – Woolverstone Marina – which has both swinging moorings and pontoon berths. It is on the port hand, between Cathouse and green No. 7. Visitors' berths are, in the main, on the hammer heads of the outer pontoons. A little further upstream are more berths for visitors immediately round the port corner. The harbourmaster has an office well situated so that he can see all craft, whether berthed, coming or going. Frequently there is one of his colleagues to lend a hand to visitors. The harbour staff are well informed, alert and witty to a point; friendly and co-operative to a degree. There are very good and wide-ranging boating

The River Orwell has many photogenic visions to offer: from a busy estate of floating des. res's . . .

services. The well-stocked chandlery is at the top of a short, well-stepped but demanding hill. On the domestic front, next door, there are modest facilities for food and drink.

Upstream, the buoyage can be a bit difficult to spot above Cathouse, with a number of greens being difficult to isolate from their confusing backgrounds, especially with incipient mist. However, a reasonable middle-of-the-road track is to make for the middle arch of the 'new' road bridge with its air draught of 40m. Look out for blind green No. 11, just before the bridge, where there is a dogleg. In poor visibility it is easy to make an error, since some of the buoys are numberless.

Almost immediately after Woolverstone, towards the NE bank, by the unmarked green buoy between Prior and Mulberry, there is a green beacon that tells of a small broken down jetty, dangerous pipes and stakes, and slightly further upstream there are some standard diamond beacon cautionaries.

On the southwest side, along Downham Reach and then Freston Reach, the scenery all round becomes staggeringly beautiful – especially when the sun is in the right quarter. It is especially so on the south bank where, by the red Deer Park buoy, it is no longer little deer but big cows that are to be seen grazing graciously and gracefully in the splendid park. Standing proud and brave are castles, red brick walls and halls and palaces. Then, to change the ambience utterly and abruptly, there is a hostelry at neighbouring Freston where you can put your foot in the door; or get your feet under the table. It is called the Boot Inn.

Not far upstream of the bridge come the first signs of the commercial works and docks that, from here on, are to take over the river. However, our interest lies on the west bank where there is still a residue of small-town-atmosphere. It is Fox's Marina, known now as it has been for years. It is the penultimate of

the marinas, easily spotted on the port hand by the red No. 12. The approach channel has now been dredged to take vessels up to 2m at all states of the tide, and the stake/piling is clear to follow. General expansion has been the order of the day, but the old order of well-organised, fast and friendly service has not changed; nor have its bills yet escalated out of sight. It is charmingly tucked away, if that is how you can describe a marina with more than a 100 berths. It is situated in a quiet corner that gives immediate access to a splendid pub and a general stores.

Not long ago, it was almost impossible to find a 'chance' berth in the marina, but now chances are better. Over the years, it has 'suffered' all kinds of sea changes. It has been known variously as Fox's, Ipswich, Oyster and other sobriquets; it has been part and parcel of all kinds of big-bang financial wheeling/dealing; but it has never ceased to improve its skills, its services, its facilities, its facade and its image. It is a welcoming and efficient place, with power and water on all pontoons; new toilets, showers, and yacht spray centre (always one of the specials). Diesel and gas are available. There is a splendid chandlery, one of the best on the East Coast. The new man at the helm, responsible for much of what has changed and improved in the recent past is John Munns.

It is also possible to approach the Ostrich Yacht Club which maintain premises north of the marina. Shoresides and waterfronts can be well sussed out from the road bridge while en route for shopping. It also has its moorings in the river.

Doubles was a quaint shop until it was taken over. It is no longer quaint, but the range of goods is good. I visited the much older Ostrich (1612) the first time I came here, and cannot forget the joy with which I read the following: 'I Thomas Pimper, drank 2 cups of Sack with my friend J. Hotlip 8th May 1698 in this house and 6 cups this day April 1702.' Nearly 300 years on, sack butting has to be on its way out as the Ostrich makes inexorable upwardly mobile moves.

At one time, Fox's was virtually the head of navigation for leisure craft except for those daring skippers who were prepared to take their own and their boat's chancy chances in the Cut. Having seen it at both high and low water, I would never take *Valcon* within spitting or barge-pole distance (nor even the dinghy, for it is dingy at best and hazardous at worst). In any case there is now no need, since there is the new Neptune Marina, so a foray almost into the centre of the city can at last be achieved by boat.

How pleasantly surprising to have a new and attractive marina in such a splendid old spot. It is a small family concern and, while it is not yet fully developed, it is an ongoing concern. It has been running for some time and is on the way up. The many attractions of the noble city of Ipswich make a visit to this friendly and efficient marina a desirable must for those cruising the River Orwell.

. . . to all the charms of a nearly isolated week-end retreat.

The unmistakable 'new' Orwell road bridge (air draught 40m), navigable through the obviously largest 'middle' arch.

Bottom Over the years, Fox's Marina has 'suffered' all kinds of sea changes; and has been known variously as Fox's, Ipswich, Oyster and has frequently attracted other sobriquets – but Fox's is the one that sticks.

Angela Swann, one of the directors, is usually there to welcome visitors at tide time, and you could not wish for a warmer welcome. The marina has over 100 pontoon berths alongside with a minimum depth of 15ft . . . and is expanding.

Its services occupy the ground floor of the well-known and much-missed chandlery and sailmaking building of Whitemore's. There is a snooker bar and club room – an unusual combination. There is also a pleasing walk to the Tolly Cobbold Brewery and pub on Cliff Quay. Neptune Marina provides the following navigation information:

When entering or leaving Neptune Marina, contact the Orwell Navigation Service (Ipswich Port Radio) VHF Channel 14 to check approaches to the lock specifying your destination as Neptune Marina. The marina can be seen directly ahead of you as you pass through the lock gates identified by a large red 'Visitors' Berths' sign. Marina staff can be contacted on VHF channel 37.

Entry through lock gates – Locking times for leisure craft wishing to enter or leave the Ipswich Dock are now as follows:

Arrival may be made during the period 2 hours before to 40 minutes following high water.

Departure may be made from 2 hours before and up to high water This may be varied by special arrangement.

Vessels leaving should have no difficulty in arranging departure to coincide with the level time, however do

The 'new' Neptune Marina is an attractive family-run growing concern. It has been running for some time; and is on the way up. Ipswich Dock was once a Mecca denied to all but a few privileged yachtsmen. Things have now improved dramatically, and a great deal of the dockland area has been given over to leisure and pleasure.

remember that the movement of the lock gates is tide-sensitive

Commercial craft have right of way at all times and skippers must obey the lock signals (red and green lights) and the lock-keeper's orders.

If you arrive outside the lock opening times the Neptune Marina lay-by pontoon, situated just above Fox's on the port hand, is available to clients.

When planning your cruise, telephone us if visiting and seeking a berth. Minimum alongside depth of water at Neptune Quay 2·5m.

It is possible to navigate to Ipswich at all states of the tide. The lock is 91m by 15·2m and is manned 24 hours; but the lock crew is mustered only between 2 hours before and 1 hour after HW. Yachts are asked to navigate at levels between the river and the wet dock, as and when these occur. That can vary from as much as 2 hours around tide time, to no level being achieved at all. Harbour staff will instruct.

Ipswich Dock was once a Mecca denied to all but a few privileged yachtsmen. Things have now improved dramatically, and a great deal of the dockland area has been given over to leisure and pleasure. Already completed are the differing premises of the Consular Building and Mortimer's on the Quay. Both are appealing from the outside, but Mortimer's has added delights inside for connoisseurs of fish.

More new buildings and refurbishments have made this area, by the attractive old custom house, quite unrecognisable. Not even Prince Charles would be likely to suggest that what has happened to the old malt kiln can be described as carbuncling. The old custom house is of great interest. I am indebted to the Ipswich Maritime Trust for the following information:

The Old Custom House, as it has come to be known, flanking the Common Quay, is one of the finest buildings in Ipswich. Within this is a spirited carving of the Borough arms with the lion rampant and three half ships or hulks. The origin of the arms is not known but they probably date from the first charter granted to the borough by King John in the year 1200. The lion symbolises the crown and the three half ships can also be found in the arms of the Cinque Ports in Kent. The blazon was confirmed during the reign of Queen Elizabeth I in 1560 and augmented with the seahorse supporters and a crest with a demi-lion carrying a ship in full sail. The seahorses are mythical beasts with the head of a horse and the body of a fish.

With the Ipswich Dock Act of 1837, the River Orwell, which opened out into a wide expanse of water below Stoke Bridge, was contained within the New Cut and the Wet Dock created with an entrance lock from New Cut East. The outer end of this can still be seen and the row of keepers' cottages, now the harbourmaster's office. The Wet Dock was opened with little ceremony on a wintry afternoon on 17 January 1842. This was done by closing the gates for the first time. The first vessel to pass through the lock was the brig *Zephyr* with a cargo of coal from the Tyne.

Ipswich town is packed with interest and there is much to explore. I would like to draw attention to three attractions in particular. The first is the Amberstone Bookshop at 49 Upper Orwell Street; a bookshop with the care of the Olde Worlde but with all the swiftness and efficiency of the new. The

IPSWICH
52°03'N 01°09'·7E

Charts Admiralty 2693. Imray Y16. OS Landranger 169.

Tides
Dover +0120

Tidal access
HW –2hrs to HW +¾hr. Call Ipswich Port Radio on VHF Ch 14 before arrival; then Neptune Marina to arrange a berth, VHF Ch M, 14. Lock is manned from -2hrs to HW+1hr.

Authorities
Harbourmaster ☎ 01473 231010. Radio VHF Ch 12, 14, 16 (24 hrs). Call *Ipswich Port Radio*.

Locking signals
Day
Ball at masthead south end of west pier head – Proceed outward
Ball and flag at masthead - Proceed inward
Ball at yardarm - Dock closed
Night
Light on mast at south end of west pier head for inward-bound vessels
Light on pole at north end of east pier head for outward-bound vessels
Green light - Vessels to enter lock
Red light - Lock closed

Neptune Marina
☎ 01473 215204/780366. Radio VHF Ch M, 14

Tidal access
HW -2hrs to HW + ¾hr
Ⓥ (Visitors' pontoons) 🚻, ▣, ⚓, ⚡, ⚓, Provisions, D, P, Engineer, Repairs

---

second is the Magnus Fish and Game shop at 14 Tacket Street. They all know almost all there is to know about what they sell; and they love it. The third is what must be one of the best ironmongers (hardware, as I am told it is known in today's jargon) in the UK – Martin & Newbury. Long may they be with us; for they are among the last of the few.

The Stour

This is what I wrote in the third edition: 'In conclusion, the Stour is no place for those in search of sophistication or comprehensive facilities; nor for that matter those who want no more than a safe and relatively comfortable berth. It is, in essence, a singular chapter in an eclectic book, suited best to those who are used to taking and suffering pains, but who still remain susceptible to the very real pleasures of shoal-draught art and craft. The fact that I am not a fully paid up, card-carrying member, will, in the long run I am sure, rebound only to my loss.'

I now write: 'Veni, vidi, vici' – except that, in my instance, it was a case of 'I came, I saw, I *was* conquered'. So, after being able to spend over a week in the lower and upper reaches of the Stour, I now defer to all my early critics and confess that I have quite changed my mind: the river, pure and simple, converted me and overcame my previous prejudiced.

And so, to start again, I was straightway lucky at the mouth, for I was in the presence of not only two huge Russian merchant ships (looking as threateningly great and impossibly grand as only they can) but also of two equally magnificent examples of Thames barges. They were all at ease; and following in the massive wakes of the Russian and the calm ripples of the barges, I slowly made my way past Shotley Marina and Parkeston Quay.

The area near Shotley is an interesting and rewarding part of the river, bringing together many aspects of thriving commerce: entrepreneurs hard at work on their mobile phones; business if not merchant venturers practising their craft; pleasure seekers; as well as those princes of sea-traffic and all the land trappings that accompany the ever-busy, ever-growing Haven Ports.

During the Napoleonic Wars, Nelson anchored by Shotley; and, in the 14–18 war, Harwich was significant again as a naval station. After the war, 150 German submarines came to surrender there. Shotley Point, was the site of the one-time infamous training ship HMS *Ganges*, which stood until 1976. It was named after the 1821 sailing ship. The area was also famous for the Thames barges that it built.

Overall, the river extends for 35 miles between Harwich and its (now weeded-up) source. The 25 miles above Manningtree are acknowledged as among some of the most beautiful in England, if not the world. They certainly had their appeal for some painters' eyes, having been immortalised by Constable and Gainsborough, in their pieces of rural, natural and quite unpainterly scenery.

It is reported, or reputed, that Horace Walpole called it 'the charmingest place by nature and the most trumpery by art,' that he had ever seen.

The *Admiralty Pilot* says of the Stour:

. . . flows into Harwich Harbour from W, provides communication with Mistley and Manningtree, 8 miles above Harwich. Its banks are from ¼ to 1 mile wide, but the navigable channel is reduced to a width from 1 to 3 cables by drying mud flats extending from the banks; these mud flats are intersected by creeks. There are dredged depths of 7·2m off Harwich, thence the depth decreases irregularly as the river is ascended. The channel winds but is well marked. There is only about 0·5m when nearing Mistley.

The 10 miles from Shotley to Manningtree start off being pretty bleak and featureless, and there is little in the shoreline foreground that is of interest; but, before the headland of Erwarton Ness is reached, the church at Erwarton stands out among the few trees in the background as if to mark the beginning of something special in view. The hall is an Elizabethan manor house, and is worth a special viewing if you feel like anchoring and crawling off for a stout walk.

When given time and the right light in which to view the locale, it shows itself to be varied in its scenery with, in fact, some splendid views across the river. Erwarton Ness stands out as an isolated peninsular with some high ground round it. Near the jetty, the solid muddy shore is fairly close-to, and it is not difficult to get ashore if you have the right gear. The mud flats are a haven for black-tailed godwits and, frequently, herons attend, so unafraid that they seem almost friendly.

After Erwarton Ness, the river continues its wide spread with a narrow channel in the middle. A channel which occupies no more than a third of the totality, the rest being saltings. Passing Harkstead Point, with its wooded bank of many dead trees leaning at dramatic angles as if signifying something not at rest, we come to Wrabness Point to the south and the vast Holbrook Bay. They are marked by cardinal Holbrook and the green Horse buoy. About a third of the way into Holbrook Bay there is anchorage in which a craft up to a metre will stay afloat most of the time.

The Royal Hospital School stands out as conspicuously as a sore thumb on the hand of a surgeon. Preferential treatment is given to boys with a seafaring family background, especially orphans. It is actually part of Greenwich Hospital, started by William and Mary in the 17th century and first got under way in 1712 in Greenwich Palace. Try as I may to be generous, I cannot but find it lacking in aesthetic appeal – in fact, its massive tower looks downright ugly.

However, exactly the opposite must be said of the scenery, and also of the modest buildings that cluster in small parcels on the shoreline between Wrabness Point and Nether Hall. It is all quite miniature in magnitude, its eminence being based in its peculiar quality. Nearby is a safe, well-protected anchorage just by the moorings at Wrabness Point, with 2·0m at low water. Shore access is easy at all times, though the village is achieved only after something of an uncompromising uphill walk.

Truly, let it be said that it is only the peace and quiet that can in any way justify or compensate for the narrow and tortuous channel that wends its way through the broad stretches of the river from there to the barrier at Cattawade. Mistley and Manningtree can be approached at high water, preferably on spring tides, with the buoyed channel being strictly observed with an additional eye on the sounder. Commercial vessels navigate to Mistley, but that doesn't mean that anybody can. It takes a better man than I to get more than a dinghy right up to Manningtree. But I am sure that is incompetence.

In the old days, Mistley must have been a glory to behold, with all the sailing ships and barges, the well-treed banks, the gorgeous houses. I am told that the well-known aesthete and wit, de la Rochefoucauld, wrote of them thus in the late 18th century:

Grand guardians, wondrous wardens, sombre sentinels or mere lightships: what's a name..they are just imposingly splendid.

Mistley is a very pretty place consisting of rather more than 50 houses, which are so neat and well built, that it is obvious at a glance that they all belong to one man. The harbour is faced with a high brick wall to which the whalers are fixed. At the end of it there is quite a large warehouse where merchants put all they want without paying. At the end of the harbour there is a small shipbuilding yard in which I saw two forty-tonners under construction. Near the port there is a lime-kiln which has been faced with brick and made into the shape of a fort. Mistley Hall is of white brick. The drawing rooms and dining rooms are magnificent. There are nine acres of kitchen garden with fruit trees from France; large hot houses with peaches, pineapples and cherries.

Both Mistley and Manningtree lay claim to fame as head-hunters of Matthew Hopkins, Witchfinder General to the Commonwealth. His headquarters were at the Thorn Inn and, from there, he directed an operation that was responsible for the murder of some 400 souls in the name of God. During the mid-17th century, all kinds of folk, mainly female and many young, were brought there to be harassed and finally charged with the practice of witchcraft.

So successful were his persecutions and prosecutions that he became fabulously rich. The whole scene was disgusting; anyone with 'unnaturals' on their body – scars, warts, boils . . . indeed almost any excrescence – was likely to be deemed a witch. Confessions were frequent and swift – denial of light, fresh air and food and drink soon brought about misery and depletion; and when the victims seemed in an appropriate state, 'prickers' were brought in to show that they would not bleed because they had been infected by the devil.

At the end of such a session, it was no wonder that they would rather face death by drowning than try to hang on for a longer and even 'grimmer death'. The victims were immersed in water (fully, that is, in the way of John the Baptist) and if they died by drowning, they were deemed not guilty; but if they did not die by drowning, they were deemed guilty, and then died by hanging. Catch 22. It is not certain how Matthew Hopkins became immersed in his grisly career or how he met his end. He was born the son of a vicar, the Reverend James Hopkins, of Great Wenham in Suffolk. He visited The Netherlands during his youth and may have received part of his education there. He may also have witnessed the persecution of the Huguenots. Hopkins started work as a solicitor's clerk in Ipswich before moving to a shipping office in Mistley. Although he may have started hunting witches at first for financial reasons, he soon became flushed with his success and obsessed by power and, before long, he was a fanatic. He came to believe that he had been divinely appointed to his task and that he was in possession of the 'Devil's List' of English witches.

In 1647 a record was made of a son of the vicar of Wenham (supposedly Matthew's father) being buried in Mistley Church. Legend then takes over more completely – there are those who like to think he died by the sword; others from the damp from hiding in the Mistley Pools, marshes and damp cellars; and, of course, by his own schema – drowned, as it were, by his own petard.

Indeed, the facts surrounding the 'death' of Matthew Hopkins suggest an enigma as broad and as long as that of his life. It seems that he 'disappeared' sometime during the early spring to summer of 1647, and no one seems to have noted or noticed the event. Best advice is that he was quietly done away with (in his pond) by those who wished rid of him but had no wish to make a martyr of him.

So, after such unhappy tales, let tranquillity take over in my peroration. The River Stour is not for the sophisticate socialiser; nor the pontoon seeker; nor yet for the gin-and-tonic-on-the-third-storey-of-a-broom-broom brigade. No, it is quite definitely what I hinted at the beginning – it is a special in a singular chapter in an unusual book; but one that is worth searching out with all the diligence that your draught will permit.

The Walton Backwaters

It is over 20 years since I first visited the Walton Backwaters, a complex network which appears, at high water, to be one vast inland sea with one island and a few humps; yet which, at low water, reveals itself to be acres of mud flats and saltings with hundreds of creeks, channels and dykes, all ready to challenge, mystify and intrigue the navigator . . . especially a first visitor. For me, they have never lost their appeal.

On my first visit, I had been told to set a course of 345° to 350° from the Stone Banks buoy to bring into line three large white buildings. Then I was to line up the lower of the old Dovercourt lights, and the Pye End buoy would be between the left-hand buildings. I spent ages sorting out the multiplicity of possible candidates for white buildings before rejecting that approach and returning to the chart and the hand bearing compass.

In addition, I was becoming rapidly exhausted by having to contend and bargain with 101 spotted dinghies, all racing like mad. Then, in spite of all my work with white buildings, directions, charts and the hand bearing compass, I still could lay neither hand (glass) nor eye (compass) upon the elusive Pye End buoy. I jilled around for another 15 minutes knowing I had to be at least somewhere near the right spot. In the end I felt forced to admit defeat, for by now the tide was ebbing and I had visions of a forced night's vigil on the Stone.

So, reluctantly, because I lacked the confidence to do other, I steamed up to a couple of nearby boats that had been there for at least half an hour. I hailed the four fishermen: 'Where can I find the Pye End buoy?' They nudged the two boats only slightly apart to expose and display a gleaming one-eyed red-and-white monster – the Pye End buoy. Their faces were a delight to behold; and mine must have been a sight to see. During the time that I had been baffled, stymied and foiled in my search for the wretched buoy, they had been quietly replacing it after a service.

It has now been renewed, revamped and very slightly increased in size, and is the responsibility of Trinity House. In bright sunlight it winks at you from all of 2 miles away. But its notorious obscurity still exists in legend.

Years and many Pye End-probes later, I now know that there is no serious hazard in the area and calm scrutiny 'unearths' it without fuss. And, in any case, Decca and the like have, of course, rendered such a search a different kind of game.

The landmark that stands out when approaching from the south is the tower at Walton-on-the-Naze. The Medusa Channel, that leads from the Naze to Stone Banks and Pye Sand is, named after HMS *Medusa* which escaped the Dutch fleet by using this, hardly then known, short cut. It can take a long time to spot the red buoy, Stone Banks, for it does not always stand out well against the low-lying background in an unfavourable, albeit pleasant, sunlight.

In general, it is just not sensible for strangers to be navigating around the Halliday Rock Flats and Pennyhole Bay at anything less than half tide. You won't be able to get into the Backwaters before this time, and you will only risk finding the bottom fairly frequently. Should you ever make the trip to the Backwaters from the Haven Ports area, it is worth knowing that a wind-against-tide configuration will expose you to the peaks and troughs of a quite unpleasant beam sea.

The way in lies southwesterly from Pye End; the buoyed channel being entered between Crabnowe Spit and the extremity of Pye Sand, both of which dry out. Once the sands have been covered, the area is a vast desert of a sea with only the modest buoys for guidance. Once you are in the channel proper (and it does not begin to feel that way until past the tighter gate of red 6 and green 7) the way is then plain sailing.

I have always tended to the north when making my way to the first Backwaters 'gate' of No. 2 red and green Crab Knoll, and have found as much water there as in the channel itself. This cannot be said if you deviate too far to the south. Modest the buoys may be but they are extremely well maintained and supported by local good causes and benefactors. For example, green No. 5 reads 'Heather J'; while there are reds for 'Titchmarsh Marina'; 'Support the RNLI'; and the Walton and Frinton Yacht Club.

The buoys are easily observed all the way up to Island Point, the junction for Stone Point and the Twizzle or Horsey Island and the Backwaters themselves. This is how Arthur Ransome described the approach:

'Crossroads buoy,' said Roger as they passed it.

A minute or two later they had left the open bay and the *Goblin* was slipping easily along in the quiet water of an inland sea. A low spit of land with a dyke along it already hid the creek that led to the town, though they could still see the tops of distant masts. Far away, on the opposite side, was another low dyke. Standing on the deck and in the cockpit they could see bushes here and there. Ahead of them the inland sea seemed to stretch on for ever.

'What's it called?' asked Titty, from the foredeck.

Daddy smiled. 'Do you want the name on Jim's chart? I thought you'd give it a name yourselves.'

'It's a very secret place,' said Roger. 'You don't see it until you're almost inside.'

'Secret Water,' said Titty. 'Let's call it that.'

The Island Point north cardinal marks the major junction. Here goes up the cry 'All Change', for this is the parting of the ways round Horsey Island. To port is the much-used main channel that leads to the Twizzle and to Walton itself. Just to starboard, but more or less straight ahead, lies the main Hamford

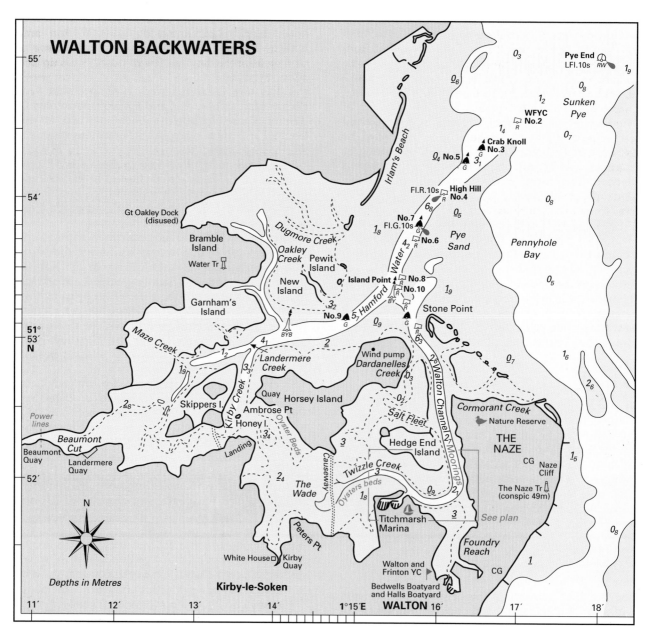

Water route between acres and acres of saltings, mud flats and the vast capriciously drying areas to the north. To the south, the down to real earth solid Horsey island is clear to see. The more used channel is the one that leads to Walton and Titchmarsh Marina, and we will turn towards that way first.

Upon entering Walton Creek, there are two red canned withies to mark the channel, just after Stone Point and by Stone Creek. The first of these, the major landmark Stone Point, is an extremely popular leisure spot for anchoring and landing. The shingle/sand is clean and steep-to and the holding ground sound provided you have the substantial tackle required for that area. The tide runs hard here for the first 2 hours of the ebb, so it is advisable to take careful soundings and give the chain good scope, for you can easily get caught out and/or taken short by Stone. Others lay off so far that the congregation from time to time extends across the fairway; with not many anchor balls in sight. Once, I was mystified by a white fender displayed in the rigging.

Now comes true island/creek/inlet territory. There are numerous very small islands and a massive area of mud and saltings: Stone Marsh Island; Horsey Island; Stone Creek; Dardanelles Creek, Cormorant Creek, Bad Luck Creek, Crab Creek and many more anonymous leftovers. Before we reach the Twizzle, it is worth noting that the area is well-protected from most weather; a safe haven with a good, deep anchorage.

These are the last places where it is possible to anchor before going up the major fairway of Walton Channel and then on to Twizzle Creek where there are so many moorings; so many discarded and broken pieces of ground tackle; and so many troublesome foul reaches that there is space for neither boat nor anchor to stay in safety.

Once past the Dardanelles and Stone Creeks, the Walton Channel runs north/south between the upstanding Naze to the east and the low-lying, diminutive Hedge-end Island to the west. In good conditions, the fairway can easily be identified by the swinging craft but, with gusty winds, the same craft merely muddle the stranger. After a mile, the channel divides; the southerly continuation becomes Foundry Reach and leads to the Walton and Frinton Yacht Club, the boatyards, and the town hard. The westerly arm, after a dramatic 90° turn, becomes Twizzle Creek – or the 'Twizzle' as it is usually known. It leads, first, to Titchmarsh Marina, then to those acres of flats known as the Wade – the vast drying area south of Horsey Island and north of the mainland.

First we will tackle Foundry, sometimes called Creek and sometimes Reach. The course is dead ahead and we find ourselves in more of a mature gutway than minor creek. The Foundry leads to that fount of all Naze knowledge, the Walton and Frinton Yacht Club. It is possible to achieve a landing from the dinghy a few hundred yards up this reach, but it is wiser and cleaner to get right up to the club's hard and/or quayside. Here we are very close to the shallows and wallows that are known as

---

The Walton Backwaters consist of a complex network of creeks that thread their peaceful ways round innumerable small islands. It can be a very curious experience, being apparently land-locked by near-joined low-lying islands with ditches, gutways and creeks infesting them. Here, we are looking at the entrance, with famous Stone Point just to the left in the middle distance.

Foundry Reach (or Creek) offers dinghy landings for a few hundred yards, but it is better to move up to the yacht club's hard or quayside. Next do or are the shallows of The Great Mere: a large area of drying patches, mud and saltings.

Walton Mere (a great space of drying patches, much mud and some saltings). The clubhouse sits at the virtual head of navigation and is the arbiter of taste for all yachtsmen in the area. The adjacent quay is extremely well kept and has beacons to show the entry. They should be closely observed and complied with. The town is very close and nearby are possible short- and long-term moorings.

At the entrance to the creek, there can be as little as 1·0m at LWS. Walton and Frinton Yacht Club undertakes the mainly thankless task of furnishing and maintaining the blind buoys in the channel. If you are a keen member of the yachting club trail, it will lead you straight to their front door and, after, right into the town. The interior of their clubhouse

is inviting with some of it laid out as if in expectation of a great event. The style is irrefutably impeccable without being decadent.

On a number of visits I have made up Foundry Creek, there have been non-U boys almost chanting 'Watch your boat for 20p, mister?' The first was of the Charles Dickens Greatly Expecting type of youth. Since I wanted to go into the town fairly smartly, I bought his offer; returning to find the dinghy hitched to another with no visible means of my being able to reach it. A couple of years later, I was approached by an apparently more trustworthy youth. His price was high at 50p, but I (naïvely if not even stupidly) thought this might guarantee a better quality of service. Again the dinghy was inaccessible. 'If a man deceive you once; shame on him. If a man deceive you twice; shame on you.'

The pontoon and drying mud berths in the attractive yacht basin are administered by Bedwell's for the Walton and Frinton Yacht Trust. Craft up to 14·0m and 1·80m draught have access for about an hour each side of high water for the 10–12 days around spring tides. However, there is no guarantee, for sometimes the water does not reach even the 1·5m mark. Berths may be allocated to visitors upon application to the boatyard, which is usually open from 10am to 4pm. It is, of course, best to telephone well ahead.

At the Town Quay there is also a small top-of-the-tide hard landing with a territorially imperative notice outlining the laws regarding the mandatory removal and obligatory impounding of boats whose owners have committed sins of commission or omission. It is packed with boats, and nearby can be seen, at the walls and gates, the sturdy defences against the flood.

This general area, made up of dry land, mud and saltings sometimes known as Walton Mere, is not one devoted to the touring cruising industry, so it just as well to call ahead of any boating visit to see for yourself what is what, and make any necessary arrangements. The buildings are singularly appealing, in spite of signs of decay, decline and deterioration.

If not creeping up Foundry Creek, or heading straightway for one of the Backwater anchorages to find a remote spot, my prime recommendation is for you to visit one of the most amenable facilities on the East Coast: Titchmarsh Marina – a most agreeable spread more or less at the head waters of the Twizzle. It used to be a quiet, low-key operation and, while it has definitely moved with the times, it is still no razzmatazz affair. In spite of its size (500+ berths) it has kept its quiet charm, but at no sacrifice to efficiency.

Generally speaking, visitors take up berths outside on the sturdy, well-maintained pontoons before the entrance, or make their way inside to ask for berthing instructions. It is also possible for small craft to moor on the inside of these pontoons. Past the entrance, to the westward, there are mooring piles. The channel to the inner moorings is usually accessible for 1·5m craft at all times but, at low water springs, with unfavourable winds and a bad barometer, there can be as little as 0·5m. In exceptional circumstances it can reduce to a trickle.

From his new crow's nest, the harbourmaster commands a view up to the Deben and, strictly speaking, he keeps office hours (although he generally stays open all hours). This new 'nest' was achieved by lifting the top of the old one by crane, waiting until the next floor was built and then just dropping it back again.

Most boating facilities are available on the spot, and there is now a small domestics section in the chandlery. From time to time you can buy not-quite-yet-landed fish at the end of the pontoon without having to pay through the nose for it. Perhaps more significantly for cruising folk, the Harbour Lights restaurant and bar is a flourishing and welcome recent addition.

For full-blown comestibles and domestics you must make the pleasant walk to the shop and pub via the marina lane to the main road. It takes no more than half an hour – dependent on age, ability and attitude. Here, you can also catch a bus to take you into Walton town.

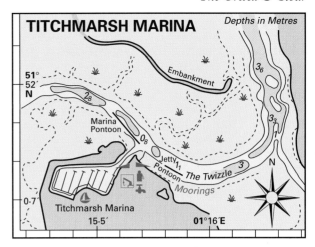

Titchmarsh Marina has not been transformed (that was never needed), but its recent expansion and refurbishment have made it even more popular than before. It is an excellent social centre from which to explore the loneliness of the Long Distance Backwaters.

All in all, it is a splendid spot for cruising people, be they novice, sophisticate or even world-weary cynics; all are assured of a truly East-Coast welcome.

So, having approached the town via the back way, it is now time to open the door. The Walton district is very flat, as the names of nearby Holland-on-Sea and Holland Haven suggest, with only the Ness for relief. Seated atop is the famous Trinity House tower, commanding the territory for miles from land or sea. Viewed from the water, Walton looks pleasing enough, but close-to it is an encounter to be honoured in the breach rather than the experience. Tourist-besotted beyond sense; specialising in Brummagem; and failing in its provision of most significant offices, it does not make for an agreeable visit. 'To travel hopefully is a

better thing than to arrive,' and if ever a place justified Stevenson's view, it is Walton-on-the-Naze.

The greengrocers and the Co-op are now in pale puce-to-pink paint, and the funhouse games shop with its lit-up-tit lights has disappeared. The plastic-covered tabletops of the 'traditional' Pie & Mash Shop ('eels stewed or jellied') are well used indeed. Otherwise, nothing seems to have changed in 20 years; certainly there is still a super-abundance of wheeler-dealer, second-hand shops. I suspect that this notice is symbolic: 'Please use this bin for general litter and wrapped dog mess. Failure to do so could cost you a £1,000.00.'

So, back to Island Point for the other route and into a perspective of quite a different kind. First comes the major waterway, Hamford Water. It is the key to the diverse and disparate channels and dykes, islands and islets, mud flats and saltings that make up the most, and the most attractive, parts of the Walton Backwaters. The first, and main, anchorage is on the south side of Hamford Water, just before the cardinal marking Oakley Creek. There are two other creeks that lead off Hamford and they are Landermere and Kirby.

While the multitude of quiet creeks has become increasingly popular over the years, it is still possible to find near-secluded anchorages where you will almost certainly be on your own. Altogether, there are ten low-lying islands in the Hamford Water group with a combined area of little more than five square miles. Many of them are separated by difficult-to-see narrow channels and, confusingly, reed-covered meres. While there is good grazing in places, and here and there the isolated brick farmhouse, much of the area is marshland, visited only by wildlife. (The Essex Wildlife Trust and the Naturalists' Society use Skipper's Island.) At one of the stations there is the legend: 'This area is managed for the benefit of wildlife. No Landing.' (Actually, just before the landing, to the southwest of Honey Island, there is deepish hole, which permits craft of up to 2·0m to stay afloat at all states.)

The Backwaters consist of a complex network of creeks that thread their peaceful ways round innumerable small islands. One could spend a week or more exploring the various waterways, although even in a dinghy many are only navigable at high tide; and this leaves little time for exploration. It can be a curious experience, being apparently land-locked by near-joined low-lying islands infested with ditches, gutways and creeks.

For an attractive first exploration, I suggest leaving the main Hamford Water anchorage (which can get rough in a brisk northeasterly) to make for the nearby Kirby Creek. It lies between Horsey and Skipper's Islands, with an entrance channel that has a substantial bar. Indeed it is a wide swathe of a bar, reaching well to the north of the islands. It is so wide, deep, shallow and misleading that even dinghies have been known to strand on it. The way in is marked by the central buoy (Fishery). Both drying side banks are marked by withies. The traditional anchorage in Kirby Creek lies between Horsey and Skipper's Island. In the creek, there are oyster layings for the first five cables to port, with the 'S Oyster' buoy designating the 'upstream' limit of the layings. They are so clearly marked that it is easy to avoid them. Sometimes it is possible to use one of the available moorings, but do be prepared to be moved along at any hour, for the indigens and other holders have a habit of coming and going at quite unexpected hours. As, indeed, does the HM Customs launch. You may think you are all alone, but that is not always the case.

When I first went to Kirby, Horsey Island sported a notice board bearing the solemn warning, 'HERE BE WITCHES'. It was a long time before the penny dropped. It was the country of Arthur Ransome's *Secret Water*, the well-known young people's adventure story published in 1939. Horsey Island was Swallow Island and my anchorage was Goblin Creek. The small landing opposite was Witch's Quay; and Horsey Mere was the Red Sea. It is intriguing to discover that his sketch maps are as relevant today as they were before the war.

I remember it as a really quiet spot, particularly in the evenings. More than once I was entertained by the sounds of grey mullet as they nuzzled and nibbled at *Valcon*'s hull. No sooner had they left me to the stillness of that secret place than another visitation took place. A wide spread of floating islets

---

WALTON-ON-THE-NAZE
51°54'·5N 0°16'·9E (No 2 buoy)

Charts Admiralty 2695. Imray Y16. OS Landranger 169.

Tides
Dover +0030

Authorities
Harbourmaster ☎ 01255 851887

Titchmarsh Marina Ltd
☎ 01255 672185/851901, Radio VHF Ch 80 (0800–2000)

Tidal access
1·3m LWS
Ⓥ (420, inc. visitors'), 🚾, ▣, ⚓, ⚡ (16 amp), ➘,
Ⓔ (nearby), ▮D, Engineer (nearby)

Walton & Frinton Yacht Club
☎ 01255 678161/675526

Tidal access
HW −2hrs to HW + 1hr
Ⓥ (60, 30 visitors' in season), 🚾, ▣ (0800–2300),
⚓, ⚡, ➘, Provisions (nearby), Ⓔ (nearby),
▮D (limited), Engineer (nearby), Repairs (nearby)

Walton Yacht Basin (Walton & Frinton YC)
☎ 01255 675526/675873

Tidal access
HW −2hrs to HW +1hr
Ⓥ (inc. visitors'), 🚾 (YC), ▣ (YC), ⚓ (YC),
⚡ (YC), ➘, Ⓔ (nearby), ▮D (nearby), ▮P (nearby),
Engineer (nearby), Repairs (nearby)

That fount of all Naze knowledge, the highly particular Walton and Frinton Yacht Club, has its clubhouse at the virtual head of navigation. It is the arbiter of taste for all yachtsmen in the area. The vast drying beds stand out clearly, while the channel is difficult to espy.

of grey-green phosphorescence covered the surface of the water. It stretched from side to side of the wide channel. The islets moved slowly towards me like an armada of water-borne wills-o'-the-wisp.

Once I got accustomed to the sight, I dropped small pebbles into the glowing swarms. The reward was a show of lights rising and falling like milky sparks in a watery way. It could have been a diminutive St Elmo's Fire.

My mind slowly emptied as I plopped stone after stone into the luminous sheen. I began to feel almost at one with those Jack o' the Marine Lanterns. I know there is a scientific explanation for that

phosphorescence, but I still prefer my own perception of that night's show of sheer natural magic.

The many creeks in the vicinity of Horsey Island are best explored by dinghy. Not only is it most enjoyable and relaxing on its own account but, from half tide to low water, it presents an opportunity to inspect the gutways when whims and deviations are at their most apparent. After which you can judge which are of the greatest appeal and take your boat without too much worry about finding bottom.

From Kirby Creek, there are three main directions to take for explorations – SE for the Wade and Kirby Quay; W for all points to Landermere and Beaumont Quays; and N for all the gutways and 'islands' off Bramble Island.

Visiting Horsey Mere and the Wade (the Causeway or Island Road) reveals that the hard itself uncovers at less than 2 hours each side of high water. Lorries seen apparently driving on the water create a strange, mirage-like, vision when seen from over the salting a mile or so away. Although much of the area is extremely soft mud, there are many patches in the vicinity that are far from unencumbered. It is satisfactory to discover that musselling here at low water can be rewarding.

Arthur Ransome's characters were also here:

'And we'll have to call all this the Red Sea.' She waved her hand towards the muddy plain with the cart road across it with withies sticking up. Already the water was creeping over the mud towards the road, a tongue of water from the east moving slowly on to meet another tongue of water from the west. 'Why?' said Roger. 'Pharaoh and the Israelites,' said Titty. 'Just the place for them. The waters divide when the tide goes down and they can rush across where those sticks mark the road, and then the water comes back from both ends and joins and sweeps them away, chariots and all.'

Now we return to Kirby Creek to foray for Kirby Quay, the key to the village of Kirby le Soken. We leave behind the anchorage by Ambrosia Point and the delightfully named Honey Island, to take the first starboard – the southerly – fork.

Even some of the smallest channels are marked by withies; but a lot of care and local knowledge is needed to interpret their actual meaning. There are withies that mark high-tide routes and withies that mark low-water gutways. Some have 'cryptic' topmarks (white, black, striped, red, green and so on) and, in addition, many lean so far away from their deep water that they misdirect. Indeed, all round are scars and trails, which flights of fancy advise were dredged or sculpted by the keel of some *Wandering Jew* or *Flying Dutchman*.

The last few cables to Kirby Quay consist of a very narrow gully which, when found, does indeed carry a decent depth; however, it takes real study and determination to master its intricacies. The close approach brings into view the large black Quay House, and its legend: 'Private quay and saltings. No access.' The channel actually leads to the back of the black house and its white neighbour; in fact, what was once a clear piece of pilotage information to 'look for the white house' should now read 'look around for a number of white houses'. From the gutway, they mostly looked bleak – all except the black house, from the windows of which beamed down the happy faces of dolls. The whole area is private, but the owners are friendly boating types. I was welcomed by the quite unexpected vision of a tall, young female figure in very modish gear. As she helped with the arduous task of getting the dinghy through the silt-soft mud, she confessed to being a sailing novice, but went on to say that her husband had mastered the gutway at all states of the tide and was quite proud of the achievement, sailing as he did in an old gaff cutter. Then the situation developed into a London bus-stop scenario. There had been no visitor before me that year – but I was followed only minutes later by another dinghy seeking out the landing. The mud here is extremely soft, so your feet can quickly sink deep. Appropriate foot and leg-

wear is essential unless your skin is to become encrusted.

From shoresides, the frontages show that they have been refurbished with care, looking much happier than they do from the rear. So the presence of 'smiling' children's toys in the windows had not been misleading after all. Not far down the lane is a miniature, black wooden cottage. Straight from a fairy tale, it has a thatched roof and red-brick chimney stack. It is known to all the *Secret Waters* characters and fans as the 'Witch's Cottage':

Away to the left was a broken down wooden fence, with a wicket gate in it, and beyond it a thatched cottage, a very small cottage of tarred black wood standing in a small potato patch. John went to the wicket gate, which stood half open . . . Somebody tapped at the window. The door of the cottage opened and a bent old woman stood on the threshold, leaning on a stick. The old woman did not answer. She began to cough, and her cough turned into a laugh and then into a cough again. She went back in her cottage. 'I bet she's a witch,' said Titty.

The surroundings are classically rural, with hedges of thistles, nettles and wild, wild flowers. Natural roses and tree-creeping plants flourish all round. It was a delight to see it still standing so prettily.

Leaving behind the path made up of large pebbles, you will arrive at a metalled road. Bordering it are large houses hidden behind high hedges and tall trees. This is the country of the gravelled drive, the large lawns set in large grounds, and the double garages with strikingly obvious burglar alarms. Their flower beds are as beautifully tended and impeccable as the properties themselves. Well kept, secluded and expensive, they are mainly contemporary in style. Those nearer to the village are older and have been refurbished – if not entirely rebuilt. They all have distinctly marked-out territorial boundaries.

Nearly at the main road, there is an edifice with an entirely different scene. It is cottage with a perfectly ordinary sign that announces, 'Vegetables to order'. In addition, it proclaims the presence of a chimney sweep who advertises himself as a 'flueologist'. No doubt the proximity of Frinton, on whose telephone exchange he is to be contacted, is the explanation for this euphemism.

Quay Lane gives directly on to the main road of Kirby-le-Soken village, where traffic and suburbia take over. There is a bus stop, a post office and general stores, and an excellent inn, the Ship ('16oz rump steak £5.50'). There are various routes to and from the Creek Head at Kirby Quay to the village. They are all appealingly different, but have in common the quality of quietness.

Now back to the Backwater. Navigating from Skipper's Island to Landermere is an arduous and tortuous business; while reaching the old Beaumont Quay is an almost impossible proposition, since there is such a confusion of islets and inlets, and so many mini-channels, some with withered withies. Towards the last of the 'afloat at all states' pools in the westerly stretch of Landermere Creek, are some well-kept, substantial mooring buoys – all clearly marked 'Private'. The owners are not, however, anti-visitors, indeed quite the opposite; so it is, from time to time, possible to use one of them. I think the whole area is totally delightful.

An entirely different locale is to be found in the waters to the north of Hamford Water and Landermere Creek. They are in the region of Bramble Island, Bull's Ooze and Oakley Creek. This outing takes us to the north, to one of the most isolated regions of the Backwaters. The main entrance can easily be discerned at any stage of the tide by the presence of the BYB cardinal.

We are now in the North Backwaters, where the main waterway runs north and south between Pewit and New Islands to the east and Garnham's and Bramble to the west. The tortuous channel permits access to craft of 1·5m for a mile or so, even at low water. It does, of course, require constant attention to soundings and surface water signs. There are plenty of sidings offering a safe anchorage. It is a really solitary spot.

The last time I searched out the nooks and crannies of these northern waters, I had made only a little progress when I heard sounds as of flipping, flopping and flapping. Turning to look, I saw, sliding and slithering down the muddy banks, a family of seals. At the water's edge, they dived to reappear close to the dinghy's stern. Like Brer Rabbit, I lay low, and was finally rewarded by the pups' curiosity overcoming any fears they might have had as they played a kind of hide and seek round the boat. It was really delightful that the present 'riparian' incumbents welcomed me with such joy.

Thereabouts is a water-skiing prohibition sign, and two stakes with radar topmarks. The huge retaining wall is in stark contrast to the wild rurality of the saltings. All the mud spits, as well as some of the banks, reach well out from their proper stations to search out your bottom. Beware.

All the creeks divide and sub-divide until there is such a plethora of disappearing ditches that one can easily become disorientated. It often seems that the creeks will continue into a veritable desert of mud – but also certainly ad libitum for those who wish to seek them out near low water. These isles and islets of mud turn themselves into amazing sculptures of nature's creation; an example to man and his artifices, as their banks and braes spread far and wide like a magical contour map.

Throughout the channels and by their headlands there are markers that are difficult for a stranger to interpret. Some have white topmarks (but it was only by trial and error that I discovered which side to leave them). Small cans and underwater spits abound and there was only one occasion when I was able to read their significance accurately; towards the head of Bramble Creek, out of the blue, appeared a standard 'gate' of one red and one green beacon. However, the chances of meeting traffic or

having to give way are remote, so their presence at all in such an isolated patch is unexpected.

Back in the main Oakley Creek, we turn off to the now-decaying jetty at Great Oakland into Bramble Creek. The first small jetty on the south side of Bramble Island is in good order and therefore, predictably, carries a notice: 'Trespassers will be prosecuted'. The rotting stumps on the other side suggest a decayed jetty and perhaps the site of an old ferry station. The stumps look like Gargantua's rotting teeth – reminders of busy days with ships and ferries and folk.

At its very head is the Old Moze Dock, but it is so long since any vessel of substance attempted the coup that it is now virtually inaccessible to all but the shoalest of craft. There are various landings in various stages of disrepair and numerous offshoot channels each attempting to search out the depths (as it were) of Garnham's.

Once more in the main creek, past the western part of Pewit Island, there comes the last, and smallest, of the great divides: Oakley Creek to the northwest and an unnamed creek that leads to Bull's Ooze, where at its most northerly it connects with Boat Creek and Dugmore Creek, finally winding its way back to the more open water opposite the Pye Sand. Intriguingly, these creeks are often parish boundaries, indicating the fervour of the founding fathers not to have their territorial advantages undermined . . . or watered down.

If the Walton Backwaters are to be properly appreciated, their secrets must be lovingly searched out, for they are almost as well kept now as they were in the days of the Real Secret Water. I have never spent an unhappy hour in the Walton Backwaters. They offer a choice of berthing or anchoring in well-protected conditions; the places likely to attract visitors are, in the main, all accessible at half tide or better; there are equal opportunities for full-blown revelling, mild socialising or almost completely disappearing into utter seclusion; and better-than-basic facilities are all within easy striking distance, with attractive walks. In addition, there are hundreds of miles of cruising waters literally on their watershed doorstep.

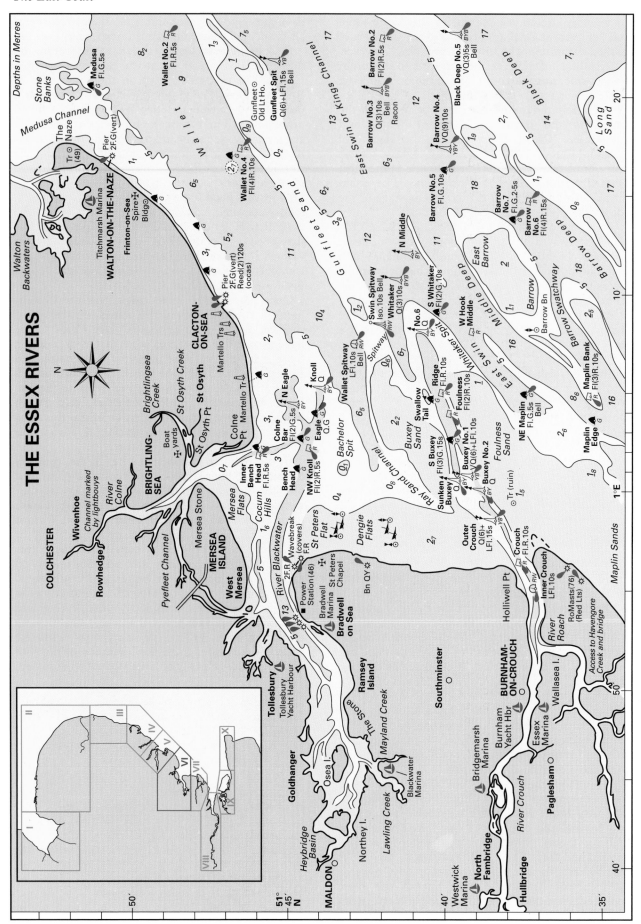

THE ESSEX RIVERS

VI. The Colne & Blackwater

From Harwich or the Walton Backwaters, it is no long haul down to the cardinal Knoll and Colne Point to reach the shared estuary of the River Colne (and on to Brightlingsea) and the River Blackwater (for the Merseas). The cardinal Knoll is in fact the key to this shared estuary which offers some of the most pleasurable leisurable cruising grounds on the East Coast. (See the Imray *Y17* chart *River Colne to the Blackwater and Crouch.*)

Moving down from the Haven Ports or the Walton Backwaters towards the Knoll there are frequent towers to be observed along that stretch of coast; but the one that stands out from all the rest, distanced geographically as well as stylistically, is the gaunt tower of the Naze. It is 24 metres high and mounted on a promontory that is itself 23 metres above sea level. The Naze tower makes an excellent landmark and is also a reminder that the ledge it overlooks reaches out shallowly for about a mile towards the green buoy marking the Medusa Channel with its overtones of doom-laden myths.

The tower is much easier to spot than the Medusa, even on radar; although, once, after tedious adjustments, I did manage to get an echo from it at just over a mile away. Moving down, we pass the pier and the reassuring presence of Walton lifeboat.

En route for Colne Point, there is no hazard a mile offshore. There is also enough to look at on land to keep a wilting crew entertained, even in the lightest of airs. To seaward there is Gunfleet Sand and the disappearing remains of the old lighthouse and beacon. Shoresides, the coast undulates gently and is punctuated by diminutive cliffs that neither threaten vertigo nor peter out into crumbling miniatures. There is a generous smattering of sandy beaches, many of which almost hummock into full-blown dunes, and a sufficiency of hills and trees to give a nicely contrasting prospect. This stretch also contains those twinned opposites Clacton and Frinton, both styled '-on-Sea'. Each has contrasting architecture – contemporary brutish vies with decaying baroque, as does the Victorian yellow-glazed brickwork with the faded greens and blues of 1930s pantiles. The concrete shades of pseudo-Bauhaus villas match the pale greys, browns and fawns of once-aspiring Edwardian maisonettes; while, for miles, high-rise towers compete with Martello towers, water towers and Grand Hotel-type towers.

Inshore, there is little tide, thus allowing close observation to be made of the shoreline without hazard. Clacton and Holland cliffs are modest, and

above them can just be picked out the bits and bats that go to make up the major and minor Hollands and Great Holland church.

Walton is about the last word in ugliness, at any rate when seen from the sea. A row of ill-favoured houses, all with a tired look, and a pier that has in the classic phrase, 'seen better days' (just like the entertainment in fact). From the sea, Walton offers nothing to tempt the cruising man ashore; and from the land nothing really changes.

No doubt much to its chagrin, Frinton-on-Sea can hardly be separated out from Walton. Certainly, on the map, there is complete contiguity. However, in terms of culture there could hardly be a stronger territorial divide; a frontier even. There is no doubt

---

RIVER COLNE
51°47'·95N 01°00'·70E (Brightlingsea)
Charts Admiralty 3741, 1975, 1183. Imray Y17.
OS Landranger 168
Tides
Dover +0050

CLACTON (ST OSYTH)
St Osyth Boatyard ☎ 01255 820005
Tidal access
HW ±2 hrs (Brightlingsea)
Ⓥ (50+, 5 visitors'- drying), 🚾, ⚓, ⚡, ⌇ (nearby), Provisions (nearby), ⊕ (by arrangement), Engineer, Repairs

---

BRIGHTLINGSEA
Tides
Dover +0050
Authorities
Harbourmaster ☎ 01206 302200. Radio Brightlingsea Port Radio VHF Ch 68 (0800–2000)
Facilities
All usual facilities available.

WIVENHOE
Tides
Dover +0115
Ⓥ

COLCHESTER HARBOUR
☎ 01206 827316. Radio Colchester VHF Ch 68, 11, 14, 16 (office hours and HW -3hrs to HW +1hr)
Note
Tidal barrier at Wivenhoe may impede navigation.
Facilities
✉PO, ⚓, public house

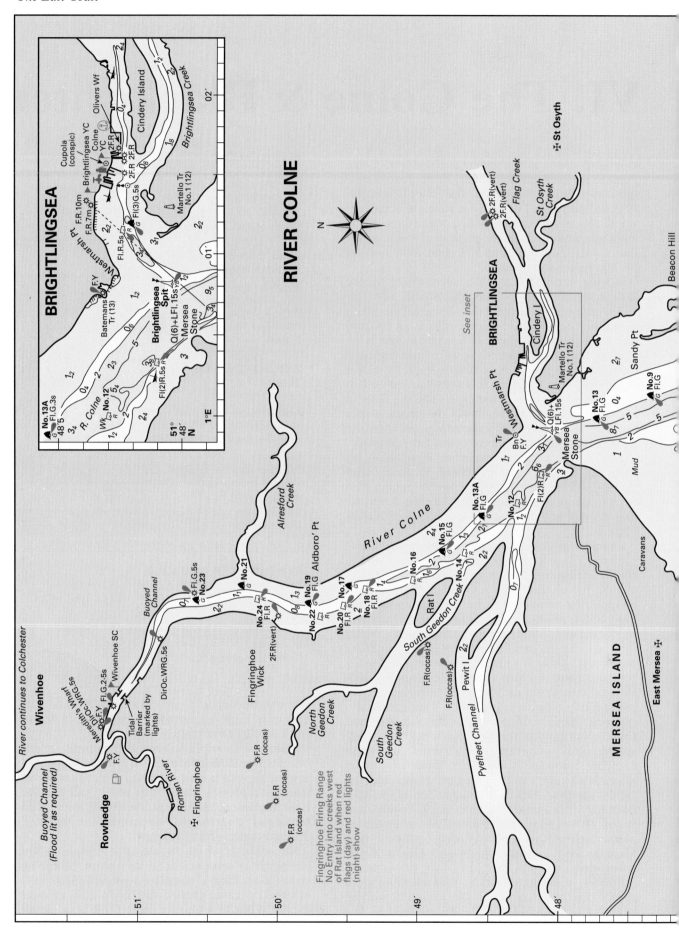

BRIGHTLINGSEA

Cupola (conspic)

Brightlingsea YC

Colne YC

2F.R 2F.R

2F.R

Cindery Island

Brightlingsea Creek

Westmarsh Pt

F.R.10m

F.R.7m

Martello Tr No.1 (12)

Oliver's Wf

F.Y

Batemans Tr (13)

Brightlingsea Spit

Q(6)+LFl.15s

Mersea Stone

Fl.R.5s

Fl(3).5s

Fl(2)R.5s

No.13A

Fl.G.3s

R. Colne

Wk

No.12

Buoyed Channel (Flood lit as required)

1°E

51° 48' N

RIVER COLNE

N

River continues to Colchester

Wivenhoe

Meredith's Wharf

F.Y

DirOc.WRG.5s

Fl.G.2.5s

Wivenhoe SC

Tidal Barrier (marked by lights)

DirOc.WRG.5s

2F.R.(vert)

Rowhedge

Roman River

⚓ Fingringhoe

F.R (occas)

F.R (occas)

F.R (occas)

Fingringhoe Firing Range
No Entry into creeks west
of Rat Island when red
flags (day) and red lights
(night) show

Buoyed Channel

Fl.G.5s

No.23

No.21

Alresford Creek

Fl.G Aldboro' Pt

No.24 Fl.R

No.22 Fl.R

No.19 Fl.G

No.17

No.20 Fl.R

No.18 Fl.R

River Colne

Fingringhoe Wick

Rat I

North Geedon Creek

South Geedon Creek

No.16

No.15 Fl.G

No.13A Fl.G

No.12

Fl(2)R

See inset

Tr Westmarsh Pt

Bn F.Y

Q(6)+ LFl.15s

Mersea Stone

No.14

F.R(occas)

Pewit I

F.R(occas)

South Geedon Creek

Pyefleet Channel

MERSEA ISLAND

East Mersea ⚓

BRIGHTLINGSEA

Martello Tr No.1 (12)

Cindery I

2F.R(vert)

2F.R(vert)

Flag Creek

St Osyth Creek

⚓ **St Osyth**

No.13 Fl.G

No.9 Fl.G

Sandy Pt

Beacon Hill

Mud

Caravans

118

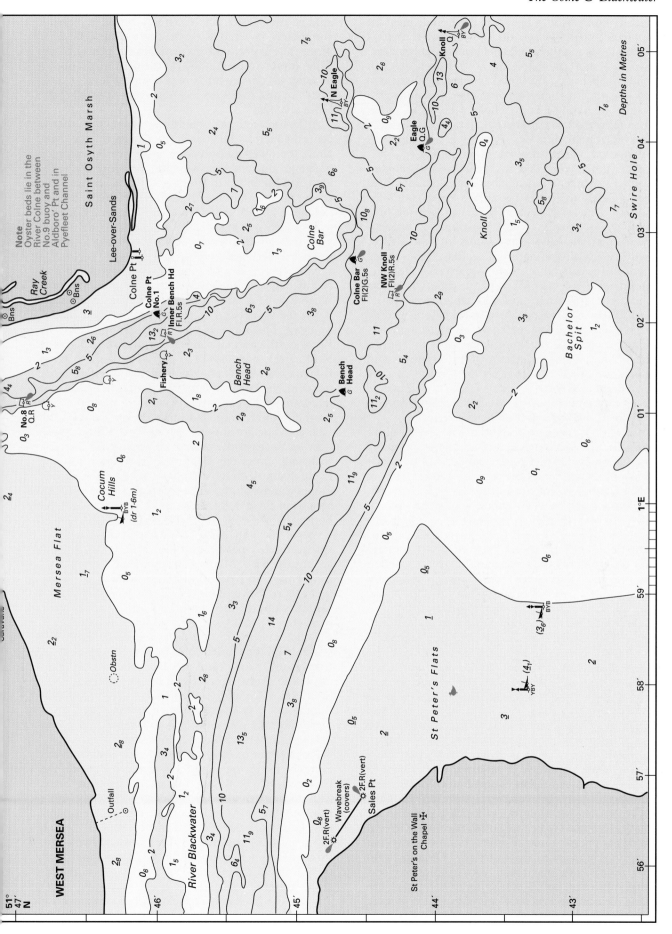

WEST MERSEA

51°
47′
N

Mersea Flat

Saint Osyth Marsh

Lee-over-Sands

Note
Oyster beds lie in the
River Colne between
No.9 buoy and
Aldboro' Pt and in
Pyefleet Channel

Ray
Creek

⊙ Bns

⊙ Bns

Colne Pt

Colne Pt
Colne Pt No.1

Inner Bench Hd
Fl.R.5s

Fishery

No.8
Q.R

Cocum
Hills
(dr 1·6m)

Obstn

Outfall
⊙

River Blackwater

Bench
Head

Colne
Bar

Bench
Head
G

Colne Bar
Fl(2)G.5s
G

NW Knoll
Fl(2)R.5s
R

Knoll

N Eagle

Eagle
Q.G
G

Knoll
Q

Bachelor
Spit

Swire Hole

St Peter's Flats

St Peter's on the Wall
Chapel ✠

Wavebreak
(covers)
2F.R(vert)
Sales Pt
2F.R(vert)

2F.R(vert)

Depths in Metres

N

1°E

that Frinton is a more colourful and pleasant experience than Walton. In the season, the effete dilettantes who inhabit what is virtually an enclave, have to suffer the intrusion of a better class of holidaymakers . . . but holidaymakers nonetheless, and that must be an offence to their yellow-gloved aristo/plutocratic feelings. How could it be other, when even the taxi drivers must wear suitable attire (and that includes a tie, even in a hot summer) 'because our clients of substance require it'!

The shoreline is scattered with multi-coloured beach huts while, a little behind it, the dated houses and a faded tower or two make their claim for sobriety. One establishment has what seems to be a small white lookout tower. Pope-hatted, pagoda-style creations also top some of the larger Victorian/Edwardian hotels. They have those small windows typical of the servants' quarters of the time. (Quarters, did I say? More like eighths or garrets even, as I know from personal experience when I worked at Scarborough's Grand Hotel.) The architecture of many of these establishments is mundane at best, but in keeping with the public image that Frinton attempts to espouse and broadcast. Much of this must be a waste of time since the more recent tower-blocks now dominate – straight triangulations of concrete, reminiscent of Corbusier, but without his talent or style.

As crab pots begin to abound out at sea, we move down parallel to a long sea wall and flatlands; going past the renowned golf course, Holland Gap, Sandy Point, Chevaux de Frise Point to Holland Haven, which is neither Dutch nor a haven as such. Here, overlooking the area for miles, is a huge skeletal radar tower. In the area known as Copperas Ground, for a mile or so I found myself surrounded by extraordinary brown patches. At first I thought they were only on the surface, but closer inspection showed that they were some inches in depth. Perhaps they were floating relics of the classic Copperas?

Once past the tall mast, the beach huts begin. While they start out fairly thin and well scattered, they soon become an agglomeration – only to be challenged by the sea-front houses that are such a feature of Clacton-on-Sea. The sea wall is still with us, but the houses get more and more splendid as we move towards the core of Old Clacton – some of them are absolutely spectacular. The pier stands out in a strange way: it fronts a large yellowish edifice and comes out towards us as if on jagged concrete ramps. There is a near-conical tower that suggests a melting ice cream cone immediately in front a sandwich.

Clacton-on-Sea is almost as much a paradise for tourists as it used to be; they often used to be known as 'day-trippers' – but 'tripping' is now something else entirely. Viewed from the sea, Clacton is no great shakes, although it might aim to emulate Great Yarmouth. But, as in that latter place, there are many pleasure seekers who still patronise it in spite of all the competition from cheap Spanish hotels.

And it must said that Clacton's beach is seldom completely covered with the over-tanned flesh of prone humanity; and there is always plenty to do when it rains. The seafood department might not be as fresh as one might expect – but at least it does exist . . . and there are still purveyors of whelks and other shellfish.

At length we leave behind the macrocosm that is central Clacton. The beach huts begin to take over, while the dwelling houses provide a really complex melange: ancient and modern; low-squat/tall-rise; high-flat buildings in black and white, cream, off-cream and red brick with red tiles. Namely, a huge hotchpotch of Victorian and contemporary British styles. This melange finally gives way to the sandy bays that go all the way to Colne Point, to which there is a close inshore passage.

Next, we set out to spot the cardinals Knoll and North Eagle, or the green Eagle and the red North West Knoll; if you want to be further out, then down the Wallet and on to the red and white Wallet Spitway. From the Wallet, you then pick up the Knoll north cardinal and leave it to starboard, or the North Eagle and leave it to port. The thing to avoid is mixing the Knoll and the Eagles; something easily done in the mist and broken waters that are not uncommon hereabouts. Then it is more or less northerly towards the red Inner Bench Head for the Colne; or the green Bench Head for the Blackwater.

From the east, the passage to beware of is the one that cuts across the Colne Bar to the north of the Eagle bank and its attendant marker the North Eagle. Careful study of the charts and a survey of the area from the dinghy at low water will show that the bottom is likely to be encountered in all kinds of unexpected spots. The Colne Bar itself is a wide-spreading manifestation, an unshapely accumulation of holes, bumps and braes that frequently and unpredictably follow in close succession. Such considerations, together with a careful study of the chart, will put off all but the reckless.

There are many approaches indeed: from the south; from the Crouch; and from the Blackwater. A risky route runs from the Blackwater, and goes inside the green Bench Head to skirt the old target by Mersea Flat and Cocum Hills. I have seen craft caught on a falling tide when cutting off Bench Head, having got too close to Mersea Flat, and having to pay the penalty of a full tide.

Perhaps the most intriguing short cut is from the Crouch, using the Ray Sand channel through the Buxey Sand. However, for smaller-draught boats with no more than 1·5m, with a good forecast and a rising spring tide, you may feel like exploring this best known of them, Ray Sand (or Rays'n) which saves the long haul round the Spitway. Years ago, there was much more water in the channel than there is now, perhaps as much as a couple of metres at low water.

It can be a challenging experience, even with a rising spring tide with the weather not entirely

It is not difficult to see why it is seldom easy for a visitor to slip in to a mooring at Brightlingsea. Across the water, and almost equally as popular, lies Pyefleet creek.

against you. The wind seems to funnel itself in a strange way through the Spitway and brings with it short, sharp shocks of waves that accost the boat on the beam. The channel is narrow and the bottom uneven. Deciding on the right course is not easy. Perhaps the best way is to sort it out from the configuration of the three Buxey cardinals: No. 1, No. 2 and Sunken. This may or may not work according to the day of the month or the luck of the draw. My experience of this cut, is that the more difficult of the tasks is the spotting of the Buxey beacon. I never yet had a quiet crossing, and locals have told me that it is always likely to be 'a bit lumpy'. They have also told me that lots of boats have been caught out when a troublesome sea washes over the first sandbanks, builds up in the Big Dip and breaks even more ferociously after.

There are variations. The first is to cross the Whitaker Spit with one eye on the Whitaker beacon and the red Ridge buoy; and the other on the sounder. The second is to negotiate the miniature channel by the Knoll and Batchelors Spit. However, you need to keep your eye on the sounder for, between Mersea Flat and Bench Head, there are inconspicuous hazards.

Mostly, these byways and non-highways take you over entirely, or partially, drying sands and a few times I have been shown the way by 'locals with special knowledge' when they themselves have lost the track. This is no condemnation of their skills which are far in excess of mine. I am making the point that these channels are difficult and can be confusing, and even dangerous, for the stranger. Most of the professional fishermen know their exits and entrances extremely well; and, in addition, need only wring out a wet dishcloth to get across the bar.

On balance, I don't think that first-timers should try these channels at all. They may challenge those who want to search out every last swatchway but, on passage, they seldom save enough time to justify the anxieties. Such 'short' cuts, here or in the Wash, cannot be worth the attendant risks. They are best left for fine days in a substantial dinghy with a powerful outboard. Then channel exploration, fishing and sightseeing can be happily and safely combined.

The entrance to the Colne is between the St Osyth Stone Point Martello tower to the east, and Mersea Stone, the extremity of Mersea Island, to the west. Rising some 32 miles away in the northwest of Essex, it is no more than a muddy trickle above Colchester at low water. Its 11 miles of tideway run down to the sea through extensive mud flats, saltings and detached banks.

Once the Colne Bar buoy has been identified, the channel right up to Mersea Stone and Brightlingsea is easy to identify. Watch out for the substantial tidal set across the entrance. It is worth keeping an eye on your wake with the Bar buoy astern to make sure you aren't drifting off. There is shoal water to each side, and it is best to maintain a central course in the channel. The beacons marking Colne Point, Mersea Stone and the measured half mile are all clear to see.

The clubhouse and the pubhouse are popular places – especially at week-ends. Fortunately, there is an excellent water-taxi service for those who need post-liquid-prandial assistance.

Some very small fishing pots and markers are to be met in the channel.

There is a long pretty sliver of sand on the east bank once past the corner known as Lee-over-Sands, on the edge of the St Osyth Marsh. This is clearly visible as we move past Inner Bench Head and the channel becomes enclosed and we no longer feel that we are out at sea. The sand strip shows the way razor sharp, past the green beacons and on to the cardinal, which seems to be an impossibly long haul. We now approach the caravan park at Point Clear, after which there are more classic holiday huts. If seen at the top of the tide, this stretch then becomes one of the prettiest, low-lying, low-key approaches in the area (an area that has almost a surfeit of them). While the 'hills' are no more than modest, they are decorated with trees, bushes and greenery that form an attractive border to the wide estuary mouth. The bright holiday huts take the eyes almost compellingly to Bateman's Tower and the entrance to Brightlingsea Harbour to the north of which it stands. The Martello tower is almost hidden from view but the church can be seen fairly well. The cardinal at the entrance is not a giant of its class but its stands out well enough to be easily observed. The final sand spit before the entrance is completely rural, without buildings of any kind. The entrance opens up to show red and green buoys, easily detected, unless obscured by what is a very busy sailing/surfing area. Sometimes a little bleak, but with a considerable amount of variety in its scenery, Brightlingsea's real appeal is to be found not in the locale, but in its community.

Brightlingsea may be small, but it is a thrivingly busy place and, like Topsy, just keeps on growing. The approach into the harbour is problem free if

you note that it has little more than a metre at low water. Access is restricted to 90 minutes or so after low water if you want to be on the safe side. Otherwise there is no difficulty in gaining the main harbour.

From the river, you leave green No. 13 to starboard to avoid the spit off the south of the entrance, and then leave the cardinal to port to avoid the broader spit above it. There are red/white leading marks, both with red centres and white/grey stripes. It is not particularly easy to differentiate them from their backgrounds but, helpfully, close to them is the noticeable triangle of the yacht club station. There are also FR leading lights. Bateman's Point has a red beacon that is very conspicuous as its stands out well into the river. After leaving Brightlingsea Spit south cardinal buoy astern, keep well close to the moorings and the buoys (the first of which is lit) and watch out for the odd withy. The inner entry is a slow waltz to starboard until you are past the fishing fleet to starboard. The long lines of moorings will then come into view.

Great changes have been made with regard to the welcome and the facilities offered to visiting yachtsmen. It still cannot be said that there are plenty of spare berths for visitors, nor that there is not a difficult stream to hinder easy mooring. However, the improvement to the pontoons, and the promise of even more has done much to help. But much more has been done by the presence of a harbourmaster who sees it as a major part of his job to ensure that he meets as many visiting yachts as possible, and leads them to a suitable berth. Moreover, he will then adeptly tie up and be ready on the pontoon to help with your lines. There is a notice: 'Visitors call Channel 68 for assistance and instruction'. The harbourmaster is a veritable gent, and his assistance a veritable luxury.

(While mentioning radio, it is something of an irritation that French and Dutch stations come in much more strongly than do the British. Indeed, communications with the coastguards on VHF Channels 02, 88 and 62 are generally poor in parts of the Stour, the Crouch, the Roach and the Blackwater. However, there are plans to correct this shortcoming by the erection of new aerials.)

In the recent past Brightlingsea has had lots of troubles, some of its own making and others not; but all related to environmental issues and the welfare of cattle. Some of the 'demonstrations' led to 'protestations' that got out of hand. The harbourmaster told me not just what he had seen, but what he had experienced 'hands on'. What will no doubt give readers cause to pause for thought is that he himself became a frequent target, not only for abuse, but also for bricks and broken bottles. He was pilloried, called an Enemy of the People, and the fences round the dockyard were covered in black oil. Indeed, in the town, many of the windows were defaced by posters conveying the message that all animals should be protected. The question of the export of live animals elided into environmental good causes, mad cows and scrapied sheep. I felt there would soon be a league for the defence of mad dogs. As Gladstone said, 'There is nothing quite as dangerous, quite so ferocious, quite so terrifying as a mad sheep.'

Back to the sanctuary of the piles and the pontoons. If you are unlucky and have to find a mooring for yourself, keep to the centre lanes and the Cindery Island (northerly) side. The far lane, which is to starboard when entering, does not carry enough water for boats with more than 1·5m

draught. A good plan is to take the north side on the way in, then turn and come back via the centre channel. If you have entered on a rising tide you will also have the advantage of stemming it while you inspect the trots.

There is a ferry that runs constantly round all the pontoon to take visitors to the shore at the yacht-club jetty. Passengers are indeed lucky to have such a co-operative, friendly and charismatic man at the wheel. He runs the ferry during the summer months and, in the winter, charters a boat in the Caribbean – often to locals. In the depths of English winters he is to be found there himself. In general, from Easter to October, on Fridays to Sundays, his times are 0830 to 2030, but sometimes you can cajole him to run even later than 2300 for an occasion of special revelry. His launch is known as 'Kevin's Taxi' and he listens on 68/37/M/P1.

There is also a boat service from Brightlingsea hard to Stone Point. For a small consideration the boatmen will pick you up and drop you at your boat, or vice versa, for those who want walk up to St Osyth's (see below).

There is water at the YC jetty and the key is held by the barman at the club. It is no longer permitted to anchor in the north channel. During the week, commercial ships use the wharves at the new development. On one of the pontoons there was an intriguing converted ex-lifeboat. True, all boats are compromises, but this was a splendid hybrid, looking still, but only half, like a lifeboat with the other half being an excellent representation of a Scottish trawler.

The Brightlingsea Harbour Commissioners' Laws proclaim the following:

You are advised that your anchored vessel could cause unnecessary difficulty to the navigation of the larger craft using Brightlingsea Creek. Anchoring north of moorings in the outer reach of the creek or in the north low-water channel east of the public causeway is not recommended at any time. Visitors' moorings are available in the south channel.

I saw an example of a cruiser causing inconvenience by having been left moored in danger at the quay when a coaster was coming in to that very place. The harbourmaster towed it away to a place of safety, and immediately took a line to a yacht that was apparently without steerage of power. It was installed at the posts for repairs to be carried out and then left on the tide. The following morning, after a Pan-Pan-Pan call, the same yacht was brought back in by the local inshore RNLI. No injury to person or damage to the vessel had been sustained but, ironically, the yacht was named *Tout va Bien*.

Seen when approaching at water level, the Wivenhoe Barrier looks like a serious example of over-kill; but those who live there know better. However, it does contrast dramatically with the rest of the small riverside port – much of which still enjoys living in the near past.

Before the final head of navigation can be reached, Cindery Island and the romantically and temptingly named 'Pincushion' must be negotiated. Cindery Island itself has a spit out to the west that extends for a very long way. Many strangers find themselves stranded, even with flat rubber-bottomed dinghies, which are pigs to haul on mud.

There is a boatyard at St Osyth which is navigable with care +/- 2hrs high water. The channel is narrow, the tides run hard and it is particularly important to follow very closely not only the indications of the buoys and withies but also the markers themselves. The accompanying chartlet (for which I am grateful to Andrew Harman at St Osyth Boatyard) will be of assistance. You may prefer to walk to the famous St Osyth Priory, but the channel permits an intriguing access by boat.

During the dissolution of the monasteries, most of the buildings were destroyed, but part, including the gatehouse, is still there. St Osyth was rich, after being founded by a Saxon princess. Come the Danes she was given the choice between death and servitude. She rejected slavery and had her head promptly removed. Legend has it that, rather like a dead chicken, she kept alive long enough to parade with her head right up to the doors of the church where she, somewhat tardily, dropped dead. In later times, it is not without import that Brightlingsea was at one time a Cinque Port, when it was part of the brotherhood of the Kentish Borough and Port of Sandwich.

When I first visited Brightlingsea, nearly 20 years ago, it was developing in the town and market-place, as well as at the quayside. The quayside is still thriving, but the core seems now to be decaying. There are many examples of posters in shop and office windows displaying the plaintive legend, 'Use it or lose it!'. Timelessly, almost, it is possessed of amazing architecture; many of the buildings being ancient pieces in their own right, but also with a mix of the ancient and modern in such a way that dates become irrelevant and blending is all. Charming!

Those shops that have remained and survived in the town offer good food and services. For example, there are two very good chandlers; there is a real wet-fish shop and three excellent butchers; a Chinese take-away near the outskirts that dispenses its wares from the deep interior of an old cottage; and one of the most attractive fish'n'chip shops, in all its floral glory, that I have even seen.

Back in the creek, the wildlife is also interesting, as hypnotic herons stroll around with the sounds of birdsong always present in the background. Even the swans were gracious and friendly – and, by swans' standards, neither condescending nor greedy.

Outside in the river again, immediately opposite the entrance to Brightlingsea, there is a sound anchorage between Mersea Stone and the lit red can buoy marked 'Wreck'. This is Ms Driscoll's letter on the subject:

The wreck which you mention off East Mersea is not the steamer *Lowland*, mined during the Second World War, but the *Lowlands* built in Sunderland in 1888, which went on the mud about 1918, being put there when she was about to sink. To date I haven't been able to establish the exact year when she was put there but it was between the end of 1917 and the autumn of 1921, which narrows it down. It's a long story that I won't tell you here or this letter, already long, will get totally out of hand.

This anchorage suffers from no disadvantage but neither does it possess the charms of the one round the corner in the popular waters of Pyefleet Creek. This area of the main river is extremely busy. You are likely to come across all kinds of traffic, from the most unstable of youthful dinghies and the most acrobatic of windsurfers, to stubborn small coasters apparently ignoring everything but, in fact, not missing a trick.

Pyefleet Creek

There is no longer an olde-worlde feel here. The working boats, nets and huts that were strewn hither and yon are now gone. Its ambience is still extremely pleasant, but no longer has the impact on me that it had nearly 20 years ago. Then it was the first proper anchorage I ever found in *Valcon* and I stayed there for much longer than I had intended. I even risked running out of gas and water (there is no facility here) just because of its quiet, spellbinding magnetism. It has a *genius loci* all its own. When the setting sun threw its rays on the fishermen's huts, the steeply slanted angles made them into monuments of picturesque decay and a real inspiration to the imagination. In the overhead brightness of high noon, it was unhappily obvious that, in the absence of the magic of long shadows, they possessed no more than the spirit of a broken-down shambles; but they were not built for midday inspection. It was really at night, when their textures were chased in and out of relief by a cloud-caught moon, that huts, boats and nets became transformed into history made manifest and grew in stature until they were dramatic emblems of centuries of local tradition.

It is one of the most charming anchorages on the East Coast, of enduring appeal to most East Coast yachtsmen. However, there can be a most unlikely and also most unpleasant 'sea state' when an unfavourable wind (of no more than, say, Force 4 or 5) is over the tide. The creek is such an apparently protected haven, that it would seem that nothing could disturb its calm. But, when the wind is funnelled and the tide is tunnelled, an eccentric configuration of rips and whirls is set up that causes confusion among the ranks of even the best-laid plans of those at anchor. Indeed, I was myself sadly involved in one such 'local difficulty' when I was last there.

My next visit will take us away from the 'favourites' and well up into the creek where there is, of course, the possibility of drying out, but much

Rowhedge looks pretty enough – and it is a friendly place; but there are two sadnesses: the lifeboat trade has gone and with it wooden boat-building; and there is no guaranteed safe berth except at High Water.

less a possibility of disturbance of the kind I have described. Just to intrigue you, there are some floating objects covered in black plastic that are not at all apparent in their function.

Pyefleet is also special insofar as it draws an entirely different kind of visitor – Christian foot soldiers come to bow before the shrine of Sabine Baring-Gould. Sightseers, tourists and pilgrims alike make what is a long shoresides trip to what is now a rather dull edifice of a one-time place of worship. Folk come from as far away as Horbury Bridge near Wakefield, where the Reverend Sabine started his sombre ministry, surrounded by the classic mills and deep, dark waters that lend the north country its gloomy satanic reputation. No wonder he created 'Through the Night of Doubt and Sorrow', 'Now the Day is Over' and 'Onward Christian Soldiers'. Perhaps he even called the fishermen to become fishers of men. It is not only the profane who turn to the ever-open arms of the nearby Dog & Pheasant.

Last note – oyster beds still rule, OK? They are marked by red buoys or withies with red topmarks.

If Pyefleet isn't far enough away from the rough and tumble for your taste, there is a possible navigation round Rat Island. In the main river, there is another red wreck buoy that is not shown on the charts. The first, more southerly, channel is marked by the red No. 14 buoy, and takes you in sight of the North and South Geedon Creeks and Fingringhoe

Marsh. The whole area is restricted: when it is not active as a killing field, it comes into its own as a nature reserve. I still think that provision should be made to permit leisure craft into these westerly creeks. Generally speaking, the presence of yachtsmen usually does nothing but improve conditions for wildlife in the area. The red No.16 marks the beginning of the 'No Speed Limit' area.

Going upstream, the scenery improves, becoming really pretty – especially when viewed at the top of the tide. There are occasional houses and farms, with dead silver trees standing out from the living green ones – a fantastic scene for water-colour artists. They are also an inspiration to the imagination; these dead and scraggy fingers might well be the cursed masts of witches' boats, sailing who knows where, when the devil's wind blows?

Even as far back as Pyefleet, the red flags centred on Fingringhoe Firing Range have been obvious and abundant, and they continue well on the way upstream.

Fingringhoe Wick has a pretty headland with picnic areas, seats and a sandy beach. Both it and the headquarters of the Essex Wildlife Trust seem unhappily placed in such a warlike environment.

Also on this south headland, are red beacons that mark the small broken-down jetty that looks more like a construction of breakwaters for the protection of oyster beds. It is not to be approached, as the hazardous area stretches a few cables into the river.

Further up, on the starboard hand to the east, comes Alresford Creek. The green No. 21 marks the limit of low-water navigation for craft drawing more than 1·5m and very little is gained from going up from Pyefleet. The channel is well buoyed but, since it is extremely narrow, it is important to follow the laid-out track exactly. Almost the slightest deviation will cause a churning-up of the silt-soft mud of the riverbed.

The creek allows craft in for a couple of cables at tide time, and there is good dinghy access and landing further in. Unless you are deeply into the ways of swatch and shoal, it is perhaps better not to try to anchor in the creek itself but to use the stretch between the two greens – Nos. 19 and 21. The entrance is marked by numerous buoys of contrasting colours, shapes and sizes. You must, of course, keep well clear of the channel; hoist a good anchor light; and be prepared to find the soft bottom. It is a very small 'stream' with a great deal of allure to that very small group – the initiated.

There is a large sand quarry just inside the creek on the north bank. Landing is difficult there. In the river there are some moorings for modest craft. A little further upstream there is a boathouse with two nearby gaffers looking somewhat sad and jaded. Upstream of them is a splendid red-brick, red-tiled mansion house residence. Magnificent! Back at the entrance, just a little upstream, there are often groups of bathers who sometimes venture right into the channel.

Valcon seldom reaches seven knots so there is always a wry smile when I pass a speed limit notice, as here, prohibiting anything in excess of eight knots. After Alresford Creek, the channel takes a marked dogleg, with four red cans to mark it. On the eastern bank the scenery takes on a pleasant image with miniature beaches (sandy strips really) backed by attractive bushes and trees.

The channel is particularly well buoyed upstream with lots of reds and a few greens. Because of the magical mystery tour ahead, it would be nice to offer the instruction: 'Follow the yellow brick road' to reach 'Never Never Land', 'Somewhere over the rainbow'. And why would it?

The reason is Wivenhoe. At first glimpse, this tiny port is a busy big-ship stop. Second sights and later thoughts confirm this impression; but with the qualifying criterion that it is, in addition, something quite other. The ballast quay and sand quarries are unmistakable; the WRG beacon is outstandingly obvious. They all herald the approach of the tidal barrier that protects the small community of Wivenhoe. Sitting proud, and apparently impervious, amid the lorries and the quarrying is a semi-timbered red-tiled mansion.

It is important not to deviate from the centre of the channel when you are getting close to Wivenhoe because the banks on both sides are host to a variety of obstructions and some wreckage. By the sand and gravel works, the channel is on the port hand and very close-to. Otherwise the approach is central and generally straightforward with the Wivenhoe Sailing Club moorings appearing to starboard. There is sometimes a visitor's mooring to be found on the E side of the channel. Occasionally the upstream head

of the swinging mooring buoys is left unoccupied and reserved for a visitor. I have still to find it vacant. On my last visit, the club's officers were kind to offer a place set aside. But when I reached my allotted spot, it was to find that I had been usurped by a visiting 'foreigner'.

The new Wivenhoe 'dam' is a massive concrete 'wall' with a hole in the middle. Not as big as the Thames Barrier, nor as stylish, it is nevertheless appropriate and efficient. It is impressive from downstream, and the red and green pillars are plain to see.

Wivenhoe, from time to time, is not only extremely busy with its own and visiting yachts, but also very occupied with the commercial traffic that passes through en route for Colchester at the head of the navigation, or has business in Wivenhoe itself. At high water therefore, it behoves skippers to make sure that a really efficient traffic watch is being kept. You can get some useful assistance from the harbour radio officer who will be pleased to inform you of the traffic he knows of and expects in the river.

And now to the nub of it all – the small non-commercial quayside that makes Wivenhoe the wonder that it is. It is such a popular spot that seldom indeed will you be able to find a vacant berth. If you are lucky enough to do so, you will moor up bows-on (there is insufficient water at the edge to moor up stern-to) and will need a ladder or plank to get ashore. There is little sign of any improvement or even simple repair work, so the riverside moorings are not being enhanced. This is no doubt all part of a dark plot on the part of the indigens to keep Wivenhoe quiet, but it must be hoped that the waterfront will not be allowed to drift into decay.

To arrive at Wivenhoe by water is to come close to a sympathetic encounter with the marriage of our maritime and riparian heritages. These two aspects are firmly held in the hands of time. Locals, guests and visitors alike try to keep one foot in that past and the other in the present – while trying not to fall into the hands of the future. The shopkeepers have a cavalier, if not eccentric, attitude to opening (bad mark) and closing (bad mark cancelled) times.

This is all symbolically presented in concrete form in the eyecatching cluster of stylishly modernised houses which contrast so clearly with their neighbours, a clutch of older cottages in an excellent state of repair and decoration. There is a public house blessed with an exterior of charm and character and an interior suffused with warmth and welcome.

You will frequently see an assembly of wooden boats moored bows-on to the jetty and, as if directing the whole scene to suit their own special vision, a coterie of painters, complete with stools, easels, shawls . . . and straw hats, absorbed as if preserving a vision of a world that was about to be devastated. They may have a mission.

I hope that, while the details may change over the next few years, the essence will linger. This intriguing riverside village is known to the Admiralty as a sub-port of Colchester.

Next up the river on the port hand comes the small village of Rowhedge. It has some shops, a pub or two, a few hundred feet of wharf space and a public quay. In spite of the presence of a first-rate hostelry, that quay is not as hospitable as it looks. Most of the Colne is soft mud; and much of the ground by that tempting quay is also soft mud but there is a shelving collection of concrete blocks, bricks and other impedimenta that makes it an unpleasant spot. Even if you manage to bottom without disaster, you are likely to dry out in a most uncomfortable manner.

Slightly further upriver on the port hand there is another spot that seems to invite mooring lines – right on the corner towards the end of the village. The corner is in fact one of the last places to moor; coasters have been known, more than once, to swing too far, too fast and so do serious damage, not only to the boats, but also to the corner itself. It is best to arrange any trip to Rowhedge to be a top of the tide visit, leaving well before the ebb starts to run out on you.

There is no hazard proceeding upriver to Colchester. Indeed, the waterway is floodlit whenever appropriate for traffic. It is accessible to 1·5m craft from about 2 hours before high water. I have always found it an hospitable spot, with helpful and friendly harbour staff. The mud is so malleable here, that it takes only a single tide for you to make a mud berth for yourself. All the facilities that the charming town of Colchester have to offer are with easy walking distance.

The port services about 100 big ships a month but the harbourmaster is still ready to dispense advice to those few remaining yachtsmen who want to stay there for a tide or two. Indeed, my most recent communication from harbourmaster Captain Harris confirms that there are still no dues for visiting pleasure craft. A disappearing joy!

Adding to this, Ms Driscoll's aforementioned letter continues:

At Colchester, the general rule is that nothing going away moves until on the high water, so going up on the ebb is extremely unwise, apart from the tide pushing your head away at each bend as it strikes your port bow.

The Colne has four major mooring choices to offer – an anchorage in Pyefleet Creek; a berth at Brightlingsea; a perch at lotus-land Wivenhoe; or a mud patch at Colchester.

The Colne is not the longest river in the world – being no more than 15 miles at most – nor is it the most beautiful, but it does possess splendid anchorages and attractive ports of call. It is a river to be neither missed nor rushed. Give yourself time to enjoy it.

The Blackwater

You reach the River Blackwater from the Wallet itself, or the Wallet Spitway. The surrounding coastline has few high-rise attractions. It is from such flat, plain ground that the defunct Bradwell power station rises. Together with its massive water-wall outfall, it is the most noticeable landmark in the area, and usually grimly silhouetted against a background of classic unrelenting North-Sea grey. As I said in an earlier version, 'Look on my works, ye mighty, and despair!'. We do; we do!

The actual entrance lies between Mersea Flats to the north and St Peter's Flats to the south; both areas living up to their names. The navigation from the Knoll to Bench Head and then on to the Nass beacon, where the river proper begins, is problem free; though it can feel a long haul from the Knoll to the Nass, with little to inspire on the way. Many are the constructions, some resembling concrete barges, topped with red markers and lights, that make up the wavebreak off Sales Point. From here on, the main attraction is the deep and regular water channel, atypically deep and regular for the East Coast, that leads to the Nass. Its beacon is as well known and significant on the East Coast as is the Chichester beacon on the south. Leaving the Nass, the course takes us into the river with Shinglehead Point to starboard, and Bradwell to port.

When the banks noticeably begin to close in, it becomes clear that it is going to be a river not to be missed. Nor is it a river to be rushed, for it possesses unique attractions. Some of the river's most intriguing attractions are Mersea, Osea Island, Heybridge Basin and Maldon. While this last is the drying head of the navigation, it is still nowhere near the source of the river which is more than 30 miles away.

So, back to the Nass for a cruise of discovery. For 1·5m craft, access to the Nass beacon is problem free at all states of the tide; and once that uniquely slender, unmitred cardinal has been identified, the question is: where now – right, left or centre?

To starboard are the classic fleets, islands and marshes that make up the very popular area of West Mersea, the Quarters and Tollesbury. The channels tend to be narrow, shallow and tortuous, not so deep as wells, nor so wide as church doors; nevertheless enough. They will serve; and serve they

---

RIVER BLACKWATER
51°45'·30N 00°55'·00E (½ mile south of Nass bn)
Charts Admiralty 3741, 1975, 1183. Imray Y17.
OS Landranger 168

Tides
Mersea Quarters: Dover +0100; Osea I: Dover +0115; Maldon: Dover +0115

Authorities
Harbourmaster ☎ 01621 856726
River bailiff (Maldon Quay) ☎ 01621 856487
Ⓥ Maldon Quay

One of the most noticeable features at West Mersea is Packing Marsh island: easily identified by the black hut on its northern end. It can be left to either hand: to port being Thorn Fleet and to starboard Mersea Fleet. As can be seen, Packing is the order of the day: various craft in various sizes and various states cover the water – while cars, dinghies and detritus abounding ashore.

do, through the maze of oyster beds and moorings that are, in their discreet ways, territorial reservations. Indeed, some are staked out as in the old Gold Rush days – and guarded with as much fervour. Fortunately, there is no evidence of the use of fire arms, although that was not always the case when vandalism, bed-rock plundering and smuggling were the practice of the day. There are channels and marshy banks to be explored by the hour if not the day around here; and all best done by dinghy because of the profusion of oyster beds. The main channels skirt Sunken Island and lead (slowly but ultimately) to the hamlets of Salcott and Virley, that well-known double act. The others are the Ray and Strood at the back of Mersea which get little publicity and hardly a dozen boats in a year.

The lower ends of the Ray and the Strood, together with the ins and outs of Pye Fleet, Tollesbury Fleet and Goldhanger Creek are such that, in their day, smuggling was an obvious moonlighting vocation. Nary a chance was given to

HM's opposition, and many there were who were executed by the sinister knife in the name of HM Contraband.

The old Strood causeway dries and, about every 8 hours or so, it is possible to walk across to Mersea Island. It is important to keep to the narrow hard strip, for the mud comes close and is of the softest, clinging all-embracing species. Mersea Island is well worth a visit, being hilly in the main and offering lovely views. The land rises steeply about West Mersea village, which has an old Norman church, grey stone and flint, with Roman brickwork let in. Landing is possible at King's Hard, which leads up to West Mersea village. This 'King's' area stretches nearly a third of a mile to Besom Fleet, a narrow, shallow strip of water between the Mersea shore and Cobmarsh Island. The Fleet can offer a short cut on the top of the tide. It is essential to get the timing right, since both ends of the gutway can dry out. However, for those in the know or with the right shoal craft it is a neat route from West Mersea to the Blackwater.

At first glance, the moorings seem all over the place, and first-time visitors, especially those unused to navigating through masses of occupied and unoccupied laid moorings, may find it confusing – and the boatmen are not always obvious to strangers. It would seem a good idea to take a berth

WEST MERSEA

West Mersea Yacht Club ☎ 01206 382947

Tidal access

24hrs (LWS: some restrictions at landing stage)
Ⓥ (300, inc. visitors'), 🆆🅒 (nearby), 🅟 (club hrs),
⚓ (nearby), ⚓ (club), Provisions (nearby),
Ⓖ (nearby), ⛽D (nearby), ⛽P (nearby), Repairs

West Mersea Marine ☎ 01206 382244

Tidal access

24 hrs
Ⓥ (swinging & post), 🆆🅒 (nearby), ⚓, ⚡ (nearby),
⚓ (nearby), Provisions (nearby), Ⓖ (nearby),
⛽D (nearby), Engineer (nearby), Repairs (nearby)

at one of the two nearby marina facilities and search out moorings and anchorages by dinghy. In such ways are the most appropriate places for one's own boat discovered, good relationships developed, and the interests of nature, the working community, and all other locals and strangers served. Mersea has now been taken over by the Maritime and Leisure Group that already runs the Blackwater Marina at Maylandsea. If it does as good a job here as it has done there, the future for the visiting yachtsman looks rosy.

A red pillar buoy with a black topmark marks the beginning of the Tollesbury and West Mersea Channels. The latter lead to Sunken Island and Salcott Channel. Although there are many trots to be encountered ahead, the main Salcott channel, which is to the northwest, appears first and is obvious. Then there comes Packing Marsh Island which is easily identified by the black hut on its northern end. It can be left to either hand – to port is Thorn Fleet (with a small creek running off to the northwest known as Little Ditch); while to starboard is Mersea Fleet. Near the middle of Packing Marsh Island and the black hut, the water tends to drop away for two to three cables but shortly returns to a good depth. The quayside and landing at the busy West Mersea headquarters are packed with various craft in various sizes and various states. The cars, dinghies and detritus that abound can also be described in the same way. While there are some vessels of substance on the trots, most are occupied by modest sailing craft. It is good to note that many fishermen are still working from here, most of them with boats that are well-kept joys to look at.

The main channel from the Nass beacon is westerly to pick up the white buoy with red topmark. A careful study of the chart is required from here on, as there are many confined channels. The obvious one leads to South Channel, and on to the very head of the gutway where stands Old Hall Farm, which is approached, if at all, by the eponymous Creek.

Tollesbury Marina gives the following navigation details:

Enter the River Blackwater (Bradwell Power Station conspic to Port) and steer as for Mersea Quarters leaving the Nass beacon to port. After passing two red buoys to port, steer WSW and enter Tollesbury Channel marked by buoys (Red Port). Pass between No. 3 Red and No. 4 East cardinal and steer to leave No. 5 Green buoy (marking southern end of Great Cob Island) to starboard. Steer, keeping to the centre of the South Channel (marked by withies), passing close either side of any boats on moorings, leaving Little Cob Island to starboard. After passing five mooring buoys of Woodrolfe Boatyard, enter Woodrolfe Creek and keep to the centre of the channel. (Tide mark at entrance to Woodrolfe Creek will indicate depth of water on harbour sill.) The yacht harbour entrance will be seen just south of the prominent white buildings of Woodrolfe Boatyard.

Craft should not enter Woodrolfe Creek until the tide gauge, south of Woodrolfe Boatyard moorings, shows enough water to clear the harbour sill. Anchor clear of the channel to pick up a WB mooring if awaiting the tide. If not directed to a berth, visitors should moor at the jetty on the starboard side after entering the inner harbour under the 5-ton derrick, where a list of vacant berths is shown.

Craft using the Woodrolfe Boatyard moorings at the leavings in Tollesbury Fleet South Channel should not raft up more than two abreast. If the moorings are taken, craft should anchor clear of moorings and in the centre of the channel, in the North or South Channels or Tollesbury Fleet.

The harbour is tidal, access being over a sill with a depth of 7½ft at mean high water (about 10ft HW springs and 5½ft HW neaps). The harbour is dredged to an average of 7ft below sill level. Depending on weather conditions, access is available from 2 hours either side of HW springs and 1 hour either side of HW neaps. HW Tollesbury is 1 hour after HW Dover.

When I was last there, when the buoys were easy to locate and follow; they were, nevertheless, still going to be renewed. Inside, the entrance has been widened and dredged, with some new berths. It is no longer quite as necessary for visitors to keep their eyes open and their speed down for there is no space for grand manoeuvres and not a lot for correcting errors.

Hereabouts, you begin to see what is almost hidden from the Blackwater, as the headland of Shinglehead Point becomes very noticeable, and the important landmarks of white houses with their near-butterfly roof formations, are unmistakable.

The withies are in the best East Coast tradition – still trying to spout. Equally traditionally, there are oyster layings, some marked only by indifferent withies. Great Cob Island and the two channels on either side are clear to see. The south channel is the marked favourite and, towards the well-marked Quarters Spit, are the mooring trots and the courtesy waiting buoys. The last green buoy before the withies is not numbered. In early morning or late evening mist, the red and greens do not stand out as much as they might, and these are to be improved in keeping with those mentioned above.

Once 'inside' and moving directly towards Tollesbury Fleet, you will find no pomp, panoply or

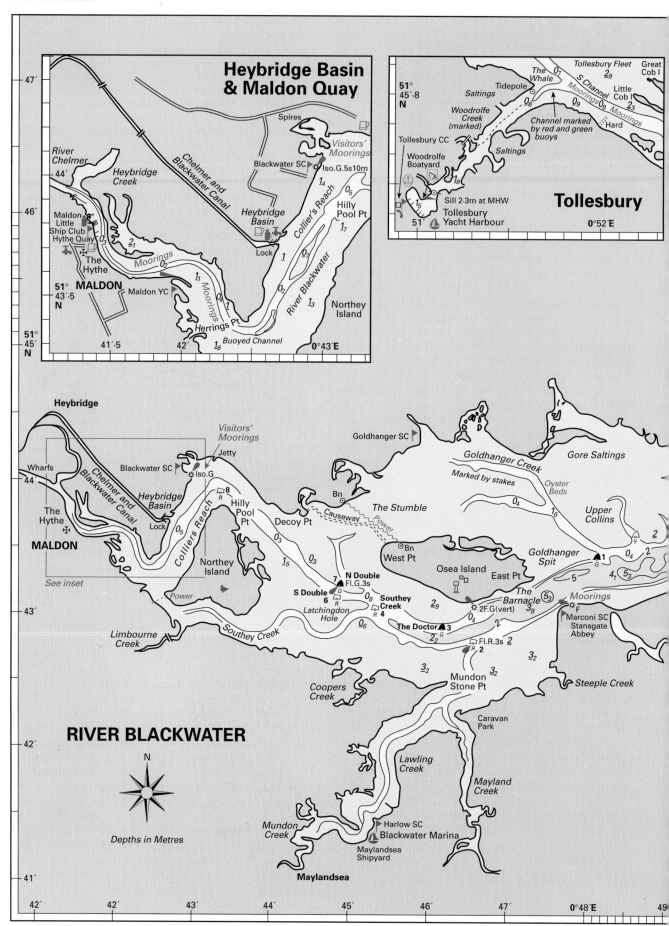

Heybridge Basin & Maldon Quay

47'

Spires

River Chelmer

Chelmer and Blackwater Canal

Heybridge Creek

44'

Blackwater SC

Visitors' Moorings

Iso.G.5s10m

46'

Maldon Little Ship Club
Hythe Quay

The Hythe

Heybridge Basin

Lock

0_3

2_1

0_2

Collier's Reach

1_4

0_5

Hilly Pool Pt

1_7

51° 43'.5 N

MALDON

Maldon YC

1_1

0_1

Moorings

2_7

1

River Blackwater

Northey Island

1_3

0_2

51° 45' N

Herrings Pt

Buoyed Channel

1_6

41'.5

42'

0°43'E

Tollesbury

51° 45'.8 N

The Whale

0_1

Tollesbury Fleet

2_9

Great Cob I

Saltings

Tidepole

S Channel

Moorings

0_6

0_9

0_8

Little Cob I

2_3

Woodrolfe Creek (marked)

Tollesbury CC

Channel marked by red and green buoys

Hard

Saltings

Woodrolfe Boatyard

1_9

1_5

Sill 2·3m at MHW

51°

Tollesbury Yacht Harbour

Tollesbury

Tollesbury Yacht Harbour

0°52'E

Heybridge

Visitors' Moorings

Jetty

Goldhanger SC

Goldhanger Creek

Gore Saltings

Wharfs

Chelmer and Blackwater Canal

Blackwater SC

Iso.G

8
R

Marked by stakes

Oyster Beds

44'

The Hythe

Heybridge Basin

Lock

Hilly Pool Pt

Decoy Pt

Bn

0_4

1_6

Upper Collins

2
Y

MALDON

0_5

Collier's Reach

0_3

Causeway

Power

The Stumble

0_4

2

1
G

Northey Island

1_5

0_3

West Pt

Bn

Osea Island

Goldhanger Spit

0_4

2

5_3

See inset

7
N Double
Fl.G.3s

0_6

5

4_1

43'

Power

S Double

6
R

Southey Creek

2_9

2F.G(vert)

The Barnacle

5_3

Moorings

F

Limbourne Creek

Latchingdon Hole

4
R

0_6

3_8

Marconi SC
Stansgate Abbey

Southey Creek

The Doctor 3

0_4

2_2

3_2

0_6

2
G

Fl.R.3s 2

2
R

Coopers Creek

3_2

Mundon Stone Pt

3_2

Steeple Creek

RIVER BLACKWATER

42'

N

Caravan Park

Lawling Creek

Mayland Creek

Depths in Metres

Mundon Creek

Harlow SC

Blackwater Marina

Maylandsea Shipyard

41'

Maylandsea

42' 42' 43' 44' 45' 46' 47' 0°48'E 49'

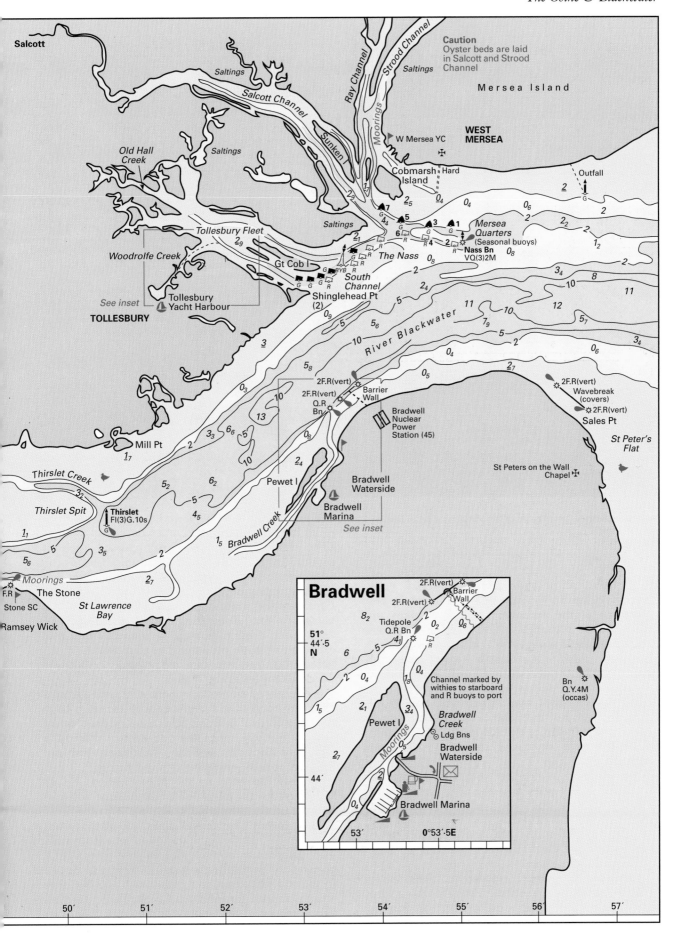

Salcott

Saltings

Saltings

Salcott Channel

Old Hall Creek

Saltings

Caution
Oyster beds are laid
in Salcott and Strood
Channel

M e r s e a   I s l a n d

Ray Channel

Strood Channel

Saltings

Moorings

W Mersea YC

WEST
MERSEA

Cobmarsh
Island

Hard

Outfall

2

0₄

0₄

0₆

2

2₅

▲7
4₄
G

▲5
G

3
G

▲1

Mersea
Quarters
(Seasonal buoys)

2₂

1₂

Tollesbury Fleet

Saltings

2₉

6
R

4

2

Nass Bn
VQ(3)2M

0₈

Woodrolfe Creek

2₉

Gt Cob I

G
BYB

The Nass

0₈

3₄

8

11

2₁

R

G R

G   G   G   R

*South
Channel*

2

2₄

3₄

10

12

See inset

TOLLESBURY

Tollesbury
Yacht Harbour

Shinglehead Pt
(2)

0₉

5

5₆

River Blackwater

11

7₉

10

2

0₆

3₄

5

3

10

5₈

0₄

2₇

0₃

10

0₅

2F.R(vert)
Wavebreak
(covers)

2F.R(vert)

Sales Pt

13

2F.R(vert)

2F.R(vert)

Q.R
Bn

Barrier
Wall

0₈

Bradwell
Nuclear
Power
Station (45)

*St Peter's
Flat*

Mill Pt

1₇

3₃

6₆

5

2

10

2₄

Pewet I

Bradwell
Waterside

St Peters on the Wall
Chapel

Thirslet Creek

3₂

5₂

6₂

5

Thirslet
Fl(3)G.10s
G

4₅

Bradwell
Marina

See inset

Thirslet Spit

1₁

5

3₅

2

1₅ *Bradwell Creek*

Bn
Q.Y.4M
(occas)

5₆

2₇

Moorings

F.R

The Stone

Stone SC

*St Lawrence
Bay*

Ramsey Wick

Bradwell

2F.R(vert)

2F.R(vert)

Barrier
Wall

51°
44´·5
N

8₂

Tidepole
Q.R Bn

2

0₂

0₆

R

6

5

4₁

Channel marked by
withies to starboard
and R buoys to port

2

0₄

1₈

0₄

Bn
Q.Y.4M
(occas)

1₅

2₁

3₄

Pewet I

*Bradwell
Creek*

Moorings

Ldg Bns

0₅

Bradwell
Waterside

2₇

44´

2

0₄

Bradwell Marina

53´

0°53´·5E

Tollesbury Marina (also known as Woodrolfe's) is set in idyllic surroundings . . .

spectacle to mark your arrival or delay your progress. However, you may be slowed down by the emergence of the water/landscape that opens up before you. It is enough to arrest all but the most cynical and world weary. It is a paradigm of 'inland' waterways and a classic expression of Blackwater/backwater saltings and East Coast scenery at their flattest and bestest. Chestnut browns and bronzed siennas surround you in all shapes and shades, tints and textures; while small islands and headlands point fingers of green that search out and show the shallow creeks and channels.

The last turn is to port into the diminutive Woodrolfe Creek and on to the cilled entrance to Tollesbury Yacht Harbour. For those wishing to search out the less orthodox, there is also another channel, to the north; but goose-pimples have always made me chicken out of swanning up past the Great Cob that way.

The marina is a happy, secluded and quiet place; but not without great joyful socialising for those who wish to find it in the clubhouse and the bar. It is an ideal spot for a tucked-away weekend.

The village is close by, and the pleasant, but most of all intriguing, walk will take you within sight of three chandlers and the parish council open-air swimming pool. The ancient buildings of the waterside are set off well by weatherboarding, and there are many occasions when you can stand and think yourself straight into one of the old masters. Closer to the village there begins a strange and fascinating combination of a modern industrial estate intent upon presenting an olde-worlde, craft-based image and a genuine olde-worlde, craft-based village intent on being 'with it'.

It offers good shopping opportunities, with a most excellent butcher and a grocer who carries a large selection of 'deli' fare and other esoteric eats; in fact a most unlikely range for the corner shop of a remote and tiny village. Sadly, 'Marjorie's: Fish and Fashion' is now something of a red herring.

We now go back to the Nass beacon. To its southwest lies the deep-water channel that will lead into the upriver Blackwater. The big ships that used to lie at anchor have now all gone, and all that is left to observe is the power station and its barrier wall. The perspective of this wall as you approach it changes so that it often appears to be a large vessel. In the end, of course, it explains itself and becomes a useful marker for Bradwell Creek. There is a tide-gauge beacon at the 'outlet' of the creek that leads

TOLLESBURY

Woodrolfe Boatyard (Tollesbury Marina)
☎ 01621 869202, Radio: VHF Ch 80 (M)

Tidal access HW ±2hrs

Ⓥ (240, visitors' berths vary), 🆆🅲, 🅿, ⚓, ⚡, ⚓
Provisions (nearby), Ⓒ, 🛢D, Engineer, Repairs

Tollesbury Saltings Ltd ☎ 01621 868624

Tidal access HW ±2½hrs

Ⓥ (120, 6 visitors'), 🆆🅲, 🅿, ⚓, ⚡ (some),
Provisions, Ⓒ (nearby), Engineer, Repairs

BRADWELL-ON-SEA

Bradwell Marina ☎ 01621 776235
Radio VHF Ch 80 (M)

Tidal access HW ± 4hrs

Ⓥ (300 pontoon, visitors' vary), 🆆🅲, 🅿, ⚓, ⚡, ⚓
Provisions, Ⓒ, 🛢D, 🛢P, Engineer, Repairs

. . . with an equally idyllic route through the approach channels. This is a fine area for classic saltings and withies *par excellence*.

to Bradwell Marina. It can be easily seen once you are past the barrier wall. However, it can only properly be read if you approach it from a position inshore of the barrier wall.

A starboard-hand buoy marks the spit at the bend in the Creek, and the leading marks are still in place on the shore. The marina channel is well marked by the new red buoys – the old beer cans having unhappily gone to the great cellar in the deeps! The buoyage is very easy to follow, making the last approach straightforward. There are green withies, and one pointed green cone to indicate the tight dogleg. The short channel into the marina itself tends just to port of middle, with a small spit to starboard when you first turn in. The channel is well marked by withies port and starboard. The turn into the marina, upstream with moorings all round and the remains of the once-working quay on the port hand, is marked by the last red buoy. The actual entrance is through a narrow channel, clearly marked with substantial red-and-green withies. You will need just a little better than half tide if you draw more than 1·5m. Note that, even on neap tides, the ebb can flow swiftly.

It is interesting that Bradwell is registered as 'Port Flair'. I have never heard of anyone call it by that name, but it is appropriate for a facility that, although it is set in completely rural surroundings, manages to keep about itself an air of the cosmopolitan. The chandlery is small, but the

Bradwell Marina is usually busily quiet and quietly busy. It has an intriguingly ambivalent ambience: in the midst of a truly rural patch (sceptics please note the location of the post office) it manages to achieve an atmosphere of cosmopolitan gregariousness.

service is larger than the premises, and almost anything can be obtained within a day or two.

The Essex police vessel, *Alert*, can be seen on its berth at the marina. In 1995, it was frequently called upon to deal with the 'troubles' at Brightlingsea. Often, the police had to prevent or deal with animal lovers who were attempting to throw themselves in the water in front of commercial shipping. One of the officers says, 'I don't really have a view; but I don't like eating baby flesh, if you get my drift.'

I have been made more than welcome at Bradwell Marina many times and oft; and recent changes have served only to improve the general atmosphere. The club serves meals at down-to-earth prices (seven days a week, customers willing) and there is some table service. I did not find the food or wine list in any way outstanding, but everyone else did. It certainly helps to take the sting out of being weather-bound. Many yachts use the upper reaches of the Creek itself, either for mooring or for anchoring. Their masts can be seen for a long way up the creek and are also outstanding from the river.

The creek rejoins the Blackwater via St Lawrence Creek, just before the easterly beginning of the eponymous Bay. I have never succeeded in getting

through but, perhaps on the right tide on the right day, I shall be able so to do.

There is a narrow path from the marina to the tiny hamlet of a village called Bradwell Waterside. Once, it was all-over tarmac, but now it is breaking up and falling apart. What is to be said in its favour is that it has become completely overgrown with wild flowers, wild weeds and natty nettles. This is not the route to take when returning from a long, late night at the Green Man, when the nettles and the potholes would make it an obstacle course, with deep ditches awaiting you. There is a longer, but less encumbered, route along the bank.

The Green Man is no longer Green; much more mustardy, or perhaps the colour of Dengie Pie. The Captain's Table offers 'All you can eat for £12.50 – and we do take Visa'. However, it never opens before 12 noon.

The 'centre' of the community is at the top of the slight hill, and is only a few minutes' walk away. The old traditional village 'corner shop' has been converted into a studio by James Cooper. He paints in various media, including oils, and enjoys a number of styles. His background is unlikely for a painter – he was a policeman who wanted to go into law but, having failed to be called to the Bar, now calls his own tune.

The 'new' village shop is to be found (that is if you can find it at all) to the left of the T-junction at the top of the hill. There is an arrow, but it does need to be interpreted with some discernment and discretion. You should move on past the green on the left-hand side and down a narrow lane where you will see a notice: 'Nuclear Electric. No visitors allowed'. (I pondered for a long while why they should stipulate such a command when the last thing that anyone would be likely to want to do is visit a Nuclear Electric site.) Do not despair. The shop will appear when you reach the old house at the end of the lane. The shop and post office are in its forecourt. The small shop offers a small range of goods, but does so with amplitude and friendliness. Much of the counter display consists of home-made sweet-toothed fantasies, strange marmalades and jams. There are second-hand books for sale at 10p each, with proceeds going to the Great Ormond Street Hospital for Sick Children. The lady told me, with justifiable pride, that they had raised over £400 by 1995. It is open almost every day from 0900 until at least 1300, except Sunday, when it closes at 1100. This is not a guide to shopping on the Blackwater, neither is it intended to be, but this shop offers such a recherché experience that it should not be missed by any visitor.

Back at the top of the hill, there is another delight in store for those who like to pursue the phenomenal. It is the small chapel of St Peter:

In 653 AD St Cedd sailed from Lindisfarne in Northumbria, itself an outpost of Iona in Scotland, as part of the great Celtic Christian mission. All that remains of his little monastery today is this simple chapel which attracts 14,000 visitors each year.

Back at the marina, I was able to leave my berth a good 2 hours before high water (with a 5·9m tide) with never less the 1·0m below the keel. Once out in the channel again, and heading upstream, it may appear tempting to cut the corner by the beacon, but it is right on the edge of the spit and must be

The tidal waters veritably rush in over the cill at Tollesbury Marina. Note the substantial depth gauge.

fully rounded. Further upriver, the low water level is marked by withies. Since many of them are submerged at high water, it is not a good idea to go too near the sides, unless one of the regular East Coast fogs demands you pick them up for navigating.

The old Radio Caroline vessel sits just by a white buoy with a red top and the No. 12 just after the creek. No. 5 Yellow marks the spits by Mill Creek and Mill Point to the north. Although not in the best of repair, the 'good ship Caroline' is still red and bright – at home to visitors, if you please, via a trip boat from the marina. It still has enough of an aura to remind one of those days when 'Bliss it was that dawn to be alive, But to be young was very heaven!'. And indeed, Caroline headed a revolution – the consequences of which it could never have foreseen and probably never imagined. Today, broadcasting has spawned so much trashy transmission with so many puny presenters, that it is good to be reminded of the times when programmes used to be programmes – namely, properly defined 'schemes of events to provide entertainment' – and not what we have today . . . opiates for the masses. It might have been illegal; it might have been immoral; but it kept us on our ears and it didn't make us fat.

The entrance to the shallow St Lawrence Creek is 2 miles SW of Bradwell power station and is marked by a small red buoy. It almost joins Bradwell Creek and is a nice hidey-hole for getting out of the main channel on the less broadly muddied side. Just across the water, after Mill Creek, comes the more well-known Thirslet Creek, marked by its unusual beacon buoy that, in turn, marks its spit.

Many yachts have been caught out by the fact that these banks with their extensive spits stretch further out into the river than someone not used to the muddy ways of East Coast cruising might think. Make sure that you don't set a course that lines up Thirslet beacon and the very small conical green Goldhanger buoy when proceeding to or from the power station. If you are at all unsure, it is better to keep to the south shoreline, with an eye open for the withies which also mark far-reaching oyster layings. I have been so intrigued by birdwatching, wanting to get just that bit nearer, that I have only too often found myself stirring up muddy waters.

Both Thirslet and Goldhanger Creeks provide quiet anchorages just within their entrances. Neither offers a spectacle of natural splendour, but both have elements of barren grandeur and furnish silence and seclusion. By using the dinghy and stout wet-gear boots you can find numerous landings at all these creeks and plenty of quiet country walks to the not-too-distant local communities. *Ordnance Survey Pathfinders* are useful guides.

While the different kind of beacon at Thirslet is not difficult to spot, the green Goldhanger, marking the farthest easterly extension of Osea Island, is not easy to pick out from its background. Sometimes it looks yellow, and can be easily confused with the yellow conical/barrel Collins 2, 3 and 4 that sometimes stand close enough by to mislead. Recently, one of these buoys was moved by order of Trinity House, but the stout local fishermen were not about to have any of their traditional marks moved at the whimsical order of some absent water-lord. It was cut adrift, and the powers that would like to have been, were overpowered by the powers that be. It has been back on-station for some time now.

Recently, my eye was taken by the appealing sight of what looked like basking seals. In my enthusiasm, I almost went into shoal water to look at them from closer quarters. As I approached, curiosity and disappointment set in as I discovered nothing other than what looked like a fleet of oil drums covered in black plastic. Later, I asked around for information, but the locals I spoke to knew nothing about them. Perhaps they weren't going to put it around, or perhaps I just picked the wrong locals, but I never learned of their purpose.

So, if not intending to prowl into the inner depths of the floating mud and spreading saltings that make up the huge foreshore of the southern side of the mainland, we keep to the port hand. The deepest water is to be found, first, in the middle of the river coming up from Bradwell to Thirslet. Then it tends to the southwest as we head for the Sailing Club off the Stone where there are some visitors' moorings. The deepest water then runs westerly towards the old jetty on the south bank of Osea Island. To the east of the Stone is the expanse of shallow water known as St Lawrence Bay. It can be approached by shoal craft by turning into Lawrence Creek about a mile downstream, almost opposite the Thirslet beacon. Nearby are Ramsey Marsh and Ramsey Island, both popular with holidaymakers. Indeed, the whole area round the Stone is devoted to leisure, pleasure and water sports, as witness the plethora of moorings belonging to the local sailing clubs, and the shoresides assortment of short-order holiday accommodation.

It is not always easy to identify exactly what's what on the Stone shore – caravans, masts, chimneys, bungalows, boats and trees all combine to create a backcloth of potential confusion for the stranger in what is a low conglomerate of miniature palaces of pleasure; that is except for the long, low, flat symmetrical building with its identical windows all in straight lines . . . very neat. The triangular racing marks of the Stone Sailing Club stand out clearly as does the outstanding white hut. On the western end of the (not really) island, there is a fixed navigation mark flown by the Marconi Sailing Club. Along the shore, there is a sea wall in front of which there are a few moorings. These are followed by a string of larger moorings, a landing stage and posts for the Marconi Club, with space for visitors. The red mooring buoys are solid men. In fact, they are so substantial that it is possible to confuse one of them with the red No. 2 marking Lawling Creek. Especially so, since it tends to be partly camouflaged against the vast expanse of its low-lying background

An almost concealed, secret winding staircase leads up to the watch tower where everything is on view – and most everything in the marina and nearby waters can be observed. It may look a little bleak – but the welcome is warm.

Rounding Stansgate Point to the southwest presents a good open view of the remains of the Abbey which, from the anchorage at Osea Island, makes an even more splendid sight in the changing lights of the passing hours. The Abbey has more or less returned to the land. It is said that, some decades ago, an old stone coffin was used by the farmer as a water trough – presumably for his horses or taking a rude bath, rather than for baptism.

Osea Island was known to the Romans and inhabited in Saxon times by a fisherman and three serfs who guarded 60 sheep. After 1066 it was given to a nephew of William the Conqueror. In 1903, one Mr F N 'Brewer' Charrington bought it to build 'Temperance Town', but his plans came to nought. He did however turn his own home on the island into a 'retreat for gentlefolk who had fallen into the drink habit'. In the Second World War it was used by the navy, but more recently it has gone back to private ownership.

At low water it is possible to walk over to the Goldhanger mainland from the northwest tip of Osea Island, just above West Point, where there is a causeway. I have heard that, not only did the inmates move across whenever they could, but that sheep farmers had a *ram*pant trade with the sinful sufferers. The farmers smuggled the booze across in accoutrements disguised as sheep accessories. Eventually, the prohibition was broken just as it was in the States, so perhaps it should have been called sheep-legging.

I for one have questions to ask about the present occupation, having always found the island to present something of an enigma. To start with, the pillbox still squats as a sinister sentinel or guardian; but guardian against what? Neither the Germans nor the Dutch, who, while arriving in large numbers, do not do so in threatening mode.

I never feel that I have understood its mysterious ambience. Nor have I pierced the veil that hides (what I imagine to be) the clandestine events that take place behind the blind and blinded windows of that single sombre edifice. Windows that seem to stare blankly like the sad, bad eyes of the long dead. I have never experienced a hospitable gesture from any human soul, nor sensed the possibility of 'Welcome' on the doormat – that is, should any visitor happenstance to get that far. Another cause for interest concerns the apparently temporary denizens who propel, from time to time, unusual vehicles that move in unearthly ways. One of them seemed to fly like a bird. Over the years, for me, the house has carried the stamp of the disappointed founder. Indeed, I wonder if he sits there like some Miss Havisham or a phantom from one of Tennessee William's more eerie works. Adding to the general air of mystery and magic are the silver trees, all in varying states of death and decay, that draw startling attention to themselves as they stand out against the greens of their neighbours; apparently more alive and alert than the actual living.

I find Osea Island hypnotic in its apparently endless enigma and its fascinating, if chequered, history – ancient and modern. In less cabalistic terms, it appeals because of its attractive anchorage, just below the pier, where the agreeable sandy beach is steep-to and backed by trees. The ebb and flood both run fast; but not too fast to let us see the jellyfish that often come by in huge numbers.

The pier still reaches out as if in hope that one day regular traffic will arrive again. However, it seems highly unlikely that it will survive much longer. It is skeletal and looks to be in a very insecure state, but its fixed green beacon lights are in good shape. The pier is virtually opposite the red No. 2 buoy, and it is important to anchor well to the east of a line between the pier and the buoy in order to avoid the shallows known as the Barnacle. One to two cables off is a good position. The deepest part of the channel, which is narrow at this point, is midway between red No. 2 and green No. 3 (the unnamed Doctor) which stands just off the island.

There is a shallow channel to the north of Osea Island, which is found by leaving the green Goldhanger Spit buoy to port and moving northwest for about ½ mile. If you then continue on that course until stakes and withies mark a channel you will find Goldhanger Creek itself, with the Goldhanger Sailing Club at the very 'head of the navigation'. The 'main' channel is found by leaving Goldhanger Creek about ½ mile before the sailing club and tending to the southwest. This will take you across the Stumble; across the Causeway; and back into the river. The channel to the village of Goldhanger was used in the past by barges. Nowadays it is only local craft in search of peace or fishing who attempt to search out its mysteries. Any

**BLACKWATER MARINA
(LAWLING CREEK)**
☎ 01621 740264
Radio
VHF Ch 80 (0900–2300)
Tidal access
HW ±2½hrs (1m)
Ⓥ (168: 150 swinging moorings, 20 visitors'), [WC], 🚿, ⚓, ⚡, ⚓, Provisions, Ⓖ, ⛽D, Engineer, Repairs

such manoeuvre for a visitor is a top-of-the-tide job, and must not be taken without much forethought and an equal amount of caution, for it can be a fraught affair for a stranger.

There are two more pleasing anchorages in Lawling Creek just across the water. The creek is entered by the No. 2 red can buoy that marks the main river channel. It is sited at the furthest extension of the spit, off Mundon Stone Point. A yellow buoy (marked Mundon) is laid just off the Spit headland itself and is a good marker for the channel. For shoal craft with a notion for shallows, the miniature Steeple Creek which is found by following the mainland shore south from Stansgate Abbey is ideal. While a deeper proposition is the main Lawling Creek that goes all the way to Maylandsea.

At the confluence, Mundon Stone Point reaches out east well into Lawling Creek. At half tide it still shows its brown and green contours, reminding the passer-by that it is an elemental item and not to be trifled with. Across the river is the east headland of Ramsey and its holiday caravans where, tucked away, is Mayland Creek which, for a dinghy trip, goes deep into the backwaters.

There are red and orange deep-water moorings at the entrance to Lawling Creek, and sometimes they are unoccupied. At the creek head is the community of Maylandsea, where the marina is now called 'Blackwater'. It has been taken over by the Maritime and Leisure Group. The channel up to it is now plain and clear – just follow the line of moored craft up Lawling Creek, keeping close to the 'C' buoy numbers as they progress. Starting at C1, they continue up to 67, by which number you will be almost opposite the pontoons. Some of them also carry the legend 'BMC'. Those with more than average draught will find that there are big boats to offer guidance about the deep-water channel. For 1·5m craft, access across the Mundon Bar is no better than half tide, although there may be plenty of water once you have got over it.

Many of the marina pontoons are private, so it is a good idea to call ahead on VHF Ch 37. Otherwise, on arrival, visitors should go to the first pontoon. You will probably be observed and met by the friendly and efficient harbourmaster. The previous atmosphere of a deeply remote boatyard no longer obtains. The place is a veritable hive of activity, having been brought thoroughly up to date by the

Never rowdy; never raucous; never crowded; and seldom busy: the anchorage at Osea Island is one of the most pleasing on the East Coast – provided imagination doesn't take over and people your craft with sinister ghosts.

new management. There are full facilities for contemporary cruising needs: serviced pontoons; major workshops and boatyard; a well-stocked chandlery; and a new bar and restaurant. It is a most attractive proposition for a weekend visit.

Shoresides, the truth will out – it is something of a strange if not actually weird place. Not without charm and attraction, but definitely unusual.

There are better than basic facilities in the village which is a short and attractive walk away. The appealing, willing and friendly greengrocer is still in the village: 'Oh, yes, guv. We're still here. Always will be. Where else would we ever be?'. He is a sailing man to boot.

There are other facilities to try out – the General Lee public house, the fish'n'chip shop (the 'Chip Inn'), general store, hardware store, a visiting butcher, a carpet shop, a hairdressers, a 'Cockney Girl' clothes shop, and a bakery known as 'The Golden Platter'. The service, if not speedy, is friendly – and anyway, who wants to rush in that part of the woody, muddy backwoods and waters? There are buses to Maldon and Chelmsford.

Back in the Blackwater, speed limit buoys and racing marks from here onwards literally litter the

scene, almost taking over from the standard navigation marks. They are, however, fairly easy to spot; very helpful since the channel not only narrows but also wanders at will in the still confusingly broad waters of the flats.

Off the main channel to the south is Copper's Creek, just past the Doctor buoy. It is a channel for dedicated mud crawlers and, as such, offers an almost watertight guarantee that once you are there you will be left alone. It is only too easy to get neaped. A little further upstream, the Southey red No. 4 buoy marks the entrance to the creek. It is a modest fellow, as is his senior upstream, No. 6, who is, however, much sprightlier, brighter and altogether redder in aspect. The creek, which has a centre yellow buoy, leads you first to Latchingdon Hole, which is the furthest point upstream where craft can lay afloat through the tides. But there is more . . . this creek also takes a southern passage round Northey Island. Such a trip is an excursion to be made by dinghy or mud waders. It is definitely an interesting one since there is more land to be seen from that side of the island than from the north, which is mainly saltings. It passes over a causeway marked some time ago by yellow beacons.

Going past the green and red 'North and South Doubles' there is a yellow buoy with a red-and-white pennant standing off the spit by West Point on Osea Island, and the power lines are well marked by their beacons. The southern point of Goldhanger, Decoy Point, is marked by a buoy bearing the legend, 'Osea Road'. There was once a decoy pond here to catch ducks for sale in town. In this area, where the river is quite wide, the water tends to become shallower but gains depth again once the narrower leg going up to Hilly Pool Point is reached. The red can buoy (No. 8) just off the point is not easy to spot against the moorings and shoreline; but the Blackwater Sailing Club flagstaff is a good enough mark once you have passed the green North Double No. 7 buoy. The plentiful speed limit buoys also tend to give some indication of the channel. However, there are, in addition, dinghies and other small craft in the area to add even more colour to what is generally a fairly confusing panorama. There is another signpost to help you pick up the red No. 8 and that is the long and low white building of the Blackwater Sailing Club. The buoy appears just on the upstream side of it.

We are now in a popular sailing spot, to which testify the many boats and boathouses, some of these being in the classic tradition. The Sailing Club

marks the end of the buildings before the settlement that is Heybridge Basin hoves into view. Approaching it, the 'headland' of Northey Island stands out brown and dark green against the pale sands and sea wall on the north mainland.

Heybridge Basin

After No. 8 buoy, the river turns dramatically to port and shortly leads to the lock basin at Heybridge. There is one large mooring buoy upstream of the lock and a good number of slightly less substantial ones. Many of them are completely high and dry at low water – not even a cupful. An alternative is to anchor on the other side of the river where the holding ground is good. Although the lock is usually operated only for about an hour before and after high water, the keeper does have his eye on the river most of the time and will call you to the approach so that you can tie up to the staging as soon as possible. The channel to the lock entrance is now much less of a dogleg than it was; approached best from the south then tending to the west. You pass one green sapling of a withy, apparently in such poor health that, ailing and failing, it leans over almost at 45°. To see it at low water, having faithfully trusted it as a true mark when coming in, is to note it carefully for reference on the way out.

Heybridge Basin, where the one-time thriving Chelmer and Blackwater navigation meets the Blackwater river. Entry is restricted to tide times – and there are only brief windows then. The authorities prize and price themselves highly – but the place is of a singular milieu.

Now we are inside – let credit be given where it's due and homage paid where deserved. Heybridge Basin is an extraordinary place; in my experience, unique in the UK. It is still enjoying something of a high and holiday. Its popularity has increased with cruising folk but, in spite of the fact that fees have increased to reflect this popularity, it seems to have done nothing to deter visitors. Since it is not always possible to get a berth on demand or by chance, it is wise to phone ahead.

The Basin is attractive in most of the usual postcard ways, but it also a one-off. The only other lock in any way remotely like it is West Stockwith on the River Trent, all the way up in the frozen north. There is no shop, but there are the two pubs: the Jolly Sailor and the Old Ship. You pays your money and you takes your choice, but the Old Ship Inn cannot be beaten for quantity. It has 'local' jazz with strange equipment, a particularly idiosyncratic attitude to melody, and an eccentric approach to harmony. If you are interested in people as well as places, there will be no shortage of intrigue and entertainment.

The James McMillan Boatyard and Chandlery specialises in fastenings of all kinds; the owner is also a contact for horses, second-hand cars, a range of boats, and his chandlery section is excellently well stocked. His strength, however, lies in his endearing charm. There are plenty of engineers to be easily found in the area; but there is no possibility of gas or fuel. Heybridge is not without boatbuilding history. The famous racing yacht *Jullanar* was built here in 1875, inspired by one E H Bentall, an agricultural tool merchant. She was among the fastest in her day.

I was pleased, on my last visit there, to find that George, the ex- and now 80 year-old lock-keeper

The chick weed et al once lay so thick on the water that a (not very bright-eyed) dog walked on as if it were a lawn. It wasn't bushy tailed either on exit.

was still there and active with his fishing boat *Lady Joan*. When he saw that I was single-handed, he insisted on pulling me through the lock and tying me up next his own boat. I sat and pondered on the thought that I may or may not be doing the same for someone else at that age. How ponderous can one get?

There are plans for the lock to have new doors fitted, perhaps even with up-to-date signals. There is no loo or shower associated with the lock, but there is mains electricity and water. The fees for just locking in and out are very high; so, once inside, it makes sense to stay there for a couple of days at least, and make it a worthwhile proposition.

Sadly, there is no really regular bus service to the basin – sometimes it arrives and sometimes it departs, but one is well advised to consult the operators at length before planning a trip to Maldon. By dinghy you can get to the small township of Heybridge within minutes, and will no doubt come across a lot of wildlife on the way. After the original stint of bankside moorings, the Chelmer & Blackwater canal settles down into quiet countryside peace. The lilies are beautiful in season and there seems to have been little chick/duck weed of recent years. The only sounds are likely to be the

The approach channel to Maldon makes its sinuous progress, resembling an effete poet's verse as it dribbles thinly down a quarto page.

Above Just to the right of middle can be seen the few places at Maldon's renowned quay where modestly sized leisure craft can find a haven of a mooring for anything more than a few hours. Betterment for such craft is said to be in the pipeline.

MALDON

Heybridge Basin ☎ 01621 853506

Tidal access

Sea lock, HW ±1hr

Ⓥ (200, inc. visitors'), WC (nearby), ⛽, ⚡, Ⓖ, D, P (by arrangement), Engineer, Repairs

Hythe Quay (Maldon District Council)

☎ 01621 856487/0860 456802

Tidal access

HW ±2hrs

Ⓥ (moorings from river bailiff; visitors' pontoon), WC, ⛽, ⚡, ↘ (quay), Provisions (nearby), Ⓖ (nearby), D (nearby), P (nearby), Engineer (nearby), Repairs (nearby)

Maldon Little Ship Club ☎ 01621 854139

Tidal access

HW ±1½hrs

Berths T S

Blackwater Sailing Club ☎ 01621 853923

Tidal access

HW ±2hrs

WC, 🚿, ⛽, ⚡, ↘, Ⓖ (nearby)

splash of the oars; the occasional plop from a fisherman's cast; or the sound of ducks instructing their ducklings. On one occasion, I came across a single mother with ten chicks in line astern who, within seconds, was seeing off a lurking male. There are also swans in attendance. They can look threatening, as is their matchless way; but they always stop short of attempting to eat the dinghy. One family had six grown-up and very active cygnets. A little further up the canal is the quite different experience of a large Tesco store, with a small landing only yards away. It is also a pleasant walk along the canal bank to Heybridge and then into the town. The canal is no longer what you would call 'navigable' by anything much more substantial than a canoe. The aforementioned Ms Driscoll says:

> Heybridge Basin used to have a little shop by the lock (Old Ship side) and down the Lock Hill and round the corner was a sizeable double-fronted shop, Pam's Stores, and a small butcher's shop. In the Basin, too, used to lay Dutch and Danish eel boats when Kuitjen's live-eel business was situated there.

When moving up to Maldon, there is a dramatic turn to be made from southeast to northwest at Herrings Point. The channel is clearly marked by red and green buoys; just as well since, jutting right out from the mainland, are three huge lumps of concrete. In 1961, the Maldon ballast company, A J Brush Ltd, put a Scotch crane on the headland, hoping to load here instead of at Maldon. It never got off the ground and the crane was removed. Locals still call it 'The Crane'. Happily, the channel goes nowhere near them.

Decades ago, any sortie to the quay at Maldon had to be strictly planned and just as strictly executed; for it was business and barges – first, last and almost only. Sometimes you could manage to get a berth by going up with the tide, and sneaking into a cranny or hanging on, by grace and favour, to something much larger; and that was, of course, more by luck that good management.

If you draw more than 2·0m or more, you will need to take care. There is never more than 3·0m at the best spring tides in Maldon and neaps can be down to less than 1·50m by the jetties; although there is about 0·50m more in the channel itself. Perhaps the best plan nowadays is to wait over a tide or two at Heybridge (which is, after all, no hardship) and get local advice. You can also phone Maldon for a modus operandi right up to the quay.

You need to know that there is no harbourmaster as such at Maldon. There are two significant positions – the river bailiff, a post currently occupied by Nigel Harmer; and the river warden, currently Chris Reynolds-Hole. Nigel, an ex-sailing-sailor-marine has made great progress on behalf of visiting leisure craft and, recently, there have been some major changes. There is now a 'floating' pontoon. True, it is modest but it is also efficient and substantial enough to take a few boats each tide. There is also a new river bailiff's office block and workroom. Last, but perhaps most importantly for yachtsmen, there are full shower and toilet facilities. Electricity is also available, but you may need a really long power line. There are plans to improve that situation. All in all, there is a marked change in the welcome that a yachtsman is likely to receive from the quay. Whether you are met by the bailiff himself, or the river warden will make no difference: you will get a warm welcome and as much help as you seem to want.

Immediately shoresides, on the famous Hythe, there are three hospitable venues – the Maldon Little Ship Club; the thoroughly modernised Jolly Sailor; and the quite traditional Queen's Head. One weekend offered, on Saturday, a 'Midsummer Xmas' party in the Queen's Head; on Sunday, the Salvation Army, jazz, an oil-drum band and fireworks; and, on Tuesday, Morris Dancing, complete with black leather jackets and pseudo Harley Davidsons holding a chapel outside the Jolly Sailor. Later in the week there was the ritual Ride of the London Cabbies, circuiting the town centre in their annual appeal to raise money for children's hospitals.

Back at the quay, there are more and better facilities for yachtsmen than one might expect in such a small town. Almost next the quay is an excellent chandlery and, close by, plenty of really co-operative boatyards, engineers and sailmakers. The Felixstowe Oyster Company is at the head of the quay. When Chris, the water bailiff, as welcoming and charming as ever, insisted that I should be introduced to the processes (that is, preparation and consumption), I hesitantly agreed. I was offered oysters with the traditional slice of lemon and have been addicted ever since.

It is but a short, steep climb to reach the beginnings of the High Street. Once at the top, joys are immediately to be seen abounding: first-rate Indian and Chinese take-aways and restaurants aplenty; a good motor spares and plant hire with *Calor Gas* at the corner. In particular, there is an splendid bookshop, All Books, at 2 Mill Road. The shop is filled to bursting with all kinds of books; and for any reader of same a visit must be obligatory. Nearer to the centre is a most helpful old-fashioned ironmongers while, in the centre itself, the town is littered with real food shops – bakers, butchers, wet fish shops and a very good deli. The gamut is there to be run, from Yamahas and BT mobiles to home-made brawn, to smoked-on-the-premises haddock, to not very exciting hand-made crafts. All Saints church stands out, as does the 15th-century D'Arcy Moot Hall. It is often cap-doffingly referred to as The D'Arcy Tower. It now contains the remnants of previous high office; the Great Mace and the Police Station, for example. How are the mighty fallen.

Maldon is an altogether special and splendid experience. It is, as it were, required reading; certainly more than worth its place on the front cover of the first edition of this East Coast pilot.

VII. The Crouch & Roach

The main navigational aids for the entry into the River Crouch are the red and white Wallet and Swin Spitway buoys. On either side of them, are the cardinal Knoll, at about 3 miles to the northwest from the Wallet; and the cardinal Whitaker at about 2 miles to the southeast. Some beacons and some of the many Whitaker buoys will also be seen. Once you have confirmed the buoys for your track – provided you take care to follow the route indicated by the River Crouch buoyage – there is no hazard up to Burnham-on-Crouch. Visitors should note that the better water has, in the past, always seemed to tend southerly in the river. It seems that the Swallowtail has been growing over the past couple of years, so it is important to keep an eye on the sounder when approaching it. It is also wise to do so until past the four Buxeys – Plain as well as Sunk. In the Buxey area it may be best to tend to the north, since it usually leaves the better water that side when the channel does shift.

The alternative is to use the Ray Sand Channel (frequently pronounced 'Rays'n'). This takes you on a southwest course from the green Eagle buoy or the cardinal Knoll past the Buxey beacon. This last marker should be left about ½ mile to the east. Then the move is towards the cardinal Outer Crouch, tending if anything to the west. (For more details on this passage see page 120 in the chapter on the Colne.)

An Essex landfall is neither inspiring nor dramatic, merely a slow growth from shallow waters into grey, low-lying flats. Maplin, Foulness and Buxey offer little of what is usually understood by the words 'land' or 'sand'. In any case, there is a good chance that they will be shrouded by one of the area's regular mists. Foulness Point and Holliwell Point stand out only a little from the surrounding water, though the former is slightly heralded by the odd shapes and horseshoe that make up the high ground known as the Cockle Banks.

As and when the coastline begins fully to emerge, it does so as a muddy waste, broken only by sewer outfalls, pylons, factory chimneys and spasm after spasm of bathing huts and caravans. It is sad that we have not left the area to living things who would have put it to better use than we. I was neither encouraged nor uplifted on my first visit to read on the chart: 'Caution: firing area. Experimental firing is frequently carried out off the Maplin and Foulness Sands. While this is in progress, no vessel may enter, or remain in the area.' Firing itself is bad enough, but 'experimental firing'? The caution went on: 'Obstructions to navigation, sometimes

BURNHAM-ON-CROUCH
51°37'·47N 00°48'·33E (Burnham Yacht Harbour)
Charts Admiralty 3750, 1975, 1183.
Imray Y17, Y7, Y6, C1. OS Landranger 168
Tides
Dover +0115
Authorities
Harbourmaster ☎ 01621 783602
Radio
VHF Ch 80 for Crouch Hr Mr launch (0900–1700, w/e); also Ch M

Burnham Yacht Harbour
☎ 01621 782150/785848
Radio VHF Ch M
Tides
Dover +0130
Tidal access 24hr (2·5m min)
Ⓥ (350: pontoon; 30+ visitors'), 🚻, ▯, ⚓, ⚡, ➘,
Provisions (nearby), ⊕, ▮D, Engineer, Repairs

Crouch Yacht Club ☎ 01621 782252
Tidal access
24hr
🚻, ▯, ⚓, ⚡, ➘

Rice & Cole Ltd ☎ 01621 782063
Tidal access
24hr
Ⓥ (half-tide & deep-water swinging moorings; visitors' vary), 🚻, ▯, ➘, Provisions (nearby), ⊕, ▮D, Engineer (by arrangement), Repairs

submerged, may be encountered within the area. beacons of no navigational significance, with or without lights, may also be erected.' Nothing endearing in that.

It is a good, long haul from the Whitaker buoy to Holliwell and Foulness Points and then there are still 4 more miles to Burnham. That long finger of Holliwell Point takes ages to become anything substantial. Exemplary of man's creative abilities are the concrete lookout/pillbox to the north and, to the south, all the paraphernalia of the Foulness Firing Range and Great Shell Corner.

Once the madness of the Foulness antics are behind us, on the south bank come three small headlands, each named 'Corner': they are known as Ware, Crouch and High. Much scrutiny is needed to spot and designate them by the naked eye. Then, 2 miles or so below Burnham, also on the south bank, comes Nase Point. The opposite headland (directly to the west) is Wallasea Ness. It is marked by a permanent yellow spherical buoy carrying a

Burnham-on-Crouch is often called Britain's 'foremost' yachting centre. No more than 100 years ago, it was almost unheard of, its only claim to anything being that it had good oysters. Now, after phenomenal growth, it has seemed impossible, year upon year, that another boat could find a berth.

radar reflector. It also needs to be well rounded before entering the Roach from upstream, particularly after NE winds when the buoy can be blown back on to the very muddy sands it marks.

No more than ½ mile upstream of Wallasea Ness, is the commencement of the Horse Shoal, now marked not only at its west end but also by the cardinal Horse Shoal. It is followed shortly after by green No. 1. Leisure craft can progress close-ish to the banks on either side of Horse in a least depth of 4·0m. However, the Horse itself carries no more than 0·6m. It is followed by the four dramatically striking spheres of the easily recognisable yellow buoys that mark the power cable. These are not to be confused with the yellow racing buoys, many of which are only laid in the summer season, being taken up in the winter. These markers are easy to spot in the Crouch as well as in the Roach. They frequently make good courses from spit to spit. The last leg into Burnham-on-Crouch is marked by the much improved close buoyage system consisting of all greens.

The buoyage, of course, helps to delineate the fairway but, in spite of the new Burnham Yacht Harbour and the refurbished Essex Marina, there seem to be just as many yachts at river moorings as when I first tried to find my way through them nearly 20 years ago. Indeed, at first glance, you get a vision that proves the truth of the old saying, 'Can't see the wood for the trees'. For the first-time visitor, especially one used to small havens, the boats will seem to be more plentiful than the water in which they sit. It seems barely possible that there is room for them all to swing. Its growth has been phenomenal. No more than 100 years ago, Burnham was an almost unheard-of somnambulant settlement. Its only claim to anything was that it had oysters. It was, of course, the now much-debated Southend railway line that brought it into the outside world. It wasn't long before it was discovered by the London Sailing Club and the Royal Corinthian Yacht Club. Soon after came what is now known as the Royal Burnham Yacht Club. In the early 1990s there were barely more than 500 yachts to be found there. Now, catch and count them if you can.

Burnham-on-Crouch is often called Britain's 'foremost' yachting centre. Many Yorkshire racing/yachting types who have learned their sailing skills under conditions more arduous than those usually encountered on the Crouch would, however, be sure to challenge any such claim. Be that as it may, there is no argument about it being very busy.

The newest marina on the Crouch is Burnham Yacht Harbour. It has substantial clean pontoons and, for once, they are visibly well labelled for those entering. It has all the facilities you would expect of an up-to-date marina. It has 24-hour access and there is usually someone to direct you to a berth and take your lines. The whole facility gets full marks for being at the top of the list in quantity and quality. In particular, it has one of the best chandlers in the country.

The other marina is across the river. It also has 24-hour access to its long outer pontoons. It is the long- and well-established, and now refurbished, facility of Essex Marina at Wallasea Island. Since dredging, drying out has more or less been mastered and the new pontoons offer fully floating berths even at big LWS. There are comprehensive boating facilities, including fuel. Petrol can also be obtained – not a frequent feature of marinas. Late night/early morning fishermen often arrive and prowl the pontoons – and not always silently even at 0300! After the recent renewal of the bar/restaurant/disco facilities, the troupe of feral cats has now dispersed. Domestic shopping and chandlery are available, but only basically so. Nearby, and generally around on the water, are the staff of Trevor W Taylor Marine Services, who will handle boats up to 16·8m LOA, 2·40 draught and 35 tons. They have a cat, but it is of a very different order; namely the kind that gives the orders while the yard runs around after it. In general the passing years have seen many improvements at Essex Marina. Much has been done to improve access, especially with the pontoons having been brought up to date; and with the continuation of the restoration and renewal, Essex now has much of which it can be justifiably proud.

A bonus for the real sailing fraternity in the recently established Wilkinsons Sail Ltd at Quayside – Cindy's.

If you favour a swinging mooring for a visit, the usual plan is to take the first convenient buoy, then go ashore for advice and instruction. This can come from the boatyards or the clubs. Another way is to phone Crouch Harbour Authority's harbourmaster before you visit. The authority maintains a launch that patrols the river. Its VHF channels are 16 and 80 when not on the river but, when they are on patrol, they listen on Ch 11. The Authority's Burnham Office hours are 0930 to 1100.

Shoresides, in Burnham-on-Crouch, you can find all the shops you are likely to need, and in an old lay-by near the sea wall, you can get as wide a range of first-rate fresh fish as you could ask for. Once, Burnham was an acquired, delicate taste; appealing to those with a penchant for the expensive and the extravagant. The days are long gone when one might see the Rolls Royces double parked in the Main Drag. Things have undoubtedly changed over the past 20 years. It must have been with shouting and screaming that Burnham was forced to face the millennium. Once away from 'Top Street', the shops become even more interesting and have more to offer in goods and character. There is a new 'super'-market (Fiveways) at the crossroads. Down the hill there is fresh bread and a first-rate butcher. The tower of St Mary's church is supposed to have been 20ft taller than it now is; topped with a spire to serve as a navigation mark for ships in the river. It was reputed to be the tallest in the area until the 1702 storm brought it to its knees.

For many people, it is the clubs and the racing that form the main attractions of Burnham-on-Crouch. There are certainly ideal conditions for racing, with most of the 10 miles to the Whitaker likened to the open sea with little to diminish the winds from the estuary. There are merits from the cruising point of view as well. In particular, you can stay afloat right up to Stow Creek and so use the stretch as a viable staging post. From the water, there is indeed much to extol on the Crouch.

Some cruising men still insist that there are good anchorages to be found both above and below Burnham. With the Baltic Wharf commercial traffic in addition to all the leisure craft, Burnham itself is just too busy for any anchorage to be a sensible proposition. The only prudent anchorage is well above Burnham and, possibly safest and best, no further downstream than Cliff Reach.

One of the first places of note and to catch the eye after quitting Burnham is the community at Creeksea. There used to be a ferry here, at the point where the mud reaches out well into the river. The Creeksea sailing club has its HQ close by the slip and the yacht moorings are easily spotted. It is marked by green Fairway buoy No. 15. Just across the water, is Lion Creek which, after much mud

. . . and that is in spite of the 350 extra berths made available when the 'new' Burnham Yacht Harbour was opened.

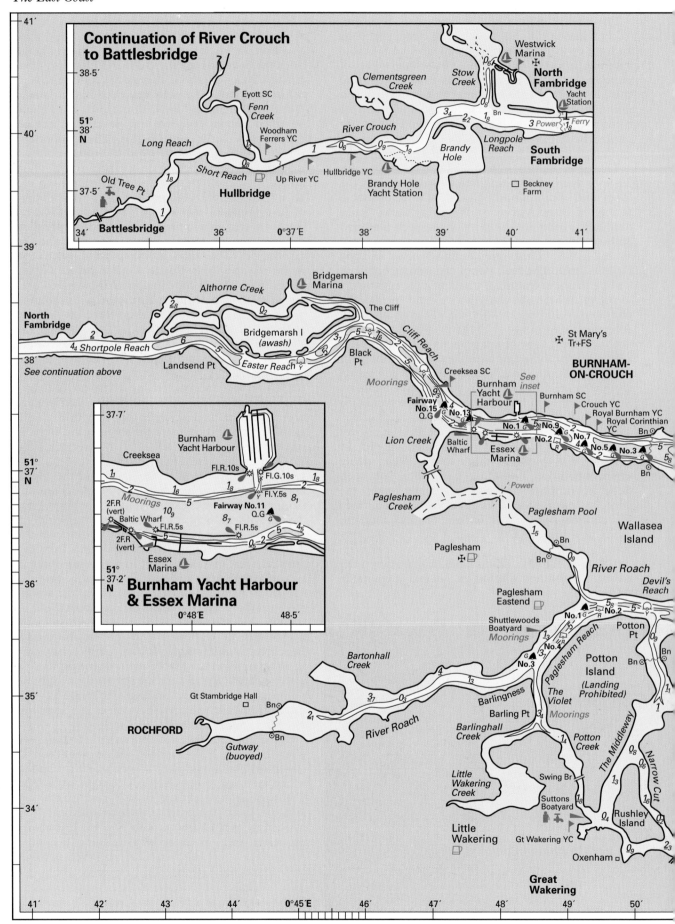

Continuation of River Crouch to Battlesbridge

Eyott SC

Fenn Creek

Clementsgreen Creek

Stow Creek

Westwick Marina

North Fambridge

Yacht Station

Woodham Ferrers YC

River Crouch

Long Reach

Short Reach

Old Tree Pt

Battlesbridge

Hullbridge

Up River YC

Hullbridge YC

Brandy Hole Yacht Station

Brandy Hole

Longpole Reach

South Fambridge

Beckney Farm

Bn

3 Power

Ferry

51°
38′
N

North Fambridge

Althorne Creek

Bridgemarsh Marina

The Cliff

Bridgemarsh I (awash)

Shortpole Reach

See continuation above

Landsend Pt

Easter Reach

Black Pt

Cliff Reach

St Mary's Tr+FS

Moorings

Creeksea SC

See inset

BURNHAM-ON-CROUCH

Fairway No.15
Q.G

No.13

Burnham Yacht Harbour

Burnham SC

Crouch YC

Royal Burnham YC

Royal Corinthian YC

Bn

No.1

No.9

No.7

Lion Creek

Baltic Wharf

Essex Marina

No.2

No.5

No.3

Bn

Burnham Yacht Harbour & Essex Marina

Creeksea

Burnham Yacht Harbour

Fl.R.10s

Fl.G.10s

Fl.Y.5s

Moorings

2.F.R (vert)

Baltic Wharf

Fl.R.5s

2.F.R (vert)

Fairway No.11
Q.G

Fl.R.5s

Essex Marina

0°48′E

48.5′

51°
37.2′
N

51°
37′
N

Paglesham Creek

Power

Paglesham Pool

Wallasea Island

Paglesham

Bn

River Roach

Devil's Reach

Paglesham Eastend

No.1

No.2

Potton Pt

Shuttlewoods Boatyard

Moorings

No.4

No.3

Potton Island (Landing Prohibited)

Bartonhall Creek

Paglesham Reach

Barlingness

Barling Pt

The Violet

Moorings

Gt Stambridge Hall

Bn

ROCHFORD

Bn

Gutway (buoyed)

River Roach

Barlinghall Creek

Potton Creek

The Middleway

Narrow Cut

Little Wakering Creek

Swing Br

Suttons Boatyard

Little Wakering

Gt Wakering YC

Rushley Island

Oxenham

Great Wakering

0°45′E

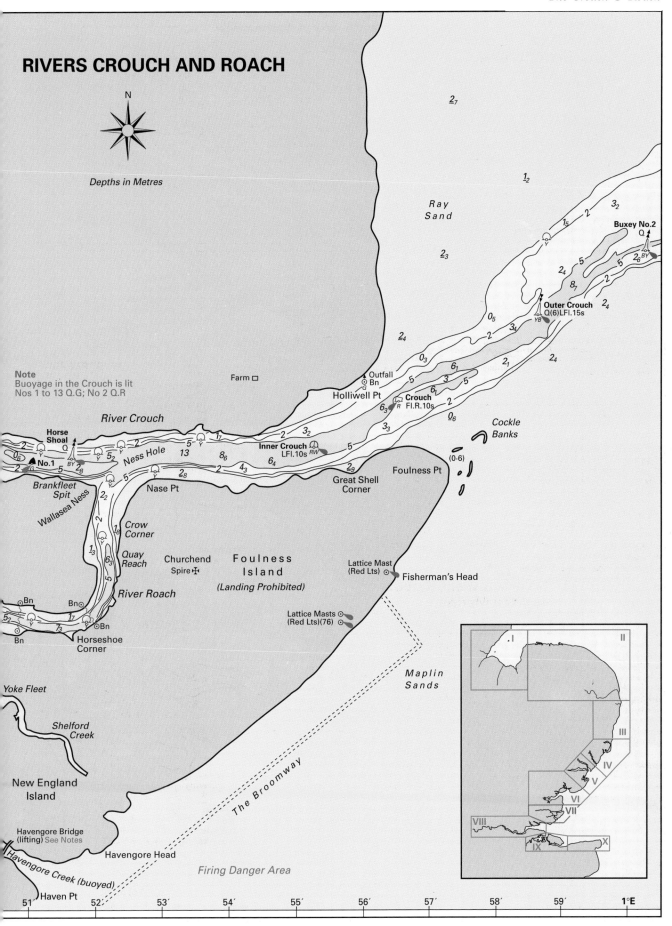

RIVERS CROUCH AND ROACH

N

Depths in Metres

The Crouch & Roach

Ray Sand

Buxey No.2

Outer Crouch
Q(6)LFl.15s

Note
Buoyage in the Crouch is lit
Nos 1 to 13 Q.G; No 2 Q.R

Farm

Outfall
Bn

Holliwell Pt

Crouch
Fl.R.10s

River Crouch

Cockle Banks

Horse Shoal

No.1

Ness Hole

Inner Crouch
LFl.10s

Brankfleet Spit

Wallasea Ness

Nase Pt

Great Shell Corner

Foulness Pt

Crow Corner

Quay Reach

Churchend Spire

Foulness Island
(Landing Prohibited)

Lattice Mast
(Red Lts)

Fisherman's Head

Bn

Bn

River Roach

Bn

Horseshoe Corner

Lattice Masts
(Red Lts)(76)

Yoke Fleet

Maplin Sands

Shelford Creek

New England Island

Havengore Bridge
(lifting) See Notes

Havengore Creek (buoyed)

Havengore Head

Haven Pt

The Broomway

Firing Danger Area

I II III IV V VI VII VIII IX X

WALLASEA ISLAND
Essex Marina ☎ 01702 258531
Radio VHF Ch M

Tides
Dover +0130

Tidal access
24hr

Ⓥ (400; 100 moorings; visitors' berths), 🅦🅒, 📋, ⚓, ⚡, Provisions, Ⓖ, ⬤D, ⬤P, Engineer, Repairs

NORTH FAMBRIDGE
North Fambridge Yacht Centre
☎ 01621 740370. Radio VHF Ch M

Tidal access
24hr (2·5–3m)

Ⓥ (120 deep-water swinging, inc. visitors'), 🅦🅒, 📋, ⚓, ⚡, ⟍, Provisions, Ⓖ (nearby), ⬤D, Engineer, Repairs

West Wick Marina Ltd
☎ 01621 741268, Radio. VHF Ch M (1000–1700)

Tidal access
HW ±5hrs

Ⓥ (180 pontoons, inc. visitors), 🅦🅒, 📋, ⚓, ⚡, ⟍, Provisions, Ⓖ, ⬤D, Engineer, Repairs

ALTHORNE
Bridgemarsh Marina
☎ 01621 740414

Tides
Dover +0120

Tidal access
HW ±5hrs

Ⓥ (195 pontoons, 4 visitors'), 🅦🅒, 📋, ⚓, ⚡, ⟍, ⬤D, Engineer, Repairs

HULLBRIDGE
Brandy Hole Yacht Club
☎ 01702 230320

Tidal access
HW ±4hrs

Ⓥ (some drying, swinging, inc. visitors'), 🅦🅒, 📋, ⚓, ⟍, Provisions (nearby), Ⓖ, ⬤D, Engineer, Repairs

crawling, becomes Paglesham Creek. It is an anchorage used by some, and it does offer protection from winds other than from the north. Unless you are uncommonly careful or lucky you must be prepared to take the ground. You are not likely to be accosted here for Lion Creek is seldom visited.

Opposite top
On the other side of the River from Burnham Yacht Harbour (though not on the other side of the tracks when it comes to providing berths, services – and a swinging social life) is the well-known and long-founded Essex Marina.

Bottom
Upstream, well removed from the Crouch's metropolis, the singular facility of Bridgemarsh Marina. Run in a idiosyncratically charismatic style, it offers a rural contrast to the downstream operations.

Quiet spots can also be found further upstream. One of the inducements to attract you is the sheer romance of their names – Cliff Reach, Black Point, Brandy Hole and Landsend Point. The first really handsome anchorage is Cliff Reach; an attractive spot where the modest rise of cliffs, little more than 15m, helps distract the mind. There is usually a good show of colour in the redness of the cliff, and the variety of foliage from the numerous bushes and tiny trees. On my last visit, at very low water springs, I discovered some foul patches when searching close to the bank, so it is as well not to approach too near and to keep a good watch. It is only just over a mile up from the No. 16 Fairway buoy.

Just upstream, and across the river from Black Point is the east entrance to Althorne Creek. First impressions suggest merely a nascent creek, little more than a mature dike and not very hospitable. Closer inspection determines differently to reveal a well-marked channel offering a warm invitation. There is a spit that reaches far out but, provided you take note of the conspicuous red beacon, it will not trouble you. The entrance channel is well marked by three red cans, has good depth and is entirely unencumbered.

The island has had its troubles – in the late 1890s, it was inundated by a high tide that took away or killed most of the animals. There was another just before 1930, that ended with a like result. Since then, life has been, if not quiet, at least not overly threatened by the invading sea.

The warm invitation I mentioned stems from the efforts, enterprise and aspirations of John and Ray Walker to establish an 'X marks the spot, A1 place'. They run an informal but still tight little ship of an enterprise called, modestly enough, Bridgemarsh Island Marina. The entrance round the bight now carries 1·5m at LWS thus allowing most leisure craft access at most states of the tide, and quite similar to such places as Bradwell and Westwick. Through the creek there is a very fast tide that cleanses, scours and flushes so there is no problem of silting, though initially the pontoon area needed dredging to prevent boats taking the bottom at low water.

Bridgemarsh Marina is a singular, particular and highly personalised operation. There is none of the anonymity of the G&T GRP boat parks . . . not with the Walkers in charge. I first met them on their traditional old Dutch schooner. It was on the slip and from the deck high above, John passionately declaimed, 'We own the river from our moorings to the jetty, but nobody ever mentions us. So far as the magazines, pilots, guides and all that lot, we might as well not be here. Though we have been here now for years and years. As I said to one editor, What if somebody had a heart attack just off the island? They could land here. There's a telephone. The ambulance could get right to the slipway. But they wouldn't know. They'd have a corpse on their hands, wouldn't they? It could definitely save a life.' Well, hopefully, this report will settle the account. There is a large range of boats in the marina – some of them quite out of the ordinary . . . and some very substantial stuff. Pontoons and facilities have been improved and much has been refurbished. Visitors are made personally welcome. It is a superb spot for those who want to leave behind the bustle of Burnham. It is good to see that the walls in the area are being fully restored. From the river, there are many signs with the legend: 'Bridgemarsh Island. Private!'

It is only a five-minute walk up the lane to the hinterland for Althorne Station, which has single-line trains at better-than-hourly intervals. Bridgemarsh Island itself consists mainly of saltings with most of it covered most of the time. Landing is prohibited and since some of its 'banks' are dangerous to approach, it can hardly be described as a prime attraction of an island. Some mud spits are marked by withies. In spite of what John and Ray say, there are signs of silt at the west end of Althorne Creek. Between Shortpole Reach and Stow Creek there are many unpleasant obstructions on the north bank. They are all clearly marked by withies which are fully visible most of the time, but it is no place to go in search of a bankside mooring at HW when they are not all obvious.

Back in the river, there are additional places where the anchor may be used with care. Opposite Bridgemarsh Island there are suitable spots in Easter Reach, on the Upper Raypits south side between Black and Lansend Points. Nearby is the seasonal buoy 'Canewdon'. The old village of that name still exists, and is notable because it was about there that Canute camped, and not far away is the site of the warfare with Edmund Ironsides.

Opposite Black Point there are two yellow buoys. The more southerly of the two is the bigger, while the other is flagged. The southern yellow marks the eastern limit for water-skiing along Easter Reach and Upper Raypits. Along the water's edge, there are the remains of many stagings, jetties, breakwaters and the like. They continue to the end of Bridgemarsh Island and are all well marked by beacons. Near Landsend Point there is another Yellow buoy carrying a pennant with the legend, 'Essex Marina Yacht Club'.

Just above Landsend Point comes the delightfully named Shortpole Reach. Near the north bank is the western ('rear') entry to Althorne creek that runs right round Bridgemarsh Island. There is a marker in the form of an oil drum in extraordinary shades of blue, red and yellow. Carrying the label 'Bridgemarsh Island' it is usually found, if found at all, on its side in a state of decay. I tried to work out the ins and outs of the actual channel it marked, if it marked any at all. However, I was so confused by the proliferation of gutways and dykes, poles and withies, that I dared not attempt an entrance. Many of the withies must be special marks for crabs, eels or oysters; and it will be only a select few locals who are privy to their purpose. I retreated in despair.

Any approach to these strange signposts should be made by dinghy; as should any attempt to make a

The splendid isolation of Hullbridge where the remains of the old causeway to Woodham Ferrers is still to be seen (centre left and right) .

round trip of the island. The withies are classic East Coast tackle: slender, crooked, leaning over and trying to grow back into life again. The disposal and configuration are suspect and hairy. A lure and a deception, they should be left well alone. All these stretches carry constant reminders of the 8-knot speed limit. Sometimes they proliferate.

By the time you reach North Fambridge the moorings have become extensive, but it is still possible to anchor in Longpole Reach, well below the moorings. It is worth seeking advice on good spots from the North Fambridge Yacht Station (see below). On the north shore, there is a conspicuous white hut. Now a private retreat, approachable only by water, it used to be a hospital for lepers; while the North Fambridge Yacht Clubhouse was, more predictably, the ferryman's abode. It has now been raised a metre to prevent flooding and there has not been a ferry service for some time.

Yachting at Fambridge goes way back. Even before the turn of the century there were well nigh 50 yachts moored there. Just about that time, Francis Cooke, Sir Samuel Pechell and his friends dined and wined at the Ferry Boat (more wining than dining I suspect, but all for two old shillings) and they decided on the risky venture of founding the Fambridge Yacht Club. Their venture succeeded. They once sailed past Stow Creek and made the following comment: '. . . a cul de sac running inland for about a mile. We could sail up there if we wanted to, but as it leads to nowhere we do not think it worth while'. How things have changed!

It was back in 1981 that the North Fambridge Yacht Station started life; but its attitudes to service and courtesy go back to those earlier days of knights and nights in the Ferry Inn. The Yacht Station has installed a new pontoon access to the river and established the additional service of a launch taxi for yachtsmen on Friday nights to Sunday nights and on public holidays. A long finger of a catwalk reaches down to the new solidly piled pontoon that is afloat at almost all states of the tide. There is not quite enough water for a 1·50m vessel to stay afloat at low water springs, but the bottom is very soft mud. There is a water point on the pontoon and, of course, access to the mainland is much cleaner and easier. They try to keep it free so that craft are able to water up at any time. The clubhouse has also gone in for refurbishment with its clean lines and double-glazed windows – with a double-vision stunning view. The station is easy to spot from downstream because of the white watchtower and the line of trots that demand you to follow them. Visitors are permitted to use vacant ones, observing

the usual courtesies. Seldom are they charged for this privilege overnight or at weekends. It is an extremely pleasant spot with unusually vivid dawns, nebulous dusks, and intense sunsets. It is an excellent place for keen photographers and painters.

Between North Fambridge Yacht Station and Westwick Marina, on the north bank, is the conspicuous white hut. It is equidistant between the two mooring facilities. It is no distance to Stow Creek where the pile marker seems as if it must mark the centre of the channel so far out is it from the bank. But then, the mud spit reaches out no less far. It is not a tide gauge, but is kept in a good state of repair and is immediately obvious once you have opened the creek. It carries a speed limit sign. You can leave it close to starboard upon entering. At the entrance to the creek, there is a water tower at the top of the hill which, when in line with the entrance beacon, marks the track of the channel. There is no hazard in the area and the limiting factor is draught; if you draw more than 1·5m it is better not to approach the Creek until 2 hours after low water. Starboard withies mark the channel in Stow Creek and also the sharp dogleg that turns to starboard (the east) into Westwick Marina at the 'head' of the creek. They should be well observed for the spit they mark reaches far out. There is a 'T' hammerhead at the entrance, much used for dinghy rallies, but usually available for visitors to enquire about berthing. After this, the piles and pontoons are obvious. There are fingers to the north and the south of the main pontoon. The ones on the south are the deeper and those to be used by visitors.

Westwick Marina was established in 1971, ten years before its NFYS sister. There are continuing improvements here: as well as new pontoons, mains water and power have been installed with all the skills, expertise and materials that an (ex) aficionado of the building, haulage and tin-plate recovery trades can muster. The marina can usually accommodate visitors, for whom there is spacious car parking, but groups need to make prior arrangements. Whatever the state of its business or workload you can be sure of a warm and enthusiastic welcome. You will notice that the pontoons are swept every morning, mainly because of the over-friendly ducks, and that there is carpeting in place where needed. Their thoughtfully designed loos are spotless. In particular (a small matter this, but serious when you want water) their hose fittings are among the smoothest running in the country. There is a clubhouse where you will receive a welcome so near to the rapturous that you may need assistance when it comes time to leave. It is no exaggeration to describe Westwick as immaculate and efficient; but with none of the clinical anonymity that often accompanied those qualities. They now dredge the marina throughout the winter to try to solve the East Coast's own age-old 'Forth Bridge' problem – the silt.

Westwick is a place of character and characters, with the overall ambience of a boating preserve. It is

The north Fambridge Yacht Station (with refurbished clubhouse) that goes back to the end of the last century and the days of Sir Samuel Pechell's carousing at the Ferry boat.

Further up the River Crouch, berths, anchorages and moorings become less exoteric – moving almost into the exotic as with the charms of Westwick Marina.

in fact something of a sanctuary for a number of ducks. Sadly the china goose, Charlie, is no longer among the incumbents, having disappeared without trace. In spite of being a 'foreigner', he was almost the leader and symbol of the proliferation of local wildlife.

Local life of an entirely different calibre must be tasted at the Ferry Boat. Dearly departed the ferry may be, but local life, soul and party all proceed apace in this very special pub. Times, barrels, pumps and the clientele may have changed, but there is still an air of history and mystery about the place.

North Fambridge, where the single-line trains cross at the station, is less than a mile distant. There is a post office and a pub in the village. For really first-rate shopping you should go to the 'new village' of Woodham Ferrers (in any case, its design, layout and some of its architecture make it worth a visit in its own right).

A little further upstream comes the nicely named Clementsgreen Creek to the north, where there is a possible anchorage just inside the wide entrance. Its main use is as a base for water-skiing, and it has a specially installed station just for that.

Leaving the creek and its extensive spit on the starboard hand, the river runs into Brandy Hole Reach where, in the proximity of the far-reaching saltings, the Yacht Station maintains its deep-water moorings with a gathering of really substantial craft; and where, in Brandy Hole Bay, you will find a pleasant anchorage. This is the farthest point upriver where you can hope to stay afloat. The Brandy Hole Yacht Club offers you the hospitality of its moorings as well as its clubhouse. It asks you to gain permission from the Club's HQ (just upstream) or its ferryman first.

The area is quite charming and the local yachtsmen most welcoming, provided you don't want to stay too long, for there is a waiting list and congestion here as elsewhere. The clubhouse is a lively, going proposition that is open all the time except Mondays. The waitresses are dressed in the classic frills and black and white of the best establishments. It has a most welcoming atmosphere.

The club uses VHF Ch 37. Diesel is available in cans and the shops are a mile away. There is mains water at the pontoon, which dries to a hard, flat bottom. The club has two very good – and very busy – ferrymen.

Immediately after Brandy Hole, the river becomes crowded with moorings. At the Anchor pub, there are two slips. One is large and the other small, and they are matched by a pair on the other side. Both carry notices: 'Crouch Harbour Authority. No water- or jet-skiing without a licence issued by the CHA'. As the land maps confirm, there used to be a full-blown Causeway here from Woodham Ferrers to Hullbridge. I was told that it is perfectly feasible to walk across the river from the car park to the pub without even getting damp. That, I take it, is a bit of local pride to be taken with a pinch of sea salt. The river has now become very pretty, and to add a hint of a holiday feeling, there are two sandy patches at this point, with proper beach huts; and to confirm its connection with past and typical activities of the river, there are old boats as used by old-fashioned fishermen. From here on, the moorings begin to thin out and tail away. Noticeably, there are some select properties, each with their own mooring arrangement at the bottom of their riverside patch.

On the north is a small deviation known as Fenn Creek. There is a horse bar in mid-stream at the entrance, after which the better water tends to the south bank. There are some small beacons marking small headlands. There are also some stumps by the banksides to the east that can appear, from some perspectives, as if they are mini-beacons. They are to be avoided. Upstream a little distance is the Eyot Sailing Club. It is a small, very attractive new wooden building with an amazingly steep slipway. The club does not dispense alcohol (I wonder how long that will last?) but you are always welcome for a cup of tea and a chat. Motor cruisers drawing no more than 2'6" and can take the ground are frequently seen there. Many leave their boats and take to the dinghy to go further upstream, right into the middle of the rural countryside (25ft is the maximum possible LOA and bilge keels are the craft best suited). The buoys are racing marks: F is Farm and D is Ditch. However, they also mark the deepest water. For those who cannot get their craft into the Creek, there is usually a vacant buoy in the river close to the entrance. There is also a pleasant anchorage just off, out of the fairway. Whichever method you try, there is no way of avoiding drying out.

Back in the main river, the next features – if that is what they should be called – are an overhead pylon, a few moorings and a small jetty with room for two boats on each side, and a nearby caravan park on the north side. Next comes Short Reach, followed by Long Reach which turns to the west at 90°. Green buoys apparently mark the severe dogleg; but they are in fact racing marks (although they do, sometimes, also mark the deep water). 'Cruise it and see' is the rule. After these buoys, the river begins to twist and turn more and more tightly as it progresses. The channel becomes narrow, heavily weeded on each side and is little more than a mature stream: a veritable backwater experience. The names – Spitty's Reach and Oldtree Point – do nothing but support this feeling. The charts don't even hint at the myriad bends, turns and angles that must be negotiated; nor at the abundance of wildlife growing up or flying down on each side, above and below the water.

The actual head of the navigation is very pretty, and has an outstanding blue and red iron bridge; a classic old mill; and a boat-building yard. Water and fuel can be obtained and the pub in the township is not far away. There are barges of all kinds nearby: new, old, decaying and decayed. In some of the tiny creeklets there are Dutch-type barges that look as if they harbour live-aboards.

The *Hazel May*, all neat and nice, cast off and went downstream on the top of the tide, with a load of passengers on board. She occupied almost the whole breadth of the channel, and was not herself a substantial vessel. Legend has it that boats with even more than 2·0m reach Battlesbridge at high water springs, but I imagine it would be a hairy, twisty, bottom-raking job indeed. *Valcon*'s twin screws don't like less than a good 2·50m and I had some difficulty in manoeuvring in the narrower, shallower parts. It was really something of an exacting passage but it did permit a good look at the world beyond the banks and braes. Shallow river-water-reading expertise is called for.

I decided to turn round and leave the moment I arrived (not the easiest of manoeuvres at the head of navigation) since I was not sure I would lie easy at low water. It also meant going down on the ebb, another practice I don't care for at all in a restricted waterway that I don't know. I like the upper river a lot, but would personally prefer to go there by the grace and favour of local hospitality . . . or in a dinghy.

The Crouch is undoubtedly a river of contrasts: offering tremendous variety in its width, depth and speed; town, village and rural countryside; cruising, racing and just messing about; surroundings that are mundane, pretty and outstanding; and clubs that range from some of the largest and most sophisticated to the smallest and least pretentious in the country. The choice is there for the taking.

The Roach to Havengore

There are two ways into the River Roach and they could hardly be more different. The first uses the River Crouch and enters the Roach just below Burnham between Nase Point and Wallasea Ness. The second requires a passage across the shallow Maplin Sands to negotiate the high bar of the 'Broomway-Broomroad'. This is the key to the 'front door' of the new Havengore lifting bridge which permits entry into the Roach via Havengore Creek.

RIVER ROACH
51°36'·95N 00°52'·24E (Brankfleet buoy)

Charts Admiralty 3750, 1185. Imray C1 Y17. OS Landranger 178

Tides
Dover + 0110

HAVENGORE CREEK
51°33'·59N 00°50'·62E (Havengore Bridge)

Charts Admiralty 3750, 1185. Imray C1 Y17. OS Landranger 178

Tidal access
No access possible when bridge is closed.
Min depth 1·5m near HW
Speed limit 8 knots

Authorities
Range officer ☎ 01621 292271 (ext. 3211)
Operations officer ☎ 01621 292271 (ext 3436)

Radio
Range officer (Shoe Base) VHF Ch 72, 16 (office hours)
Havengore bridge-keeper (Shoe Bridge) VHF Ch 72, 16 (HW ±2hrs)

Notes
DTEO SHOEBURYNESS-HAVENGORE BRIDGE
The bridge is manned for HW ±2hrs in daylight hours (½ hr after sunset, ½ hr before sunrise and, during BST, 1 hr after sunset and 1 hr before sunrise). The bridge-keeper may be contacted on ☎ 01702 292271 ext 3436 during these hours, or on VHF Ch 16 (working Ch 72). Outside these times, information on bridge opening can be obtained 24 hrs in advance by contacting the Range Operations Office (☎ 01702 292271 ext 3211/3212) or calling *Shoe Radar* on marine Ch 72 in working hours. Outside normal working hours, this information is available from MoD Police on ☎ 01702 292271.

Shoeburyness Range
Usually active Mon–Fri 0600–1700 LT. 24 hours' notice of proposed passage across range should be given.

PAGLESHAM
Shuttlewoods Boatyard ☎ 01702 258885

Tidal access
24 hrs (2m at LW)
Ⓥ (100 swinging, some drying, 15 jetty moorings, 15 visitors'), ⓦⒸ, ⚓, ⚡, ⚓, Provisions, ▮D, Engineer, Repairs

The requirements for crossing the Maplins and getting through Havengore Bridge are very clear and plain – if not entirely simple. Fine and settled conditions with a good spring tide are prerequisites; and a boat of no more than 1·40m draught with the person at the wheel having more than a little experience of navigating in shoal waters. If those conditions are met, then the Havengore project should be all right.

However, that will be Journey's End; let us start with the entrance to the Roach from the Crouch. It is well up towards Burnham, and lies between the downstream easterly spit, Nase Point, and the upstream westerly Brankfleet, that extends way out from Wallasea Ness. As I mentioned in the preceding section on the Crouch, it is important to respect the yellow buoy off Wallasea and to keep to a central channel when entering the Roach, since Brankfleet Spit and Nase Point both extend well into the river from their respective roots. Cutting corners here is a fool's game. Keep an eye on the sounder until well into Quay Reach, since the depths vary quite a lot, and quite quickly.

For example, there is the deep Ness Hole followed by a small half bar. Better water follows for a time but only to become shoal again before finally developing into a channel proper, well after Crow Corner in Quay Reach. Thereafter, you carry plenty of water until you are well past the boatyard in Paglesham Reach. The yellow racing buoys that abound in the Crouch and the Roach, marking the spit ends and turns, are a most useful adjunct for the cruising stranger.

The Roach can be an attractive alternative when the Crouch is suffering inclement weather, with an inhospitable 'sea state' blowing up so that it takes on all the aspects of the North Sea's grey-white horses. However, help is at hand, as the silent movies have it. You have only to move into the Roach, steam round a few bends, and there will be every chance that you will find some shelter. Take note, though, that Paglesham Reach is not beyond having its moments – especially when it blows up from the northeast. However, there are some good holes before we get to the Reach for Paglesham.

Indeed, the Roach is well blessed with such hiding places, for its anchorages proliferate. For example, there are four very good ones in the first two legs (which are also the first 2 miles) of the river. The first comes just past Brankfleet Spit towards the west bank. The second is a little further on, towards the opposite, easterly, bank in Quay Reach. (While there is a residual jetty, just past the old quay towards the east bank, the construction no longer completely resembles its previous fabrication, so it is necessary to keep an eye open or you may steam straight past it.) The third is tucked away on the bend, by Whitehouse Hole, off Horseshoe Corner, at the end of Quay Reach and at the beginning of Devil's Reach.

The Fleet itself takes you down to the Middleway, the Narrow Cuts and on to Havengore. The fourth

It is possible, on the tide, to visit Rochford, head of the Roach navigation. All the way up, the river becomes a very modest, if not indeed a minor affair. In spite of its sometimes commercial use, caution must be exercised if you are not to stray from the straight and narrow. There is little in the way of attractive scenery. Two buoys unexpectedly appear on the scene near the end of the navigation: a red and a green marking a submarine cable. There is little to fire the spirit at Rochford and, if you propose to visit, you must be prepared to take the ground almost straightway. It is not a trip to be recommended, except in a tender, day-boat or dinghy.

Back in Paglesham Reach, before actually setting off for Havengore, we'll take a brief look at some of the other anchorages in the creeks. For the first, we must retrace our steps even further. Back at the entrance to Paglesham Reach, we turn out attention to Paglesham (where else?) Pool. Where the main reach bends to the southwest, the Pool carries straight on for a short while before it turns to the northwest. Past 'Pill Box' Point, withies mark both banks and the entrance. Caution is, of course, required since it dries completely after the first three or four cables and, shortly after that, the bottom becomes foul. An exploratory low-water foray makes all things clear. Paglesham Pool finally leads, via the muddy channels and gutways, into Lion Creek which then makes an exit into the Crouch opposite the Creeksea Sailing Club. It is perhaps not so pretty as others, but it is close – and little visited.

Another possible anchorage is to be found in the stretch known as the Violet. It starts at Barling Ness and runs up on the west side to Barlinghall Creek; while, to the east, it is bordered by Potton Island. The good holding ground is well protected, and most craft will stay afloat at all states. Care must be taken not to impede the movements of the small fishing fleet – some of the boats are in fact quite substantial. The presence of their buoys means that you are not entirely at liberty to anchor where you will.

Most other creeks are not suitable for anchoring unless you want to spend a fair amount of each tide on the mud. Creeks of this kind proliferate round Potton and Rushley Islands. They are probably best described as 'Creeks Navigable by Tender Only'. They include Shelford, Little Wakering, Fleethead, Bartonhall and the upper part of Barlinghall. With the exception of Bartonhall, which is not a prime candidate, they all make for a good day's holiday – fine for messing about in boats with children. Their foremost and singular attributes are their remoteness and usually unchallenged privacy. So, let me bring this section to a close by confessing my preference. It is the short stretch that consists of the lower reaches of Barlinghall Creek. I find it the most appealing and sheltered venue in the Roach. It is, of course, removed from all contact with 'civilisation', but anyone cruising this area will, from the outset, surely have wanted to get away from it all.

The other, 'navigable creeks' are not serious candidates for pottering. They are of interest because they afford access to Havengore and the crossing to the Thames Estuary. The choice starts at Potton Point. If you want to visit Paglesham before going on to Havengore, the route to be taken is: Paglesham Reach down to the Violet; and then across the old, hard ford at Great Potton. It is not only the Ford itself that dries high and proud, it is the rest of the channel as far down as Rushley Island. There is little point in trying to get across at anything less than an hour or so before high water. Between the Ford and Wakering there is a swing bridge. The keeper will, in all likelihood, be at his post, raring to go, for he is a bright and considerate master who takes a delight in working his bridge. You must keep well to the centre here for there is an extensive shoal patch to westward, on the Wakering side.

The alternative routes from Potton Point don't separate until Rushley Island. The part of the route that is held in common is, first, the stretch down Yoke Fleet. This reach doesn't quite dry until close to Shelford Creek; a completely drying gutway that runs away somewhat tortuously to the southwest. Yoke Fleet then becomes the Middleway, which itself runs straight down to the southwest tip of Rushley Island. As it does so, it passes the junction with the Narrow Cuts, shortly after the dammed-up New England Creek on the east bank. We shall return to that shortly.

The boatyard pontoons and moorings, all of which dry out, can easily be seen on the mainland opposite Rushley Island to the west. Although it is the base of the Wakering Yacht Club, there are still many more moorings here than one would expect. Unless you know the area well, it will be difficult to get all the way through without touching bottom. After this the course to the Havengore bascule bridge crosses another ford as it wends and bends its way south and west on its ½-mile journey to Journey's End.

As the appellation would suggest, the Middleway is wider than the Narrow Cuts. The Cuts are straighter (though not more straightforward) and also shorter – by a good ½ mile or so. They are not only (predictably) narrower, but also (perhaps less predictably) shallower. There is little room to turn and even less for any manoeuvre that is more than minor. Once you have started on any of the tidal approaches to the bridge (be it on the way in or out), unless you are prepared to get quite stranded, you are committed to completing the undertaking.

All these channels should be used as near as possible to high water; certainly on a rising tide (preferably around springs); and all must be navigated with precision. There is no need to promulgate advice for each one separately for they all require the same procedures – one eye on the sounder, the other on the banks and a third on the stretch just in front! In other words, treat all the stretches as shoal and make sure that you have plenty of power . . . and some in reserve.

Whatever approach is used to reach Havengore itself, it is important to know that the tides are eccentric and can race through the creeks at a cracking pace. You need to be confident of your power and your ground tackle; otherwise it is better to stay in Yoke Fleet or Paglesham Reach. Many visitors are taken unawares when they discover that the tidal streams run in both directions for each tide; just like the River Swale across the estuary. This is how it occurs: before the Broomway is covered, the flood comes from the Roach, running southeast. Once it is covered, it comes from the estuary and runs northwest. The reverse occurs on the ebb. All the changes happen about 1 hour each side of high water. The tide stands no more than two to three minutes, and sometimes not at all.

On leaving the creek for the Broomway-Broomroad, you are straightway approaching the highest ridge of the drying sands. Vehicles use this stretch which is sometimes referred to as the military road. Most recently, the channel has been, roughly, a mild dogleg – port, starboard, port.

The general approach from seaward is to pick up the East Shoebury buoy and then set a course for the red-and-white (vertical) can buoy that is the current major replacement. Then you will see a line of small buoys to be left to port when making the last approach to the bridge. On the way out, deeper-draught boats go on to just north of the Blacktail Spit buoy, while shallow ones can make for the South Shoebury. All passages must be close to high water.

It used to, take the keeper seven to eight minutes to open the bridge once he reached the final stage in the over-all process – pressing the button. But, before he did so, he had to close the road barrier by hand and operate the traffic-control lights. There was never any way in which you could get through 'at the drop of a hat'. You had to be properly prepared since the ebb and flow through the bridge are very strong, frequently taking strangers by surprise and pinning them against the bridge.

The new Havengore bridge is fitted with a boom to the underside of the bascule, thus preventing free passage when the bridge is not manned. What a relief it is that the new one opens in 90 seconds, as opposed to the seven minutes it took the old one. Here are the details as promulgated by the range operations officer of the Defence Test & Evaluation Organisation (DTEO):

The bridge is manned for 2 hours either side of high water in daylight hours. Daylight is deemed to be half an hour after sunset and half an hour before sunrise, but during British summer time 1 hour after sunset and 1 hour before sunrise.

Whilst the bridge is manned, the bridge-keeper may be contacted by telephone ☎ 01702 292271 ext 3436 and on marine radio Ch 16 (working channel 72).

Outside these times, information regarding the possibility of the bridge being opened can be given 24 hours in advance by contacting the Range Operations Office ☎ 01702 292271 ext 3211 or 3212 or calling 'Shoe

Radar' on marine Ch 72 in working hours, Monday to Friday.

Outside normal working hours, this information is available from the Ministry of Defence Police ☎ 01702 292271.

In addition the following information may be of help. Passage is not allowed through the bridge at night. Generally speaking, it is best to try for a weekend when there is usually no firing. Occasionally there is firing at night. Red flags are displayed on Havengore Bridge and at frequent intervals along the sea wall between Shoeburyness and Foulness Point; also on the south bank of the River Crouch and the east bank of the River Roach when firing is in progress or is about to take place. Passage is prohibited when flags are displayed and approach is dangerous, especially from seaward.

The old Imray *Pilot Guide to the Thames* Estuary said:

Traffic in and out of the creek is entirely controlled by firing practice. Facilities are granted to proceed during firing by permission of the Officer Commanding Shoeburyness Garrison, and every consideration is given in this respect.

Firing takes precedence, and the planning officer or bridge-keeper should be contacted at least 24 hours in advance. As one keeper said: 'We all try to co-operate as much as possible, but you would be amazed how many people just turn up, thinking they can get through at any time never mind the firing. Me. I'd be worried stiff once I heard those bangs'.

It is difficult to get definitive information about the best route and approach to Havengore from the sea. For example, I have interviewed skippers with 1·10m draught who have pronounced it to be 'OK'. In the main they had very fast motor cruisers that, if anything, drew less and not more than a metre. I traced one skipper whose draught was 1·4m and he said, 'Oh no! it was far too dodgy ever to try again.' I also heard around and about of boats of 1·8m that had been through, but to this day I have not been able to trace one of them. I think the point is straightforward: if the conditions are fine and settled; if there is a biggish spring tide; if your boat falls into the appropriate draught; and, generally speaking, if you know what you are doing, then the Havengore route will be worth trying.

However, it is worth noting that the local fishermen advised very strongly against *Valcon* crossing the Broomway once they knew she drew more than 1·5m under way; and that the bridge keeper at Havengore said, 'On a 5·5m tide, the maximum draught is 0·8m; on a 6m tide, 1·8m boats have been known to get through and others have foundered but you must know what you are doing . . . and exactly where you are'.

VIII. The Thames

Nelson is reputed to have said that, in terms of navigation, the Thames Estuary is one of the worst areas around the coast of the UK, being as tricky as a fox and as dangerous as a tiger. I can find no reason to disagree with his perceptions.

I remember thinking of estuaries as modest tracts of water, with almost all river mouths as fairly narrow affairs, like the Humber at Spurn Head. Certainly, it was no broad expanse of potentially rough exposed waters with no land in sight in any direction. It was not until I had spent a few years cruising that I really came to grips with the enormity of the Thames Estuary. I had read about it while still preparing *Valcon*; but reading is one thing – reality is another.

The *Admiralty Pilot* describes the Thames Estuary this way:

From the Naze (51°52'N 1°27'E) SW to Shoeburyness (51°31'N 0°47'E) S to Garrison Point (51°27'N 0°45'E) E to North Foreland (51°23'N 1°27'E) N to the Naze.

Joseph Conrad says this

Forthwith a change came over the waters, and the serenity became less brilliant but more profound. The old river in its broad reach rested unruffled at the decline of day, after ages of good service done to the race that peopled its banks, spread out in the tranquil dignity of a waterway leading to the uttermost ends of the earth. We looked at the venerable stream not in the vivid flush of a short day that comes and departs for ever, but in the august light of abiding memories. And indeed nothing is easier for a man who has, as the phrase goes, 'followed the sea' with reverence and affection, than to evoke the great spirit of the past upon the lower reaches of the Thames. The tidal current runs to and fro in its unceasing service, crowded with memories of men and ships it has borne to the rest of home or to the battles of the sea. It had known and served all the men of whom the nation is proud from Sir Francis Drake to Sir John Franklin, knights all, titled and untitled – the great knights-errant of the sea. It had borne all the ships whose names are like jewels flashing in the night of time, from the Golden Hind returning with her round flanks full of treasure, to be visited by the Queen's Highness and thus pass out of the gigantic tale, to the Erebus and Terror, bound on other conquests – and that never returned. It had known the ships and the men. They had sailed from Deptford, from Greenwich, from Erith – the adventurers and the settlers; kings' ships and the ships of men on 'Change'; captains, admirals, the dark 'interlopers' of the Eastern trade, and the commissioned 'generals' of East India fleets. Hunters for gold or pursuers of fame, they all had gone out on that stream, bearing the sword, and often the torch, messengers of the might within the land, bearers of a spark from the sacred fire. What greatness had not floated on the ebb of that river into the mystery of an unknown earth! . . The dreams of men, the seed of commonwealths, the germs of empires.

The sun set; the dusk fell on the stream, and lights began to appear along the shore. The Chapman lighthouse, a three-legged thing erect on a mudflat, shone strongly. Lights of ships moved in the fairway – a great stir of lights going up and going down. And farther west on the upper reaches the place of the monstrous town was still marked ominously on the sky, a brooding gloom in sunshine, a lurid glare under the stars.

'And this also,' said Marlow suddenly, 'has been one of the dark places of the earth.'

Heart of Darkness
Joseph Conrad

The Cruising Association Handbook puts it another way: 'The estuary is notorious for its short, steep seas when the wind is against the tide, and the worst seas occur with northeasterly winds. It is much encumbered with shoals which are subject to frequent changes.' *Chambers Twentieth Century Dictionary* describes an estuary as the 'Tidal mouth of a large river'; and, from the Latin, comes 'aestuarium/aestus: burning, boiling, commotion, tide'. Marrying these ideas conjures up something of the singular experience that is the Thames Estuary.

It is easy to underestimate how really rough and tough this estuary can be; even with its apparently safe, home coastal waters. Such conditions are in stark contrast to the friendly image that can be enjoyed from the alcoholic warmth of the Victoria-to-Brighton buffet car.

The Thames rises in Inglesham, Gloucestershire and, from there, through its 44 locks down to the mouth of the estuary it runs for nearly 200 statute miles. At London Bridge, the Thames is still quite obviously a river. You can see easily from one bank to the other and the distance between them is no more than 240m. At Woolwich, hardly any distance down the river, it is already much wider at 450m; and by the time you are downriver as far as Gravesend it has grown to 1300m, nearly a mile. We should consider the Thames below the comparative safety of St Katharine's Dock veritably to be a major seaway, with many channels and many approaches.

There can be little doubt that the easiest approach is from the Medway, via the estuary's soft underbelly as it were. Heading London-wards from the Medway takes you past Sheerness, past the partly submerged wreck of the ammunition carrier, *Montgomery*, and past the usual conglomeration of big ships in the anchorages awaiting the tide. The approach is then by Nore Sand through its Swatchway along the south bank by Yantlet Flats.

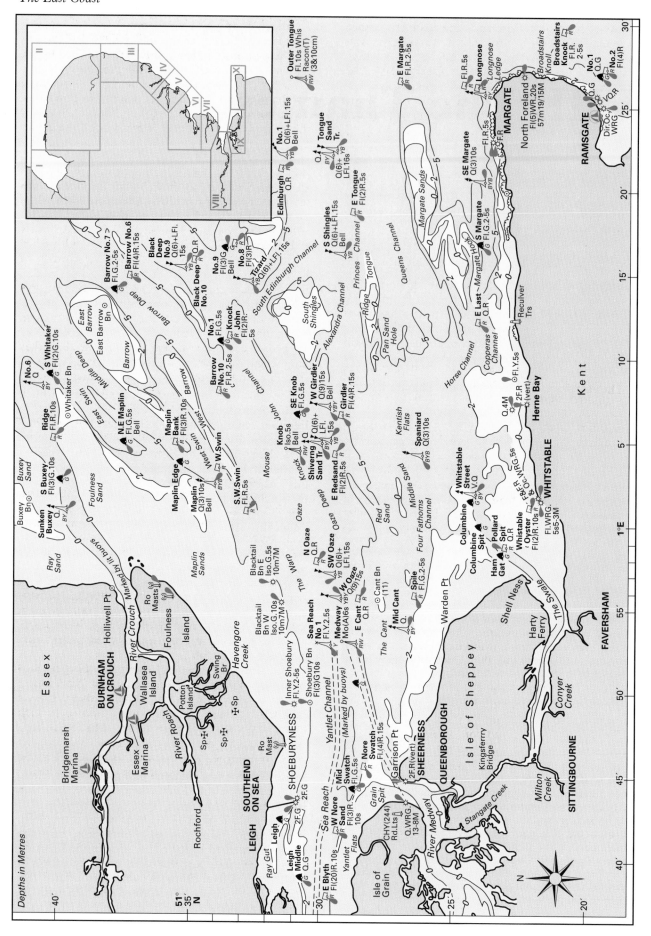

From the North Foreland, the inshore passage through the South and Gore Channels, past Whitstable and the Isle of Sheppey, and across the Four Fathoms Channel to the *Montgomery*, is a straightforward passage. Sea conditions can often make it very uncomfortable; the shallowness of the whole of the area encouraging the slightest of winds to create the roughest of waters. More than once I thought I was a bit pathetic having decided that a Force 4/5 wind against the tide was too much of a good thing for a crossing from Ramsgate. It was only after a number of such tough passages that I met up with three round-the-world sailors – at quite different times – to discover that they shared Nelson's view. Nothing now shakes the cautious attitude with which I approach an estuary passage; and I would urge all readers to take a similar view.

The alternative routes from the North Foreland are the 'outer passages' as shown in the channels (pages 162–166). The main ones are, of course, reliable and safe for all-comers, noviciate or sophisticate. I must confess that I have not used the South Edinburgh Channel, nor the Alexandra. Imray's old pilot guide says this about the latter: 'The channel is not recommended for use by day, and should never be attempted at night' (and I would add an emphatic '!' to that).

Another 'inshore' approach to the Thames is through the Wallet and Swin Spitways into the East Swin off Foulness Sand down the West Swin past the Maplins. After this it is a short leg into the Warp and on to Sea Reach No. 1. We are then left with the larger main channels from the north – the East Swin or King's Channel into Middle Deep or Barrow Deep and then down to the Maplins again; or the really wide Black Deep down to Knock John and more or less straight on to Sea Reach No. 1.

These minor channels may be tempting for a skipper who feels like a change; but they can be very lonely. It is not like being in a main channel where, should a mishap occur, you could be fairly confident of help being, if not at hand, at least not far away. I prefer that reassurance when negotiating the maze of chances that make up the Thames Estuary.

Sea Reach itself is the first stretch of the Thames that is noticeably a 'river' – although it is still quite a distance from the bank. The Reach is well named. It begins between Maplin Sands and the Cant just before Shoeburyness, and continues to be a mighty seaway until well past Mucking No. 1. From Sea Reach No. 1 right up to Sea Reach No. 7 there is little to rivet the eye ashore until you can pick out the usually dim and misty outline of Shoeburyness. Way across the mud flats, halfway between the Ness and Southend Pier is the small yacht club in Thorpe Bay known as 'Halfway'. It has one visitors' drying berth.

Then Southend long pier looms into view. Plans for a marina have been mooted for many a year, but nothing concrete has yet been laid down or even come forward. Crown property is involved. While it is possible to moor at the pier, in the words of Mr

Reader, Director of Engineering Services, 'there is only limited facility at the Pier for visiting yachts'. All the moorings in the vicinity are controlled by the individual local yacht clubs. In settled weather, it is probably best to anchor off and take the dinghy if you have in mind to taste the delights of Southend. Tucked away, in the little shelter that is afforded by the pier are the Thames Estuary and Alexandra Yacht Clubs, both of which retain moorings for visitors.

Next, however, comes something of a change with Leigh-on-Sea, Canvey Island and Holehaven. On my first visit to the area I was completely put off by noticing on the chart, just by Canvey Island, 'Chapman Explosive Anchorage'. Of course, I knew of bad holding and foul ground, but the idea of an explosive anchorage was too much. Personally, I have always found it difficult to pick out London Stone or the entrance to Yantlet Creek. For me, this side of the river is perhaps best banished to the relative obscurity of mud flats, saltings and marsh gas; although I have met skippers who speak well of the place – and one or two are proud to tell how they have found hook-dropping spots to stay afloat at all states of the tide. Insofar as it is dominated by tall chimneys, it just is like a Medway rivulet; but in all other respects it resembles any other East Coast muddy creek. For those skippers emboldened by a stout craft with bottom-taking qualities and who have an interest in creeping in and out of holes, havens and creeks, there are indeed some classic 'better oles' to be found in the vicinity. My most vivid memories are of the plaintive cries of the birds.

Leigh-on-Sea and Hadleigh Ray are favourites with those who know the waters; these areas have yacht clubs and plenty of facilities within easy reach. Benfleet, Small Gains and Tewkes Creeks are also in favour with those who possess a goodly portion of that telling factor, local knowledge. The clubs at Benfleet, Essex, Island and Leigh-on-Sea all have moorings in the vicinity. There are anchorages in the area – Ray Gut and Hadleigh Bay, for example – but it is wisest to get some detailed information from one of the clubs.

Leigh-on-Sea is approached via Ray Gut, marked by the green Leigh (also known as Low Way) just to westward of Southend Pier. This leads in its own inimitable fashion through Marsh End and Leigh Sands to the all-change junction for Hadleigh Creek (also known as Ray) and Leigh Creek. Although the creek is buoyed, the moorings are probably the surest way of guiding yourself in; if that is what you have to do. A far better way is to thumb a following ride with a sister vessel near the top of a tide.

There is deepish water in Hadleigh Creek and this tends to make Hadleigh and the nearby stretch to Smallgains Creek perhaps more popular than Leigh, thus explaining the multiplicity of buoys, beacons, marks and markers as well the plethora of moorings. However, there is a very good anchorage in the vicinity, so long as you avoid the few low spots that are to be found. It is true that, when the tide is over

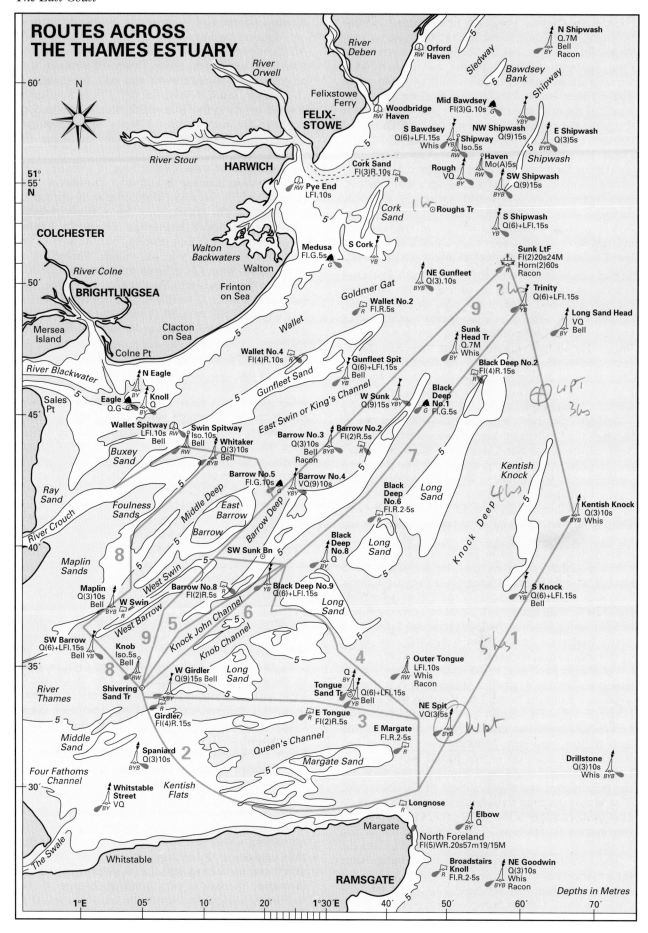

ROUTES ACROSS
THE THAMES ESTUARY

River Deben

River Orwell

River Stour

N Shipwash
Q.7M
Bell
Racon

Orford
Haven RW

Sledway

Bawdsey
Bank

Shipway

FELIX-
STOWE

Felixstowe
Ferry

Woodbridge
Haven RW

Mid Bawdsey
Fl(3)G.10s G

NW Shipwash
Q(9)15s

E Shipwash
Q(3)5s

S Bawdsey
Q(6)+LFl.15s
Whis

Shipway
Iso.5s
RW

Haven
Mo(A)5s
RW

Shipwash

HARWICH

Rough
VQ BY

SW Shipwash
Q(9)15s BYB

Cork Sand
Fl(3)R.10s R

COLCHESTER

Pye End
LFl.10s RW

Cork
Sand

Roughs Tr

S Shipwash
Q(6)+LFl.15s
YB

River Colne

Walton
Backwaters

Medusa
Fl.G.5s G

S Cork
YB

Sunk LtF
Fl(2)20s24M
Horn(2)60s
Racon

BRIGHTLINGSEA

Walton

NE Gunfleet
Q(3).10s

9

Trinity
Q(6)+LFl.15s
YB

Mersea
Island

Frinton
on Sea

Goldmer Gat

Wallet No.2
Fl.R.5s R

Long Sand Head
VQ
BY
Bell

Clacton
on Sea

River Blackwater

Colne Pt

Wallet

Sunk
Head Tr
Q.7M
Whis

Black Deep No.2
Fl(4)R.15s R

Sales
Pt

Wallet No.4
Fl(4)R.10s R

Gunfleet Sand

Gunfleet Spit
Q(6)+LFl.15s
Bell YB

W Sunk
Q(9)15s YBY

Black
Deep
No.1
Fl.G.5s G

N Eagle

East Swin or King's Channel

7

Eagle
Q.G BY

Knoll
Q
BY

Wallet Spitway
LFl.10s RW
Bell

Swin Spitway
Iso.10s
Bell RW

Whitaker
Q(3)10s
Bell RW

Barrow No.3
Q(3)10s
Bell
Racon BYB

Barrow No.2
Fl(2)R.5s
R

Black
Deep
No.6
Fl.R.2·5s R

Long
Sand

Kentish
Knock

45′

Buxey
Sand

Barrow No.5
Fl.G.10s G

Barrow No.4
VQ(9)10s YBY

Kentish Knock
Q(3)10s
BYB Whis

Ray
Sand

Foulness
Sands

Middle Deep

East
Barrow

Barrow Deep

Black
Deep
No.8
Q
BY

Long
Sand

Knock Deep

River Crouch

Barrow

SW Sunk Bn

40′

8

Maplin
Sands

West Swin

Barrow No.8
Fl(2)R.5s R

Black Deep No.9
Q(6)+LFl.15s YB

S Knock
Q(6)+LFl.15s
YB
Bell

Maplin
Q(3)10s
Bell BYB

W Swin
R

West Barrow

9

5

Knock John Channel

6

Long
Sand

SW Barrow
Q(6)+LFl.15s
Bell YB

Knob
Iso.5s
Bell

Knob Channel

4

Outer Tongue
LFl.10s
Whis
Racon RW

35′

8

Shivering
Sand Tr YBY

W Girdler
Q(9)15s Bell YBY

Long
Sand

Q
BY

Tongue
Sand Tr
Q(6)+LFl.15s
Bell YB

NE Spit
VQ(3)5s
BYB

*River
Thames*

Girdler
Fl(4)R.15s R

E Tongue
Fl(2)R.5s R

3

E Margate
Fl.R.2·5s R

Drillstone
Q(3)10s
Whis BYB

Middle
Sand

Spaniard
Q(3)10s
BYB

2

Queen's Channel

*Four Fathoms
Channel*

Kentish
Flats

Margate Sand

30′

Whitstable
Street
VQ BY

Longnose
R

Elbow
Q
BY

Margate

North Foreland
Fl(5)WR.20s57m19/15M

Whitstable

Broadstairs
Knoll
Fl.R.2·5s R

NE Goodwin
Q(3)10s
Whis
Racon BYB

The Swale

RAMSGATE

Depths in Metres

1°E   05′   10′   20′   1°30′E   40′   50′   60′   70′

ROUTES ACROSS THE THAMES ESTUARY

BUOYAGE

Plans read from bottom to top

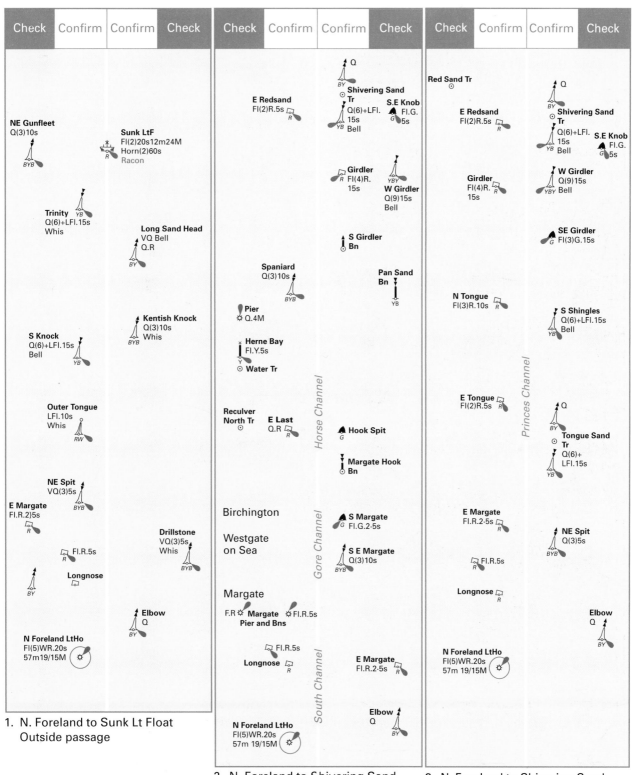

1. N. Foreland to Sunk Lt Float
   Outside passage

2. N. Foreland to Shivering Sand
   Towers via Gore Channel and
   Kentish Flats

3. N. Foreland to Shivering Sand
   Tower via Princes Channel

Check	Confirm	Confirm	Check		Check	Confirm	Confirm	Check		Check	Confirm	Confirm	Check

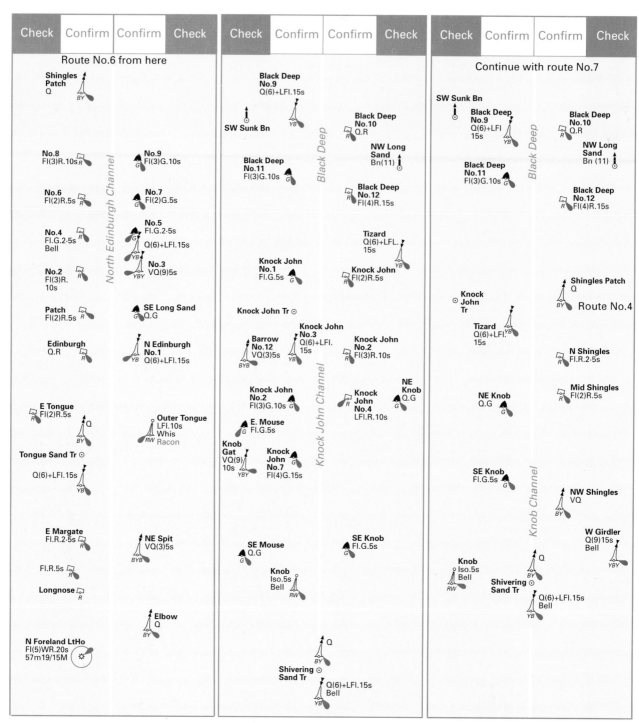

Route No.6 from here

Shingles Patch
Q
BY

No.8
Fl(3)R.10s
R

No.9
Fl(3)G.10s
G

No.6
Fl(2)R.5s
R

No.7
Fl(2)G.5s
G

No.4
Fl.G.2·5s
Bell
G

No.5
Fl.G.2·5s
G

No.2
Fl(3)R.10s
R

Q(6)+LFl.15s
YBY

No.3
VQ(9)5s
YBY

Patch
Fl(2)R.5s
R

SE Long Sand
Q.G
G

Edinburgh
Q.R
R

N Edinburgh
No.1
Q(6)+LFl.15s
YB

E Tongue
Fl(2)R.5s
R

Q
BY

Outer Tongue
LFl.10s
Whis
Racon
RW

Tongue Sand Tr ⊙

Q(6)+LFl.15s
YB

E Margate
Fl.R.2·5s
R

NE Spit
VQ(3)5s
BYB

Fl.R.5s
R

Longnose
R

Elbow
Q
BY

N Foreland LtHo
Fl(5)WR.20s
57m19/15M

5. Shivering Sand Tower to Black Deep via Knock John channel

Black Deep
No.9
Q(6)+LFl.15s

SW Sunk Bn
YB

Black Deep
No.10
Q.R
R

NW Long
Sand
Bn(11)

Black Deep
No.11
Fl(3)G.10s
G

Black Deep
No.12
Fl(4)R.15s
R

Tizard
Q(6)+LFl.
15s

Knock John
No.1
Fl.G.5s
G

Knock John
Fl(2)R.5s
R

Knock John Tr ⊙

Knock John
No.3
Q(6)+LFl.
15s

Barrow
No.12
VQ(3)5s
BYB

YB

Knock John
No.2
Fl(3)R.10s
R

Knock John
No.2
Fl(3)G.10s
G

E. Mouse
Fl.G.5s
G

Knock
John
No.4
LFl.R.10s

NE
Knob
Q.G
G

Knob
Gat
VQ(9)
10s
YBY

Knock
John
No.7
Fl(4)G.15s

SE Mouse
Q.G
G

SE Knob
Fl.G.5s
G

Knob
Iso.5s
Bell
RW

Q
BY

Shivering ⊙
Sand Tr

Q(6)+LFl.15s
Bell
YB

6. Shivering sand Tower to Black Deep via Knob Channel

Continue with route No.7

SW Sunk Bn

Black Deep
No.9
Q(6)+LFl
15s
YB

Black Deep
No.10
Q.R
R

NW Long
Sand
Bn (11)

Black Deep
No.11
Fl(3)G.10s
G

Black Deep
No.12
Fl(4)R.15s
R

Knock
John
Tr ⊙

Shingles Patch
Q
BY   Route No.4

Tizard
Q(6)+LFl.
15s
YB

N Shingles
Fl.R.2·5s
R

NE Knob
Q.G

Mid Shingles
Fl(2)R.5s
R

G

SE Knob
Fl.G.5s
G

NW Shingles
VQ
BY

W Girdler
Q(9)15s
Bell
YBY

Knob
Iso.5s
Bell
RW

Q
BY

Shivering ⊙
Sand Tr

Q(6)+LFl.15s
Bell
YB

4. N. Foreland to Black Deep via N. Edinburgh Channel

5. Shivering Sand Tower to Black Deep via Knock John channel

6. Shivering sand Tower to Black Deep via Knob Channel

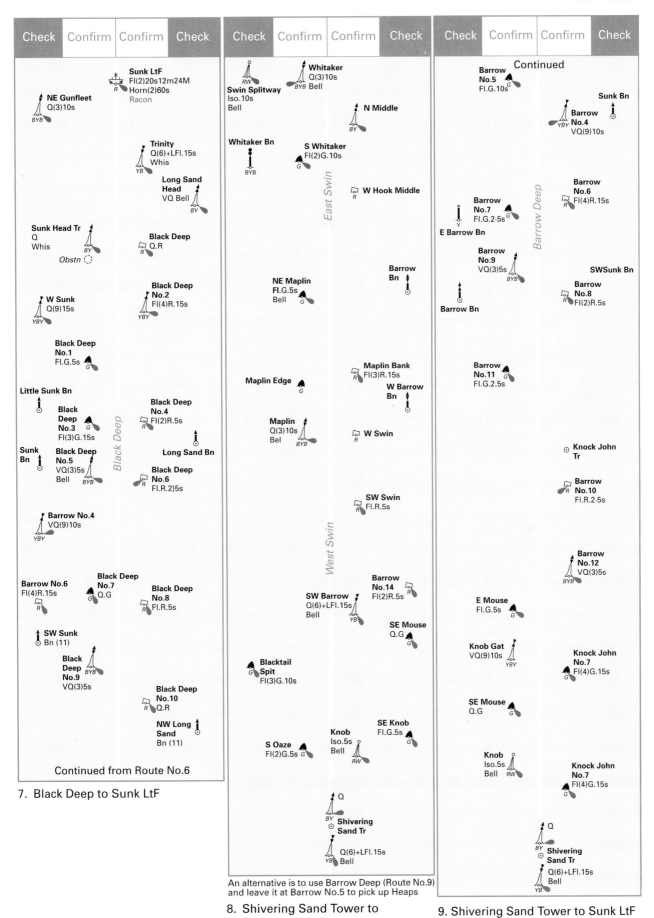

Check	Confirm	Confirm	Check

NE Gunfleet
Q(3)10s
BYB

Sunk LtF
Fl(2)20s12m24M
Horn(2)60s
Racon

Trinity
Q(6)+LFl.15s
Whis
YB

Long Sand Head
VQ Bell
BY

Sunk Head Tr
Q
Whis
BY

Obstn

Black Deep
Q.R
R

Black Deep No.2
Fl(4)R.15s
YBY

W Sunk
Q(9)15s
YBY

Black Deep No.1
Fl.G.5s
G

Little Sunk Bn

Black Deep No.3
Fl(3)G.15s
G

Black Deep No.4
Fl(2)R.5s
R

Sunk Bn

Black Deep No.5
VQ(3)5s
Bell
BYB

Long Sand Bn

Black Deep No.6
Fl.R.2)5s
R

Black Deep

Barrow No.4
VQ(9)10s
YBY

Barrow No.6
Fl(4)R.15s
R

Black Deep No.7
Q.G
G

Black Deep No.8
Fl.R.5s
R

SW Sunk
Bn (11)

Black Deep No.9
VQ(3)5s
BYB

Black Deep No.10
Q.R
R

NW Long Sand
Bn (11)

Continued from Route No.6

7. Black Deep to Sunk LtF

Check	Confirm	Confirm	Check

Swin Splitway
Iso.10s
Bell
RW

Whitaker
Q(3)10s
Bell
BYB

N Middle
BY

Whitaker Bn
BYB

S Whitaker
Fl(2)G.10s
G

East Swin

W Hook Middle
R

Barrow Bn

NE Maplin
Fl.G.5s
Bell
G

Maplin Bank
Fl(3)R.15s
R

W Barrow Bn

Maplin Edge
G

Maplin
Q(3)10s
Bel
BYB

W Swin
R

West Swin

SW Swin
Fl.R.5s
R

Barrow No.14
Fl(2)R.5s
R

SW Barrow
Q(6)+LFl.15s
Bell
YB

SE Mouse
Q.G

Blacktail Spit
Fl(3)G.10s
G

SE Knob
Fl.G.5s

S Oaze
Fl(2)G.5s
G

Knob
Iso.5s
Bell
RW

Q
BY

Shivering Sand Tr
Q(6)+LFl.15s
Bell
YB

An alternative is to use Barrow Deep (Route No.9)
and leave it at Barrow No.5 to pick up Heaps

8. Shivering Sand Tower to Whitaker Buoy

Check	Confirm	Confirm	Check

Continued

Barrow No.5
Fl.G.10s
G

Sunk Bn

Barrow No.4
VQ(9)10s
YBY

Barrow No.6
Fl(4)R.15s
R

Barrow Deep

Barrow No.7
Fl.G.2·5s
G

E Barrow Bn
Y

Barrow No.9
VQ(3)5s
BYB

SWSunk Bn

Barrow No.8
Fl(2)R.5s
R

Barrow Bn

Barrow No.11
Fl.G.2.5s
G

Knock John Tr

Barrow No.10
Fl.R.2·5s
R

Barrow No.12
VQ(3)5s
BYB

E Mouse
Fl.G.5s
G

Knob Gat
VQ(9)10s
YBY

Knock John No.7
Fl(4)G.15s
G

SE Mouse
Q.G
G

Knob
Iso.5s
Bell
RW

Knock John No.7
Fl(4)G.15s
G

Q
BY

Shivering Sand Tr
Q(6)+LFl.15s
Bell
YB

9. Shivering Sand Tower to Sunk LtF via Barrow Deep

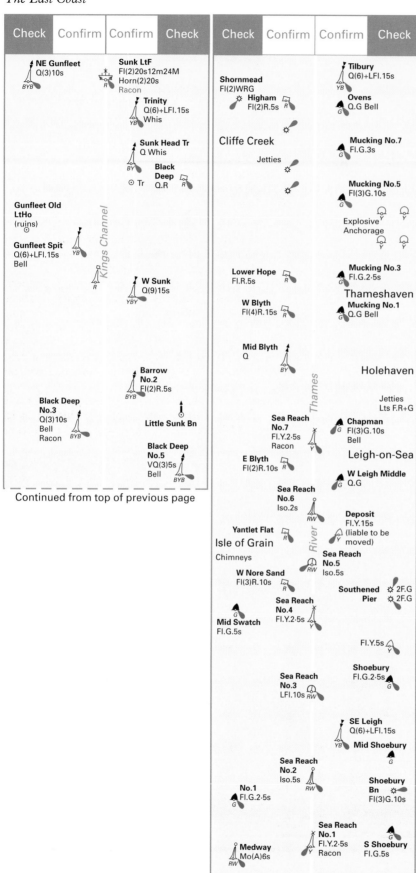

Check	Confirm	Confirm	Check	Check	Confirm	Confirm	Check

NE Gunfleet
Q(3)10s
BYB

Sunk LtF
Fl(2)20s12m24M
Horn(2)20s
Racon
R

Trinity
Q(6)+LFl.15s
Whis
YB

Sunk Head Tr
Q Whis
BY

⊙ Tr   **Black Deep**
Q.R
R

Gunfleet Old LtHo
(ruins)
⊙

Gunfleet Spit
Q(6)+LFl.15s
Bell
YB

Kings Channel

W Sunk
Q(9)15s
YBY
R

Barrow No.2
Fl(2)R.5s
BYB

Black Deep No.3
Q(3)10s
Bell
Racon
BYB

Little Sunk Bn

Black Deep No.5
VQ(3)5s
Bell
BYB

Continued from top of previous page

Shornmead
Fl(2)WRG
☼ **Higham**
Fl(2)R.5s
R

Cliffe Creek

Jetties

Tilbury
Q(6)+LFl.15s
YB

Ovens
Q.G Bell
G

Mucking No.7
Fl.G.3s
G

Mucking No.5
Fl(3)G.10s
G

Explosive   Y   Y
Anchorage
Y   Y

Mucking No.3
Fl.G.2·5s
G

Lower Hope
Fl.R.5s
R

W Blyth
Fl(4)R.15s
R

Thameshaven
Mucking No.1
Q.G Bell
G

Mid Blyth
Q
BY

Thames

Holehaven

Jetties
Lts F.R+G

Sea Reach No.7
Fl.Y.2·5s
Racon
Y

E Blyth
Fl(2)R.10s
R

Chapman
Fl(3)G.10s
Bell
G

Leigh-on-Sea

W Leigh Middle
Q.G
G

Sea Reach No.6
Iso.2s
RW

Yantlet Flat
R

Isle of Grain

Chimneys

W Nore Sand
Fl(3)R.10s
R

River

Deposit
Fl.Y.15s
(liable to be moved)
Y

Sea Reach No.5
Iso.5s
RW

Southened Pier   ☼ 2F.G
☼ 2F.G

Sea Reach No.4
Fl.Y.2·5s
Y

Mid Swatch
Fl.G.5s
G

Fl.Y.5s
Y

Shoebury
Fl.G.2·5s
G

Sea Reach No.3
LFl.10s
RW

SE Leigh
Q(6)+LFl.15s
YB
Mid Shoebury
G

Sea Reach No.2
Iso.5s
RW

No.1
Fl.G.2·5s
G

Shoebury Bn   ☼
Fl(3)G.10s

Medway
Mo(A)6s
RW

Sea Reach No.1
Fl.Y.2·5s
Racon
Y

S Shoebury
Fl.G.5s
G

The Thames: from Sea Reach
No.1 to Tilbury Cardinal Marker

BASILDON
Pitsea Hall Country Park ☎ 01268 550088/
581093

Tidal access
HW ±3hrs
Ⓥ (100, end-on-end; visitors' by arrangement), 🚾,
⚓, ⟋

CANVEY ISLAND
Benfleet Yacht Club ☎ 01268 792278

Tidal access
HW ±1½hrs
Ⓥ (250 drying; visitors' by arrangement), 🚾, 📄, ⚓,
Ⓖ (nearby)

ERITH
Erith Yacht Club ☎ 01322 430040/332943

Tidal access
24 hrs
Ⓥ (swinging moorings; visitors') 🚾, ⚓, ⟋,
Provisions (nearby)

THURROCK
Thurrock Yacht Club ☎ 01375 373720

Tidal access
24 hrs
Ⓥ (swinging moorings only), 🛢D (nearby),
🛢P (nearby), ⚓, 🚾, ⟋, Provisions (nearby)

BENFLEET
Benfleet Yacht Club ☎ 01268 792278

Tidal access
HW ±4hrs, 1·8m at HW
⚓, Ⓖ, 🛢D, Provisions (nearby), Repairs (nearby)
Ⓥ as for Thurrock

the sandbanks, conditions can cause rocking and rolling of craft; but for the best part of 6–7 hours of each tide, it is a comfortable spot.

There is less water as you move up to Benfleet bridge through the narrow buoyed channel. Benfleet Yacht Club will afford you a warm welcome, and there is the possibility of a berth at the slip or by its barge. In the clubhouse there are showers, drink and some food. If you want to visit, give them a ring beforehand and it is possible that someone will be able to meet you to guide you in.

There is no doubt that these places are packed with interest and redolent of our history and heritage. However, any skipper thinking of visiting

The multitude of mini-channels and gutways of Benfleet Creek are here seen to good advantage – reinforcing the notion that it is wise to get advice before entering. The moorings are almost as dense as the houses in the background . . .

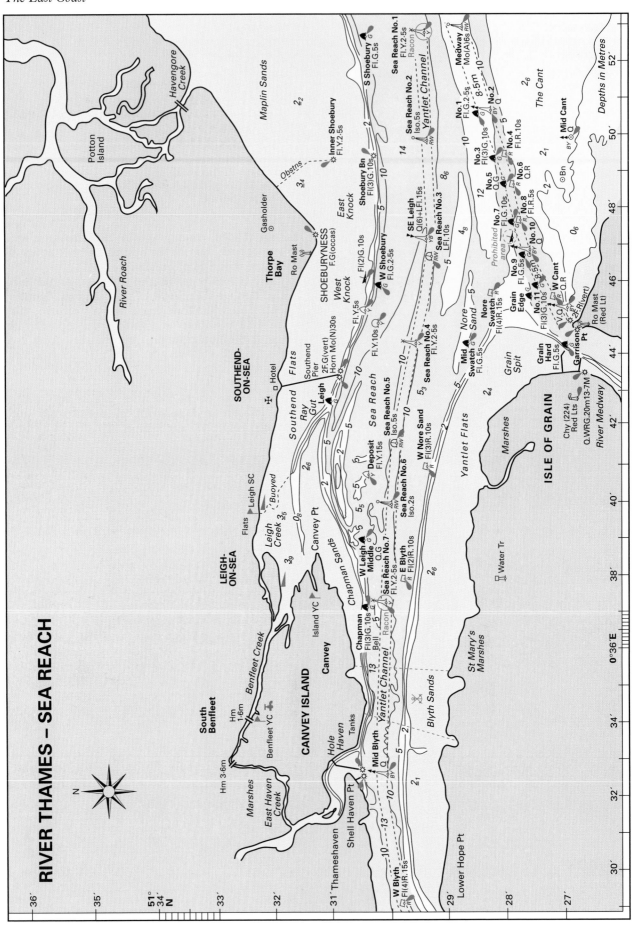

RIVER THAMES – SEA REACH

Depths in Metres

LEIGH-ON-SEA
51°32'·5N 0°40'E

Charts Admiralty 1185, 1183. Imray C1, C2, Y6, Y7. OS Landranger 178

Tides
Dover +0125

Authorities
Harbourmaster (Leigh) ☎ 01702 710561
Harbourmaster (Southend) ☎ 01702 611889

Radio
Port Control London VHF Ch 12

HOLEHAVEN
51°30'·55N 00°33'·50E

Charts Admiralty 2484, 1186. Imray C1, C2, Y7

Tides
Sheerness +0010, Dover +0140

Note
A busy spot. Inaccessible to boats drawing more than 1m, except between HW ±4hrs.

Authorities
PLA Piermaster ☎ 01268 683041

Radio
Canvey Patrol VHF Ch 12

Facilities
⚓ (by arrangement), ⚲ (nearby), Provisions (nearby)

for the first time would be well advised to research charts and tide times conscientiously.

In the summer of '95, I wished that I had been able to do so, for I had planned a long-delayed foray into Ray Gut to pay my respects to the many clubs between the pier and the north of Canvey Island. Eventually, wind against tide put paid to that; but not before I had had a full frontal close-up of Southend Pier and made three attempts to find the buoys that would lead me safely through the surfing crests to the comparative still (but not necessarily running deep) waters of the inner channels. As *Macmillan's Almanac* puts it: 'all are buoyed, but

. . . while nearby Leigh on Sea seems to be a rustic riverside community that knows not the meaning of municipality.

echo-sounder is invaluable'. Later, I was told in 'certain terms' that wind against a flood tide makes a safe entry possible only with good local knowledge. I also tried anchoring by the pier, but found that too daunting. So, sadly, I had to move on and miss out on visiting all the friends from this area whom I have met while cruising elsewhere. To be upfront, I felt quite pathetic about my failure.

In spite of Holehaven's off-putting first appearance, I crept in early one morning and took refuge in the deep water immediately behind the jetty. Anchoring was easy; the hole was deep and the

The upper reaches of Holehaven show not a single sign of having any connection with oil tankers or the troubled waters of the Thames.

water as thick as the cocoa I was drinking. It was easy to see why it had been granted the status of 'haven'.

The next stopping place is Holehaven, the well-named refuge that created the eponymous community. It is not far upstream, nor from the main channel, being merely tucked in behind a jetty. The Holy Haven itself is not easy to spot, but the vast tanks of Shell Haven towering above it are unmistakable.

Holehaven gets its name from two Holes: the 20m deep one just outside, that causes strong currents, and the 4m+ one about ½ mile inside (in fact, some old pilots give the depth in excess of 20ft, but I was unable to find any trace of such a depth). Just inside by the jetty where I anchored, however, there was plenty of water. It was only when I looked as far as I could see through the binoculars that I saw that the course got more difficult. So, if you want to go much further up than where I was, you must needs take care, for the channel is narrow and not easy to discern. Indeed, when the tide is in, the whole area

is covered, and it takes some expert knowledge to navigate the gutway. So, caution is called for – or a friendly local. However, there is little to tempt a cruising crew, unless they feel they must search out the ultimate . . . every time.

It is possible to get a mooring or to anchor in the creek, but it is best to check with the harbourmaster for advice and instruction. You may even be allocated a swinging mooring. The main reason for calling is the presence of the classic 'olde worlde' pub, the Lobster Smack (which everyone calls 'Becky's') where 'fings ain't changed from wot vey used ter be'.

GRAVESEND
51°23'·6N 00°23'·00E
Gravesend Canal Basin

Tides
Dover +0150

Tidal access
Lock opens HW –1½hrs to HW (0700–2100).
☎ 01474 352392

Moorings
Contact Gravesend Yacht Club ☎ 01474 533974
Ⓥ (80, 15 visitors'- swinging), ⚓ (by arrangement), ⚓, ⚡, 🏪, 🚾, ⚓, Provisions (nearby), Repairs

RIVER THAMES

Charts Admiralty 3319, 2484, 3337. Imray C2, C1.
OS Landranger 176, 177, 178

Tides

Dover +0250. Diff on HW London Bridge: Tilbury
−0400, Gallions Pt +0200, Hammersmith Bridge
+0035, Kew Bridge +0050, Richmond Lock +0050
Note Caution tide can run at 3–4 knots

Authorities

PLA chief harbourmaster ☎ 0181 855 0315
Harbourmaster (upper section) ☎ 0171 265 2656
Harbourmaster (lower section) ☎ 01474 560311
Duty officer Woolwich ☎ 0181 855 0315
Port Controller Gravesend & London Port Control
Centre ☎ 01474 560311

Radio

Port Control London VHF Ch 12 (sea to Sea Reach
No. 4 buoy), 68 (No. 4 buoy to Crayfordness), 14
(upriver from Crayfordness). Patrol launch *Thames
Patrol* VHF Ch 12, 13, 14, 16, 6

Fuel

Diesel from Thames refueller barge on N side ½
mile E of Tower Bridge: 0900–1600 Mon–Fri,
☎ 0171 481 1774. VHF Ch 14 *Thames Refueller*.
Fuel barge *Freddy* of Westminster Pier: 0900–1600
Mon–Fri, ☎ 0831 451260 VHF Ch 14

THAMES BARRIER

Authorities

Barrier Control ☎ 0181 855 0315

Radio

Woolwich Radio VHF Ch 14, 22, 16 (contact must be
made when passing Margaret Pt (inward) and
Blackwell Pt (outward)

Lights

Amber – proceed with caution; red – navigation
prohibited

Located at Woolwich Reach, the Thames Barrier
protects London from flooding. There are 9 piers
between which gates can be rotated upwards from
the riverbed to form a barrier. The piers are
numbered 1–9 from N to S, the spans are lettered
A–K from S–N. A, H, J and K are not navigable;
C–F, with a depth of 5·8m, are for larger vessels; B
and G, with 1·5m, are for small craft/yachts,
westbound via G and eastbound via B.

Details of the Thames Barrier transit arrangements
are contained in PLA *Notices to Mariners*, published
from time to time, available at all PLA offices and
posted at Teddington, Richmond, Brentford, Bow
and Limehouse Locks.

Note The Barrier is completely closed for testing one
day a month. Individual spans are tested weekly.

In 1622, Canvey Island was in danger of
becoming a marsh or perhaps even a morass. One
John Croppenburgh, a Dutchman, reclaimed the
island at well below sea level with deep dykes. He
was rewarded for his efforts to the tune of one-third
of the island and, with many of his cronies, he
settled there, living to a ripe old age and only
outdone in longevity by his brilliant sea-wall works.

Then the slog of the slowly narrowing river
Thames continues with a more chilling than thrilling
leg up to the green Mucking No. 3, the buoy that
marks the marshes and flats of the northwest bank.
The red Lower Hope marks the point of that name,
where the river takes a dramatic turn more or less
directly to the south. Whichever way you interpret
the ambiguously titled 'Lower Hope Point' (lower
geographically or just lower in hopeful
expectations?), it does nothing to ameliorate the
pretty bleak area that it is. Along Lower Hope
Reach, small craft are advised to keep to the south
on ebbs and the north on floods; and not overlook
the works between Muckings 5 and 7.

Then comes the congestion that is Gravesend and
Tilbury. Gravesend, which comes first, is not a
particularly well-known resort but you can, in fact,
ease into the basin of the now disused Thames and
Medway Canal from 2hrs before high water. The
lock is unmanned at other times. About 300m above
the Canal Basin is the landing at the causeway.
General facilities, and a few moorings, abound in
the vicinity, including the Customs House and the
Yacht Club.

The onset of Tilbury marks the beginning of the
heavy commercial aspect of the river, and all leisure
craft are well advised to keep away from this busy
container port. On the north shore just upstream of
the Port of Tilbury Grain Terminal, however, is the
small but extremely welcoming Thurrock Yacht
Club.

As one would expect, the buoyage is excellent
right up to Tilbury, where it stops. Any hazard
upstream is due, not to the lack of buoyage, but to
the constraints created by the debris, garbage and
litter that accumulate and drift down the river,
consisting of all the nasties you can imagine. Serious
threats are lengths of rope and nylon/plastic sheet
and, at the other end of the spectrum, hugely rafted
oil/water-logged/clogged sleepers. They look somewhat akin to sleeping crocodiles – half submerged
and just as well camouflaged. It is probably worth all
the complications of having a crew, just for someone
to keep a debris watch.

This may seem something of an exaggeration in a
'peaceful' river like the Thames, but some of the big
ships, as well as the police, customs, pilots and the
like, can move so much water in their progress that
their bow waves and stern wakes can require the
exclusive, full-time attention of the skipper for a
long time. I remember, on one occasion near
Coalhouse Point, being overtaken by a Russian ship.
Its wash was so tremendous that I nearly surfed a
couple of times. The natural surging and resurging
from the banks was still continuing when I had to
contend with a small collection of coasters and
yachts working in both directions – coasters wanting
to overtake but not going quite fast enough unless I
cut down, and yachts doing their best to manoeuvre
under sail – in unfitting circumstances.

The chances are that you will also be accosted by
other traffic – the police and/or customs. Provided

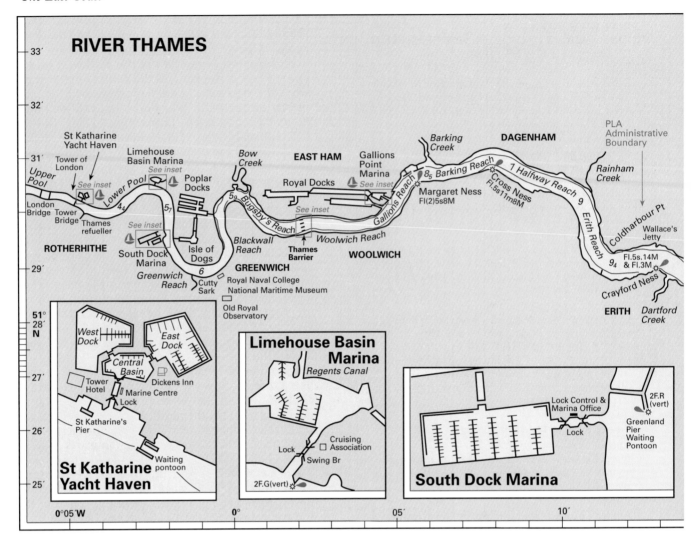

RIVER THAMES

GALLIONS POINT MARINA
51°30'·27N 00°04'·76E
☎ 0171 476 7054 radio VHF Ch 68

Tidal access
HW ±5hrs

Access to City via Docklands Light Railway.
Woolwich via Ferry and foot tunnel.

Facilities
Ⓥ (90 pontoons, visitors' by arrangement), **WC**, 🚿,
⚓, ⚡, ↘, Provisions, Engineer, Repairs

LIMEHOUSE BASIN
51°30'·5N 00°02'·17W

Tidal access
HW ±3hrs 1m over lock sill
Note Entrance through lock 0800–1800. Waiting
pontoon outside Limehouse Basin provides access to
the Grand Union Canal

Lock office (BW) ☎ 0171 308 9930

Radio
VHF Ch 80

Moorings Cruising Association ☎ 0171 537 2828

SOUTH DOCK MARINA
51°29'·64N 00°01'·80E

Tidal access
By lock: HW ±2hrs (2m draught). HW ±4hrs (1m
draught). Lock manned 24hrs.

South Dock Marina ☎ 0171 252 2244

Radio
VHF Ch 80 M

Facilities
Ⓥ (300, visitors' by arrangement), **WC**, 🚿, ⚓, ⚡, ↘,
Provisions (nearby), 🛢D (fuel barge), Engineer
(by arrangement), Repairs (by arrangement)

ST KATHARINE YACHT HAVEN
51°30'·30N 00°04'·26E

Access
Access is via a tidal lock 38m x 9m and draught of
5m −2 to +1½hrs London Bridge: 0600–0230
Mar–Oct; 0800–1800 Nov–Feb; lock closed
Tues/Wed; waiting buoys downstream.

Authorities
Harbourmaster ☎ 0171 481 8350

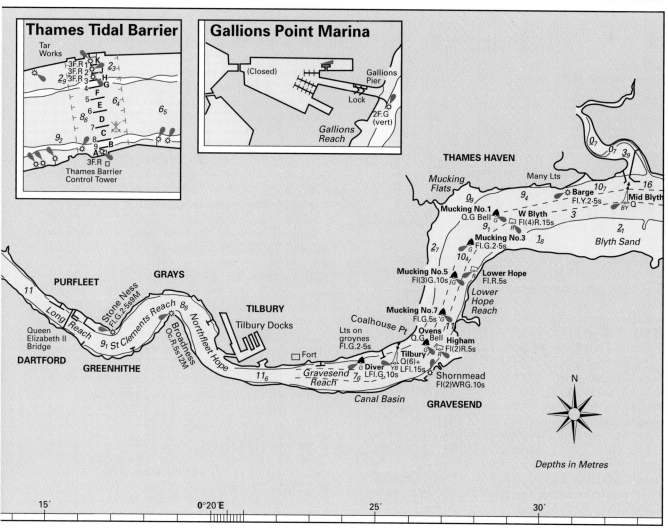

Thames Tidal Barrier

Tar Works

3F.R 1 K
3F.R 2 J
3F.R 3 H
G
5 F
E
D
C
B
A
3F.R

Thames Barrier Control Tower

Gallions Point Marina

(Closed)

Gallions Pier

Lock

2F.G (vert)

Gallions Reach

THAMES HAVEN

Mucking Flats

Many Lts

Barge Fl.Y.2·5s

Mid Blyth

Mucking No.1 Q.G Bell

W Blyth Fl(4)R.15s

Mucking No.3 Fl.G.2·5s

Blyth Sand

Mucking No.5 Fl(3)G.10s

Lower Hope Fl.R.5s

Lower Hope Reach

Mucking No.7 Fl.G.5s

Coalhouse Pt

Ovens

PURFLEET

GRAYS

Stone Ness Fl.G.2·5s9M

St Clements Reach

Lts on groynes Fl.G.2·5s

Q.G Bell

Higham Fl(2)R.5s

TILBURY

Tilbury Docks

Broadness Oc.R.5s12M

Northfleet Hope

Tilbury Q(6)+ LFl.15s

Queen Elizabeth II Bridge

Fort

Diver LFl.G.10s

Shornmead Fl(2)WRG.10s

DARTFORD

GREENHITHE

Gravesend Reach

Canal Basin

GRAVESEND

N

Depths in Metres

15′   0°20′E   25′   30′

Radio
St Katharine VHF Ch 80 M

Facilities
All usual facilities

PIERS
Piers where landing can be made by arrangement
Piers with ★, contact PLA Central Booking Service
☎ 0171 265 2666.
Greenwich Pier, Tower Pier★
London Bridge City Pier   0171 403 5939
Charing Cross Pier★
Westminster Pier★
Lambeth Pier   0171 839 2164
Festival Pier★
Cadogan Pier   0171 349 8585
Putney Pier   0171 378 1211
Kew Pier   0171 930 2062
Richmond Landing Stage
Hampton Court Pier   0181 781 9758

---

you are on lawful business or pleasure, it is always encouraging to discover that these officers get around much more than one might expect. (I recall in the middle of winter being visited early in the morning at an anchorage up the Deben by a customs man who greeted me with: 'Didn't see you here yesterday morning sir; just wondered if you were all right?' Heavy-hinted if not heavy-handed.)

On my first trip up the Thames, my first visit was from a police launch. I had noticed that it had been ambling along behind for a while, so gave it a call on VHF. The launch was alongside and a River Police officer jumped on as if boarding a bus. No fuss. We chatted about this and that, partaking of the inevitable cup of tea, but it wasn't long before we got down to the day's agenda: checking the serial numbers on *Valcon*'s gear. It was all put so politely, that it seemed impossible that I might have been the target of their investigations. 'We like to know who's passing through our patch and what they've got on board. If some of it should later, sadly, turn up on another vessel, we know where it belongs, don't we?' When the police vessel came to pick up its man, I noticed that there was a customs launch almost in tow. Clearly, they were in cahoots . . . and a good thing too!

Bridge depths and clearance heights, central spans

Bridge	Depth (m)		Clearances (m)		
	MLWN	MHWS	MHWN	MLWN	MLWS
QEII Dartford		54·1			
Tower lowered)	6·5	8·6	9·8	14·4	15·3
Tower (raised)	6·5	42·5	43·7	48·3	49·2
London	2·5	8·9	10·1	14·7	15·5
Cannon St Rail	3·5	7·1	8·2	12·8	13·6
Blackfriars Rail	2·9	7·0	8·1	12·7	13·5
Westminster	1·9	5·4	6·6	11·1	11·8
Albert	2·1	4·9	6·0	10·5	11·0
Ham'smith	1·5	3·7	4·8	9·1	9·4
Twickenham		5·9	7·1	8·5	8·5
Richmond		5·3	6·5	7·9	7·9

In spite of the attractive-sounding names of St Clement's or Fiddler's Reach and Erith Rands, there is little to attract hereabouts, for the area tends towards the busier and dirtier aspects of river life. It is here, between Crayford Ness and Coldharbour Point, that, somewhat surprisingly, but nevertheless a thankful relief, the Erith Yacht Club has its HQ.

The further upstream we go, the more interesting does it become, and there are quite a few items of note to entertain on the way: the Dartford road bridge which has closed the river to tall ships; the enormous trumpet-shaped vents that mark the infamous Dartford Tunnel; Henry Ford's factory at Dagenham; and Barking Creek's imposing guillotine-gated entrance. Then comes Gallion's Reach, with its locked entrances for Queen Victoria, Royal Albert and King George V Docks. This once-busy area is now coming to life with the London City Airport, and a multiplicity of modern developments. For the benefit of the yachtsman, there is the new Gallion's Point Marina, situated in the London Docklands, downstream of the Woolwich Ferry on the north side.

Gallion soon gives way to the wide, long Woolwich Reach, and this holds two obstacles for the mariner. The first, although the less noticeable (and all the more hazardous for that) are the ferries that ply from Woolwich. The area is just as grim and grotty as it was over 40 years ago when I 'served' in the arsenal. In those days, I was doing my best to be a WO3 in the Royal Artillery attached to the Education Corps, but was really beginning to discover how to educate myself. The good old Woolwich free ferry had a certain charm (and it was not a case of *'Je ne sais quoi'* – it was more the undoubted possibility of 'picking up a bit of stuff', only slightly more euphemistically referred to as 'Getting On and Getting Off': the title of a book in which I was, many years later, to describe what was often a maladroit procedure).

The more noticeable of the two comes second – although, in fact, it is second to none. It is the striking Thames Flood Control Barrier. I can never look at it without its nine hooded piers reminding me of the ceremonial garb of some gargantuan

cardinal. However, there is nothing mystical about its workings. (For the regulations covering navigation through the barrier please see the details on page 171).

Between Woolwich Reach and Bugsbys Reach, on the South Bank, is the Greenwich Yacht Club, which maintains one visitors' mooring and makes available others when possible. After this, it is almost possible to make a complete circumnavigation of the horrendously famous Isle of Dogs. Only a few metres separate the West India and Millwall Docks and the rest one from another and thus from the river – otherwise it really would be an island. At the southernmost bend in the loop, the skyline is impressively punctuated by the grand buildings of the Royal Naval College, with the *Cutty Sark*, and Sir Francis Chichester's *Gipsy Moth* lying nearby.

About halfway along Limehouse Reach, on the W bank opposite the Isle of Dogs, is the recently developed project, the Marina at South Dock. Its lock opens +/-2 hours HW and there is a shore-linked waiting pontoon to the north at Greenland Pier; midway between Greenwich and Tower Bridge.

Limehouse Reach is topped at its northerly end by Limehouse Lock and Basin. This gives access to the

TEDDINGTON LOCK
This is the tidal limit of the river. Worked daily on a 24-hour rostered-duty basis. However, if you plan to arrive at an unsociable hour, it would be courteous to advise the lock-keeper in advance ☎ 0181 940 8723.

RICHMOND LOCK
Operated at all times when the sluices are in position under the three central spans of the footbridge. Hold off close to the lock which is against the Surrey bank and await the lock-keeper's instructions. The sluices are raised for clear passage through the footbridge from 2 hours before to 2 hours after HW except during the winter 'draw-off' period when passage under the sluices is available at all times, subject to the depth in the channel. Advice on timingFor advice on timing ☎ 0181 940 0634.

GRAND UNION CANAL AT BRENTFORD
This entrance is via Brentford Creek which leads to Thames locks that open from 2 hrs before HW to 2 hrs after (1600–2200). For information and advice ☎ 0171 560 8942 ext 31. The Grand Union Canal is controlled by British Waterways (BW) and a licence is required for navigation. For more information from BW ☎ 01923 226422

USEFUL CONTACTS
Brentford and Thames Lock ☎ 0181 560 1120
British Waterways ☎ 01923 226422
Port of London Authority ☎ 01474 562200
The Environment Agency ☎ 01734 535000
Chiswick Quay Marina ☎ 0181 994 8743

Regents Canal, and thence the River Lee. As such, it falls under the jurisdiction of BW, and a licence is needed. The lock has recently been revamped to make it more appropriate for leisure craft. Limehouse Basin, now the HQ of the Cruising Association, provides access to the inland waterways. It is run jointly by the Association and British Waterways. A happy marriage for all Thames cruising folk – and especially for visitors.

Around the corner at the head of the straight of Upper Pool is Tower Bridge. I have fancied blowing the ship's whistle for it to open, but I have never been able to raise the funds for the raising of the bridge (the thousands of pounds Sterling required demands a sterling effort that I cannot manage).

But what most yachtsmen want to open hereabouts are the lock gates into St Katharine Haven; known to most as 'Saint Katts'. They open +/-2 hours either side of high water. An arrival outside these times can leave you with an uncomfortable stay on the temporary moorings between the lock and HM President Pier, to which there is access at all states of the tide. The constant wash of passing vessels demands stout tackle to withstand the onslaught. Once inside, the mirror-calm waters of this Thames Mecca reflect the benefits and luxuries of its location and essence.

The Thames is not the widest, nor the fastest nor the longest river in the world. Nor is it the most beautiful, the most dramatic or the most treacherous; but it does possess a singularity charm with a variety of features that few other waterways can challenge. It is in its individuality, in its variety and, perhaps above all, in its history that it can lay claim to everlasting fame and to glory in being simply, Old Father Thames.

The River Medway is a waterway of contrasts; and such upstanding commercial fingers dominate the scene . . .

IX. The Medway & Swale

The Mighty River Medway rises in Sussex, from where it runs both north and east from its source at Turner's Hill near East Grinstead to the Thames estuary 60 miles away. It may rise in Sussex, but it is, in essence, a Kentish river, dividing the Kentish Men in the NW, from the Men of Kent in the SE. It flows through the famous, classic Medway towns of Maidstone, the county town; Rochester; Chatham; Strood and Gillingham.

It is about 6 miles from the red and white pillar of the Medway safe water buoy to the navigable entrance. This lies between Grain Hard and the famous Garrison Point at Sheerness, on the very edge of the Thames Estuary. At this point we are still 'all at sea' and it is 'plain sailing'; but, once past Garrison, everything alters. From here on, the River Medway has a great deal to offer in variety and contrast, with the major and most dramatic change coming at the guardian gates of Allington Lock. All below is tidal and mainly exposed to the elements; while all above tends to be calmer, more rural and altogether more picturesque. The tidal stretch offers good sailing, quiet anchorages in the marshes and saltings, and an excellent choice of marinas and

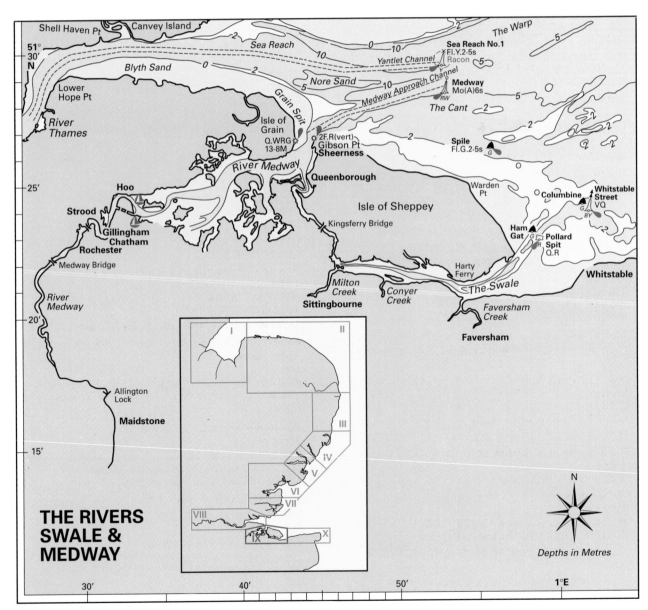

RIVER MEDWAY
51°27'·00N 00°44'·60E (off Garrison Point, Sheerness)
Charts Admiralty 3683, 2482, 1835, 1834. Imray Y18. OS Landranger 178
Tides
Sheerness: Dover +0130; Upnor: Dover +0145
Authorities
Harbourmaster (Sheerness) Medway Ports Ltd
☎ 01795 561234
Non-tidal River Medway Environment Agency
☎ 01732 838858
Radio
Medway Navigation Service:VHF Ch 74, 16, 11, 22, 73 (24hrs) ☎ 01795 663025

GILLINGHAM
Gillingham Marina ☎ 01634 280022 Radio VHF Ch 80 *Gillingham Marina*
Tides
HW Dover 0115
Tidal access
Locked basin HW ±4½ hrs
Ⓥ (250 tidal, 250 afloat, visitors' varies), WC, 🖼, ⚓, ⚡, ↘, Provisions, ⊙, ⬤D, ⬤P, Engineer (weekdays), Repairs

Medway Pier Marina ☎ 01634 851113
Radio: VHF Ch 80
Tidal access
HW ±4hrs
Ⓥ (60, 6 visitors'), WC, 🖼, ⚓, ⚡, ↘, Provisions, ⬤D, Engineers, Repairs

Hoo Marina ☎ 01634 250311
Radio: VHF Ch 80
Tides
HW Dover +0133
Tidal access
HW ±2½hrs
Ⓥ (120 pontoons, 10 visitors'), WC, 🖼, ⚓, ⚡, ↘, Provisions, ⬤D, Engineer, Repairs

Mariners Farm Boatyard ☎ 01634 233179
Tides
Dover +0130
Tidal access
HW ±2 hrs
Ⓥ (14 half-tide, 100 ashore), WC, ⚓, ⚡, Engineer, Repairs

Medway Ports Ltd
Radio
VHF Ch 80
Six visitors' buoys above Rochester Bridge on Strood side.

Medway Bridge Marina ☎ 01634 843576/826134
Tides
HW Dover +0130
Tidal access
23hrs
Ⓥ (160 pontoons, 4 visitors'), WC, 🖼, ⚓, ⚡, ↘, Provisions, ⊙, ⬤D, ⬤P, Engineer, Repairs

Port Medway Marina ☎ 01634 720033
Radio
VHF Ch 80

Tidal access
24hrs (sometimes low on springs)
Tides
HW Dover −0133
Ⓥ (90+, visitors' by arrangement), WC, ⚓, ⚡, ↘, Provisions, ⊙, Engineer, Repairs

Otterham Creek Boatyard ☎ 01634 23179
Tides/Access
As Mariners Farm Boatyard.
Ⓥ (drying), WC, ⚓, ⚡, ⬤D, Engineer, Boat Repairs (Specialises in insurance work)

HALLING
Elmhaven Marina ☎ 01634 240489
Tidal access
HW ±4½hrs
Ⓥ (30, 2/3 visitors'), WC, 🖼, ⚓, ⚡, Provisions (nearby), Engineer, Repairs

Medway Cruising Club ☎ 01795 842410
Tides
Dover −0125
Tidal access
24 hrs
Ⓥ (visitors' by arrangement), WC, 🖼, ⚓

Allington Lock (Environment Agency)
☎ 01622 752864
Tides
Dover −0130
Tidal access
HW +3hrs to HW −2hrs
Ⓥ (3 visitors'), WC (nearby), ⚓, ↘ (nearby), Provisions (nearby), ⊙ (nearby), ⬤D (nearby), ⬤P (nearby), Engineer (nearby), Repairs (nearby)

ROCHESTER
Beacon Boatyard ☎ 01634 841320
Tidal access
HW ±3hrs
Ⓥ (pontoon/mud, 2 visitors'), WC, ⚓, ⚡, ↘, ⬤D, Engineer, Repairs

Hundred of Hoo Sailing Club ☎ 01634 250102
Tides
HW Dover +0144
Tidal access HW ±5½hrs
Ⓥ (50 mud, 1 visitors'), WC, 🖼, ⚓, ⚡, ↘, ⬤D

Medway Yacht Club ☎ 01634 718399
Tidal access
24hrs
Ⓥ (250, visitors' varies), WC, 🖼, ⚓, ☎, Provisions (nearby), ⊙ (nearby), Engineer (nearby), Repairs (nearby)

Whitton Marine ☎ 01634 250593
Tidal access
HW ±2hrs
Ⓥ (80 mud, visitors' by arrangement), WC, 🖼, ⚓, ⚡, Provisions (nearby), ⊙, ⬤D, Engineer, Repairs

Lower Halstown Yacht Club
Tidal access
HW ±1½hrs
Ⓥ (swinging, 4 visitors'), WC, ⚓, ⚡, Provisions (nearby), ⊙ (nearby)

moorings. The Dutch sailors who nowadays visit the river to enjoy all this are more welcome than they were when they came as invading 'tourists' in 1667.

From Havengore it is a straight southerly course across the Maplins to the Medway. From the Crouch and further up, the passage runs through all the Swins down to the Warp before gaining the river. From the Thames, after passing Blyth Sands and Yantlet Flats to the south, Mid Swatch is left starboard and a course set for Nore Swatch. Then it is straight on to No. 11, leaving Grain Edge to starboard. The flood tide here will urge you on to Grain Spit and its encumbrances. It should therefore be given good clearance, since it is easy to go aground here.

From the North East Estuary, it is a long haul from Black Deep, through Knock John and Oaze Deep, before the Medway is reached. From the North Foreland, the deep-water route takes you northwards towards the Tongue Sand Towers and then through Princes Channel past Shivering and Red Sand Towers to the Medway red and white pillar safe water mark. Close in to the Kent coast is the famous 'overland route' via the Kentish Flats and past the old Wansum outlet near Reculvers. Then you go through the Gore Channel and the Hook Spit/East Last gate, past Whitstable Street until you identify the Spaniard. It is almost due west for the Spile through the Four Fathoms Channel off the Isle of Sheppey. Finally you cross the Cant. There is not a lot of water here and it is wise to keep an eye on the depth sounder as well as a good lookout for the not-so-easy-to-spot beacons. While it is a relatively straightforward piece of pilotage, it can, at tricky states of the tide, make demands if you draw much more than a metre. An alternative, after the Spaniard, is to head north for Shivering Sand Towers, into Oaze Deep and then west for the Medway.

Once in the big ship channel, it is best to stay just outside, tending southerly of the paired buoys. There is ample depth. By following this route you avoid the wreck of the *Richard Montgomery*, the US Liberty Ship that went down in the 1939–45 war, fully loaded with ammunition. She sits, to everyone's discomfort, a little north of the channel near Sheerness Middle Sand between buoys No. 7 and No. 9. She is well marked by the buoys which designate the prohibited zone. Her topsides and searching uprights rise awesomely out of the water.

The Medway Ports Authority begins westward of a line from Shell Ness to Seasalter Sailing Club close by Whitstable. Garrison Point, mentioned earlier as the real point of entry, is unmistakable with its radar station tower and old Admiralty signal station behind. The other landmark is the equally unmistakable 244m-high Grain Power Station chimney on the western shore. It is unwise to pass too close to Garrison Point, as there can be a powerful tidal rip just off its steep-to shore. In addition, ferries berth just inside the Point, often with tugs in attendance, demanding additional vigilance.

The river and its approaches all carry navigation buoys in conformity with IALA System 'A', and the navigable channel all the way to Upnor is clearly marked and easy to follow. This is just as well since the middle reaches of the river are bounded by extensive mud flats and saltings. These offer many secondary channels to the Hoo and Rainham areas, but they all cover at high water. The channels should be approached with caution. Before a deep penetration, perhaps the best course is to use one of the better-known and more well-established, anchorages and search out the highways, byways and gutways by dinghy before taking the mother craft. Strangers should be particularly beware of straying too far from the main channels on a falling tide. The ebb can run away very fast.

Once past Queenborough Spit, the river broadens out dramatically and here the contrasts begin, with High Rise Grain and Oil to starboard and Flats to port: marshes, saltings, creeks and gutways. You are never far away from the old world of the muddies, the wet cow grazers and the salt shepherds, the latter epitomised by the presence of Shepherds Creek just to the south of Deadman's Island at Swale Ness. Deadman's takes its name from the remains of the many prisoners from the Napoleonic Wars who died, victims of the plague. However, no refuge exists there and deeper water must be looked for further westwards.

. . . while others, more squat, are reminders of when other institutions dominated the river.

Stangate Creek

This, the first creek to port, is marked by Stangate Spit cardinal, and the run up to it follows the large dolphins, 8 10 and 11. The entrance is wide and deep and the main channel gives access to the smaller creeks. The first is the 'Medway' Sharfleet – not to be confused with its little 'Swale' sister. It is on the starboard hand after the green buoy that marks an old wreck. At first it carries deep water but, after a huge 'S' bend, it begins to peter out behind Burntwick Island and above Slayhills Marsh, into the drying gutways of Ham and Captains Creeks. The area between Nos. 7 and 8 BW beacons is a favourite one for quiet anchoring. Since the ebb can rip fast here, substantial ground tackle is essential.

Continuing south in the deep water of Stangate leads to a fork off Slaughterhouse Point; to port is the Shade which gives onto Funton and Bedlam's Bottom. It is a desolate area with wrecks and hulks all round. A more hospitable welcome is to be found after taking the starboard turn. Leaving the large dolphin to port, straight ahead can be seen Seagull Island, marked by a small red pole. Just to the north is a small watering hole used as a staging post by the Lower Halstow Yacht Club, whose HQ is at the very head of Halstow Creek. Since there is water for little more than 90 minutes a tide, it is important for Yacht Club members to be able to reach a decent 'staging post'.

For those with gutway feelings for a drying (nearly dying) creek, it is possible to get across to Half Acre Creek via Medway and Kingsferry Saltings and across Ham Ooze; but most skippers will want to return to the Stangate junction and make for Sharp Ness and No. 14 Red. The river bends to the SW and if you continue in that direction you will leave the main channel for Half Acre and the RW Fairway that marks the tri-parting of the ways for Otterham, Bartlett and Rainham, and South Yantlet Creeks. This last offers a drying channel to the main river just south of Darnett Ness marked by four RW buoys.

Otterham Creek

There has been a boatyard at Otterham Creek for many years, but it was derelict for decades. Now the wharf has been rebuilt, the buildings repaired and the creek dredged to give access 2 hours either side of high water. Moorings and storage facilities are available most of the time, and there is water, electricity and diesel at the yard. As well as making a feature of wooden boat building and restoration, the Otterham Creek Boatyard undertakes osmosis repairs and specialises in wood epoxy treatment.

Otterham Creek is well buoyed to port and starboard up to Woodgers Wharf, after which craft should stay the same distance from the bank as the last port-hand buoy before rounding into the dock.

Visiting yachts should telephone beforehand if possible, Rod Bryant will be pleased to hear from you.

Rainham Creek and Saltings

It is difficult to get deeper into saltings and gutways than those that are found in the Rainham area. You must, of course, be prepared to take the ground since there is water for only very limited periods, but, as in all these creeks, the mud is soft and, to many, inviting. There is a warm welcome to be found unexpectedly tucked away on this quiet backwater, at a facility known as Mariners Farm Boatyard.

Mariners Farm offers tidal moorings for craft up to 12m and storage facilities ashore for craft of any size. Many owners choose to do their own fitting-out in the informal atmosphere. There are haul-out facilities for all types of craft, including deep-keeled yachts and catamarans, with a travel-hoist and the boatyard's slipway. Cranage is up to 7 tons. Water and power are available in the yard, where there are full toilet amenities. A restaurant and a pub serving meals is within walking distance.

Access to the tidal moorings is 2 hours either side of high water, and there is a choice of ways in. From the west: from Gillingham Reach No. 26 buoy, enter Bartlett Creek between the Red Can and the B/W beacon on the SW tip of Nor Marsh. The Mariners buoy (red can) will be visible ¼ mile to the SE. Leave this close to port and follow the channel markers ¼ mile SW to the yacht moorings and slipway. From the east: go from No. 16 buoy, via Half Acre Creek into Bartlett Creek. From the red can buoy at the upper end of Bartlett and lower end of Rainham, the Mariners buoy (red can) will be visible (¼ mile WSW) Leave this to port and follow the port and starboard (oil-can topped) withies ¼ mile SW to the yacht moorings and slipway. When close, the two trots of moorings clearly show the fairway channel.

For the north side of the river we return to a position just after Stangate Spit where, on the north bank, the first item of interest to yachtsmen is Colemouth Creek where there are some yacht moorings with ancient rights. Just round Elphinstone Point there is a deep pool with water access at almost all states of tide. It would be a magnificent spot for a fully afloat marina, except that there is no road access.

That does not apply to Stoke, where Rivermaye has moorings right at the head of the creek. The entrance across Stoke Ooze and past Stoke Ness is marked by a small green buoy just past Green Stoke No. 13. Among the saltings, there are 150 berths (max. LOA 10m) some 50 of which are alongside. They are all mud berths with access better than 2h +/- HW. There is fresh water but no electricity here; a large launching slip that is much in demand; a floating dry dock; and massive hard standing. The

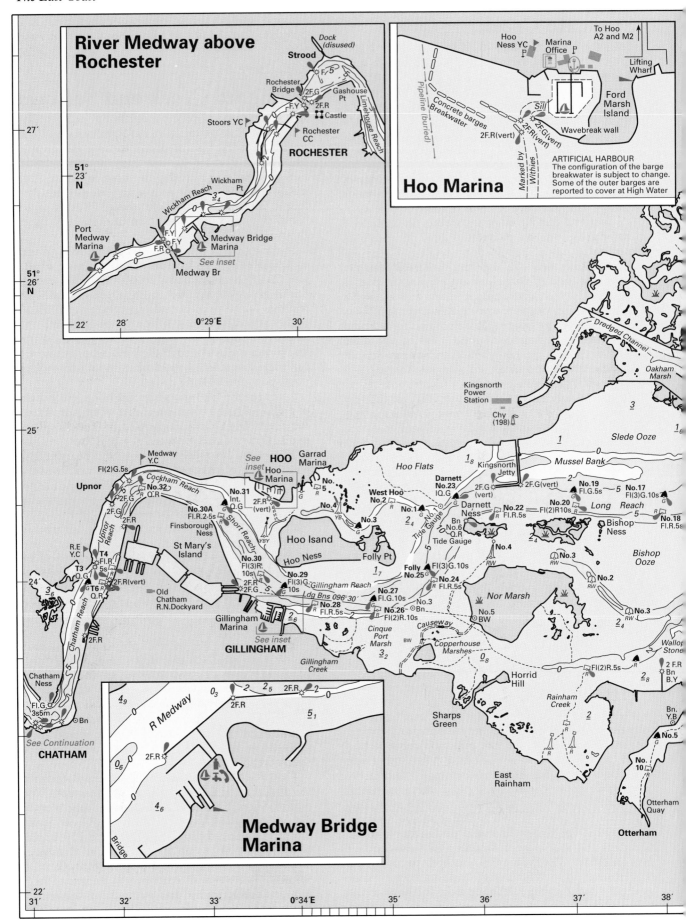

River Medway above Rochester

Dock (disused)
Strood
F.5
Rochester Bridge
2F.G
2F.R
Gashouse Pt
F.Y
Castle
Limehouse Reach
Stoors YC
Rochester CC
ROCHESTER

51° 23′ N

Wickham Reach
Wickham Pt
3 4

Port Medway Marina

F.Y F.Y
F.R
Medway Bridge Marina
See inset
Medway Br

51° 26′ N

22′   28′   0°29′E   30′

Hoo Marina

To Hoo A2 and M2
Hoo Ness YC
Marina Office
Lifting Wharf
Pipeline (buried)
Concrete barges Breakwater
Sill
Ford Marsh Island
2F.G(vert)
2F.R(vert)
2F.R.R(vert)
Wavebreak wall
Marked by Withies

ARTIFICIAL HARBOUR
The configuration of the barge breakwater is subject to change. Some of the outer barges are reported to cover at High Water

Kingsnorth Power Station
Chy (198)
Dredged Channel
Oakham Marsh
3
Slede Ooze
1 6
1
0
Mussel Bank

Medway Y.C
Fl(2)G.5s
Cockham Reach
No.32
Q.R
Upnor
2F.G
2F.R
R.E Y.C
T4
Fl.R.5s
T3
Q.G
T6
Q.R
2F.R(vert)
Chatham Reach
G
2F.R
Chatham Ness
Fl.G 3s5m
Bn
See Continuation
CHATHAM

Uphor Reach

See inset HOO
Hoo Marina
No.31 Int.Q.G
2F.R(vert)
No.30A Fl.R.2.5s
Finsborough Ness
St Mary's Island
No.30 Fl(3)R.10s
2F.R
2F.G
Old Chatham R.N.Dockyard
No.29 Fl(3)G.10s
Gillingham Reach
Ldg Bns 096°30′
No.28 Fl.R.5s
Gillingham Marina
See inset
GILLINGHAM
Gillingham Creek

Garrad Marina
No.5
No.4
No.3
YB
Hoo Isand
Hoo Ness
Folly Pt
1 7
No.27 Fl.G.10s
No.26 Fl(2)R.10s
Bn
No.3
Cinque Port Marsh
3 2

West Hoo
No.2
No.1
2 4
Bn No.6 Q.R
Tide Gauge
Folly No.25 Fl.R.5s
Folly Fl(3)G.10s
No.24 Fl.R.5s
No.5 BW
Causeway
BW
Copperhouse Marshes
0 8

Hoo Flats
1 8
Kingsnorth Jetty
Darnett No.23 IQ.G
2F.G(vert)
Darnett Ness
Tide Gauge
No.4
Nor Marsh
Horrid Hill
Sharps Green
East Rainham

2F.G(vert)
No.22 Fl(2)R10s
2
No.20 Fl(2)R10s
No.19 Fl.G.5s
5
No.17 Fl(3)G.10s
Long Reach
5
No.18 Fl.R.5s
Bishop Ness
No.3 RW
Bishop Ooze
No.2 RW
No.3 RW
2 4
Fl(2)R.5s
2 8
Wallop Stone
2F.R Bn B.Y
Rainham Creek
2
Bn. Y.B
No.5
No.10
Otterham Quay
Otterham

Medway Bridge Marina

R Medway
0 3
4 9
2
2 5
2F.R
2
2F.R
5 1
2F.R
0 6
0
4 6
Bridge

Gillingham Marina

R Medway

Depths in Metres

W Basin

Moorings
2F.R(vert)

2F.R (vert)

Lock
E Basin

2F.R(vert)
2F.R(vert)

Commodore's Hard

Segas S.C

Grain Edge

Grain Spit

W Cant
Q.R

V.Q

Grain Hard
Fl.G.5s
Garrison Pt

2FR(Vert)
Horn(3)30s

Garrison Pt
(Rd Lt)

SHEERNESS

Fl(2)G.10s
Bn

Sheerness Harbour

North Kent
Q.G

South Kent
Fl.R.5s

Queenborough Spit
Q(3)10s

Pontoon

Isle of Sheppey

Stoke Ooze

Colemouth Spit

Stoke Ness

Bee Ness

Stoke No.13
Fl.G.5s

No.12
Q.R

Z1
Fl(2)10s

Z2
Q.

Saltpan Reach

Swale Ness

Queenborough Pt

W Bulwark

E Bulwark
Fl(3)G.15s

Dn
2F.G

Stoke No.14
Fl.R.5s

Stangate Spit
VQ(3)5s

Burntwick I

Dn
Fl.R.4s

Q.R
Dn

QUEENBOROUGH

2F.R(vert)

Fl.G.3s
Fl.R.3s

No.1
Q.WG

No.2
Q.WG

No.4
Iso.R.3s
10m3M

S3
Fl.G.

S2
Q.G.

Stangate Creek

Sharfleet Creek

Bn
BW

No.16
Bishop
Fl(2)R.10s

Bishop Spit

Medway Saltings

No.3
Q.WG

S4
Q.R.

2F.R

2F.R

Bn
Q.16m5M

Rushenden Marshes

Ham Ooze

Kingsferry Saltings

S5
Fl.G.5s

Half Acre Creek

Fairway
Mo(A)10s

Barge

Ham Green Saltings

Millfordhope Creek

Slaughterhouse Pt

Chetney Hill

River Swale

Long Reach

S6
Fl.R.5s

No.2

No.4

No.3

No.6

No.8
Bn.Y.B

Millfordhope Marsh

Millfordhope Saltings

Twinney Creek

Halstow Creek

Barksore Marshes

Funton Reach

Bedlam's Bottom

S7
Q.R

DirVQ(4)R.5s5M

Fl(2)R.10s

QG.7m

Fl.G.3s10m

Ferry Reach

Kingsferry Bridge

2F.G(vert)9m7M

2F(vert)11m10M

Twinney Saltings

Funton Creek

N

Lower Halstowe
Chy

Brickworks

RIVER MEDWAY

Gillingham Marina's locked basin is seen at top centre; with the tidal section just under; and under that, the facilities of Medway Pier Marine – an often overlooked port of call.

yard is run in the most informal of manners by the manager Peter Tyler.

Shortly after Stoke, comes diminutive Humble Bee Creek and massive Bee Ness jetty while, out in the river, there is a foul area marked by the red and green Bulwarks, just to starboard of the main channel. Tucked away between Bee Ness and Oakham Jetty is East Hoo Creek, leading to Slede and at the head to Damhead Creek and the wharf by the oil refinery. While you can stay afloat, it is a bleak and inhospitable spot, with some areas foul and encumbered. After Slede Ooze, come the Kingsforth works which mark the end of Long Reach and the beginning of Pinup Reach, with Hoo Flats and its tide gauge to starboard and Darnett Ness Fort to port.

The looming dark-grey mass of Darnett Fort brings decision time – left and southerly down the main river, or straight ahead and westerly across Hoo Flats? Following the main channel, it is not long before trot after trot of leisure craft seem completely to cover the surface of the river. This near-saturation mooring, much of it fore-and-aft, continues more or less non-stop up to Rochester

Bridge and, since most folk take this route, we will do the same.

Leaving Darnett Ness to port, the fort on Hoo Island at Folly Point is soon abeam to starboard, with Cinque Port and Gillingham Marshes to port. Here are to be found the Medway Cruising Club, the Strand and the SEGAS Sailing Club. Most first-time visitors on this, the Gillingham Reach, will be on their way to one of the two main marinas on the river – Gillingham or Hoo.

To Gillingham first, where the marina comes in two versions: the locked basin and the tidal berths. They are, of course, linked but not directly connected by water. The locked entrance to the inner basin of Gillingham Marina is directly off the main river on the south bank of Gillingham Reach. It is conspicuously indicated by huge gas holders, but they in no way compete with its dramatically impressive office and clubhouse block, built in an unmistakable Bauhaus-*manqué* style. In keeping with its undoubted upmarket image, the establishment also operates a private helicopter landing-pad. The marina facilities include floating pontoon moorings, mud berths and a locked basin. Diesel is available at the river-front entrance at tide-access times (generally +/-3 hours HW). Visitors are welcome and asked to book at least 24 hours in advance.

In the locked basin, boats are afloat at all states of the tide with access up to 4·5h +/−HW. Boats up to

The encircling arms enclose Hoo Marina cilled basin. Whitton and Stargate boatyards can be seen immediately above; while at the very top is the far-reaching jetty of Kingsnorth power station.

23m LOA can be accommodated. Water and electricity are available at all berths. The tidal basin, with its soft mud berths, has all the facilities of the locked basin, but with only 2h +/−HW access at springs. Deep-water moorings are available for arrival and departure at low water. Boats up to 13m length and 4m beam can be lifted out by the 20-ton lift which is fitted with a mast crane.

On arrival, skippers should make initial contact through VHF Ch 80 to the lock-keeper, or to the boatman who may be in attendance at tide times. You are asked to specify whether you are calling the lock or the marina. Security staff are on duty at all times and there are all the facilities a visitor could want for shopping, boating, eating, drinking or generally socialising at large. There is no ambiguity at Gillingham Marina; from the moment you arrive, you will know who and what to expect. Once having perceived this, no visitor ever goes away disappointed.

Medway Pier Marine is the mooring facility immediately next Gillingham Marina. It is one that is often, quite undeservedly, overlooked by speedy travellers. While it shares with the marina the approach to its tidal basin, it is in fact a very different kind of operation. It may be small, but it is no small-fry experience, being quite noteworthy for its laid-back atmosphere and informal service. The characterful location is run in an unique and singular style by Dave Harris. This remarkable patch, on the eastern arm of Gillingham Pier, was originally the site of the Royal Naval Diving School. During the war, the berth flourished, being on active service. It went into decline later, and the original landing stage and connecting bridge were removed. After this, it was only predictable that the slips would fall into complete disrepair.

Medway Pier Marine not only rebuilt the old timber slipways and the river wall, but also reconstructed a new landing stage and bridge. An additional landing stage was completed in 1988. There are berths for some 50 craft around the landing stages, where they enjoy a 'tidal window' of some 8 hours on the outer stage. On spring tides, the landing stages ground onto soft mud. There is electricity and water, with toilets and car parking ashore. Slipping and workshop facilities, together with an inspection cradle go to complete the work area, where the unceremonious atmosphere is blended with a great deal of happy DIY.

Down the road apiece again is DC Marine. This establishment provides a facility that is of great importance for skippers of motor vessels, especially those with less than capacious fuel tanks, as it is one of the main sources of diesel on the river. DC Marine also operates mud berths and moorings. It has some 50 deep-water moorings and about a dozen drying pontoons (most of which have been snapped up and are now permanently taken). Somewhat unusually, it is beam that is the restricting factor here, not LOA – 3m beam is the maximum. It is a source of sad complaint and some reproach against persons known and unknown to

DC Marine that, up to 1984, there was as much as 2·5m at LW springs; now there is 1m of mud; all of which has been caused by changes in the flow of water in the river due to a decade of developments, which are many and various in the area.

The first thing to note, back once more on the Hoo trail, is that the marina at Hoo is different from Gillingham Marina and Medway Marine in many ways. Mainly, however, it differs insofar as it cannot easily be spotted from the main river, so no one ever finds himself at the sill that sits guardian at the entrance to the marina by chance. It is only to be discerned by those who follow, not the yellow brick road, but one of the two approach channels, neither of which is without its twists and turns, but both of which are susceptible to basic pilotage skills; and, as in all the creeks, the bottom of the channel, much of which dries at LWS, is almost universally soft mud and only occasionally foul at the edges.

For the first route, we return to Folly Point and Darnett Ness, where there is the B/W No. 1 beacon with its tide gauge, just below Green Darnett No. 23 and just above the Green No. 1 that marks the entrance to Middle Creek (the channel to use to cross Hoo Flats). The channel goes to the north of west for 400m to Red No. 2; then to the south of west for 500m to Green No. 3 (just before which there is a 6m-deep pool); it is then 300m northwest to West Hoo No. 4 cardinal, warning all visitors to keep south. It is here that there is yet another parting of the ways. Through a few small craft moorings, 550m to the west, are the port and starboard beacons that mark the channel gate by the old causeway off Ford Marsh Island. They are not always on station, but it is unusual for both to be absent. Once through, it is easy to pick out the white-topped port withies that mark the main channel entrance to Hoo Marina. So, having detoured for a while, we turn back to the other channel, back to West Hoo No. 4. Red West Hoo No. 5 is 400m to the northeast from the cardinal at the head of West Hoo Creek. It is the last marker buoy before Hundred of Hoo Sailing Club, Stargate Marine and Whitton Marine.

The real alternative is, of course, the main approach channel, for which you leave Chatham Docks to port and Hoo Ness to starboard and after Red No. 30, move northwest as does the river itself, into Short Reach. Very soon after, there will appear, just to the northeast, three blue deep-water mooring buoys and, to the northeast of them, four orange Hoo Marina holding buoys. Once these have been identified and approached, it is easy to pick out the marina approach channel which is extremely well marked by white-topped port-hand withies (each bearing an unlit reflector).

Improvements and refurbishment (not to mention tak-over by Maritime and the group that has done such sterling work at Maylandsea) have made Hoo Marina a smart new-looking facility. As well as the long-existing and time-honoured mud berths, there are now pontoon berths that stay afloat at all states of the tides, in depths controlled by the sill. There is deep-water access for 4½h +/−HW. Visitors are welcome and can contact the harbourmaster on VHF Chs 37 and 80. Electricity and water are

Parking spaces like this abound at low water on the Medway and its approaches.

available to all berths and there is a comprehensive range of facilities nearby, including an A100 charismatic caff-style café; the always friendly Hoo Ness Yacht Club; MAGS is one of the best-stocked chandlers for many a mile. In addition, it is no more than a short and rewarding walk to the well-kitted-out village; while, for those not up to such land-bound exercise, there is a regular bus service.

Close by is Whitton Marine. If Hoo Yacht Harbour is to be found in secret waters, then Whitton is in them deeper still. The basic approach is straightforward, along the same channels just described above for Hoo Marina. If you use the approach from Short Reach, you leave the Hoo withies once the red, small craft, mooring buoys and the causeway beacons hove into view, and then head east for about 400m; after which it will be easy to pick up the West Hoo No. 4 cardinal. After the Red West Hoo No. 5, the marina will be in sight almost dead ahead to the north. Whitton Marine has nearly 100 pontoon mud berths for boats up to 11m, with access times of 2h +/−HW. There is a slipway for launching and recovering boats, and work below the waterline can easily be undertaken between tides. A large hardstanding area is available for storage and DIY tasks as well as repair work which can be carried out by the yard. A tug is available for hire, and there are dry docks that will accept vessels up to 37m. There are toilet facilities and a small cafe.

Next in line in these backwaters is Stargate Marine, immediately next the berths of Whitton. It is an amazing establishment of a boatyard that has been working for 12 years, specialising in repairs and refurbishment to barges and other traditional craft, be they steel or wood, river, estuary or full-blooded sea-going vessels. There are two dry docks for craft up to 36m x 7·5m and 30m x 6·7m. The proprietor, Bob Deards, is known as being mad about boats; in other words he is a genuine 'enthusiast' and keenly proud of his pitch pine and oak wood-cutting gear – jealously guarding its reputation. It is a spot where other yachties, boaters and general enthusiasts foregather for a good browse and long crack with anyone who is in the mood. However, Stargate does not offer facilities for 'ordinary' leisure craft.

Back on the main river, we approach Cockham, Upnor and Chatham Reaches. These stretches of the river are especially rich, with the strikingly picturesque woods at Cockham coming down to the shore and the old fort of Upnor Castle standing out dramatically. Eyecatching in its own less striking way is the veritably ancient slipway that lurks close by. The well-known Ship and Pier pubs both present their attractions to the passing eye as they stand each side of the white, weather-boarded chandlers, the Cabin Yacht Stores. It too has its own landmark in the large tree just across the way. On the other side of the river, on the south bank, are the lock gates of the dockyard basin. The berths inside accompany the new estate homes and offices; and it now, sadly, seems unlikely that the much-vaunted/promoted marina will actually come to be.

Rochester Bridge, the watershed of the Medway where fine calculations are required to balance air draught, water draught, High Water and Low Water.

The most notable establishment on the east bank is undoubtedly Chatham's famous dockyard. From the 16th century to no more than a decade ago, it was one of our most important naval bases. Its history of boat-building and refitting spans the contrasting eras of HMS *Victory* and nuclear-powered submarines.

Along this stretch, there is a riverbus service with calling points at Sun Pier, Rochester Pier, Laser Quay and Strood Pier. Skippers with leisure craft who have in mind to use any of these piers for embarking or disembarking passengers must keep watch for the approach of the riverbus, and are permitted to stay only briefly. In particular, the boat must be attended by a competent person at all times. It is worth noting that adequate depth (2·0m) can be a problem near LW.

Sun Pier has recently been refurbished, and now stands out only slightly less than its more commercial neighbour Texas Homecare, giving an indication of the proximity of city life. Situated between Sun and Ship Piers, Ocean Care Services is an important chandlery and service station. Its recently moved pontoon may be used for visiting its chandlery or taking on diesel. The shoresides chandlers is glisteningly attractive, and the new position of the pontoons now provides access at virtually all states of the tide.

Further upstream, the inimitable Lloyds holds court, with the classic gun on its eponymous wharf. Many of the moorings in this reach are private yacht berths, in general belonging to the RNSA and the RE. Applications for use of these buoys, other than for an overnight rest when vacant, should be addressed to the River Inspector, Port of Sheerness.

Limehouse Reach, Bridge Reach and the Port of Rochester are the busiest commercial stretches on the river, with many wharves for large sea-going ships. There is also a dense collection of barge moorings. The 60 mud berths for leisure craft hereabouts belong to Letley Moorings of Sufferance Wharf. The boatyard with its dry dock and slip also has 26 alongside moorings for residents. There is never a vacancy, and no chance of a visitors' berth. Derek Wickham, the proprietor, is not easy to contact on the phone; but if you do manage to track him down, you might find yourself in serious competition with his parrots. However, as he says, 'We've been here so long doing the same thing that everybody knows us – where we are and what we do so that isn't a problem.'

Cruising upstream, the last haven before Rochester Bridge is Lemon's Boatyard, quite close to the bridge, just downstream of Strood Pier. It has mud pontoons and maintenance facilities. Tidal access is limited because the location of the yard is well above average middle-tide heights. However, this limiting factor is properly reflected in the charges.

Baker Marine in Rochester High Street is one of the oldest chandlers in the Medway towns, dating

back to 1947. It also sells dinghies, Johnson Outboards, International Paints, and is a Bombard Inflatable stockist. As well as this, it has an engineering workshop for outboards and a water-ski department.

The spit on the bend at the end of Limehouse Reach is known as Gashouse Point. Close inspection of the damaged red beacons on the spit is not required to convince skippers of the need for caution; especially since big ships may be manoeuvring and swinging here. In days gone by, this part of the river was a busy centre for oysters and shrimps, but it now deals almost exclusively with commercial, including many foreign, cargoes. Once round the bend, Rochester Bridge, with its famous restrictions of heights and depths, comes dramatically into view.

From Garrison Point to Bridge Reach, the River Medway affords many contrasts, some entirely pleasurable and some potentially hazardous; but there is one special place where the combination of air and water draught, bridge heights, depth of water and tide race demands special consideration. That place is Rochester Bridge, where, at critical tide times, there is no room for error and little for manoeuvre.

Tidal streams in the River Medway range from around 1·5 knots at neaps to around 2·5 knots at

Looking upstream from Rochester bridge: at left, the church, castle and HQ of the Rochester Cruising Club; at right, the Strood Yacht Club and, close by, yards and moorings various; and towards centre top, Medway Bridge and the eponymous Marina . . .

. . . here viewed more closely.

springs, with the velocity varying greatly from reach to reach. The two fastest patches are to be found off Garrison Point and through Rochester Bridge, where there is a clearance of 5·96m at the centre of the middle arch at MHWS and a clearance of 11·9m at low water (chart datum). While this permits passage to all but higher-masted vessels, at low water there can be as little as 0·9m in places. Since the riverbed is encumbered with parts of the old bridge, grounding could be a hard experience. It is recommended that passage under Rochester Bridge should not be attempted by vessels drawing more than 0·6m at MLWS.

Above Rochester Bridge the depth improves briefly in certain places towards the south bank as far as Rochester Pier. After that, it shoals considerably, with an average depth of 0·9–1·2m at low water. Although craft up to 1·5m draught can, in the hands of a 'local expert', find their way to the mudbank-knuckle at the M2 bridge, the channel is constantly changing, and should not be attempted without up-to-date advice or knowledge. Such local knowledge is not, however, without its contradictory aspects: there are those who maintain that craft with 1·5m draught can reach Snodland (5 miles upstream) at low water springs, and those who say Rochester Bridge is the limit. The general consensus of cautious opinion dictates that the safe rule for navigating upriver with such draught is 3 hours either side of high water.

All the clubs and marinas above Rochester are within three miles of the bridge. After them, the next realistic calling/resting point is not reached until Allington Lock, nearly 10 miles distant. Getting to the clubs and marinas on this tidal stretch requires no special planning; but the trip to Allington demands a more rigorous schedule. There must be not only enough depth of water in the river, but also enough headroom under the bridges, the limiting bridge being the old Aylesford Stone Bridge which allows 2·9m at MHWS. It is also necessary to arrive when the lock is open. Each skipper will work out his own mathematical salvation, but a good basic rule is to leave the Rochester/M2 bridge section 3 hours before HW and slowly creep up with the tide. There is no point in an unnecessary rendezvous with the bottom, and a slow speed permits a proper lookout for the debris that frequently haunts the upper reaches of the river – especially after big springs. Some of this detritus can be lethal, for it ranges from lengths of industrial plastic to sodden sleepers floating on, or (worse) lurking just below, the surface. The channel follows a predictable course: tending to the centre on the straits and the outside at bends. There are red and green beacons marking many of the small headlands. It is worth remembering that, in some places, there is never a lot of water beneath you, even at HW.

But first, back to Rochester. Immediately after the bridge, there is much to catch the eye, as commerce, industry and urban chaos are left behind for the green shoots of country life as rustic/rural/riparian aspects begin to burgeon. On the port hand, there are outstanding features. Rochester Castle and Cathedral stand on the heights, surveying the river pontoons and shoresides clubhouse of the refined station of the Rochester Cruising Club, home to many motor cruisers. One of the largest clubs on the river, it is busy throughout the year, with an office staffed Tuesdays and Thursdays 0900 to 1400. Visitors are welcome, provided they telephone well in advance.

The Rochester Cruising Club organises the annual Admiral of the River Medway Cruise during which the Admiral and his Water Bailiff cruise those parts of the river that lie within his jurisdiction; that is, from Hawkwood Stone to Garrison Point. In spite of being an extremely colourful, relaxed and enjoyable cruise-event, dignity and formality are not without their place, as exemplified by the firing of cannons, the dipping of ensigns, and the bugler sounding the 'alert' and 'carry on'. With water cannon shooting up and light aircraft flying past, this processional cruise is, for many river-folk, the highlight of the River Medway's year, attracting as it does around 50 'official' boats and at least a further 50 more accompanying craft in attendance. This annual event takes place over a weekend towards the end of July, at a date suited to tide times and dignitaries alike.

On the other side of the river are the new and well maintained pontoons of Strood Yacht Club, a splendid improvement and development upon the previous distribution of moorings. The club, which is devoted equally happily to motor vessels as well as sail, extends a welcome to visitors (who are asked to phone in advance). The club owns its own patch, its large clubhouse and its own maintenance facilities. There is only one water-bugman in the otherwise calm surface of the ointment – members are not pleased when they are reminded that they are sandwiched between masses (or, as some would have it, messes) of barges-cum-boats-cum-houses. Immediately downstream is Temple Boatyard and upstream there is Castleview.

The M2 bridge commands the river for miles, with the well-known eponymous marina (Medway Bridge Marina) virtually at its feet. One of the marina's most beneficial services to the motor-boat fraternity is fuel, both petrol and diesel, available from its waterside pontoon pumps (a facility unique on the river). The marina is home to a vast variety of craft, from the smallest of dayboats to the largest of barges. The majority are medium-range cruisers in the modern idiom. The office is well staffed and you will get a welcome whether you call in face to face, phone up or call in on VHF. Chandlery, maintenance and engineering facilities are all available on site, although their presence and capabilities do change from time to time. There is a large slip and 16-ton cradle hoist. Domestics and socialising are well catered for. The Inner Dowsing Lightship Restaurant has been established for some time now. More orientated towards cruising, the

Medway Motor Yacht Club (now incorporating the Medway Bridge Cruising School) is deemed to be the most active motor-cruising club on the Medway. It is also an approved RYA Training Establishment. The clubhouse is situated at the top of the marina near the chandlery and opens on Friday evenings from 2030. Visitors are made welcome.

Up the (steep!) Borstal Hill is a useful collection of shops. There is also a pleasant riverside walk/bike leading directly to the shopping heart of Rochester, which is blessed with pedestrian precinct and a first-rate market.

A recent change is that *Volvo-Penta* agent, John Hawkins Marine, has moved downriver from Elmhaven to Medway Bridge Marina. John has also taken over the Ship's Store Chandlery ☎ 01634 840812. After a succession of mediocre organisations, it will be a relief to see it flourish.

The engineering operation of GMS Medway is based in the marina where it is a *Sabre*, *Mermaid*, *Perkins* and *Yamaha* agent. Les Goodall is the sole proprietor: a Yorkshire boatman through and through with extraordinarily winning ways with engines, no matter how old or recalcitrant. You can rely on him to respond to your call with as much alacrity as is possible when you have a long queue a'waiting; and if it is a bona fide SOS, you should not be in trouble for long. Les is not given to unnecessary flummery: his word may be short to the point of pithiness, but it is his bond. He, and his efficient wife/secretary, Liz, can be contacted on ☎ 01634 844114 and 0860 31115.

Also on the same patch, comes Beacon Boatyard. It is situated in a creek in Wickham's Reach, just downstream of the marina. Access is gained by following the inside of Medway Bridge Marina's pontoons until the creek opens up on the port side. There, at the mouth of the creek, is a visitors' soft-mud pontoon berth with access 2hrs +/–HWST.

I am grateful to a local cruising enthusiast for the following up-to-date comments:

> Anybody passing Medway Bridge Marina now cannot fail to have their visual senses assaulted by the concrete and brick monstrosities that have been built on the river bank immediately facing the marina. The buildings house an 'entertainment centre' offering bingo, nightclub, bars, restaurants and doubtless other noisy attractions. The main centre opened on 9 May 1996, and is to be followed soon by an adjacent building accommodating, according to local rumour, ten-pin bowling, ice-skating and other activities. Fortunately perhaps, the facilities are not presently accessible from the river, although there is talk of a jetty being installed and a ferry run from Medway Bridge – the prospect of old ladies crossing the river to play bingo in the short, sharp wind-against-tide chop in this shallow reach fuels the imagination! Berth-holders at Medway Bridge have tolerated the noise and dust of construction for the last 18 months. Now they will have to tolerate indefinitely the noise of

occupancy – and car headlights beamed across the river every night!

The once-settled atmosphere of this stretch of the river may change even more if, as promised, two additional bridges are built alongside the existing crossing – one for the Channel Rail Link and another to accommodate the widening of the M2 motorway from two to three lanes. The crossings may appear more like a giant tunnel when viewed from the river!

Further up the river on the left bank is Port Medway Marina. This project is now well-established and flourishing just upriver of the Medway Bridge, on the north bank site of the old Auto Marine yard, where there has been a wharf since the 17th century. Work started in 1990 on over 700m of fully serviced floating pontoons, 600m of quayside moorings, and three slipways. There is a 16-ton hoist; vast hard-standing; and, a quite unusual feature this, a visiting chandler. It is all run by Dave Taylor as a family business – self-motivating, self-servicing and well-nigh self-sufficient. Close by are the village shops and, closer still, the village pub, the White Hart. Dave is an 'enthusiast'; while he has, as one would expect, an interest in boats and boating, his real passion and penchant are for marinas. Most youngsters in their early teens tend to dream of train driving, jet flying or alighting on Mars. No such flights of fancy for Dave. He kept his feet firmly on the water and aspired, not to dreaming spires, but to running his own marina. He puts his all into the place in every way. The facilities continue to grow: Dave has a genuine love of old working boats and recently acquired the *Rochester Queen* which he has opened as a marina restaurant and bar. If you fancy whiling away a brief moment romanticising about the beauty of rivers in general and the Medway in particular, Dave Taylor is your man.

Cuxton Marina comes next; close upstream on the same side of the river. It has 50 pontoon berths for craft up to 12m. There is a concrete slip, plenty of hardstanding and a 12-ton hoist. Ian Pearson, a salt of the river with his own classic boat on site, is usually on call. It is as close to all the domestic facilities as its downstream neighbour Port Medway.

Skiing is not normally permitted within the 6-knot speed-limited area but, just upstream of the marina, a stretch of water has been allocated for water-skiing. Predictably enough, it is opposite the site of the Kent Boat & Ski Club. Visitors to the river are often startled when confronted by speedboats towing skiers in all directions. The local practice is to keep to the middle of the river and the ski-boats will happily pass you bankside-to. Skippers who have in mind to be experimental with time and tide should bear in mind that, in this area, it is possible to walk across the river at LWS with little more protection than gumboots.

Elmhaven Marina is the last harbour/haven on the tidal Medway; last, that is, insofar as it is the one furthest from the estuary, and therefore the last reliable and/or sensible stopping place before the lock at Allington. Visitors are made welcome by prior arrangement. Elmhaven has some 300m of pontoon berths for craft from 6–10m, a slip, hardstanding and a crane. It also has one of the prettiest river sites, looking at its best from upstream, where it sits at the foot of one of the best white land-lubbed cliffs this side of Dover.

Working boats still go to Snodland and beyond where Reeds paper is piled high. At one time paper was brought by barge, but the area now has no connection with such romantic notions; the looks of the river are sadly spoiled not only by the pile upon pile of paper (pulped by the hand of nature's weather if by none other) but also by the breakers' nearly broken vehicles and equally declining buildings that attract the eye and detract from the appeal of the opposing bank. There is only one moored barge left on this stretch of the river, and it is in a terminal state.

The intriguingly named Snodland is also host to the Brookland Lake, which was created when gravel deposits below the original marshland were excavated. The site is a registered common and is now available for use by local residents of Snodland and other visitors. It is popular for wind surfing and sailing and the banks, verges and reed beds provide a home for many types of wildlife. Common to this site are the mallard, tufted duck and mute swan which are present for most of the year. The area is also an important site for breeding reed warblers.

Happily, after a mile or so, and in keeping with the Lake project, the river becomes more of a rural thing and vistas open up to show the surrounding scenery as it becomes quite dramatically changed – and for the better. However, accompanying this improvement, stride for stride as it were, is the pollution that is the bane of the upper tidal reaches.

After hints of water-coloured painterly scenery, with rolling English countryside and obligatory church with stone tower and belfry at Wouldham, New Hythe has some striking contemporary architecture to contrast dramatically with the Norman bridge at Aylesford, where the Carmelites first settled in 1242. Aylesford, with its bridge and multitudinous swans, is one of the most strikingly beautiful spots on the Medway. No more than a mile upstream is Allington Lock and the consequent end of the tidal river.

The attractive non-tidal River Medway above the lock at Allington reaches as far upriver as Tonbridge. Readers with a special interest in cruising this area will probably wish to know of *The River Medway*, also published by Imray, and written by the author. It has the advantage of a series of specially drawn maps and chartlets from the lock to the head of navigation.

The Swale

This is going to be a complicated and convoluted chapter because the Swale is a complicated and convoluted river: it has two mouths; three heads of navigation; two tidal streams; and two directions of buoyage. Now read on.

The River Swale, in the Thames Estuary, is the stretch of water that separates the Isle of Sheppey from the mainland; offering a passage between the island and the north coast of Kent from Shell Ness to Queenborough. Although superficially wide in places, the river never offers a broad passage and, between Spitend Point and the Ferry just to the east of Milton Creek, the channel is intricate and narrow. Although a short stretch of waterway (no more than 12 miles or so) the Swale is not at all straightforward, for its ebb and its flood flow simultaneously in two opposing directions. Thus, where most rivers have only one mouth, the Swale has two: the mini-estuary of the West Swale close by Whitstable; and the confluence with the Medway near Queenborough. The stream runs easterly for a lot longer than it runs westerly – a fact worth knowing if you want to conserve fuel, or sail in light airs. Since its tidal streams ebb and flow so contrarily, separating at different places at different times, it can be very confusing on a first visit.

The river is one of the most important areas for birds in southeast England. It has, for some time, been designated a Site of Special Scientific Interest (SSSI) because of its international ornithological significance. It supports large flocks of geese, ducks and waders which have bred in the far north of Europe. These birds depend on finding vast areas of mud and saltings where they can feed and roost completely undisturbed. The summer season sees other rare and vulnerable species nesting on the islands, most of which carry conspicuous notice boards forbidding landing.

The river and its approaches are marked by navigation buoys in conformity with the IALA System 'A'. In the West Swale, the direction of the lateral buoyage is inward from Queenborough Spit to Milton Creek, where it changes. In the East Swale, the direction is inward from Swale Ness to

Milton Creek. The buoys in the West Swale are fully lit. In addition there are directional beacons for the negotiation of Loden Hope and Long Point; and leading lights in Horse and Ferry Reaches for Kingsferry Bridge. The buoyage in the East Swale is blind westward of Faversham Creek.

A cruise from the Kent coast to Maidstone via the River Swale offers a variety of experiences: there is an interesting, if brief, coastal passage (perhaps also going round the outside of the Isle of Sheppey to start with); a busy commercial waterway; two highly contrasting rivers; a multitude of quiet creeks; and a tour of the riparian aspects of 'The Garden of England'. What's more, you can get away from it all yet have all that you want readily to hand, for nowhere along the cruise will you be really far away from some small village (like Conyer), a busily thriving town (like Maidstone) or one of the dozen or so marinas or moorings that lie between Harty Ferry (just inside the Swale) and Allington Lock (just below Maidstone).

You will also encounter a great cross-section of vessels – from the huge commercial tankers and container vessels that bear down in an amazing juggernaut fashion, to the fleets and flocks of sailing dinghies that skirt and flirt with incredible agility as their bows' whim takes them. There are also rotting hulks to contrast with the splendidly maintained Thames barges, some of which are still performing miracles under sail. Also the range predictably runs the gamut from enormously expensive modern motor cruisers to tiny, neatly converted fishing boats of a grand old age but always with a known history.

The area is also a great one to sail but only if you have plenty of time, since the vagaries of the British climate will make it extremely difficult to negotiate the narrow (and often tortuous) channels that make up a substantial part of the cruising grounds. Seldom is the wind of the right strength to get anywhere at all under such conditions; and even when it is, it is probably coming from the worst possible direction and, in any case, will probably die round the next bend because of some vast windbreak in the form of a power station. Although it is quite a delightful area for the use of sail – unless your time is ample – a reliable motor will serve you best in these parts . . . although the sailing buffs of the Swale will take hot issue with me here.

For the eastern entry to the Swale, there are two approaches. First, from the North Foreland, where you can go outside Margate Sands through the Queens Channel, or inside them through the Gore Channel and the Hook Spit gate. Second, from the north from the Red Sand or Shivering Sands Towers down to the Spaniard. In any case, the next marker must be the cardinal Whitstable Street. Unless you are lucky and have good visibility, you may find it difficult to identify either the aforementioned cardinal or the following green Columbine and the green Columbine Spit since they tend to get lost in the confusion of the low-lying coast behind them.

QUEENBOROUGH
51°25'·01N 00°44'·29E

Charts Admiralty 1834, 3683, 2572. Imray Y14, Y18, Y7, C1. OS Landranger 178

Tides
Dover +0130

Authorities
Harbourmaster ☎ 01795 662051

Radio
Medway Radio (VHF Ch 74) for traffic information
Sheppey One (VHF Ch 74) for berths
Call *Queen Base* Ch M, 80, M2 for water taxi in season

The general approach to the Rivers Medway and Swale, with famous Garrison Point at top left centre.

Since both Pollard and Columbine Spits are inhospitable places, and since the 2 or 3 miles in this approach to the Swale can be as boisterous as any waters in the neighbourhood, it is worthwhile taking things slowly until the Ham Gat and Pollard Spit buoys have been confirmed. With these two in sight, the Swale entrance offers no serious problem or hazard; the challenges come when you try to find your way into Conyer Creek for the first time or try to get up to Faversham on the top of a big spring tide when there is little to indicate the presence or absence of channel or saltings.

The waters in the close approach can be quite exceptionally, and unexpectedly, boisterous. It can come as a nasty jolt to strangers to find that, 2 miles inside apparently protected waters, they are being exposed to rougher conditions than 'outside' in the Thames estuary. Care should be taken not to wander out of the main channel, for not only is there a drying creek in Ham Gat but wreckage and oyster beds abound.

Shell Ness stands out clearly and, while this stretch can be tough on the way out, it is seldom difficult on the way in. The first sign of human habitation is to be found there, at the most easterly point of the Isle of Sheppey. Unexpectedly, there are some small houses – robust homes for the stalwart, the sturdy and strong. It is only those who can face the bleakness of exposure to the northeast winds without flinching that would dream of living here.

You next need to make a visual check on Sand End light buoy. Soon after Sand End come the wreck buoy, off Horse Sand opposite Faversham Creek, and the north cardinal marker that denotes the spit at the entrance to the creek.

It is followed by a green buoy by the wreck off Horse Sand and the Faversham Spit north cardinal, after which the river narrows into its classic shallow channels, mud banks and saltings.

However, before we explore these, we come to the anchorage and moorings at Harty Ferry, where the Ferry Inn at the end of the hard on the Isle of Sheppey is as famous for its water as it is for its alcohol. It is a well-established hostelry, going back nearly a thousand years. The hard reaches out far

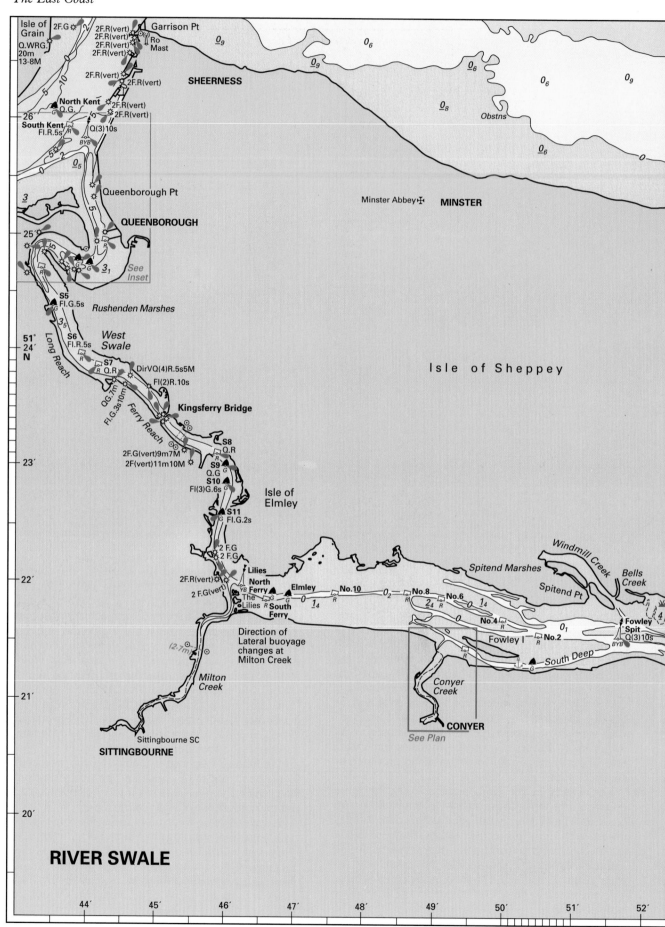

RIVER SWALE

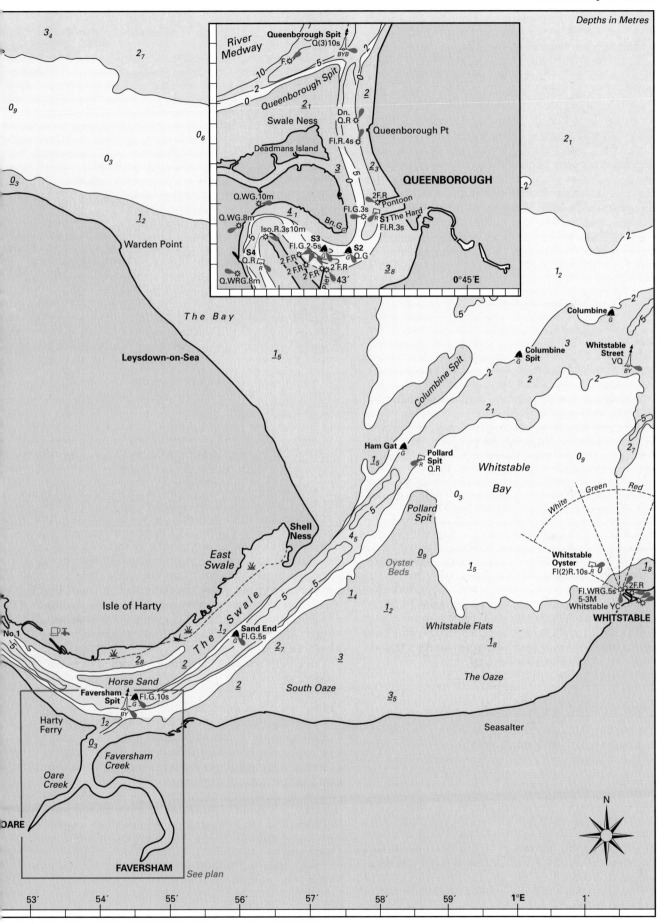

Depths in Metres

3_4

2_7

River Medway

Queenborough Spit
Q(3)10s

BYB

2

0_9

F.☆

10

5

2

0_6

2_1

0_3

Queenborough Spit

Queenborough Spit

2

0

2

2_1

Swale Ness

Dn.
Q.R ☆

Queenborough Pt

0_3

Fl.R.4s ☆

Deadmans Island

3

5

2_3

QUEENBOROUGH

2

1_2

Q.WG.10m ☆

2F.R
Pontoon

Warden Point

Q.WG.8m ☆

4_1

Fl.G.3s ☆
☆ R

S1 The Hard
Fl.R.3s

2

☆ Iso.R.3s10m

Bn.G.

S3
Fl.G.2·5s ☆
G

S2
☆ Q.G

3_8

5

S4
Q.R
☆
R

2 F.R ☆ G
2 F.R ☆ ☆ 2 F.R
Pier

2

Q.WRG.8m ☆

43′

0°45′E

The Bay

1_5

5

Columbine
G

2

Leysdown-on-Sea

1_5

**Columbine
Spit**
G

3

**Whitstable
Street**
VQ
BY

2

2

Columbine Spit

2

2_7

2_1

5

Ham Gat
G

**Pollard
Spit**
Q.R
R

*Whitstable
Bay*

0_9

2_7

1_5

0_3

White Green Red

**Shell
Ness**

*East
Swale*

5

4_5

*Pollard
Spit*

*Oyster
Beds*

0_9

1_5

**Whitstable
Oyster**
Fl(2)R.10s
R

1_8

Isle of Harty

5

5

1_4

Fl.WRG.5s
5-3M
Whitstable YC
2 F.R
☆

5

The Swale

1_2

Sand End
G
Fl.G.5s

1_2

WHITSTABLE

No.1

2_8

2

2_7

Whitstable Flats

1_8

Horse Sand

3

1_2

**Faversham
Spit**
G
Fl.G.10s
BY

2

South Oaze

3

The Oaze

Harty
Ferry

1_2

3_5

0_3

*Faversham
Creek*

Seasalter

*Oare
Creek*

N

OARE

FAVERSHAM *See plan*

53′ 54′ 55′ 56′ 57′ 58′ 59′ **1°E** 1′

into the river, so wellingtons or waders are a good idea – as is a really long painter for the dinghy.

On the mainland, there is another hard, much used by local fishermen and yachtsmen to launch dinghies for the swinging moorings. At first glance there is a gay abandon of buoys, but close inspection shows that they belong to one of these: Hollowshore Cruising Club; Brents Boatyard; Youngboats; Barry Walpole; and visitors. Harty Ferry is a hospitable spot, no charge being levied on visitors, and unoccupied buoys may be picked up so long as the usual courtesies are observed. It is something of a mistake to ask for advice or permission from one of the occupied buoys – if they are strangers you learn nothing and, if they are local, the answer often comes: 'They are all private; and the owners are coming back on the tide.' The stream can be fast just here, and picking up a buoy single-handed is best undertaken on the last of the flood, before the ebb starts to run.

This is generally a quiet spot in spite of its well-protected charm, which one would think would make it a crowded area. It is also one of the few places on the Swale where you can stay afloat at all stages of the tide and, in addition, it is close to the exit for the North Sea or the Channel.

In true English style the nomenclature lingers on although there has been no working ferry for years, and it still features on all the charts, maps and guides. Recently, there has been much talk about the river ferry at Harty Ferry going into operation again. It has been defunct since the late 1940s, but there was hope it would have been reinstated by the beginning of the 1995 season. I saw a vessel with the legend 'Ferry' clear for all to see. However, upon trying to hitch a ride of the master, I was quickly and sadly disabused. 'The council has been mucking us about!' is the euphemistic translation. So, perhaps next year . . . or the next.

There is many a skipper who considers his summer as of naught if he has not picked up a buoy, or better, anchored off, and rowed ashore (for outboards, even classic Seagulls, are frowned on hereabouts) to that special house on the Isle of Sheppey which dispenses liquors.

Faversham Creek

Faversham Creek is entered by leaving the north cardinal marker off Faversham Spit, known locally as Creek Mouth buoy, the proper distance from its proper side. This has not always been the case, but it has been moved and now marks a channel that is central. There was never a lot of room for manoeuvre and there isn't now, but at least visitors can feel more at ease when entering. It is important to give a good clearance to the wreck on the starboard hand, since half of it is well on the river side of its beacon.

Once past the wreck, the marker to look for is the white board on the boatyard shed. This board gives

Faversham Creek, near the head of navigation, is a veritable conglomeration of craft of all kinds with its most special blend being a farrago of Ancient and Modern – in beings, in boats, and in beer.

a good leading line down the main channel, which is shared by Oare and Faversham Creeks.

This board will lead to the junction (see chartlet) where there is a spit (on the starboard, west bank) opposite the boatyard that reaches far out into the stream. If you are proposing to go into Oare Creek to try for a mooring on one of the jetties belonging to Barry Tester (whose yard is called Hollowshore) you steam straight ahead, keeping fairly close to the post marking the end of the boatyard slipway. This will clear all obstacles. There are not many moorings at Hollowshore, with most taken by local sailing craft. It is best to contact Hollowshore's master before arriving.

Hollowshore is an intriguing boating community made up of the Tester boatyard; Bell Boats and Rigging (working on the *Cutty Sark*); and the Hollowshore Cruising Club's HQ. Sadly, the famous Shipwright's Arms was closed for a period but, happily for its dedicated clientele, it is now back in business. Once a notorious spot for smugglers, there still lingers about the area an air of 'brandy for the parson and baccy for the clerk' and some say there is always the chance of a late, late drink nearby. It is a remote spot, without much in the way of mains power or water, and is most easily reached by boat, since the road is neither A nor B, but is no longer X, Y, Z.

The general facilities at Barry Tester's Hollowshore boatyard are basic but Barry will get you out of serious trouble if he can. There is, however, a phone by the clubhouse. The jetty is comfortable, well protected and with access better than half tide.

Provided you do not draw too much, it is safe to moor to the steps by the Shipwright's Arms. For a good long time now, there has been a motley collection of underwater items here, rendering it quite a tricky spot. For really shoal craft at the top of the tide there will be no anxiety, but for visitors it must surely be best to anchor just off and use an inflatable.

I can think of no better mooring place than Hollowshore moorings; indeed, they must rank as among my favourites on the southeast coast. Barry Tester has got it right: 'We're trying all the time to

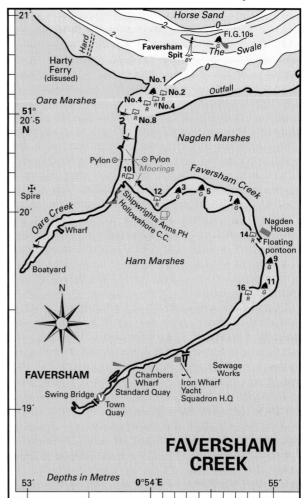

FAVERSHAM CREEK

FAVERSHAM CREEK
Charts Admiralty 2482, 2571. Imray Y14
Tides
Dover +0133
Tidal access
HW ±2hrs (max. draught approx. 3m on HWS)

Alan S R Staley (Boatbuilder) ☎ 01795 530668
Tidal access
HW ±2hrs
Ⓥ (mud, 2 visitors'), 🚻, 🛒, ⚓, ⚡ (by arrangement).
⛽D (nearby), Engineer. Repairs

Iron Wharf Boatyard ☎ 01795 536296/537122
Tides
Dover +0120

Tidal access
HW −2 hrs to HW +1½ hrs
Ⓥ (mud, 8 visitors'), 🚻, 🛒, ⚓, ⚡, ⚒, Provisions (nearby), Ⓖ, ⛽D, Engineer, Repairs

Standard Quay ☎ 01795 536040
Berthing for traditional craft only.

Brents Boatyard ☎ 01795 537809
Ⓥ (mud alongside; possible visitors') 🚻, 🛒, ⚓, ⚡

CONYER CREEK
Chart Admiralty 2482. Imray Y14
Tides
Dover +0120

Swale Marina ☎ 01795 521562
Tidal access
HW ±2hrs
Ⓥ (mud, 100 pontoon, 8/10 visitors'), 🚻, 🛒, ⚓, ⚡, ⚒ (nearby), Ⓖ, ⛽D, Engineer (by arrangement), Repairs

Wilkinson Sails ☎ 01795 521503
Tidal access
Over HW
🚻, 🛒, ⚓ (by arrangement), ⛽D, Repairs (sails)

OARE CREEK
Young Boats Marine Services ☎ 01795 536176
Ⓥ (mud, 20 finger pontoons, 5 visitors'), 🚻, 🛒, ⚓, ⚡

Hollow Shore Services Ltd (Barry Tester)
☎ 01795 532317
Ⓥ (mud, occasional visitors'), 🚻, ⚓, Repairs

---

get and keep the place just as it was 100 years ago. If people like it here just as it is, we tend to get on all right with them. But we are not a marina and can't spend our time rushing around with lots of rope and hundreds of gallons of water. Nor can we keep tugging our forelocks all the time to people who will keep calling you 'My Man' and are never likely to bring their expensive cruisers here again.'

The Hollowshore jetty is well situated for an early getaway on the tide. The last time I left there, for example, the tide started to make at 1020 (HW Dover +1220) and I was afloat at 1120. By 1130 there was enough water over the mud 'bar' of the berth to enable me to get into the channel and leave the Swale without problem.

From the Swale, you turn to port at Hollowshore for Faversham Creek. It is well buoyed, but its 2½-mile channel is narrow, and in places runs through extensive, misleading saltings so it is a good idea to go up slowly after half tide before the banks are fully covered. Between reds 14 and 16, on the east side, the bottom is foul with old timbers.

Once near the town, there are boatyards on both banks. The recently refurbished town quay is on the port hand, just below the bridge. On the north side there are council landing stages, but if you draw much more than a metre they can be tricky to negotiate since the mud shelf stands very proud on the main channel. The mud is too soft to permit even thinking of a crossing by foot, unless you happen to have arctic-type snow shoes or those legendary (and now priceless) Thames smuggling boots. If you draw over 1·5m it is worth checking with the boatyard of your choice for advice and guidance. In any case, berths are not so little sought after that chance arrivals can automatically be accommodated.

Here follow details of the candidates for berths, boats and business. Brents Boatyard, the waterfront part of the old Faversham Boatyard, is sited on the west bank just below the Albion pub. It has mud berths as well as 40 swinging moorings at Harty Ferry. There is a new development on the east bank just below the bridge, where a group of local boat owners have leased Standard Quay to provide 300m of moorings for 'traditional' craft. When asked about a completion date, they were, 'traditionally', reticent. At Iron Wharf Boatyard, on the east bank below the Anchor, they specialise in cranage and shoresides storage for DIY yachtsmen. Next door, at the Old Saw Mill on Chambers Wharf, Alan Staley (Shipwright, Boatbuilder & Sparmaker) has established his new headquarters. He is a dedicated expert with wooden boats and, not long ago, was deeply involved in the restoration of the 23m motor yacht *Coral Isle*. Refurbishment is now the order of the day. There are new piled moorings, drying of course, and not only is there a new 'administration office', but also new 'offices' so that one can squat in comfort. Sadly the resident old, old cat has died.

She was a much more likeable guardian than any computerised alarm system.

Faversham boasts another old English tradition – the brewing of ale. It is home to Shepherd Neame which is still pleased to show visitors round if telephoned in advance. Also to be sought out when the local asparagus is in season is English Asparagus; contact Mrs Carolyn Andrews, Blackbird Cottage, Luddenham, Nr Faversham, Kent ☎ 01795 532212.

Much more up-to-date is the recently built block of smart houses known as Faversham Reach. On the north bank, each is the proud possessor of a large studio-type room overlooking the river and a brand new quayside mooring just below. All in all, the town is a charming place – an ideal shopping and leisure centre. Indeed, I can find nothing but good to say about Faversham.

Back at Hollowshore, Faversham Creek possesses an arm, armlet or rivulet: Oare Creek. Leaving Hollowshore to port, after a mile or so, you reach the small boatyard and mooring facility. If you draw more than a metre you could easily experience some trouble reaching the head of navigation. The channel to Oare is a tortuous affair, but it is well marked by stout withies and, with a little local

The apparently wide entrance to Faversham Creek, which bends away to the left in mid picture; with the minor Are Creek going away to the top right. Barry Tester's boatyard can be seen dead centre at the junction.

Conyer Creek

Back in the river, after the green No. 1 buoy, there is a BYB cardinal. For the West Swale the buoy is left to port while, for Conyer Creek, it should be left to starboard. The cardinal, opposite Spit End and its marshes, marks the extremity of the far-reaching mud spit of Fowley Island. If you are on your way up the Swale, it is a case of steaming virtually straight ahead and looking out for the red buoys that mark the channel to the old Elmley Ferry.

First we go to Conyer Creek, leaving Fowley Spit to take the port fork for Conyer. Next comes South Deep, with its popular anchorage off Fowley Island by the old red beacon on the mainland. The better water tends to the south shore. It has a more restricted and difficult entry, as well as a more convoluted channel than Faversham; but it is more substantial than the miniature 'gutway' of Oare.

The easterly channel is the main one. The west is known as the 'Butterfly' and is extremely narrow with very sharp turns. It carries more water at its entrance, but since you cannot make Conyer until the main channel is open anyway, it is a pointless exercise unless you are into mud-crawling.

The main channel is better marked than before, with buoys sponsored by local groups who are to be much commended and thanked. There are still some withies but the buoys are deemed to be more reliable.

At the head of the navigation, is Swale Marina at Conyer Wharf where there have been serious improvements. At Swale marina, the lift-out is up to 10 tons and there are facilities for attention to hull, rigging and a little chandlery on site. Cindy Parker heads Wilkinson Sails. Now well established in its new, refurbished loft, it continues to gain strength and favour. The more intriguing and challenging the request the better – the size of the order is not Wilkinson's prime interest.

There are two pubs; the nearer – the Ship – is now in new hands and therefore stands a much better chance than before of attracting a wider clientele. There used to be a high-flying wine list with prices to match, and that is not what the small community or visiting yachtsmen want.

guidance, you can get a boat of 2·0m up there on big springs. Not only is it tortuous, however, it is also narrow, with its sides deeply scarred by those who have misjudged it. I remember the words of one local expert very well: 'I've been using the creek for more than 20 years and I must go out at least four times a week in the season, but I still get caught by it every year. It's a monkey!'

At the head of the navigation is an attractive village and the growing facilities of Terry Young's very personal operation, 'Youngboats'. Terry Young himself says, 'the area is most suitable for bilge and lifting keel craft to 1m'. Much refurbishment and modernisation has taken place so that there is a modern marina in an old setting. Diesel, *Calor Gas* and an 8-ton crane are available, and access is about 1½ hours +/−HW. This is no exclusive fraternity, but many of the berth-holders are members of Whitstable Cruising Club.

Above Bottom of frame is the virtual head of navigation, with, at left, the 'new' 'swish' maisonettes-with-moorings and above them Brents Boatyard. On the right, going up, is Standard Quay, Alan Staley and Iron Wharf; and, towards the top, there is one of the near-ox-bows that are a feature of Faversham Creek – and nearly cover at HWS.

Right Harty Ferry: the skipper is hearty indeed, but the ferry has been non-existent for years – although this is a recent picture . . . promise!

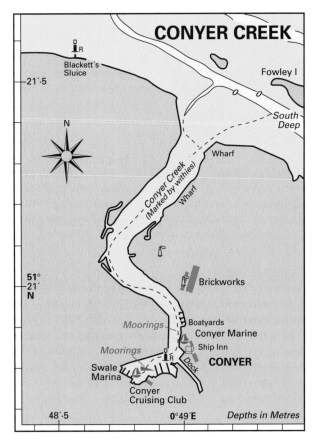

Fowley Island is the long strand and, above it, is the sheltered anchorage known as South Deep. The white area just above the right tip of the island marks the upper entrance to Conyer Creek known as The Butterfly. No time is saved by trying it (butterflies in the stomach being no fair exchange) and it is wisest to use the entrance round the other 'headland'. The creek has at last bee buoyed – many thanks to the locals.

Up the road, the Brunswick Arms continues its policy of good solid food and ale at down-to-earth prices. For proper shopping you needs must go a couple of miles down the road to Teynham. There is a bus that leaves from just by the telephone kiosk.

When quitting Conyer Creek, it is possible to regain Elmley Reach, the main channel, by making for the No. 8 red buoy that is sited between Blackett's Sluice (on the south bank) and Wellmarsh Creek (on the north). The course is roughly northwest with the channel being a double dogleg. It is a voyage of discovery to be taken on a rising spring tide, by those who do not have fixed commitments at the end of the day. The more reliable route into main Swale is to return to the BYB cardinal at the east end of Fowley Island, round the hairpin bend, and follow the red cans (Nos 2 to 10) to the west. They lead directly to the Causeway.

Approaching Milton Creek, after Green Elmley we meet the boards and buoys for the old Ferry

The Ship at the head of Conyer Creek is, predictably, a magnet to most visitors – by land or sea. It is almost as difficult to park a car as it is a boat.

hards, where I have always found less water in the channel than on the charts. It is certainly not a place for LW navigation. Nearby, on the south side, is a quiet anchorage off the Lilies by the saltings. There used to be a noticeable red stake marking the northern limits of these mud-flat/saltings, and it sent you, Willy-Nilly round the Lilly, straight into the main channel of Milton Creek. Now, there is a much more splendid marker: a South Cardinal, quite properly keeping you off the shoal ground that stretches way out into the river from the north bank. Efficient as it is at this task, it is no guide for the

Swale Marina is the absolute head of navigation for Conyer Creek. It is also the location of Cindy 'sail-maker' Parker's scintillating loft: Wilkinson Sail.

Lilies Spit, which is currently unmarked. The Spit must be studiously avoided if a safe entry is to be made into the creek.

Elmley Reach is of some importance for two reasons. First, and just to add to the potential confusion at the Milton Creek junction, it is where the direction of buoyage changes, coming inwards from both east and west to meet at the Kemsley paper mill.

Second, it is one of the places where tidal separation occurs; the other two being Kingsferry Bridge and Fowley Island. However, there is still little reliable information about exactly what happens and, as the *Admiralty Pilot* says, 'Tidal streams in the Swale are subject to considerable variations, and all data must be considered approximate.' It is important to know that both in-going and out-going streams can exceed 4 knots, mainly between Elmley Reach and Kingsferry.

In general, the stream separates as follows:

Kingsferry	HW Dover +0330
Milton Creek (the Lilies)	HW Dover +0430
Fowley Island (Conyer Creek)	HW Dover +0530

After the Lilies, the better water tends towards the wharves on the west bank. The bottom is encumbered with unpleasant objects and the channel is narrow. The chart shows the main features to be wrecks, chimneys, brickworks, hulks, wharves and a sewage works. Access is no better than half tide.

Both the poet's name and the cleansing brand are well known, but nothing could be further removed from the healthily antiseptic or the powerfully poetic than Milton, the last of the Swale creeks. True, it does lead to Sittingbourne and, while that over-busy bustling township may appeal to many, I think of it as a place to be avoided except as a matter of urgency. True, it has plenty of shops but it is also possessed of some of the ugly attributes of modern urbanisation.

The Creek has few facilities, and the only thing to tempt the visiting yachtsman is the Dolphin Sailing Barge Museum. It is where there used to be an old boatyard specialising in the building of barges. Since 1992, the wharf, the sail loft, the shipwright's work-place and the forge have been put into proper shape. There is a collection of artefacts and old photos. There are, actually, some moorings at the Museum but, as one would expect, they are intended for Thames barges – and they, naturally, take the ground well. It is thoroughly worth a long visit, but it must be favourite to make such a trip by dinghy, by foot or by car. Sittingbourne Sailing Club, which is a small-craft organisation based in the creek, has no facilities for visitors.

Perhaps the least attractive aspect of the creek itself is that its waters are redolent of unpleasantness. At the head of the creek, the water seems to thicken and the air to hang heavy. Ms Driscoll has this to say about her days there:

The channel to Oare is a tortuous affair. One local expert said: 'I've been using the creek for more than twenty years and I must go out at least four times a week in the season, but I still get caught by it every year. It's a monkey!' Terry Young Boat Services are at the head of the navigation, off the picture to the right. This section features Barry Tester's yard and mooring running from left to right; with Faversham Creek disappearing at mid left.

The smell to be found in Sittingbourne (Milton) Creek is something to do with the waste from the paper mills. It used to be a lot worse, and it would make paint go a most peculiar lead-like colour and the brass used to be covered with a strange milky sheen, preparatory to tarnishing badly. I used to cover all exposed brass with a light film of oil if bound for Sittingbourne. What it did to the human 'innards' I hate to think . . .

Queenborough to Milton Creek

Since the direction of buoyage changes here, we will do the same and 're-enter' the Swale from its confluence with the Medway. The outer approaches are described on page 160. From the Medway, you leave the Queenborough Spit cardinal marker just to starboard. The Lappel, a vast area of drying mud flats, is left well to port. Shortly after, for the first time in the area, the banks of the river approach one another so that there is a feeling of an inland waterway as opposed to a seaway. Then it is past Deadman's Island and Shepherd's Creek alongside the long line of yacht moorings that leads to the red can marking Queenborough Hard and the Creek.

Queenborough is overlooked by the Grain power station. There is no escape from its dominating edifice and, under its substantial shadow, the title 'Queenborough Harbour' must surely be something of a euphemism. After all, it is a conglomerate that starts at a line running from Swale Ness to the ruins of the pier off the point. However, it does now have a more special appeal for yachtsmen. There is a (new) old concrete lighter with a (new) old warning: 'Berthing alongside this lighter is prohibited until consent has been obtained from harbourmaster' (difficult to obey because of frequent invisibility of said master). Not only are there now two very good visitors' buoys, each capable of taking more than 12 10m craft, there is also the completely new all-tide landing pontoon, opened in 1994 to help crews coming, going, victualling, watering and/or socialising. There is a brief maximum stop-over period – and it is not intended for overnighting. There is ample dinghy parking at the side.

The Creek in Queenborough, is a small drying affair with its entrance close to, but round a bend from, the hard. The first red buoy marking the creek is situated right on the edge of the hard, and the channel buoys all sit on the edge of mud banks, as can be clearly discerned at LW. A central course is essential. After that it is well buoyed in standard red and green and runs almost into the centre of the town. It is used by commercial and fishing vessels, so, unless you really need help, you should avoid entering. However, it is being refurbished, and the locals, many of whom used to play on what was an attractive quay, are hoping it will soon regain its old glory. The boatyards are usually busy and, while their trade is mainly vested in the 'big stuff', it is just possible, with much persuasion, to get non-essential work done on small leisure craft. However, if your boat is in desperate need, you will find that you can reach the ministering angels at the quaysides on the top of the tide, and they will be very quick to get and keep you right.

Queenborough is a strange place with plenty of facilities. There is a choice of shops (though many have closed recently) and fuel can be obtained. Shoresides by the hard, there are several attractions. First there is the quaintly named pub, The Old House At Home; then the even quainter Bosun's Stores (a veritable treasure house of ships' and other stores). It is a great place for laughers and gaffers alike. You can also count on its staff for all the advice and help you may need in the area. They do all that they can to keep not just an open house, but also open hours and much 'really useful' chandlery. There are also barrels of local 'wisdom' waiting to be tapped; as well as the contact with the local HM coastguard. With its agreeable neighbour, the Queenborough Yacht Club (one of the most hospitable in the area), and the improved landing facilities, the harbour is on course for returning to popularity.

Leaving Queenborough to approach Milton Creek and the Lilies from the other direction, we come first to Loden Hope, just after the beacon on West Point. The green buoyed Horse Shoal is almost opposite the big jetty. While it may look tempting, it is not really feasible to pass on the 'wrong' side. The river then makes what must be a nascent Ox Bow as Loden Hope turns sharply from the south then the northwest before rounding on itself to face southeast. It then stays in that direction down the 3 miles to Milton Creek, after which it settles into an east-west route. Off Loden Hope and Long Point, well named and well marked with its beacon, there are fascinating views astern of the big ships back in the Medway as they seem to land-glide over Dead Man's Island.

After Loden's Bend, Long Reach and Horse Reach take us down to Ferry Reach and quite a new experience in this area – pillars that are the buttresses of Kingsferry Bridge. It is a wondrous construction to contemplate, especially when it is in the process of raising its centre, horizontal span all of a piece.

By tradition, myth and legend, you can arrange passage in a number of ways: getting in touch with the bridgemaster by telephone landline well in advance to arrange a time; calling him on VHF Ch 10; signalling with the ship's whistle (one long and four short blasts); addressing the bridgemaster by means of a loud hailer; hoisting a bucket or other suitable object in the rigging; signalling by flag; or signalling in the classic manner by the use of arm signals.

I was intrigued by all these ideas, some more than others I must confess, and so tried out a few. Much as I would have liked to have been able to recount immediate success having hoisted a 'suitable object' in the rigging, I have to report complete failure of all methods except VHF and telephone. They have

A difficult judgement: is Kingsferry Bridge the more impressive when lowered . . .
. . . or when raised?

Another of the Medway contrasts: high and low life all in one.

worked without fail every time and, as a result of checking in advance on Ch 10, I have never had to wait more than a few minutes. Sometimes the bridge opens on request, but generally, it lifts at half-hour intervals, or at the behest of a big ship. The keepers maintain a listening watch on VHF Ch 10 and will inform you of the next opening. They are extremely friendly and helpful.

Kingsferry Bridge is a road and rail bridge, unusual in that the span rises vertically, but all of a piece horizontally. It is an excellent candidate for photography. The clearance when the bridge is down is 3·3m and 29·0m when it is up. When the bridge is raised, you should add 25m to the figure on the tide gauge. The gauge is mounted on the bridge itself and is easy to read.

All inner sides of the four pillars are lit and the traffic signals are as follows:

No light	Bridge down
Q.R/Q.G	Bridge lifting
F.G	Bridge up
Q.R	Bridge descending
Q.Or	Bridge out of action

This is a busy stretch, and I once found myself negotiating four separate tugs, three sloops a'sailing, two water-skiers, and a coaster with three tugs. Wits are certainly needed at the ready.

Just south of the bridge, the half-hundred-strong Kingsferry Boat Club is a mix of sailing and motor cruising. While there is no physical clubhouse, there is plenty of the 19th-hole spirit: fresh water and friendliness are always on tap; and visitors are made welcome, whether afloat or ashore – or indeed for one of their many open-air seasonal barbecues. Mr Dewey, the club secretary, is disappointed that the Lords of the Medway will still not permit the establishment of visitors' moorings; but he recommends a quiet anchorage on the south bank between the end of their moorings and the beginning of the Ridham Dock area; it is well away from the mainstream, quiet and with good depths at most states of most tides.

The area is often busy with sea-going traffic bound for Ridham Dock and Grovehurst Jetty; neither of which is a place for leisure craft. Further down, the aptly named Clay Reach is an oppressive stretch with demolition, desolation, wreckage, remains and debris creating the deadly landscapes that are on both sides of the water. Here the channel is dead centre but, by Kemsley paper mill, it tends to the west and south until well round the long bend into Elmley Reach where the direction of buoyage changes and the tidal streams meet.

From the Lilies eastward towards Conyer Creek the channel is entered between the gate of the North and South Ferry green and red buoys. They are situated just to the west of the hard that was part and parcel of the one-time Elmley Ferry. Now there is naught but the residual and the skeletal; and that description might well be given to the narrow strip of navigable water that runs a pretty middle course through the wide flats that make up the heart of the Swale. It is not realistic to hope to float through with a 1½-metre boat at anything better than half tide; although I did once succeed in making a muddy progress all the way to Fowley on a median neap. It is easy to feel slight disorientation in the middle of this featureless stretch.

While Conyer and Faversham are the two best-known creeks in the Swale, there are others. Many of them are quite small; for example, the miniature rivulet in the saltings near the entrance by Shell Ness and the other miniatures by the Lily Banks near Harty Ferry. Then there are the slightly larger, but no longer whirling, Windmill and Bell's Creeks by Dutchmans Island, Flanders Mere and Spitend Point, as well as the three heroics at Sharfleet, Cockleshell and Wellmarsh. Sharfleet is not to be confused with the Medway Sharfleet – this is Swale style, and a different kettle altogether. Many of these smaller creeks are suitable only for wading (birds or humans) or days in the dinghy unless, of course, you have a purpose-crafted shoal boat, in which case you can have a whale, or a porpoise, of a time.

The Swale is not a long river; nevertheless, in its 12 miles, it packs in more to intrigue, absorb and fascinate than do many others, especially with its contradictory tides. It is a place of charm and eccentricity where you can find plenty of good socialising company whenever you want it. On the other hand, you can just as easily keep to your own self solus – except for wild and natural creatures that lead charmed lives in these parts. I find it a quite compelling prospect.

X. The Kent Coast to Ramsgate

We now leave behind the comparative calm of the Swale as we make our way from Harty Ferry and the cardinal Faversham Spit towards the green Sands End buoy and Shell Ness. The channel is still quite narrow as we move northeasterly between red Pollard Spit and green Ham Gat and on to Columbine Spit. It seems OK to cut straight across and there is no reason why such a track should not be used if the tides are good and the weather set fair. The proviso is that oyster beds are laid in the area outside the main channel, which goes from Pollard Spit via Columbine to the cardinal Whitstable Street. Admiralty Chart 2571 reminds us that the whole of the considerable area of shallow water is occupied by oyster beds, and that vessels grounding are liable to pay damages.

Having been guided by two local divers across those sand banks, flats and near flats that lurk between Pollard Spit and the long finger of hard, hard sand known as Whitstable Street, I have some personal knowledge of the detritus, the bits and pieces that have accumulated on the bottom – as well, of course, as the oyster beds. It is tempting to cross Whitstable Bay and make straight for the red can Whitstable Oyster; but I consider it too risky and always go right outside. Others may be less anxiety prone than I; but, from the east, I consider it essential to approach the cardinal Whitstable

Street before trying to make for one of the mooring buoys laid by the Yacht Club.

Whitstable Harbour is of an unusual and pretty design, but in the main area is packed with cargo ships up to 1,000 tons carrying stone, slag, grain, timber, steel and so on. In addition there are all the local craft employed in general fishing as well as specialising in shellfish and oysters, for which the name Whitstable is well known.

Whitstable Harbour is not the easiest place to find at the best of times, nor one to be running for at the worst of times; and, while visiting yachtsmen are not exactly barred from the harbour, Whitstable, it must be clearly understood can be used by yachtsmen only as a refuge in time of distress. The entrance is not easy to see even on the clearest of days. By night it can be particularly difficult.

The members of the Whitstable Yacht Club will do all they can to help, and will try to fix you up with a suitable mooring just off. It is only sensible and courteous to call the mooring master in advance of any proposed visit. Gathered round the front are all the usual occupations and facilities that you would expect in this small, busy little town. Chandlery and rigging requirements can be satisfied near the harbour.

WHITSTABLE HARBOUR
51°21'·83N 01°01'·56E
Charts Admiralty 2571, 1607. Imray C1, Y14.
OS Landranger 179

Tides
+0135 Dover

Tidal access
Commercial: HW −1hr; other HW ±3hrs

Caution/notes
Whitstable is a busy commercial port and yachts are expected to use it only when seeking refuge or in other emergencies.

Authorities
Harbourmaster ☎ 01227 274086

Radio
VHF Ch 09, 12, 16 (Mon–Fri 0800–1700 LT. Other times: HW −3 to +1)
Tidal information on request
WC (nearby), 🏪 (nearby), ⚓, ⚒, Provisions,
🅖 (nearby), 🛢D, 🛢P (nearby)

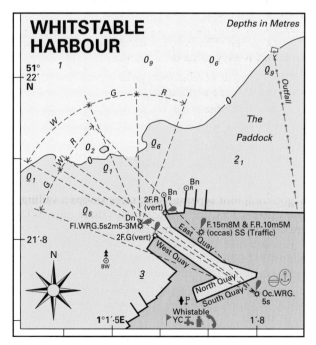

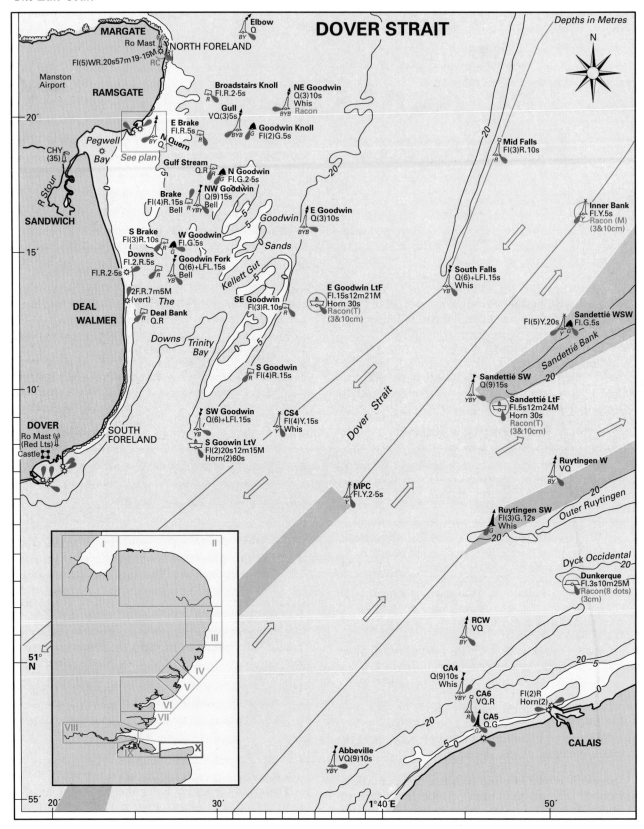

DOVER STRAIT

Depths in Metres

N

MARGATE
Ro Mast
NORTH FORELAND
Fl(5)WR.20s57m19-15M
RC

Manston
Airport
RAMSGATE

CHY
(35)

Pegwell
Bay

See plan

R Stour

SANDWICH

DEAL
WALMER

The
Downs

Trinity
Bay

DOVER
Ro Mast
(Red Lts)
Castle
SOUTH
FORELAND

Elbow
Q
BY

Broadstairs Knoll
Fl.R.2·5s
R

Gull
VQ(3)5s

E Brake
Fl.R.5s
R
BY N Quern
Q

Gulf Stream
Q.R
G

NW Goodwin
Q(9)15s
Bell
R YBY

Brake
Fl(4)R.15s
Bell

NE Goodwin
Q(3)10s
Whis
Racon
BYB

Goodwin Knoll
Fl(2)G.5s
BYB

N Goodwin
Fl.G.2·5s

E Goodwin
Q(3)10s
BYB

Goodwin

Sands

Kellett Gut

S Brake
Fl(3)R.10s
R

W Goodwin
Fl.G.5s
G

Downs
Fl.2.R.5s
Fl.R.2·5s
R

Goodwin Fork
Q(6)+LFl.15s
Bell
YB

2F.R.7m5M
(vert)

Deal Bank
Q.R

SE Goodwin
Fl(3)R.10s
R

S Goodwin
Fl(4)R.15s
R

SW Goodwin
Q(6)+LFl.15s
YB

S Goowin LtV
Fl(2)20s12m15M
Horn(2)60s

CS4
Fl(4)Y.15s
Whis
Y

E Goodwin LtF
Fl.15s12m21M
Horn 30s
Racon(T)
(3&10cm)

South Falls
Q(6)+LFl.15s
Whis
YB

Mid Falls
Fl(3)R.10s
R

Inner Bank
Fl.Y.5s
Racon (M)
(3&10cm)
Y

Fl(5)Y.20s

Sandettié WSW
Fl.G.5s
Y G

Sandettié Bank

Sandettié SW
Q(9)15s
YBY

Sandettié LtF
Fl.5s12m24M
Horn 30s
Racon(T)
(3&10cm)

Dover Strait

MPC
Fl.Y.2·5s
Y

Ruytingen W
VQ
BY

Ruytingen SW
Fl(3)G.12s
Whis
G

Outer Ruytingen

Dyck Occidental

Dunkerque
Fl.3s10m25M
Racon(8 dots)
(3cm)

RCW
VQ
BY

CA4
Q(9)10s
Whis
YBY

CA6
VQ.R
R

CA5
Q.G
G

Fl(2)R
Horn(2)

CALAIS

Abbeville
VQ(9)10s
YBY

51°
N

I
II
III
IV
V
VI
VII
VIII
IX
X

55' 20'   30'   1°40'E   50'

A careful conning of the layout of Whitstable's small harbour will show why there is little hope or place for leisure craft. All spaces are taken up by commercial fishing and coasters.

The Whitstable Street shingle bank dries for nearly 2 miles out and for up to 2·0m in places and, each season, there are unpleasant incidents and accidents among visitors. Many people walk out too far and get caught by one or other of the various pools and eddies that can be treacherous on a rising spring tide.

If it were not so busy and cramped it would be an ideal staging post for cruising craft. The town itself is a highly desirable spot for the visitor and by no means a last resort. It is a joy not to be missed. It has been well visited in the past, just like Ramsgate and the hinterland of Pegwell Bay; but holidaymakers are now more popular in the town than were the foreigners who foraged, scrounged and scavenged in the days before Domesday.

Between Whitstable and Margate there is little to catch the eye on the shoreline; the main features being Herne Bay, its pier and the modern 'contemporary-style' water tower. But then comes something different – the old Reculvers Towers. There used to be a splendid haven here when the old overland route was in existence. Indeed, it seems that, as far back as the days of St Augustus, it was possible for craft to get to the southern end of the waters that guarded the territorial borders. The

Roman name for it was Regulbium and one of the regiments posted there was known as the 1st Battalion of the Imperial Brabanters.

Navigation along this stretch is straightforward. Going eastwards, the first pair of buoys – green Hook Spit and red East Last – are close together marking the 'gate' that leads from Horse Channel into Gore Channel. The drying sands, known in the main as Margate Hook and Last, are much in evidence just over a mile offshore and are clearly marked by their buoys and beacon.

Margate's small harbour dries to about 2·0m, gently if sometimes unevenly, shelving from the head of Stone Pier to the town shore. Vessels of nearly 4m can get to this pier at HW spring tides. However, the 1960 edition of Imray's *Pilot Guide to the Thames Estuary* says this: 'Craft can only enter the harbour towards high water and, if intending to stay, must be prepared to take the mud. There is little shelter, and yachtsmen are not recommended to enter without special reason.' My own visits to the place have given me no cause to disagree.

There have been plans for the development of a marina facility at Margate for at least 20 years. So frequently have I found that what I have been told was to happen did not happen, that I can no longer utter confidently on this subject.

Margate Harbour as it is, has little to offer for cruising craft. You need a passionate interest in old stone or broken piers even to consider visiting by boat. The resort is best approached by car, and any

North Foreland lighthouse is probably the oldest in England, being erected in 1683, increased in height in 1793, and cut down to its present size in the late 1800's. Personal statement: *Valcon* has only once had a quiet passage round North Foreland.

shoresides inspection of the (sometimes) picturesque harbour at low water will tell its own story. Margate had two piers: 'Stone' that forms the harbour and 'Promenade' (also known as Iron Jetty). They are an emblem of Margate's spiky weaknesses and strident, but astute, commercialism. The place is no longer what it used to be – a pleasure and a treat for Londoners – being now quite lacking in identity, revelation or inspiration.

Moving on towards the headland, it is important to stand well clear of the Longnose. On occasions, especially in calm settled weather, it does appear as if there is a 'close inshore passage', but careful conning of the chart will show this to be extremely risky; the rocks of Longnose Spit almost reach the cardinal marker. Hardly a year goes by without some skipper clipping the corner to his lasting regret. The Foreland Lighthouse is conspicuous and perhaps the oldest in England. The light was erected as long ago as 1683, increased in height in 1793, and beheaded to its present state in the late nineteenth century.

I have only once had a quiet passage round North Foreland. There always seems to be some configuration of wind and sea to make the rounding of that corner (oh so long . . . oh so wearisome) not only confuse *Valcon* and me, but seem to turn and cant us in all directions.

Once round North Foreland, we move into the symbolically deep waters of the English Channel.

The 4 miles of coastline from the North Foreland to Ramsgate consist mainly of sheer, chalk cliffs that rise from 60–120ft, sometimes in stark perpendicularity. This in itself is enough to tell us quite clearly that we have come round the bend from the flats of the east to move into something quite different: the beginnings of the rise into chalk. The result being that the scenery improves as the cliffs come and go, being relieved from time to time by verdant slopes like those near Broadstairs and Dumpton Gap.

Close-to inspection shows that there is little that has not been built on. If time and weather permit, you will be able to muse on the site that is, by quite misguided local tradition, the setting of John Buchan's *The Thirty-Nine Steps* and also to be suitably awed, if not indeed completely subdued, by the genuine original of Charles Dickens' *Bleak House*.

Long ago, when superstition was even more rife than it is today, all craft sailing past Broadstairs used to dip their topsails to gain a blessing from Our Ladye of Broadstairs. However, that great traveller Cobbett found little that was blessed except the countryside itself. He saw it as completely in the hands of the plutocracy, with no opportunity for farmers or labourers to improve themselves. It was a region divided against itself – the impoverished living in near hovels, with the rich in mansions and huge houses.

Back in the time of the Tudors, there was a tiny pier here to provide some protection when the local boats had been dragged up on to the shore. It seems impossible to imagine, from land or sea, that Broadstairs once prospered from its business with big ships. Many of the townsfolk made their livelihood from 'foying' – that is, ferrying goods and people to and from passing vessels. No doubt the fuelling barge in Ramsgate harbour, known as *Foy*, still carries an aroma of that traffic about it. It would certainly be apropos.

Seldom is an approach to Ramsgate Harbour smooth. My experience is that it is one of the most hyperactive areas on the east and southeast coasts. The general shallowness of the coastal stretch and the plenitude of shoal banks are two important causes. Another is the exposed limb on which the harbour is perched. In addition, it is completely artificial and formed of stone piers, thus possessing none of the natural protection afforded to ports and havens of a less manufactured origin. Its immovable mass of stone stands against the irresistible force of the North Sea and the Atlantic as they conjoin in the narrowness of the Dover Strait, creating a fervent breaking swell.

However, a mile or so away from the entrance, everything is usually much calmer. At that distance, the backlash from the walls and the wakes left by the pilots die away to no more than an unpleasant memory. The improvements over the past few years have, of course, done much to help quiet this down somewhat, but not completely. Waters surrounding the North Foreland itself and the stretch to Ramsgate can be lumpy; certainly when the wind is against the tide and folk who want to go east should be prepared to spend more time in the marina than planned.

Any first-time visitor should be prepared for a difficult approach from seaward at night. It is best to try for calm, unsettled weather, of course, not only because the surrounding shallows can be unruly, but also because the town lights proliferate and offer many confusing characteristics. It is easy to confuse them with navigation lights.

The following guidance is issued by the Ramsgate Royal Harbour as advice to yachtsmen:

. . . another personal statement: my 'great adventure' began when I quit Ramsgate's harbour for what seemed, at first, like a century on the East Coast. Sally Line, now dominating not only the picture but the life of the port, was not in existence – and neither were the everlasting arms that now reach out so far. Also to be seen is the sandy triangle where Victoria trod her tiny way to the waves.

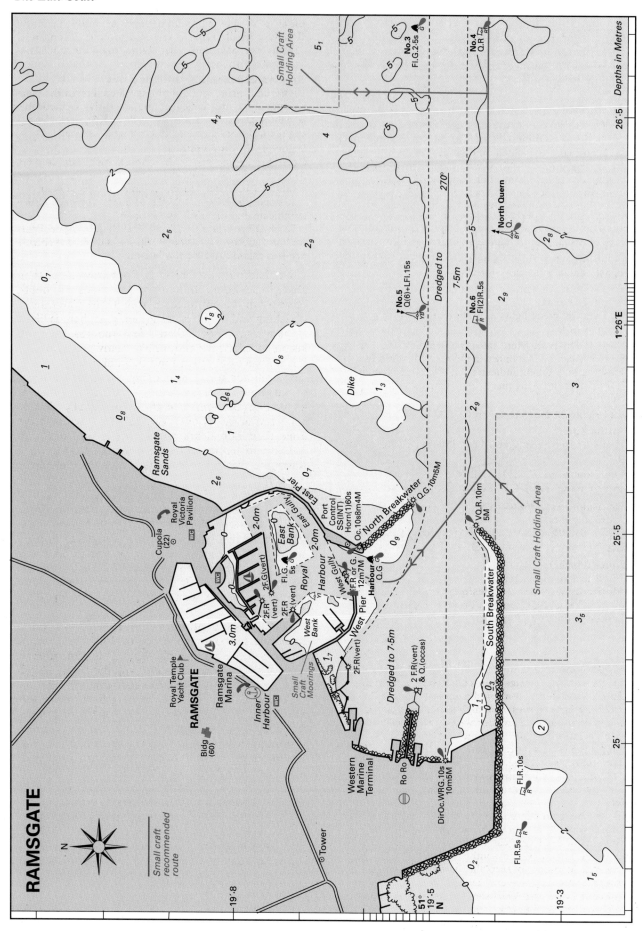

RAMSGATE

Small craft recommended route

Royal Victoria Pavilion

Cupola (22)

Ramsgate Sands

Royal Temple Yacht Club

RAMSGATE

Ramsgate Marina

Bldg (60)

Inner Harbour

3.0m

2F.R
2F.R(vert)

2F.G(vert)

West Bank

Royal Harbour

West Pier

2F.R(vert)

Small Craft Moorings

F.R or G. 12m7M

West Gully

Fl.G. 5s G

Q.G G

East Bank

Port Control SS(INT) Horn(1)60s Oc.10s8m4M

East Gully

East Pier

North Breakwater

Q.G.10m5M

VQ.R.10m 5M

South Breakwater

Western Marine Terminal

Ro Ro

DirOc.WRG.10s 10m5M

2 F.R(vert) & Q.(occas)

Dredged to 7.5m

0.9

0.3

1.1

0.2

Fl.R.5s R

Fl.R.10s R

R R

Tower

Small Craft Holding Area

Dike

Dredged to 7.5m

270°

7.5m

No.5 Q(6)+LFl.15s YB

No.6 Fl(2)R.5s R

North Quern Q. BY

No.3 Fl.G.2.5s G

No.4 Q.R R

Small Craft Holding Area

Depths in Metres

26′·5

1°26′E

25′·5

25′

N 51° 19′·5

19′·3

19′·8

RAMSGATE
51°19'·48N 01°25'·60E

Charts Admiralty 1827, 1828, 323; Imray C1, C8; OS Landranger 179

Tides
+0020 Dover

Tidal access
24hrs (Inner Marina: HW ±2 hrs)

VTS port control located on east pier
Vessel traffic service (VTS) with radar surveillance is maintained for the control of shipping and leisure craft. Port traffic signal lights and VHF Ch 14 in operation (24hrs) from port control building at entrance to Royal Harbour. All movements in Royal Harbour, outer harbour and approach channel are authorised by port control and all vessels, particularly those without radio, must observe the following port signals shown from the control tower:

- 3 vertical red lights indicate that no vessel may enter or leave
- 3 vertical green lights indicate that vessels may enter or leave.

Prior to departure from Ramsgate, permission must first be obtained before leaving the Royal Harbour. Flashing amber light indicates ferry/jetfoil movement is imminent or taking place. (All vessels should keep clear of channel.)

Call *Ramsgate Port Control* on Ch 14.

Authorities
Harbourmaster (Ramsgate) ☎ 01843 592277/540941

Radio
Port Control VHF Ch 14 (24hrs)
Dock Office VHF Ch 14 for berths

Ramsgate Royal Harbour
Tidal access 24hrs
🅥 (fingers, 200 visitors'), 🛢D, 🛢P (nearby), ⚓, ⚡, 🅿, 🆆🅲, ⚲, Provisions (nearby), ⊕ (nearby), Repairs

Inner Marina
Tidal access HW ±2hrs
Minimum depth inside basin 3m
🅥, ⚓, ⚡, 🅿, 🆆🅲, ⊕ (nearby), Provisions (nearby), Landrette (nearby), Engineer (nearby)

Navigational information
The approach to Ramsgate for commercial ferry traffic is from the East via a well-marked deep-water channel. This is used by large ferries and high-speed jetfoils, and all small craft are advised to keep well clear of such vessels, and to proceed via the recommended yacht track when approaching or leaving Ramsgate.

During transit of the small-craft channel, all yachts should maintain a listening watch on VHF Ch 14 so that the entry and departure of all vessels can be expedited safely.

When the main channel has to be crossed, this should be done as nearly as practicable at right angles.

Small-craft holding areas to the north of No. 3 buoy and to the south of the south breakwater are now in operation, in order to keep the harbour entrance clear during arrivals and sailings of ferry traffic.

All craft fitted with VHF should initially call *Ramsgate Port Control* on Ch 14 before approaching the channel and recommended track to receive authorisation to proceed to either a designated holding area or into the Royal Harbour. Small craft are required to enter Strong tidal streams set SW and NE across main channel and breakwater entrance.

Recommended yacht crossing point
Yachts and leisure craft on passage should cross the main channel in the area indicated and as nearly as practicable at right angles to the main traffic flow. Keep well clear of commercial vessels and avoid crossing close ahead.

Inner marina information
Open for approximately 2½ hours each side of HW (subject to the dockmaster's discretion as to tide, weather conditions and safety during commercial operations).

A single green light is displayed above the Dock Office to indicate that the dock gate is open.

Dock Office works on Ch 14 VHF (tidal). Signal lights (red and green) at marina entrance, control movements between marina and Royal Harbour.

The harbour staff on watch are always more than ready to advise on the state of conditions and depth of water in the entrance, as well as the movements of fishing and commercial shipping. If there is likely to be a wait of more than a few minutes, they will keep you informed; and, unlike many port controls, it is not necessary to remind them of your presence. They will not keep you hanging about for a quarter of an hour without letting you know what is happening. Shoresides staff can be equally alert to collect your fee. Some visitors seem not to have done their homework and steam in and out with little or no reference to the traffic signals; but the Ramsgate watch has an eagle eye and an elephant memory.

As far back as Roman times, a small community existed in Ramsgate, and there was a tiny harbour with a wooden pier. After the 1748 storm, when ships in the nearby Downs were dragged from their anchors, it was decided to improve the harbour as a place of refuge. Work started in 1750, with some of the work done by French prisoners of war. The lighthouse on the west pier did not fire up until 1795.

In the history of wars and rumours of wars, Ramsgate harbour goes back to 1802, and was a garrison in the Napoleonic Wars. It is remembered most of all for its part in 1940 with the 'Little Ships' saga, more than 80,000 evacuees being landed.

On the vacation trail, swimming from the beach was in fashion from back in 1780 with, of course, the obligatory bathing machines. Queen Victoria was frequently brought here (imagine that!) by her mother; and, on the proletarian side, mention is to be found in Dickens' 'Boz' sketches.

Ramsgate has all the facilities visiting yachtsmen need. Most usual supplies and services can be found along Military Road, and even the most esoteric request is generally satisfied by a simple phone call. After all, the marina is very close to the continental coast and no more than an hour or so from London. Of course, you have to pay for such proximities and the services offered.

Ramsgate is proud of its royal patronage; the Royal Temple Yacht Club enjoys an enviable

There is now no sign of the berth I first occupied. *Tempora mutantur, etnos mutamur in illis*. Onward!

position overlooking the harbour, and from it can be seen the obelisk erected to George IV 'as a grateful record of His Majesty's gracious condescension is selecting this port for his embarkation to His Kingdom of Hanover'. Today, that sycophantic tribute is surrounded by tokens of the town's changed style and status: casinos, ice-cream parlours and many, penny lanes – except that they no longer trade in pennies. Tradition and heritage are represented by the fish at the quay, the whelks, the RNLI, the extraordinary Shipwright's Arms and the superb red-brick Customs House.

Jacob's Ladder, by the car entrance to the ferry areas, will give you access to the High Road above. It was first built in wood in 1754 and, in 1826, was rebuilt in concrete. Close by is the 1881 'Home for Smack Boys'. Once up the ladder and atop the west-side cliff, the quayside, harbour and marina will appear below, on a sunny day, as if from a postcard of a Mediterranean haven. The whole panorama gives promise of the bliss of the Côte d'Azur (that is, if you are protected from the prevailing winds that incline many locals to pronounce Ramsgate one of the windiest spots in Britain).

When I first came here, I thought that was the usual kind of exaggeration to be expected from disenchanted natives. However, a few winters in the grip of the Ramsgate-to-North Foreland variety of winds soon put me to rights. Even at the height of the summer season, there is always a good chance that a NE Force 6+ will take you by surprise and then hang around for a week or more.

For anyone with a head for heights and a liking for strong air (or for the equally strong real ale that abounds in this particular part of Ramsgate) the prospect will provide entertainment for days on end; and even visiting yachtsmen should not leave the harbour without giving the view at least the once over if only for the navigationally useful perspective of the bay and the run down to Deal. With good visibility, you can see much further from that vantage point – laid out, as Eliot had it, 'Like a patient etherized upon a table'.

After Ramsgate, all things change, and the South Coast ethos slowly takes over. While it cannot properly be maintained that the harbour is geographically on the East Coast, its spirit certainly is; and in a strange kind of way we are almost back where we started, in the townships of Boston and King's Lynn. The three share much that will not be met again until a complete western passage has been made to Cornwall and its small harbours and havens. If the passage from Boston to Ramsgate be made at one fell swoop it will be a brief and demanding odyssey; but if the rivers, harbours and havens are fully explored, there must be almost enough cruising grounds to last, if not a lifetime, then at least a generation.

Index